PERSONALITY DEVELOPMENT AND DEVIATION

A Textbook for Social Work

GEORGE H. WIEDEMAN, M.D., *Editor*

SUMNER MATISON, M.A., M.S.S.W., *Associate Editor*

INTERNATIONAL UNIVERSITIES PRESS, INC.

New York

Library of Congress Catalog Card Number: 73-89439

ISBN: 0-8236-4070-1

Second Printing, 1975

Manufactured in the United States of America

PERSONALITY DEVELOPMENT AND DEVIATION

To Dr. Marion E. Kenworthy, whose ability, vision, and interest made her one of the foremost exponents of dynamic, psychoanalytically oriented psychiatry in the field of social work.

Contents

Preface

This introductory text for social workers and those in allied professions grew out of the psychiatric curriculum taught at The Columbia University School of Social Work. Over the years, we have felt the need for a book written with the social work profession in mind—one that presents a coherent picture of personality development, stressing the range from normal to pathological. The information contained in this book is available in psychiatric texts and in articles spread out in a variety of scientific journals, but it has not heretofore been available in systematic presentation under one cover.

One of our emphases is on the theories that underlie the operational aspects and treatment approaches used in the various fields of social work. A second emphasis is pragmatic in nature: we have devoted chapters to character disorders, alcoholism, addiction, psychological testing, community psychiatry, problems of aging, and learning disorders in children—all subjects about which social workers need to be informed. In many instances, social workers will be called upon to work with an interdisciplinary team that includes psychiatrists, psychologists, teachers, and paraprofessionals. For this reason, we have described treatment techniques, although we have not dwelt on those in depth.

One might fairly ask whether it is necessary or even important for the social worker to know about personality development. We are of the opinion that it is not only important but essential. Back in 1949, S. Bowers offered an evocative definition of social casework. "Social casework," he said, "is an art in which the knowledge of the science of human relations and skill in relationships are used to mobilize capacities in the individual and resources in the community appropriate for the better adjustment between the client and all or any part of his total environment." Not only is his juxtaposition of art and science to our liking; we are also in total accord with his emphasis on the interrelation of client and community. In a more recent definition of social work adopted by the Board of Directors of the National Association of Social Workers in 1970, we find a similar orientation: "The practice of social work required knowledge of human development and behavior; of social, economic, and cultural institutions, and of the interaction of all these factors." Such knowledge is a prime requisite for a professional approach to individuals, families, and groups in any therapeutic setting.

The content of dynamic psychiatry is just as essential to group work as to casework. But an understanding of group dynamics without sufficient knowledge of individual personality structure—its dynamics and pathology—would be incomplete, to say the least.

To what extent the community organizer can utilize psychiatric knowledge in his day-to-day work has also been questioned. We believe that the community organizer will be spared a great many errors and false approaches if he has some basic understanding of human development and psychopathology.

Although our emphasis is on the psychological factors in personality development and behavior, we acknowledge as well the important role of sociological factors. The two approaches, psychological and sociological, are not antagonistic; they complement each other.

Our book opens with a brief description of the theory of personality development—a description of the invisible forces and processes responsible for the highly visible phenomena we call personality and behavior. We then trace growth and development from earliest infancy through childhood, adolescence, and adulthood, to old age. Deviations in childhood development, both neurotic and psychotic, are given separate consideration. How symptoms are formed is followed by chapters dealing with each of the broad areas of pathology. We conclude with two subjects of particular importance to social workers and those in allied professions—a comprehensive survey of psychological testing, and an authoritative description of the relatively new field of community psychiatry.

A list of references of works drawn on is appended to each chapter. This seemed preferable to weighing down the text with innumerable names and dates. Most of the chapters have, in addition, a list of suggested readings for those wishing to explore in depth a particular subject, or area of development.

I express my special thanks to the contributors to this textbook, many of whom offered suggestions for chapters other than their own. Mr. Sumner Matison has been unstinting in his efforts to bring this work to completion. He has been able to bring to the task the advantages of professional social work training and his experience in various treatment modalities. I wish to acknowledge my appreciation to Mrs. Natalie Altman who did a great deal of work in preparing this manuscript for publication. I am grateful also to Mrs. Helen di Riccardo and Miss Erika Muehl, whose administrative and secretarial skills were extremely helpful. Dr. Frank Berchenko has given some excellent suggestions concerning the first four chapters, which I deeply appreciate. Mr. Steven Aoki's assistance during the last stages of preparing the text were invaluable. I am indebted to my wife Rachel H. Wiedeman, not only for her patience and support while this book was being written and edited, but also for her helpful suggestions with regard to the content and style of many of the chapters. Finally, I give recognition and thanks to the Kenworthy-Swift Foundation, whose generous grant made it possible for this project to be undertaken. The responsibility for the contents of this volume and for the opinions expressed therein belongs, of course, exclusively to the editors and the individual authors.

Contributors

Richard Burnett, M. D.
Practicing Psychoanalyst

Everett Dulit, M.D.
Director, Adolescent Psychiatry; Assistant Director of Child Psychiatry, Albert Einstein College of Medicine—Bronx Municipal Hospital, Bronx, New York.

Aaron H. Esman, M.D.
Chief Psychiatrist, Jewish Board of Guardians; Lecturer, Columbia University School of Social Work; Faculty, New York Psychoanalytic Institute.

Donald L. Gerard, M.D.
Clinical Professor of Psychiatry, Albert Einstein College of Medicine, Bronx, New York; Attending Psychiatrist, Montefiore Hospital and Medical Center, Bronx, New York.

Marion Hart, M.D.
Lecturer, Columbia University School of Social Work, New York City.

Leonard Hollander, M.D.
Director, The Child Guidance Center of Mercer County, Trenton, New Jersey.

Merl M. Jackel, M.D.
Senior Lecturer and Training Analyst, State University of New York, Downstate Medical Center, Brooklyn, New York; Consultant, Community Service Society, New York City.

Louis Linn, M.D.
Clinical Professor, Department of Psychiatry, Mount Sinai School of Medicine, City University of New York; Attending Psychiatrist, Mount Sinai Hospital; Member, Committee on Community Psychiatry, American Psychoanalytic Association.

Henry Marasse, M.D.
Associate Clinical Professor of Psychiatry, Albert Einstein College of Medicine, Bronx, New York.

John B. McDevitt, M.D.
Faculty, New York Psychoanalytic Institute; Clinical Instructor, The Masters Children's Center, New York City; Senior Research Associate, Yale University, School of Medicine Child Study Center.

Julius Rubin, M.D.
Medical Director, Community Consultation Center, Henry Street Settlement House, New York City; Lecturer, Columbia University School of Social Work; Assistant Clinical Professor, New York Medical College; Staff Psychiatrist, Veteran's Administration Hospital, Northport, New York.

Miriam G. Siegel, Ph.D.
Psychologist, Community Service Society, New York City.

Julian L. Stamm, M.D.
Clinical Assistant Professor of Psychiatry and Training Analyst, Department of Psychiatry, State University of New York, Downstate Medical Center, Brooklyn, New York.

Irving Sternschein, M.D.
Lecturer, Columbia University School of Social Work; Psychiatric Consultant, Community Service Society, New York City.

Leonard A. Weinroth, M.D.
Associate Attending Psychiatrist, Mount Sinai Hospital; Associate Clinical Professor of Psychiatry, Mount Sinai Medical School, City University of New York.

THE EDITORS

George H. Wiedeman, M.D.
M. E. Kenworthy Professor of Psychiatry; Chairman, Psychiatric Area, Columbia University School of Social Work, New York City.

Sumner Matison, M.A., M.S.S.W.
Director, Group Therapy, Rockland County Mental Health Clinic, New York.

CHAPTER ONE

Theory of Personality: Basic Givens and Assumptions

GEORGE H. WIEDEMAN, M.D.

Professionals who deal with people and their problems must know how the personality develops and what can go wrong in the course of this development. Whereas it is very important to explore the actual confronting situation with its stresses and strains, this is obviously not enough. People do react differently in comparable situations. These differences, as is well known, are due to the variations in people's psychological make-up, their strengths and weaknesses, as well as their past experiences.

How can we evaluate the personality of the one we are trying to help? Human personality and behavior are so complex that, unless we organize our observations according to some framework, we are apt to flounder. A general framework—that is, a theory of personality—will enlarge our field of observation by directing our attention toward phenomena we would otherwise overlook.

Over the years, many theories of personality have been formulated. There are theories that stress biological factors; theories that explain personality formation entirely on the basis of environmental forces;

theories that ascribe primary importance to cognitive processes—and many others.

The greatest contribution to the understanding of the normal and abnormal personality was made by Sigmund Freud. After devising a new method of investigation—the method of free association—Freud succeeded in showing that unconscious mental processes and ideas play an astonishingly significant dynamic role in our thinking, feeling, and overt behavior. Freud formulated the first comprehensive and scientific personality theory. Although his fundamental discoveries were based primarily on the exploration of the mental life of patients with emotional disorders who underwent psychoanalytic treatment, these discoveries can also be applied to normal mental functioning and can be utilized, even without the specific psychoanalytic treatment technique, in other forms of psychotherapy, in casework, group work, as well as other fields of investigation—anthropology, sociology, biography, literature, for example—fields of knowledge where the understanding of psychological processes is essential.

Givens

A personality theory must be related to the biological realities of human beings. Heredity is one of the basic factors determining personality development, structure, and function. There is frequent controversy over the relative importance in human development of heredity versus environment—the nature-nurture argument. Whereas it is not yet possible to evaluate accurately the extent to which nature or nurture predominates, we do know that, like all other living organisms, human beings develop in accordance with what is contained in their genes. The totality of this genetic information can be regarded as a set of predispositions that, through interaction with the environment, eventually become manifest in physical appearance and psychological organization. In addition to the various inherited predispositions that make up the constitution, certain other predispositions are laid down as the result of environmental influences during pregnancy and early infancy. Although these latter predispositions, which are either congenital or acquired very early in life, are not determined by heredity, they may be considered quasiconstitutional in that their effects are relatively stable, i.e., are very difficult to modify in later life. Freud (1905) conceptualized the interaction of hereditary predisposition with the environment as a "complemental series." A hereditary predisposition to a mental illness, for example, may not become manifest in a favorable environment, whereas a less marked predisposition may result in illness if the subject grows up in unfavorable conditions.

Just as nature and nurture interact, so do maturation and development. Maturation, primarily a biological process, is relatively independent of environmental factors as long as these do not exceed the adaptive capacity of the growing child. Under normal conditions, the child will grow, learn to walk, to talk, and acquire other skills according to a genetically determined timetable. Development is the result of the interaction of the maturing child with his specific human environment. This interaction leads to the formation of his unique personality.

Hartmann (1939) introduced the concept of the "*average expectable environment,*" which can be defined as the set of conditions that, within a range characteristic of a particular historical, socioeconomic, and cultural period, is compatible with normal growth. Adequate nutrition and mothering are part of an infant's average expectable environment—so important, in fact, that marked interference with either leads to delayed or inadequate mastery of such basic and necessary functions as sitting, standing, walking, and talking. Even under normal nutritional and hygenic conditions, inadequate mothering results in distortions of personality development, with ensuing disturbances of interpersonal relations (Spitz, 1945, 1946). The younger the child, the more sensitive it is to deviations from the average expectable environment.

In our efforts to understand psychological phenomena, we must assume the operation of the law of causality, just as we do when we investigate physical phenomena. The application of the law of causality to psychic events does not in any way conflict with the basic fact that all mental activity has a biologic substrate and depends on complex biochemical processes in our central nervous system. Even if we achieved a full explanation of the neurophysiological processes underlying memory and thinking, we would still have to examine specific thoughts and memories in order to understand their psychological significance.

Our mental life, like any natural phenomenon, is not determined by a single cause but by many—that is to say, it is multidetermined. The laws of causality, which we observe in our everyday life, simply state that everything that occurs is determined by a necessary chain of prior events—in effect, is multidetermined. In applying the laws of causality to mental life—i.e., what we call psychic determinism—it is necessary to keep in mind that the greater part of our mental life is unconscious and yet has a great impact on our conscious acts, thoughts, and feelings. Many mental phenomena seem to be unconnected and unrelated to those trends of our psychic life of which we are aware. Memories and thoughts may come up as if out of the blue; slips of the tongue or of the pen (parapraxes) are unexpected, puzzling; dreams may show unacceptable attitudes and wishes; delusions and hallucinations of psychotics seem inexplicable. Before the recognition of a dynamic unconscious mental life, all these phenomena were considered "accidental," the result of some "disordered" brain activity, and therefore not especially worthy of scientific attention except insofar as they could be explained somatically. With the application of the psychoanalytic method of investigation, these "accidental" and "disordered" phenomena could be made causally intelligible, first by the assumption and then by the proof that by far the greater part of our mental life was not accessible to our ordinary awareness.

Mental processes and content that are outside our awareness can be either preconscious or unconscious. Those that can be recovered by directing our attention to them are called *preconscious;* those that cannot are called *unconscious*. The descriptive qualities conscious, preconscious, and unconscious are not sharply delineated from each other, but can be observed in all possible gradations, from the clearly conscious to the deeply buried and not recoverable unconscious.

That many of our thoughts and memories are unconscious was known before Freud. His great contribution was the discovery that unconscious aspects of psychic life continue to influence thoughts, feelings, and behavior, that derivatives of unconscious psychic content may emerge in a more or less disguised form in dreams, neurotic symptoms, and parapraxes.

The division of mental phenomena according to their accessibility to awareness formed the basis for Freud's first theory of personality. According to this "topographic" theory, the systems Conscious, Preconscious, and Unconscious constituted the psychic personality. The topographic theory was superseded by the structural theory. In the structural model, the three psychic structures—id, ego, and superego—are defined, not by the degree of accessibility to consciousness, but by other criteria (which will be described shortly). The structural theory has given us a more complete and consistent understanding of the psychic personality than the topographic one. It explains more satisfactorily intrapsychic conflict and its role in normal development and in disease, as well as the individual's relation to reality. Both theories, however, topographic and structural, are based on the recognition that a vast amount of mental content is unconscious.

Assumptions

The dynamic point of view maintains that mental activity, whether conscious or unconscious, is due to an interplay of psychic forces. The energy of these forces is derived from the instinctual drives. The two broad categories of instinctual drives are the sexual and aggressive. The sexual or libidinal drive is mainly manifest in sensuous, affectionate, friendly feelings and strivings, the aggressive in self-assertion, competitive strivings, destructiveness, and hate. Drive energy—sexual and aggressive—is invested in the mental images of persons and things or in ideas. This is called cathexis.

Dynamic and energic processes take place within what we conceptualize as psychic structures, which are established in the course of development. We might regard psychic structures as riverbeds regulating the direction and speed of the flow of water. We describe psychic structures according to their origin and their functional affinities, and we divide the various manifestations of our mental life into three such structures, called the id, ego, and superego. The id is the source of the wishes stemming from the instinctual drives and striving for gratification. The ego is the perceiving, executive, and integrative agency mediating the adaptation with the outside world; it also is the intermediary through which the instinctual wishes are gratified. It responds to the demands of the superego and acts in accordance with external reality. The superego represents the aspect of the personality related to moral and ideal strivings.

Development proceeds through a series of transformations which generally increase the complexity of the psychic apparatus. The developmental progression consists of qualitatively different processes that can be observed at various stages. This historic or *genetic* point of view, accepted in biology as the epigenetic principle, is most fruitful when applied to psychic development. Erikson (1959) describes epigenesis as follows: " . . . this principle states that anything that grows has a *ground plan,* and that out of this ground plan the *parts* arise, each part having its *time* of special ascendency, until all parts have arisen to form a functioning whole" (p. 52). In successive stages of the development of the sexual instinctual drive, different erogenous zones are dominant: first the oral, then the anal, the phallic, and, finally, the genital. This succession shows an epigenetically determined sequence. The concept of successive, qualitatively different developmental stages also applies to the ego and the superego. It should be kept in mind that earlier forms of psychic functioning are not erased, but are modified and superseded by more differentiated and integrated forms. The earlier forms still retain some of their original cathexis, and a return to these forms is observed in some normal states—in dreams, for instance, and as a part of psychopatholcgical phenomena, as in symptom formation.

The adaptive point of view, accepted in biology as a basic characteristic of all living matter, was applied to mental functioning by Hartmann (1939). All living organisms adapt to their physical environment and to other organisms. Our psychological equipment serves us in mastering reality, i.e., in adapting to a constantly changing physical and social environment. Adaptation is achieved basically in two ways; through inner autoplastic psychobiological changes or through alloplastic changes of the environment brought about by the person. The changes brought about in the environment become, in turn, part of the external conditions to which man has to adapt. "Man not only adapts to the community, but also actively participates in creating the conditions to which he must adapt. Man's environment is molded increasingly by man himself . . . by adaptation, we do not mean only passive submission to the goals of society, but also active collaboration on them and attempts to change them" (Hartmann, 1939, pp. 31-32). In line with our developmental point of view, we can discern forms of adaptation whose direction coincides with developmental progression, and regressive types of adaptation which are characteristic of psychopathological states. There are times, however, when psychologically regressive—i.e., primitive forms of psychic functioning—serve a positive adaptive role contributing to artistic and scientific creativity. Ernst Kris (1952) described this as "regression in the service of the ego."

These five metapsychological points of view do not exist in isolation from one another; they are interrelated. We observe psychic structure genetically. Structural concepts would be static without dynamic and economic (energic) considerations; the adaptive point of view presupposes all the others. Together, they furnish us with the conceptual tools to establish the connection between man, the biological organism, and man, the social being.

Psychic Systems

When Freud (1923) originally introduced the structural theory, the terms structure and system were not sharply differentiated, but were both defined as the specific arrangement of component parts forming a complex whole. "Structure," however, usually had static connotations, whereas "system" had dynamic and functional ones. The term structure refers to a specific orderly organization of various parts. System, as used at present, includes, in addition, differentiation, integration, goal directedness—i.e., adaptation—the storage of information, and the maintenance of a homeostatic balance by the use of feedback mechanisms. A consideration of these additional functions, which, together with the orderly arrangement of parts, characterize system, is necessary for any psychological theory that aspires to being more than mechanistically descriptive. We therefore prefer to describe ego, id, and superego as systems rather than as structures.

In the nineteen-forties, a new branch of science, cybernetics, came into being. It was an interdisciplinary approach, dealing with the communication of information or data and control through feedback mechanisms in machines, living organisms, and social organizations. Cybernetics made the development of data-processing machines and computers possible and formed the basis of modern system-theory. According to cybernetic thinking, a system has four general characteristics: boundaries, structures, functions, and history (Buckley, 1968). If we regard the respiratory and circulatory systems of the body as illustrative examples, these four features are readily discernible. We observe the anatomical boundaries, the physical structures, the specific physiological functions, and a history from embryonic beginnings to adult forms.

The psyche and its component systems cannot be described as concretely as the somatic systems of the body. The boundaries between id, ego, and superego are less clearly delineated than, for instance, the boundaries between the circulatory and respiratory systems, although even these latter do not have sharp boundary lines, but have areas of interaction. Psychic systems can be considered to have transitional border areas rather than sharp boundary lines. As is the case with somatic systems, the psychic systems id, ego, and superego are open ones, in constant dynamic interaction with one another.

The *structure* of a psychic system refers to the patterns or abiding configurations within which perception of sensory data, memory, thought processes, and other mental functions take place. The *function* of a psychological system refers to the processes occurring within and between the structures, and also to the end results of such processes. These end results may become manifest in overt behavior, in feelings, and in thought. This tripartite division may seem artificial, inasmuch as our actions and thoughts are accompanied by feelings, and, conversely, our feelings influence to a lesser or greater extent our actions and thoughts. But because behavior in the widest sense—acting, thinking, and feeling—is the object of our study, it is essential that we avoid the pitfall of viewing any one of these in isolation, that we view any one of them in the context of the other two.

Inasmuch as boundaries, structures, and functions are modified in the course of time, somatic and psychological systems cannot be understood unless we approach them from a historical or genetic point of view. Let us briefly consider, for example, the establishment of boundaries between id and ego and between ego and superego. During the first two or three months of life, the infant exists essentially on a reflex level, with alternating periods of tension and relaxation related to its physiological state. It is hardly possible to speak of psychological structures and functions during this period. In the course of the early childhood years, the boundaries between id and ego are gradually established. The psychic systems continue to evolve throughout childhood and adolescence, eventually assuming a relatively stable, although not unchangeable form in adulthood.

The systems id, ego, and superego should not be mistaken for concrete anatomical regions located in parts of the brain. They are useful working concepts rather than physical entities. Their existence presupposes the integrity of the anatomical structure and physiological function of the brain, but they cannot be assigned to any specific part of the central nervous system. The concept of the three systems id, ego, and superego is inferred from the observation of human behavior.

In the course of normal development, as well as in pathological states and under conditions of stress, conflicts occur both within the systems ego and superego (*intra*systemic) and among the different psychic agencies (*inter*systemic). Conflicts, largely unconscious, arise out of the opposing tendencies of the systems id, ego, and superego. Intersystemic conflict might occur between id and superego—between an instinctual wish and the standards of conscience: If, for the sake of exposition, we personify the id and superego, then we can describe the id as saying, "Get rid of this bothersome child." And the superego replies, "I have an obligation to protect this child." Intrasystemic conflicts within the ego may be the result of an uneven development of various ego functions. The ego function of reality testing collides with the defensive ego function of projection: Reality dictates that my boss does not hate me. But because I cannot afford to admit that I hate him, I defend myself by believing that he does hate.

Inner conflicts, especially unconscious ones as they interact or are affected by the environment, play a large part in determining human behavior. It is therefore necessary for us to take a closer look at each of the psychic systems.

REFERENCES

Buckley, W., ed. (1968), *Modern Systems Research for the Behavioral Scientist.* Chicago: Aldine.

Erikson, E. (1959), *Identity and the Life Cycle* [*Psychological Issues,* Monogr. 1]. New York: International Universities Press, pp. 1-171.

Freud, S. (1905), Three Essays on the Theory of Sexuality. *Standard Edition,* 7:239. London: Hogarth Press, 1953.

——— (1923), The Ego and the Id. *Standard Edition,* 19:3-66. London: Hogarth Press, 1961.

Hartmann, H. (1939), *Ego Psychology and the Problem of Adaptation.* New York: International Universities Press, 1958.

Kris, E. (1952), *Psychoanalytic Explorations in Art.* New York: International Universities Press, Chapter 6.

Spitz, R. (1945), Hospitalism. *The Psychoanalytic Study of the Child,* 1:53-74. New York: International Universities Press.

——— (1946), Anaclitic Depression. *The Psychoanalytic Study of the Child,* 2:313-342. New York: International Universities Press.

SUGGESTED READING

Arlow, J. & Brenner, C. (1964), *Psychoanalytic Concepts and the Structural Theory.* New York: International Universities Press.

Brenner, C. (1955), *An Elementary Textbook of Psychoanalysis.* New York: International Universities Press. Revised edition, 1973.

Ellenberger, H. (1970), *The Discovery of the Unconscious.* New York: Basic Books.

CHAPTER TWO

Theory of Personality: The Id, Ego, and Superego

GEORGE H. WIEDEMAN, M.D.

The Id

The id is that part of our mental organization through which the instinctual drives find their expression. At one end, the id is open to somatic influences; at the other, it forms a continuum with the ego. From the viewpoint of the adult, who thinks in terms of logic and causality—"secondary type thinking"—the id appears to lack organization, since it functions on a primitive level, called the *primary process*. The latter term is used to refer both to the tendency, observed in our behavior, to seek immediate and complete discharge of the instinctual drives, and to a primitive type of thinking. This primitive type of thinking follows certain patterns: it is characterized by displacement, condensation, use of symbols, lack of a sense of time, and absence of negation—i.e., contradictions exist side by side. Primitive layers of the ego and superego are likewise under the sway of primary process thinking—another example of the phenomenon already mentioned that boundaries between the psychic systems are not sharply delineated, but have areas of gradual transition.

The basic element of the id is the wish that strives for fulfillment. This wish emerges into consciousness, and, together with ego interests, superego prohibitions, and the demands of reality, it motivates and determines our behavior in the broad sense—our thoughts, affects, and actions.

There are a great many physiological needs that take precedence over the gratification of the instinctual drives. Intense hunger or thirst, or a strong need for sleep, as well as other somatic needs, may prevail over any expression of sexual desires or aggressive tendencies. These physiological needs must be satisfied in order that bodily and mental integrity be maintained. The satisfaction of some vital physiological needs as, for instance, the need to breathe, cannot be postponed for even short periods of time without danger. The satisfaction of other physiological needs can be postponed for varying periods of time, but never indefinitely. The means by which basic physiological needs can be satisfied are relatively fixed—there are no substitutes for oxygen, food, and water.

The sexual instinctual drives, too, have physiological sources that exert pressure toward consummation. External objects—that is, other people, are usually needed to achieve the aim of the instinctual drive, namely, gratification and the subsequent subsidence of tension. But, in contrast to the physiological needs, gratification of the instinctual drives can be frustrated and postponed without endangering physical existence. This plasticity of the sexual and aggressive drives makes it possible to modify their openly sensuous or aggressive manifestations.

The conflicts between the id and the other mental systems are the major source of psychopathology. Memories, conscious and unconscious, have, as has been proven by repeated clinical observations, an important effect on activating or inhibiting sexual and aggressive behavior and on modifying its aim and object. Excessive frustration in the course of development and, conversely, excessive gratification, contribute to psychological fixations, to the dominance of earlier, childish modes of sexual gratification, aggressive behavior, and object choice over more adult, age-appropriate modes. An adult indulging in temper tantrums, for example, is retaining or returning to earlier forms of expression of the aggressive drives.

Psychopathology provides many instances where the fulfillment of physiological needs becomes involved in psychological conflicts.

Eating is normally regulated by physiological requirements and is accompanied by pleasure. Excessive consumption of food leading to obesity may be due to developmental fixation or it may represent a way of coping with underlying feelings of anxiety or depression. Or rejection of food due to psychological conflicts may result in emaciation in, for instance, the severe psychosomatic illness known as anorexia nervosa.

Other needs whose fulfillment is basic to the harmonious development and the maintenance of the total mental organization are either partly or entirely autonomous from the instinctual drives. The most important of these are the needs for perceptual stimulation, for human companionship, and for freedom of action (Cameron, 1963). The frustration of these needs does not cause direct danger to existence, but it may cause damage to and even disintegration of the established mental organization.

Our mental life is governed by a disposition to seek pleasure and to avoid unpleasure and pain, a tendency referred to as the pleasure-pain principle or, most often, simply as the *pleasure principle.* The younger the individual, the less is he capable of postponing the immediate gratification of his needs, impulses, and wishes. In the young child, the pleasure principle is supreme. With maturation and the development of the systems ego and superego, the capacity to postpone immediate gratification in line with the demands of reality is eventually achieved, and the adult acts in accordance with the reality principle.

The mature person *sublimates* his instinctual impulses—that is, he expresses them in modified form. The sexual and aggressive aims or goals of the instinctual impulses are turned into socially useful and acceptable ones. The relation of the subjective feelings of pleasure and unpleasure to underlying psychic tension is not altogether understood. Usually, an increase of psychic tension is related to feelings of unpleasure. But there are instances of increasing tension that are pleasurable—for example, in sexual excitement, provided a culmination or discharge of tension is anticipated. Conversely, a decrease in psychic tension resulting from the lack of appropriate sensory stimulation is felt as unpleasurable and even threatening. For example, the painful nature of solitary incarceration without any meaningful stimuli has been used as a cruel punitive measure and often contributes to severe psychological damage. It would appear that there are certain optimal ranges of psychic tension and that shifts within such ranges are perceived as either neutral or pleasurable, whereas a significant deviation in any direction beyond the optimal range is felt as unpleasurable.

The system id has "open" boundaries with the soma, the ego, and, after its establishment, the superego. It contains the memory traces from the preverbal stage that have never reached consciousness, as well as those which were established after the acquisition of language but were pushed out of awareness (repressed).

Although much of the mental content and mode of function of the id remains preserved throughout life, the system id undergoes developmental modifications, as do the systems ego and superego. The principle changes in the id system are those observed in relation to the shifting predominance of the body zones through which the sexual and aggressive instinctual drives are expressed. In succession, these are the oral, anal, and genital erogenic or libidinal zones. This epigenetically determined psychosexual development will be spelled out in later chapters.

The Ego

The term ego as used to designate a part of the psychic personality, should be clearly distinguished from the same term when used in various contexts as a synonym for the self, the conscious self, sense of identity, pride, etc. In our usage, the system ego encompasses the set of psychic structures, processes, and functions that mediate between the individual and his physical and social environment. The ego is the component of the personality serving adaptation to the external world.

Whereas the id operates in accordance with the primary process, which presses for immediate gratification of the instinctual drives, the discharge processes governing ego functions do not show the same peremptory, imperative character. Discharge of tension or, speaking in terms of experience, gratification, can be delayed. Wishes can be fulfilled in accordance with the reality situation so as not to endanger the individual's social and physical security, a regulatory tendency called the *reality principle.* In the course of evolution, the ego has become man's primary organ of adaptation and survival. Man differs in this respect from the lower animals, whose survival is to a large degree dependent on built-in, instinctive mechanisms.

Just as we assume that the instinctual drives have a somatic base which is transmitted from generation to generation, we also assume that the ego functions depend on apparatuses that have a biologically inherited, somatic foundation, as well as a psychological one. Although the development of the personality and of its subdivision the ego depends to a great extent on the interaction of the instinctual drives and the environment, the ego has its own autonomous origins, which led Hartmann to introduce the term *primary autonomy of the ego.*

The essential primary, autonomous apparatuses of the ego serve consciousness, motility, perception, memory, and thought. Their precursors are present at birth and constitute the reflex mechanisms necessary for survival. With development, the components of the ego system evolve through successive, qualitatively different stages, one superimposed upon another. Early magical forms of thinking, for example, are superseded by adult, logical forms of thought, yet the early forms are not fully relinquished and still appear in dreams, psychopathology, and the like. The mature, logical forms of thought are superordinated to the more primitive magical ones—an example of the "epigenetic principle."

The ego's autonomy from the id, however, is only relative, since, as we have seen, ego and id form a continuum and constantly interact. This interaction is as a rule collaborative or synergistic. Within the bounds of reality and the internalized standards of behavior, wishes originating in the id are gratified. If conflict arises between the ego and the id, defense mechanisms are activated. Some defenses of the ego—reaction formation, for example—develop into permanent patterns of behavior and assume a great deal of importance for adaptation. Such patterns of behavior or personality traits acquire a measure of independence from pressures originating in the id, an independence constituting what Hartmann called the *secondary autonomy of the ego:* the capacity of the ego to resist incursions from the id, and regression to earlier, more primitive states of personality organization. The extent of secondary autonomy is one of the major determinants of ego strength. Ego strength and its counterpart, ego weakness, are essentially qualitative terms used to describe the autonomy of the ego functions from the id, their efficiency in fulfilling their adaptive tasks, and the capacity to resist lasting, maladaptive regressions to primitive forms of thinking, feeling, and acting, even when coping with stress.

Under conditions of stress and conflict, regression from adult modes of over-all functioning to a dependence characteristic of childhood may occur, or neurotic or psychotic disturbances that represent various forms of regression may develop. The capacity to resist regression, i.e., to avoid returning to primitive forms of psychic functioning, is one aspect of adaptive behavior. The ability to experience temporary regression under certain conditions and for adaptive purposes is not an indication of ego weakness, but rather of ego strength. In waking life, regressive phenomena contribute to creative activities, to humor and play. Ernst Kris (1952) has described this as regression controlled by the ego. Normally, a person experiences temporary, reversible regression in the state of sleep. Incapacity to tolerate regression in sleep and dreaming may become pathogenic and lead to insomnia.

The ability to tolerate and utilize regression is a mental process which is considered an ego function (Arlow & Brenner, 1964); temporary and reversible regressive phenomena might best be viewed as general modes of functioning of the total mental organization rather than of one psychic system only. In more or less disguised forms, primitive thoughts, feelings, and impulses can be expressed in dreams without affecting the adaptation to the outside world. The regressive psychological manifestations of dreaming as well as the physiological aspects of the dream phase of sleep are necessary to maintain the integration and psychophysiological balance of the organism, as has been demonstrated with the help of dream-deprivation experiments.

Physical illness, especially if prolonged and dangerous to life, induces regression which, within limits, has adaptive value. The helplessness of the seriously ill patient makes him dependent on others; his temporary acceptance of help and care is adaptive. This regression to a more dependent mode of behavior serves a useful purpose, provided the patient is able to return to independent, adult ways of acting once the illness has passed.

Chemical substances that affect the central nervous system, i.e., various psychotropic drugs, may cause a return to primitive forms of perception, suspension of reality testing, dreamlike states, hallucinations, and other markedly regressive phenomena (see Chapter 22). Irreversible psychological regression may be the consequence of organic deterioration of the brain. Such deterioration can be caused by neurological disease, chronic use of certain drugs or alcohol, hardening of the arteries, injury, or other diseases.

Regression as a defense readily occurs in childhood. A familiar example is the toddler's loss of established bowel control immediately after the birth of a younger sibling. The older child experiences the unavoidable decrease in attention from his mother as a loss of love and defends himself against painful feelings of disappointment and anxiety by a regression to earlier modes of functioning when he enjoyed a fuller share of his mother's attention and affection.

In neuroses, regression is usually limited and selective. In psychoses, however, it may become profound and lead to primitive thought processes, interference with judgment, and disruption of reality testing. The depth of the regression depends on the amount of anxiety in relation to ego strength. In regression there is a return to earlier fixation points, that is, to a previous, less mature phase of development. Fixation may be caused by traumatic situations during the course of development, as well as by excessive frustration or gratification, or by an inconsistent alternation between the two. Aside from fixations, there may also be developmental arrests. Although these terms are often used interchangeably, it is better to consider *fixation* as the readiness to return to an earlier mode of mental functioning, and *developmental arrest* as the persistence of earlier modes of functioning in later periods of life. Fixation often refers to the persistence of early forms of psychosexual development—oral and anal—and of primitive object-relations; developmental arrest usually relates to ego and superego functions.

The ego has what we call an integrating function. In its fully developed form, this process of synthesis or organization, as Nunberg

(1955) described it, is basic to our capacity to think in causal terms, to generalize, to understand, and to harmonize the various components of our mental apparatus. It contributes to the formation of the sense or feeling of identity.

In one of his final papers, Freud (1940) made the following statement: "We know two kinds of things about what we call our psyche (or mental life): first, its bodily organ and scene of action, the brain (or nervous system) and, on the other hand, our acts of consciousness, which are immediate data and cannot be further explained by any sort of description" (p. 144). Consciousness is the cardinal mental function as well as a function of the system ego. It is stimulated by all perceptions coming from without and from within our own body. Perceptions coming from within our organism include the awareness of our thoughts, of affective states, and of pleasure and pain. Consciousness, in addition to being a function of the ego, can also be described as a sense organ superordinate to and stimulated by all the perceptual data communicated to our central nervous system. Consciousness is a reflective awareness of such data. The quality *preconscious* would refer to mental content that is not invested with sufficient psychic energy to bring about awareness. If psychic energy is expended to exclude mental content from awareness, then we consider such mental content to be unconscious.

We described consciousness as a mental function to which the perceptual functions, mediated by the sense organs, are subordinated. Perception depends on the intactness of the sense organs as well as of the receptors in the brain. The sense organs and sensory areas of the brain form the somatic side of the apparatus serving perceptual functions. The developmental, "learned," aspect of the perceptual apparatus consists in the establishment of organized patterns or schemata (Piaget) which contain the record of past experiences and form the conceptual framework for the perceptual data. Without this framework, perception becomes disrupted. Hence, perception cannot be considered a passive process, but must be looked upon as an active organizing of sensory data in accordance with pre-established patterns. If such patterns are lost, perception as a mental function becomes impossible even if the sensory organs are intact. The same applies to all sensory modalities. The destruction of the visual cortex of the brain, for example, entails the loss of those patterns and makes it impossible to recognize the visual stimuli coming from the outside world (visual agnosia), even though the eyes and nerve pathways are undamaged.

Control of motility is another ego function based on the intactness of an inborn apparatus. The somatic aspect of this apparatus consists of the central and peripheral nervous system as well as the voluntary muscles, bones, and tendons of the body. The control of motility observed in the adult evolves gradually, beginning with the reflex discharges of the neonate and eventually leading to the complex integrated and skilled movements of the grownup. Motility is under "conscious" control in the sense that certain movements can be willed and then proper nerve impulses proceed to stimulate muscles to perform the desired movement. But in order to perform such a movement smoothly, a vast number of reflex adjustments take place below the level of awareness. To pick up an object from the floor may appear a simple task, yet it requires the innervation of many muscles of the body to bend the trunk, to stretch out the hand, to clasp the object with the fingers, etc. A great deal of sensory data from our visual apparatus, from the position of our body and limbs in space, from the tension state (tonus) of our muscles, is processed below the level of awareness to effect the correct innervations of such movements.

Aside from the regulation of motility through reflexes, a constant learning of new patterns of motility takes place. The acquisition of any motor skills, whatever their nature, is achieved through learning, i.e., through the interaction of the inborn apparatus with the environment. Automatized patterns or schemas below the level of awareness are established and form another element in the acquisition of motor skills. Thus, aside from the reflex regulation of motility, a great many learned patterns become automatized, preconscious, and are essential to the control of motility. A loss of such automatized patterns, or deautomatization, leads to a loss of acquired skills. Even the simplest goal-directed movement would become slow, cumbersome, and nearly impossible, if every single detail of it had to be willed and executed without the benefit of automatized patterns. Learned automatized patterns can be likened to programs and subprograms that process various kinds of information in modern computers.

Memory as an ego function is based on the capacity of the central nervous system to establish traces of experience. It can be divided into four different aspects or grades (Klein, 1966). The first is the registration of sensory input to form traces or engrams. The second is the storage or retention of these traces—short-term and long-term storage can be differentiated. The third aspect is the categorization or location of traces within schemata. The final stage is retrieval and reconstruction of remembered data. From a developmental point of view, Piaget (see Baldwin, 1968) distinguishes "recognition memory" from "evocative memory." In recognition memory, which is established prior to the age of 18 months, the memory trace leads to the perception of a familiar person or thing only if that person or thing is within the perceptual field. Once evocative memory is established, the image of a familiar person can be summoned up without his presence.

At any level or stage of the memory function, a disturbance may be caused by interference with either the organic or psychological aspects of the apparatus that serves memory. Destruction of certain areas of the brain would be an example of an organic interference with memory function; repression, an example of a psychological interference.

Many sensory stimuli that impinge upon our central nervous system result in automatic reflex responses or unconditioned reflexes. They form the basis of animal and human behavior. In the course of development, a great many patterns—programs and subprograms in computer language—are acquired, and serve to organize perception, memory, and mobility. Thought processes, which we consider to be an aspect of the system ego, are interposed between stimulus and observed behavioral response. They offer a great advantage for human adaptation, since they are, as Freud formulated it, trial actions with a minimum expenditure of energy. Mature thinking becomes, at least to a large extent, divorced from the wishes originating in the id and leads to an evaluation of a situation and to appropriate action. The capacity to think in other than wishful terms and to anticipate the consequences of one's actions is a sign of progression from the pleasure principle to the reality principle.

Thinking, or thought process, as an ego function, is not identical with cognition or cognitive process. The term cognition is often used to include awareness, perception, knowing (apperception), and memory. Cognition, in some psychological theoretical systems, is one of the three subdivisions of mental life, the other two being conation (tendency to act) and affection (emotional life).

Precursors of thinking during the preverbal stage of development can, of course, only be inferred. It is assumed that when the infant's urgent needs and wishes are not gratified at once, he relieves his tension by hallucinating the gratification. This represents the first form of thinking. The hungry infant, after establishing the initial perceptual and memory patterns in connection with feeding, hallucinates the breast and the feeding situation. At least for a short time, the delay of the imperative unsatisfied needs becomes tolerable, and a primitive form of thinking in the form of hallucinated perceptual images is established. In the adult, hallucinatory wish-fulfillment is usually limited to dreaming.

Piaget has come to the conclusion that in early-type thinking—during the first two years of life—there is no separation between the perceived object and the action exerted upon it. For example, the perception of a rattle, reaching out, moving it, and producing noises, form a sensorimotor unit to the infant. In the course of the second year, it becomes possible for the toddler to summon up the image of the object even when it is not accessible to his sensory perception. This evocative memory (Fraiberg, 1969) presupposes the ability to form mental representations or images of external objects, whether persons or things, independently of the action exerted on them or of their presence in the perceptual field. Early sensorimotor intelligence is thus superseded by representational intelligence. The second or third years of life are also decisive for the acquisition of language. Verbal symbols—signifiers—are added to the mental representation of the object. At first these verbal symbols appear to the child as one of the properties of the object alongside of its other properties. Mental representations, evocative memory, and word symbols are basic to the development of thinking.

Consciousness, perception, control of motility, memory, and thought can be considered the basic functions of the system ego. Three other components of the ego, language and speech, perception and expression of affects, and reality testing, can be understood as elaborations and combinations of these five basic functions.

Language is an ego function of great complexity. Perception, consciousness, memory, control of motility, and thinking, are all prerequisites for the acquisition, development, and maintenance of the language function, which, although it utilizes all the basic ego functions, possesses additional physiological apparatuses of its own. There are specific areas of the cerebral cortex that must remain intact for the acquisition of language. Every child whose early maturation and development is not impeded by organic disturbances or by severe environmental deviations and trauma acquires the language of its environment. The acquisition of language cannot be satisfactorily explained by association and conditioning theories alone. Piaget's theory of sensorimotor schemata furnishes additional data for a developmental theory of language acquisition. Language and speech are not the same thing. Language is a "learned code for communication" (Rosen, 1966) that can be expressed in writing and various other ways; speech is the expression of the accoustical forms of words through the vocal apparatus. The structure of language and the availability or nonavailability of word symbols for things, processes, and actions exert a marked influence on the ability to assimilate and organize new impressions.

Perception and expression of affects refers to the subjective experience of emotions and their somatic manifestations. Physiologically, affects may manifest themselves through blushing, weeping, increased perspiration, rapid pulse rate, and the like, all of which are under the control of the involuntary, i.e., sympathetic and parasympathetic, nervous system. In addition, bodily posture, facial expression, and tone of voice all indicate the emotional state. Affects are expressed differently in different cultural milieus: in one society, the reaction to the death of a loved person may be restrained grief, in another, loud demonstrative wailing. A specific situation may preclude the expression of certain feelings; for example, it may be realistically dangerous or otherwise inappropriate to express one's anger, yet the awareness of that emotion and some of its somatic manifestations may be present. Affects cannot be unconscious in the same sense that ideas, thoughts, and memories can. They are subjective experiences perceived as pleasurable or unpleasurable. In accordance with the pleasure-unpleasure principle, we tend to avoid unpleasurable affects. The system ego has defense mechanisms and other means at its disposal to cope with unpleasurable affects, which can thus be avoided or at least mitigated.

We have spoken so far of the expression and perception of affects. How, though, are these affects generated? For the infant and small child, the answer is relatively simple: the frustration of the imperative physiological and instinctual needs generates unpleasure, whereas their gratification leads to pleasure. Basically, this also applies to the adult. The situation here, however, is more complex, because ego and superego together determine the affective state. Anticipation of danger—an aspect of the ego—or conflict with one's moral standards—part of the superego system—may turn a pleasurable instinctual gratification into a source of unpleasure by inducing anxiety and feelings of guilt.

The *sense of reality* employs and combines all the ego subsystems and is crucial to man's adaptation to his environment. The primary prerequisite for an objective sense of reality is the establishment of boundaries of the self. The term ego boundaries is frequently used in this context. (Ego, refers, of course, to ego as synonymous with self, rather than to ego as a systemic part of the mental organization.) The formation of these boundaries is a gradual process occurring during the separation-individuation phase of early childhood, when the basis of reality testing—that is, the capacity to differentiate perceptions coming from the external world from sensations, thoughts, and memories originating within—is established. Aside from reality testing proper, one's sense of reality depends on one's level of consciousness. During dreaming, for example, when external perception is largely excluded and the scope of consciousness is essentially restricted to stimuli coming from within, fantastic and unreal content may temporarily be perceived as "real." Memory is essential to the correct evaluation of reality. Any disturbance of the memory, whether an interference with the registration of new data or with recall, disturbs the sense of reality. Thought, to the extent that it includes anticipation, causal thinking, concepts of space and time, etc., also takes part in our evaluation of reality. Even the simple act of stopping a car in front of a red traffic light includes the correct perception of the color, the memory that a red light is a signal to stop the car, and the anticipation of possible dangers, an element of thought.

All the subsystems of the ego, conditioned and unconditioned reflexes, and those expressions of our physiological and instinctual needs that do not conflict with reality, i.e., that are reality-syntonic, contribute to self-preservation and the preservation of the species. Preformed, instinctive patterns that serve self-preservation in animals have, in man, largely been supplanted by the adaptive functioning of the system ego. Learning plays a role in animal adaptation, and even instinctive responses in animals depend to some extent on interaction with and modification through the environment, i.e., on learning. In man, the development of complex psychic systems, although it has biological foundations, depends to a very large extent on learning through interaction with the environment.

The Superego

The third system of the mental organization, the superego, gradually emerges out of the system ego. Its development presupposes the prior evolution of the ego functions perception, memory, and thought, as well as the capacity to identify with the care-taking adults and to internalize their demands and prohibitions. Some authorities use the terms superego and ego ideal interchangeably, while others define the two as different psychic formations. We consider the conscience (or prohibiting aspects) and the ego ideal (or the ideal strivings) two component parts of the superego. For instance, the ideal of truthfulness is bolstered by the prohibition against lying. Even prior to the oedipal period, the child learns the difference between "good" and "bad" by the parents' approval or disapproval. He perceives warnings designed to protect him from harm, such as, "Do not touch the hot stove," at first as moral demands, that is to say, in terms of good and evil. Later on, such warnings and prohibitions lose their "moral" aspects and become anticipations of danger and harm, i.e., become part of the system ego.

The child's compliance with the parents' demands for control of his urinary and bowel functions can be considered a forerunner of the superego. Control is something "good" to please the parents; lack of it is something "bad" because it displeases them. Primitive wishes for unrestrained expression of orality and anality in the young child are frequently controlled by conditioning and defense mechanisms such as reaction formation. The gradual internalization of prohibitions, that is to say, the development of the system superego, provides an additional method of controlling primitive impulses.

The ideal aspects of the superego have their origins in the first three years of life. The young child idealizes the strength and power of his parents. His own self-love (narcissism) causes him to incorporate these idealized images of the parents, and these images contribute to the formation of the ego ideal. Beginning with the oedipal period, idealization in large measure relates to moral behavior. Ideals, however, include other aspects of behavior aside from the moral ones—for instance, ideals of beauty, strength, or success. To the extent that a person is able to fulfill the ideal standards of his superego, he experiences inner satisfaction and enhancement of his self-esteem. The failure to live up to one's ego ideal leads to feelings of shame and a lowering of self-esteem. The mature adult learns to reduce the gap between ego ideal and the capacity for realistic achievement so that there can be a harmonious collaboration between ego and ego ideal. This facilitates the achievement of an optimal psychological balance and contributes to maintaining a steady and realistic self-evaluation.

During the oedipal period, the essential elements of the superego are established. They consist of the taboo of parricide, the incest barrier, and identification with the parents' basic moral standards. Identification replaces the rivalry with the ambivalently loved parent of the same sex whom the child needs and loves—and also hates and wants to be rid of. The internalization of superego prohibitions creates the capacity to experience guilt feelings, i.e., superego anxiety, whenever such prohibitions are transgressed either in actuality or sometimes just in thought. The development of the superego is thus the basic precondition for the socialization of the child and the successful adaptation of the adult to his social environment.

The development of the superego continues beyond the oedipal period. Modifications of the superego occur throughout latency, and a major reorganization takes place during adolescence. Even in adulthood, there may be shifts in the superego. For example, the acceptance of new secular or religious convictions and beliefs induces changes in the ego ideal as well as in the moral standards. Here we can again observe the close connection between ideal strivings and moral standards, the two components of the superego. Sometimes the establishment of strict new standards of behavior is based on reaction formation. This forms the basis for some successful treatment of drug addiction and alcoholism.

Even though ego ideals and moral prohibitions are closely related, they may also be in conflict with one another. In the service of achieving social, political, or religious ideals, ethical standards may be set aside or violated, expressed and rationalized by the phrase, "the end justifies the means."

Ethical standards may be more or less internalized, but socially acceptable behavior depends not only on the ethical standards, but also on social anxiety—i.e., the conscious fear of disapproval and the possibility of punishment. Almost everybody would shrink from incest or murder, but some people may engage in lying or cheating as long as they feel sure that they will not be found out. The superego may have gaps and inconsistencies. In situations of stress, some ordinarily truthful and honest people may resort to lies and other unethical behavior. In order to escape from or mollify the feelings of guilt and remorse that occur as a result of violating superego prohibitions, some people commit self-punitive acts or seek out punishment from others. Many look for forgiveness and atonement through religious practices.

Just as certain aspects of the ego, e.g., the defense mechanisms, remain unconscious, so, too, do many aspects of the superego. Frequently the causes of guilt feelings are unconscious. Attempts to deal with such unconscious sources of guilt may lead to symptom formation, accident-proneness, and may even contribute to the development of a masochistic or self-punitive way of life.

Self-observation is sometimes considered a function of the superego. It is doubtful whether self-observation can be differentiated from the capacity for reflective self-awareness, which is a cardinal component of the system ego. Self-observation leading to self-criticism is activated by actions and thoughts that deviate from one's superego ideals and prohibitions.

Basically, superego formation results from the growing child's interaction with his parents or parent substitutes. As the child establishes more and more contacts outside his family circle, other adults as well as members of his peer group serve as models for identifications and consequently for superego modifications. The superego may be even further modified as a result of the influence of various groups to which the individual may belong. These may be short-lived group formations, such as a mob, or long-term stable formations, such as political, social, or religious organizations. The changes in the individual superego may be temporary or permanent. In some instances, the individual may abandon his own superego standards and accept those of the leader or the group.

The superego also has a contribution to make to the evaluation of social reality. Reality testing proper is a complex ego function which makes it possible to differentiate the sensory stimuli coming from the outside world from perceptions, thoughts, and feelings arising from within. The superego standards—moral and ideal alike—provide us with a yardstick for judging the behavior of others. They thus contribute to our over-all evaluation of reality, if the superego organization is intact and flexible. Conversely, those with a primitive and rigid superego may misjudge the actions and intentions of others in line with their own superego deficiencies.

REFERENCES

Arlow, J., & Brenner, C. (1964), *Psychoanalytic Concepts and the Structural Theory.* New York: International Universities Press.

Baldwin, A. (1968), *Theories of Child Development.* New York: Wiley.

Cameron, N. (1963), *Personality Development and Psychopathology.* Boston: Houghton Mifflin.

Fraiberg, S. (1969), Libidinal Object Constancy and Mental Representation. *The Psychoanalytic Study of the Child,* 24:9-47. New York: International Universities Press.

Freud, S. (1940), An Outline of Psychoanalysis. *Standard Edition,* 23, pp. 141-207. London: Hogarth Press.

Hartmann, H. (1939), *Ego Psychology and the Problem of Adaptation.* New York: International Universities Press, 1958.

Klein, G. (1966), The Several Grades of Memory. In: *Psychoanalysis: A General*

Psychology, ed. R.M. Loewenstein, L. M. Newman, M. Schur, & A. J. Solnit. New York: International Universities Press, pp. 377-389.

Kris. E. (1952), *Psychoanalytic Explorations in Art.* New York: International Universities Press, Chapter 6.

Nunberg, H. (1955), *Principles of Psychoanalysis.* New York: International Universities Press.

Rosen, V. (1966), Disturbances of Representation and Reference in Ego Deviation. In: *Psychoanalysis: A General Psychology.* Ed. R.M. Loewenstein, L. M. Newman, M. Schur, & A. J. Solnit. New York: International Universities Press, pp. 634-654.

SUGGESTED READING

Freud, S. (1923), The Ego and the Id. *Standard Edition,* 19:3-66. London: Hogarth Press, 1961.

Piaget, J. (1970), *Genetic Epistemology.* New York: Columbia University Press, 1970.

Rapaport, D. (1967), *The Collected Papers of David Rapaport,* ed. M. Gill. New York: Basic Books.

Schur, M. (1966), *The Id and the Regulatory Principles of Mental Functioning.* New York: International Universities Press.

CHAPTER THREE

Theory Of Personality: Ego Defense Mechanisms

GEORGE H. WIEDEMAN, M.D.

In accordance with the pleasure principle, man constantly wards off painful and unpleasurable affects, ideas, and aspects of reality. This he does by means of the ego's defense mechanisms. These defense mechanisms are intrapsychic processes that are "carried out silently and invisibly" (Anna Freud, 1936), i.e., they are outside awareness and cannot be intentionally set into motion. Yet they bring about observable behavioral, affective, and cognitive changes from which they can be inferred. Defense mechanisms were discovered through clinical work with patients, and their significant role in relation to neuroses and psychoses was elucidated before their significance in the normal adaptive and developmental processes became clear.

The term defense, first used by Freud in the 1890's, was succeeded by the term repression, which became synonymous with defense. In the mid-twenties, Freud again returned to the more general term defense, and repression became one of the defenses among others. Anna Freud, by using the word "mechanism" in the title of her classic book, *The Ego and the Mechanisms of Defense* (1936), underscored the automatic, repetitive, and stereotyped qualities of the defenses.

Anxiety is of crucial importance in understanding the mechanisms of defense, and we will proceed first with a discussion of this very familiar affective state. Because of the colloquial use of the term anxiety, misunderstandings easily arise. Freud distinguished realistic from neurotic anxiety, viewing the former as the reaction to external dangers, the latter as the reaction to dangers coming from within. It is simpler and less confusing to refer to realistic anxiety as fear and to reserve the term anxiety, without the qualifier "neurotic," to reactions to inner dangers.

The psychological and the physiological manifestations of fear and anxiety are similar. Subjectively, fear and anxiety are unpleasurable feelings that can be described as apprehension in their milder forms and as dread and panic when more severe. The objective physiological manifestations of anxiety and fear consist of a variety of functional changes in the physiological processes controlled by the vegetative nervous system (the sympathetic and the parasympathetic systems). In the face of external danger, the usual effect of fear is to modify physiological functions in preparation for fight or flight. There may be no immediate awareness of fear in the face of serious real danger, provided one thinks he can cope with the threatening situation. Someone who finds himself about to have an accident while driving a car but can steer the vehicle so as to avoid the impending collision does not necessarily experience fear while he performs the actions to avoid the accident. After overcoming the dangerous situation, however, he may experience a delayed reaction. In such instances, the fear reaction stemming from the exposure to danger, i.e., to a traumatic situation, is temporarily warded off, permitting full concentration on dealing with the danger. After the passing of the danger, the temporarily warded-off fear reaction emerges into awareness: now it is re-experienced and mastered.

Unconscious conflicts based on past danger situations that for one reason or another have been reactivated lead to the arousal of anxiety. For example, separation may cause severe anxiety in the adult if this person experienced traumatic separation as a small child. The actual early experience would remain unconscious, but the anxiety would mobilize the defense mechanisms because an escape from an inner danger cannot be achieved by flight as if it were an external one.

Thus, defense mechanisms—a part of the ego system—protect us against painful affects—especially anxiety—which would disrupt our sense of well being and our adaptation to the environment. Small quantities of anxiety—often not perceived—serve as stimuli to activate the various defenses: this is called *signal anxiety*.

Repression was the first defense mechanism to be described and can be observed in health and disease, frequently combined with other defenses. It presupposes attainment of a developmental stage in which boundaries, however tenuous and fluid, exist between the ego and id systems. In repression, a thought, idea, or the memory of a past event is eliminated from awareness and kept unconscious because its emergence into consciousness would produce conflict and lead to anxiety. Repressed material cannot be recalled by an effort of will; it is assumed that it is kept unconscious by a constant expenditure of psychic energy, i.e., countercathexis.

Most early formative experiences from birth until about the age of five or six years succumb to repression and thus cannot be recalled. This "infantile amnesia" has an adaptive significance—the recall of instinctual derivatives and cognitive and affective aspects of the early years would be overwhelming and would interfere with integration and adaptation. In situations where repression and other defense mechanisms are weakened, a "return of the repressed" takes place and may lead to symptom formation. Early memories of experiences prior to the development of language and the rudiments of secondary-type thinking cannot in any event be verbalized; they succumb instead to "primal repression." They nevertheless contribute to the development of character traits or disturbances, to ego strength or weakness, and even to psychophysiological reactions later on in life. Infantile amnesia is considered a normal phenomenon. But, aside from its contribution to the normal integration of the developmental processes, excessive repression leads to impoverishment and distortion of the personality. A very far-reaching repression of aggressive-drive derivatives, for instance, may contribute to forming a personality lacking in the capacity for elementary self-assertiveness. An excessive repression of sexuality is a frequent source of psychological symptoms, inhibitions, and personality disorders. Conversely, the persistence of primitive, pregenital sexual-drive derivatives interferes with the dominance of adult genital sexuality. This may also lead to a disturbance of sexual functioning and to other symptoms. Not everything that is forgotten is necessarily repressed. Repression takes place when remembering would cause conflict and unpleasure. A large amount of sensory information is forgotten because it has not been integrated into long-storage memory schemata. Some complex skills that require intactness of memory and of other functions may become impaired and even lost because of lack of use and practice—for example, conversing in a foreign language or playing a musical instrument. Under normal circumstances, however, the recovery of such skills can be achieved with practice. Memory disturbances can also be due to organic changes in the central nervous system. Destruction of certain cell groups in the brain may lead to the inability to retain new sensory input; amnesia for limited periods of time may be the result of trauma, such as concussion of the brain.

Reaction formation is a defense mechanism whereby unacceptable feelings and attitudes are kept out of awareness by expressing the opposite in thought and behavior. Which of the opposite attitudes—love or hate, oversolicitude or neglect, cleanliness or pleasure in messing with dirt, etc.—would create anxiety, and therefore become unacceptable, depends on the specific situation and personality. Usually, the socially acceptable attitude becomes overemphasized and its opposite is rendered unconscious, but sometimes the reverse may be true: hostility may become the manifest attitude if awareness of love would create conflict and anxiety. Reaction formation is one of the defense mechanisms that reinforces repression and acts as a safeguard against the emergence of unacceptable impulses. Even more than other defense mechanisms, it contributes to the formation of character traits. Orderliness, reliability, punctuality, and other socially useful traits are derived from more primitive, opposite antecedents from which they have become largely independent, i.e., acquired a degree of secondary autonomy.

In the defense mechanism *isolation,* the affect is separated from the ideational content. Whereas in repression ideas are excluded from awareness, in isolation the idea remains conscious but is devoid of unacceptable affect. Normally, isolation contributes to logical, objective thinking. If our ideas and observations are affectively charged, logical and factual distortions are likely to occur. Isolation also contributes to the character trait of detachment. In those instances where the person engages in tasks that would evoke feelings of anxiety, disgust, guilt, or other unpleasurable affective reaction, isolation is the mainstay of detachment. An example would be the detachment soldiers acquire in the face of the destruction they are ordered to inflict.

Thoughts and memories are repressed; affects are dealt with differently—they may be postponed, displaced, converted, or somatized. Postponement of anger or rage is a well-known phenomenon. If anger cannot be expressed against the one in authority, it may erupt later on against someone else, for instance, one's wife and children. The anger is postponed and displaced. The desperate feelings aroused by the loss of a loved person may be temporarily postponed to protect the griever from being overwhelmed by their intensity. They are gradually expressed and mastered in the process of mourning. Displacement of affect plays an important part in the psychodynamics of the phobic neuroses, which will be described in a later chapter.

Conversion is another mechanism that deals with affective aspects of unacceptable impulses. Anxiety generated by inner conflicts is absorbed by the development of bodily symptoms which in symbolic form express through "body language" the underlying unconscious fantasies. For example, hysterical paralysis of the arm may be due to anxiety generated by very strong hostile impulses to attack and kill someone who is emotionally significant to the patient.

In *somatization,* affects are discharged through physiological channels. This may lead to psychosomatic disorders: persistent anger that cannot be expressed directly or through displacement may contribute to producing high blood pressure and eventually lead to organic changes in the circulatory system, if left untreated.

In *projection* as a defense mechanism, the affect and idea derived from and connected with impulses are attributed to another person, to a group of people, or to an institution. Natural and presumed supernatural phenomena may serve as a screen onto which are projected affectively charged attitudes. We see this in the magical thinking of early childhood and in early stages of sociocultural development. In modern man it may be part of psychopathology, or it may be a superstitious belief shared by others.

Projection arises when impulses, affects, and ideas that would cause conflict and anxiety are about to emerge into awareness. Angry and hostile impulses may be ascribed to another person or group of people so that one's own hostile behavior to them is justified as a response to their presumed hostile attitudes. A more complicated example of projection includes a preliminary reversal of the feeling of love into hate: an unacceptable feeling of homosexual physical attraction and love is turned into loathing and hate. The object of this love-hate becomes the "enemy." Not only is the homosexual inclination rendered unconscious, so, too, is the hate, which is ascribed to the other person—who then becomes the "persecutor."

Use of projection is very common in childhood. A young child whose cognition has not fully evolved into secondary-type thinking and whose reality testing is still tenuous may be firmly convinced, "It's not me, it's Johnny who broke the cup," despite evidence to the contrary. Of course, conscious shifting of blame, in children or adults, is not to be considered a defense mechanism, but simply a means of avoiding responsibility.

When someone assumes that his impulses and actions are recognized and talked about by others, even though there is no real basis for this assumption, he has what are called "ideas of reference." Especially during adolescence, ideas of reference are not infrequent, and they may contribute to defensive and furtive behavior. A young person may assume that others know he masturbates because of his complexion or because of rings under his eyes. Essentially, what are projected onto others as ideas of reference are superego standards. Persistent and prevalent use of projection as a defense leads to the impairment of reality testing, especially to the misjudgment of other peoples' attitudes, to guardedness, suspiciousness, and coldness. Projection is the principal mechanism underlying serious psychopathology in the various paranoid conditions.

The defense mechanism of *undoing,* as was the defense of isolation, was first observed in the obsessive-compulsive neuroses. In everyday life, phenomena resembling the mechanism of undoing are part of many magical and superstitious thoughts and actions. Some religious ceremonials contain elements of undoing sinful impulses and acts by prayer or penance. In undoing, as part of a neurotic illness, unacceptable thoughts, wishes, and deeds are canceled out by actions and sequences of acts, i.e., ceremonials designed to counteract them. One of the common symptoms of the obsessive-compulsive neurotic is the compulsion to wash the hands over and over again. The patient may explain this as an indispensable measure to avoid contamination with "germs," an obvious rationalization which helps to annul an unacceptable impulse or act, e.g., masturbation or even the wish to masturbate. An example of the mechanism of undoing that follows some "doing" is that of a man who invites a casual acquaintance to visit with his family. Everyone, including himself, is puzzled by his insistence of extending his hospitality to someone he feels quite indifferent to. The host, although he knew he felt guilty, was not aware that on a previous occasion he had been rather rude to this very same acquaintance. Repression was only partially successful. The insistent invitation represents an undoing of the rudeness. The close relation of undoing to reaction formation is obvious.

Denial used as a term to designate a defense mechanism should be clearly differentiated from the common usage of the word, which means saying "no" and consciously refusing to acknowledge facts and statements. The defense mechanism of denial is an *unconscious* process wherein the awareness of unacceptable facts and painful perceptions is negated. Young children are less able to bear pain and to accept unpleasant realities than adults, and denial is therefore prevalent in childhood. In adults, the sense of reality counteracts the tendency to deny unpleasant and dangerous events. Hence, when denial is activated—barring significant psychopathology—its effects are temporary and incomplete. Children and adolescents, and to a lesser extent, adults, use fantasies and daydreaming to bolster denial. Denial can also be supported by other defensive maneuvers, such as exaggeration, humor, and clowning. Persistent and massive denial of unacceptable facts is only possible if reality testing is impaired. It may be associated with delusions and hallucinations. For instance, when a beloved person dies, the bereaved may hear the voice of the deceased and converse with him as if he were still alive.

Defense mechanisms never appear in "pure" form, but rather combine with and reinforce one another. As we have already noted, reaction formation bolsters repression, and denial is often supported by rationalization of fantasies. There are similarities, but also essential differences, between denial and repression. Both defenses exclude mental content from awareness: in denial, sensory data from the external world, which also may include sensations coming from the subject's own body, is excluded from consciousness; in repression, the ideational derivatives of unacceptable instinctual drives and other thoughts that would induce anxiety are rendered unconscious.

Intellectualization is a defense mechanism wherein logical thinking is utilized to ward off instinctual impulses to avoid inner conflicts. In adolescence, preoccupation with philosophical, scientific, and religious problems may serve as an important defense against the upsurging instinctual impulses. At the same time, it may play a positive role in enhancing knowledge and intellectual performance. As early as latency, however, thinking may become sidetracked to trivial matters or pointless brooding displaying defensive or even symptomatic features. This is the case in obsessive-compulsive conditions where preoccupation with trivia, ill-founded worries, and doubting usually is part of the sickness. Even though magical thinking is part of this condition, the formal, logical aspects of thought are preserved. In paranoid ideation the sequence of thought may be governed by the rules of logical thinking, but the basic premise is divorced from reality and is delusional.

In *rationalization,* the individual finds seemingly logical and factual reasons for beliefs, attitudes, and behavior, the true motives for which he is repressing. Rationalization as a defense mechanism is not an excuse used consciously and deliberately to justify some kind of unacceptable behavior—it is unconsciously employed. The man who does not look for work, stating that there are no jobs worthy of him, when jobs corresponding to his actual skills are available, may be rationalizing out of an unconscious desire to be supported by others. Rationalization is also used to make irrational fears seem plausible. One with a phobic fear of traveling in subways, trains, or planes might say that crowding, inconvenience, and the possibility of accidents make him avoid public transportation. This rationalization would also help to cover up the irrationality of the fears and to maintain self-esteem.

Identification is a mental process frequently described as a defense mechanism. It is much more than just that, since it plays a crucial role in establishing the mental organization, character traits, and the sense of identity. It is an unconscious process wherein the child internalizes—that is, adopts as his own—aspects of the significant people in his environment. It might possibly be called the unconscious counterpart to imitation—which is conscious. The little girl may imitate the gestures of her mother, but later on she internalizes them: she has then identified with the mother. In a broad sense, identification may be looked upon as the internalization of the human environment that makes socialization possible. Identification contributes to the learning process through which such basic skills as language are acquired. Perception, memory, and other components of the ego system are prerequisites for identification. The affective or emotional bonds to those in the growing child's immediate environment stimulate the process of identification, so important in personality formation. Incorporation and introjection, frequently associated with identification, usually refer to primitive early patterns of identification based on fantasies of oral ingestion, i.e., eating up and swallowing. Incorporation can be conceived of as the primitive basis of introjection, whereas introjection is the psychological aspect of incorporation. The result of incorporation—introjection—is identification, namely, the formation of or addition to one's self-image or self-representation.

In early infancy, it is principally the mother-child relation that determines the quality of the basic or primary identifications. Later on, an ever increasing number of people become important in determining the nature of identifications. The sense of the self or identity rests to a great extent on a synthesis of multiple identifications. Sensations originating in one's own body are an important source of one's body image, which, in turn, is a significant aspect of the sense of self. The reactions, attributes, and feelings expressed by others also contribute to one's sense of identity. For example, the parents' usually unequivocal acceptance of the sex of the child is very early communicated to him and forms the basis for his acceptance of his own masculinity (or femininity).

Identifications with a feared or even hated person are frequently observed. This "identification with the aggressor" has a definite defensive value: confronted with the aggressor, the person protects himself from anxiety and feelings of inadequacy by internalizing the attitudes and values of the aggressor.

Another form of identification is identification with the lost object. By identification, the lost object is preserved within the self and the pain caused by the loss is lessened. Feelings of affection usually contain some negative feelings, i.e., at least a slight degree of ambivalence is present. This holds true as well for identifications. The identification with the lost, ambivalently loved-hated object may lead in some depressive states to an aggression turned against the internalized object, in effect, against the self, perhaps taking the form of self-reproaches, which are thinly disguised attacks against the ambivalently loved, lost person, or, in extreme cases, to suicidal acts that unconsciously represent an attack on the internalized object—the introject.

Character or personality traits acquired through identification are usually similar to those of the models on which they are based. There are, however, also negative identifications—character traits the reverse of those manifested by the parents. Many character traits are compromises between conflicting sources of identification.

In the course of development, the major identifications take place with parents or parent substitutes, siblings, and other relatives. As the child steps out of the confines of his family, first his peers and teachers, and, later on, social, political, and religious leaders contribute to his identifications. National, cultural, and religious leaders of the past may also serve as models for identification and become integrated into the person's sense of identity.

Each of us has our own typical combination of defenses. The predominance and consistent use of particular defense mechanisms put a stamp on character. The prevalence of some defenses contributes to psychopathology by interfering with the smooth functioning of the system ego. They may become part of symptoms of a neurotic or psychotic nature. Projection and denial seriously interfere with the evaluation of reality; extensive repression contributes to symptoms of conversion hysteria; isolation and undoing are observed in obsessive-compulsive conditions. In the healthy, a flexible and balanced defense system contributes to emotional well-being by protecting against the emergence of unpleasurable affects, in line with the pleasure-unpleasure principle.

REFERENCES

Freud, A. (1936), *The Ego and the Mechanisms of Defense. The Writings of Anna Freud,* Vol. 2. New York: International Universities Press, 1966.

SUGGESTED READING

Brenner, C. (1955), *An Elementary Textbook of Psychoanalysis.* New York: International Universities Press. Revised edition, 1973.

Freud, A. (1965), *Normality and Pathology of Childhood. The Writings of Anna Freud,* Vol. 6. New York: International Universities Press.

CHAPTER FOUR

The Infant: From Birth to Fifteen Months

JOHN B. McDEVITT, M.D.

The great majority of infants are born with a capacity for maturing normally—provided their needs for bodily care, intellectual growth, and social development are satisfactorily met. For learning and adaptation to take place, however, the infant's inborn biological potential must be properly stimulated. Such stimulation is best provided by the mother who, in the setting of the family, not only gives her baby her love, but also stimulates him selectively and responds appropriately to his specific needs.

In order to understand the development of the child, it is necessary to take into account both the infant's unique constitution and the attitudes, feelings, and behavior of his mother in providing care for him and relating to him. Because wide variations occur in both these essential elements in development, and because of the infant's prolonged helplessness and dependence on the mother, there is a marked variability in children's personality development as well as considerable vulnerability to psychological damage before full development has been achieved. For these reasons, some charac-

---

From The Masters Children's Center, New York City. The preparation of chapters 5, 6, and 7 was made possible in part by NIMH Grant MH 08238 and FFRP Grant G 69-458.

I am indebted to Dr. Margaret S. Mahler for the main descriptive and conceptual framework used in these chapters for an understanding of children's behavior during the first three years of life. I am also indebted to the many other writers listed in the bibliography, from whose works I have drawn liberally and at times literally. To have referred to each author on each such occasion would have been too distracting to the reader.

teristics of the newborn and of his environment will be examined briefly.

Newborns differ a great deal from one another. Some are vigorous and active, visually alert, and seemingly well organized; they give clear signals regarding their feeling states and they are easy to comfort. Others are tense and irritable: they do not mold easily to the mother's body when held and they are difficult to comfort. Moreover, some infants are placid and unresponsive; others, hypersensitive to stimuli, are difficult to quiet and to satisfy.

These variations, which are usually determined by heredity but may also result from different circumstances during pregnancy and childbirth, cause newborns to experience the world differently and to require different care. An active, alert, and responsive baby may develop well even when he is cared for by a mother who provides minimal stimulation. The same kind of mothering, however, would be less than adequate for an inactive, less responsive infant.

Characteristics shown by the newborn may also influence the mother's response to her child. The infant who readily accepts the mother's cuddling and comforting may elicit from her a warm response, whereas the infant who refuses this intimacy and is difficult to comfort may cause the mother to lose interest in caring for him. For these reasons, among others, variations in the newborn's mental and emotional equipment will exert an influence on his development in interaction with the forces of the environment.

Most of the influences of society and of the family are conveyed to the infant by way of his mother. The amount and kind of maternal care she is able to provide for him will depend on her conscious, and, more important, her unconscious feelings and attitudes about having a baby and being a mother—attitudes determined by her own childhood experiences, her personality make-up, and the degree of her maturity, as well as by reality factors such as her satisfaction in marriage, whether the baby was wanted or unwanted, and the family's economic circumstances.

The reactivation of childhood conflicts during pregnancy may make it difficult for a woman to assume the role of a mother, and may therefore disturb the pregnancy, the delivery, and the subsequent mother-child interaction. An underlying hostility to her own mother, which had its origins in her own childhood, may cause her to become anxious and uncertain in her role as a mother; or a childhood hostility to a sibling, which she has forgotten or even been unaware of, may bring about inexplicable feelings of hostility against her infant. If her wish was for a son who would compensate for her own disappointment over being a woman, she may be made unhappy by the fact that her newborn is a girl. Childhood conflicts with her mother may contribute to the onset of depression following delivery; if the depression is severe and prolonged, it will naturally interfere with her care of her baby.

Irrespective of the mother's original attitude toward her newborn, that attitude is continuously modified during the course of her child's growth and development. His changing needs and demands mobilize in her different conscious and unconscious attitudes. A particular stage in his development may arouse fantasies conflicts, and anxieties that are linked with the same period in her own childhood and thus play a role in determining her relationship with her baby.

The mother who has delighted in the care of her young infant may react with irritation or withdrawal when, as a toddler, he becomes active and begins to show some independence. Conversely, when the toddler does become more independent, he may gain admiration from the mother who did not find satisfaction in caring for him when he was a baby. One mother may have difficulty with feeding the baby or with toilet training, another with separation anxiety, sibling rivalry, or sexual curiosity. Siblings do not and cannot have the same meaning to their mother: each has unique characteristics and a particular place in the family, and each elicits from her different responses and feelings.

Not only will the mother's attitude and behavior change as her infant grows, but the impact on his development of the events occurring in his life will also vary, depending on the typical sequences and phases in his development. Every new developmental stage has its specific qualities, tasks, and vulnerabilities. Each child, in accordance with his innate characteristics and previous development, will experience and cope with each new developmental phase in his own fashion. Maternal care, therefore, must be appropriate both to the child's stage in development and to his particular individuality.

When weaning or toilet training is undertaken before the child is maturationally and psychologically ready, the impact on him will be quite different from what it would be if it were undertaken at a more appropriate time. How well a particular child will be able to tolerate such frustrations will depend, not only on his age and the manner in which these frustrations are imposed, but also on his specific sensitivities and personality development. The effect of a temporary separation from the mother, as in the case of hospitalization, will depend on such factors as the child's age and the stage of development of his object relations. When events occur that are grossly inappropriate to the child's phase of development, as well as to his individuality, he will suffer undue stress or trauma. This may interfere with progress in development, thereby creating a predisposition to psychological difficulties later in life.

To summarize: the development of the child may be looked upon as a dynamic unfolding process determined by complex interactions between the child's inner characteristics and the influences of his environment. These interactions involve the child's particular constitution and individuality, the changing characteristics of his environment—especially the physical and emotional availability of his mother—and the phase of the child's development in which specific events take place.

The Austistic Phase

Infancy, which extends from birth to approximately 15 months of age, is the period of man's most rapid growth and development. Never again will he learn so much in so short a time; never again will such dramatic physical and psychological changes occur.

During the first two months of life (the autistic, objectless, or undifferentiated phase) the infant lacks the capacity to distinguish between what is internal and external; he does not even distinguish between himself and his mother. He functions on an instinctive basis: innate reflex patterns such as sucking and crying assure satisfactory growth and development—provided the mother is ready, physiologically and psychologically, to nurture, stimulate, and respond to him.

In the beginning, the baby is totally helpless and dependent on his mother. He shows no evidence of awareness of the outside world, appears to perceive and respond only to inner stimuli, and seems to experience only feelings of quiescence and unpleasure. He is protected from the large number of external stimuli to which adults are ordinarily exposed by a relative imperviousness to these stimuli (the "stimulus barrier") and by the mother, who not only protects him from too many outer stimuli, but also provides discharge for his inner stimuli by responding to his needs. When these protections periodically fail, the newborn's quiescence is disturbed and he reacts with unpleasure. An excess of external and internal stimuli would be traumatic, disrupting the baby's equilibrium and creating intolerable tension. Excessive tension early in life may create a predisposition to anxiety at times of stress later in life, as well as adversely affect personality development.

Periodically the baby is aroused from sleep by hunger or by some form of discomfort. By his crying and fussing at such times, he communicates an immediate and insistent need for nursing or comforting. The baby's needs, however, extend beyond the relief of discomfort or hunger. Particularly important in this respect are oral pleasures such as sucking. During the first year or two, the child is in the oral phase of psychosexual development. His lips and mouth are, during this period, exquisitely sensitive, and either internal stimulation incidental to such biological processes as hunger, or external stimulation is capable of setting off the sucking reflex. The oral erotogenic zone is a source of sensual pleasure, and the act of sucking is pleasurable in its own right, independent of the satisfaction of hunger. The baby achieves both relief of tension and pleasure by way of the mouth, and he has a need to repeat these experiences. In the early months, gratification of the oral impulses takes place without regard to the mother or the external world and with no other aim than allevation of the excitation. Later, the oral impulses, which were at first the infant's only way of relating to anything external to himself, form the basis for his attachment to the mother. Satisfaction of the baby's need for vital nourishment and for relief of tension depends wholly upon the nursing and other bodily care that his mother provides.

The infant's experiences during the oral phase, however, are not limited to the feeding situation; they extend to a wide variety of stimulating, gratifying, and frustrating experiences involving other parts of the body, such as the skin and muscle. His contact with his mother includes not only the sensations of nursing, but also those of touch, odor, body position, and warmth. In the broader sense, orality refers to the tendency to take in by means of all sensory modalities whatever is perceived as pleasurable and tension relieving, as well as to eject that which is perceived as being unpleasurable. The taking in of stimuli from the environment forms one basis for learning and cognitive development and constitutes one way in which a feeling state is transmitted from the mother to the infant. The baby takes in, so to speak, by way of the mother's care, feelings of security and well-being.

The oral phase begins to wane during the second and third year, at which time sucking becomes a periodic and largely regressive phenomenon occurring at times of fatigue, stress, or frustration. During the course of the oral phase, the infant establishes a lasting association between affection, the need for others, and oral activity. At the same time the basis has been formed for later wishes to return or regress to oral dependencies during times of stress. Ordinarily, the oral impulses become less active with the transfer of libidinal cathexis to the next—the anal-erotogenic zone; they are either repressed or sublimated, the latter permitting partial gratification via displacement. Oral impulses normally continue to find expression in fantasy, play, or dreams, and in such pleasures as eating, smoking, and kissing.

As a result of the mother's care, as well as of the baby's own maturational processes, significant developmental changes begin to take place during the first two months of life. The baby adopts some reasonably predictable rhythms of feeding and elimination, sleep and wakefulness. His previous exclusive preoccupation with inner sensation gradually shifts to an increased sensitivity of the surface of the body and the sense organs. This makes possible greater sensory responsiveness to the outside world.

Between states of sleep and wakeful crying, the baby has periods of alertness, during which he pays attention to his environment by means of his eyes and ears and repeatedly makes diffuse movements and gurgling sounds. At first his facial expression is vague and his eyes are able to focus for only a few seconds at a time. Slowly he develops the ability to focus on the mother and somewhat later to follow her with his eyes. While being held by his mother, nursing at the breast or from the bottle, he stares solemnly at his mother's eyes and face. Through repetition of the experience of nursing, an association is established between nursing and the human face, and the pleasure of nursing comes to be associated with the face. Gradually a mental image of the face is established in the memory apparatus. Thereafter, the sight of the human face is "recognized," and the baby now responds to it with pleasure: he smiles at it.

The foundations of memory have by this time been established, and the baby has made his first human relationship. This is the beginning of recognition of and attachment to a mothering person. It is also the beginning of a shift from the perception of inner sensations to external visual perceptions. Looking at and smiling are the first behaviors of the infant that are actively directed. As a result of both the frustration and the gratification of inner needs, the human face and voice have by now become associated with relief from unpleasure as well as with the experience of pleasure.

Thereafter, the infant follows the movements of the human face with concentrated attention. His smile on seeing the familiar face or hearing the familiar voice slowly becomes generalized to include other familiar things or pleasurable stimuli. It also serves to strengthen the mother's attachment to him and thus enhances the pleasurable interchange between them.

The Symbiotic Phase

Although by the age of roughly two months the infant has made his first human connection, it is not until he is about five months of age that he begins to distinguish his mother from other human beings. At that time he develops a special smile and a joyful reaction at the sight of his mother, thereby indicating that he recognizes her both perceptually and emotionally as a distinct person. Between two and five months however, he does not yet have the capacity to distinguish one person from another, nor can he distinguish between himself and his mother, or between such objects as toys and his sensory and motor experiences with them.

It is assumed, however, that by two months of age the infant has developed the capacity to perceive, at least fleetingly, that satisfaction is dependent on a source outside his bodily self. It is this dim awareness, in fact, that marks the transition from the previous autistic phase to the symbiotic phase, which lasts from about the second to the fifth month. During the autistic phase the infant "loved" the gratifying experience of nursing. Now that his awareness has developed further, he "loves" a gratifying, albeit nonspecific and interchangeable, need-satisfying, and symbiotic human partner. From the infant's point of view, he and his mother are "one." The mother, is experienced as part of the self and the self as part of the mother. It is not possible to speak of the infant's having a real love object before the mother is distinguished from others and is thus no longer interchangeable, and before he begins to differentiate her from himself.

From about the second to the fifth month the infant continues to be almost completely dependent on his mother. He does become occupied, however, with his own movements, with learning the feel of his body, and with gaining control over his hand movements and coordinating these with his sucking and his vision. He continues to focus on people and things, and he can now follow them better with his eyes. He even turns his head and changes the position of his body in order to look at people or to look at his own hand. By three to four months of age he can clasp his hands together while lying on his back, and play with them.

At around the fourth month, coordination between his mouth and his hand becomes well established. The baby can then consistently and intentionally get his thumb to his mouth and suck it. This enables him to relieve tension and to gain pleasure through his own effort and initiative. He gradually begins to develop the ability to reach out and grasp a toy, which he mouths, bangs, looks at, and manipulates. Coordination between hand movements, sucking, and vision has been established. A similar coordination between hearing and vision enables the baby to listen when he sees something and to look in the direction from which he hears a sound.

The baby uses a wide variety of sounds in order to initiate social contact with his mother. He also likes to vocalize when he is alone—for example, when he is playing with his hands—and he often repeats the sounds that he makes. When he is smiled at, spoken to, or touched, he responds joyfully with smiling, cooing, and increased bodily activity. He is likely to respond most strongly to his mother, and he may even cry in protest when she moves out of his sight. He delights everyone with his responsiveness and his babbling.

It is important that the mother be able to respond affectionately, empathically, and appropriately to her baby's smiles and to his vocal and other cues, which indicate his needs and his feelings. The reciprocal affectionate display of delight and joy in their relationship, along with the mother's predictable relief of the baby's discomfort and tension through her satisfaction of his needs, brings about a mutuality between mother and child that has important consequences. As a result of repeated experiences of relief and gratification, the infant begins confidently to expect satisfaction from his mother.

He now not only recognizes the bottle and eagerly anticipates being fed, but, most important, is able to wait for the bottle for a few moments without crying. Tension can now be held in abeyance for a short period of time. The infant is able both to anticipate and to delay gratification because he remembers previous experiences of being fed and cared for by his mother. Although his memory is short, he does remember.

The infant's ability to "recognize" and remember the totality of the feeding situation, his association between the mother's face and her preparations to feed him, indicate that he is beginning to distinguish more precisely between sensations coming from within himself and percepts coming from outside himself. His ability to wait and to anticipate means that he is beginning to recognize outside reality (the reality principle) and not only his own sensations. These are the earliest rudiments of what will become the ego.

If the infant develops normally physically and if the mother is responsive to him and provides for him with empathy and consistency, he begins to gain a sense that the mother is dependable. He begins to develop a sense of confidence and basic trust that he is going to be cared for. This trust in the mother is the basis on which future love relationships and friendships will be built. It will also become one basis for the trust and confidence in himself that the child will later come to feel.

The subtle emotional climate created by the mother, her preferences and her selective reactions to her baby's indications of his needs, her ability to respond to him and to play with him spontaneously and pleasurably on his own level, her conscious and, particularly, her unconscious attitudes to him—all these play a role in shaping his developing personality. The affective signals generated by the mother's moods are communicated to her baby. Each perceives and responds to the other with feeling, thus creating a reciprocal and unfolding emotional interchange that significantly influences the infant's emotional and mental development.

The affective signals communicated to the baby may also reflect the mother's fears and anxieties, her tensions and irritations. If these are marked, if the mother is unpredictable, emotionally unavailable and overly frustrating, or if there is a serious discrepancy between the mother's temperament and the baby's rhythms, development will be disturbed. This may become apparent in the baby's moods, or it may be reflected in feeding problems or gastrointestinal upsets. It may also form the basis for later disturbances in object relations. Frustrations of oral and other basic needs can bring about an excessive longing for affection along with regressive dependency strivings, as well as a tendency toward pessimism and resentful rage later in life.

The Separation-Individuation Phase: Differentiation Subphase

By the middle of the first year, the infant has developed a specific attachment to his mother. He not only recognizes her as distinct from all other human beings, he also begins to love her. This love steadily grows: his mother's presence, the sight of her face, will increasingly bring forth joy; her disappearance will evoke disappointment and sadness. He smiles and vocalizes at his mother more readily, follows her visually more often, and quiets sooner when she picks him up after crying, indicating that a primitive "recognition memory" of the familiar configuration of the mother's face and voice, based on pleasurable past experiences, has been established.

Soon, most infants begin to respond to unfamiliar faces with some degree of apprehension or anxiety, recognizing the face as different from his memory of his mother's face. This reaction is commonly called stranger anxiety. The infant may lower his eyes, cover them with his hands, turn his face, or he may weep or scream. He is now clearly differentiating the mother from all other human beings, not only perceptually, but also as the object of his love. In time, his love for her will become as important to him as her satisfaction of his needs. By the end of the first year, once his memory of his mother has become more stable, his stranger anxiety will diminish markedly.

Prior to the fifth month, the social interchange between mother and baby had depended largely on the mother's initiative in eliciting and sustaining it. From around the fifth to the tenth month, the infant's initiative comes more fully into play: he attempts to reach out to the mother, to get her to respond to him. He likes to explore her face, hair, and mouth and to investigate them both visually and tactilely. Peek-a-boo games, which had previously been initiated by the mother, are soon set in motion by the infant. He is able to use a wide variety of sounds to signal his mother. When he wants attention, he can do something other than cry. He is able to produce many facial expressions that indicate his more complex emotions, making it easier for his mother to understand him and to recognize his specific needs.

At this very time, when the infant's attachment to his mother is growing stronger, paradoxically, his developing nature requires him to begin to detach himself from her. This marks the onset of the separation-individuation phase, which follows the symbiotic phase and which lasts from about the fifth to the thirty-sixth month. The process of separation-individuation refers to a psychological growing *away from* the undifferentiated symbiotic relationship with the mother and growing *toward* a differentiation of the self from the mother. It is the result both of maturational processes and of the child's growing awareness of his ability to function independently of and separately from his mother. Separation used in this sense does not refer to physical separation; rather, it refers to an intrapsychic process during the course of which the mother eventually comes to be represented internally as a mental representation. As a result of individuation, the self also comes to be represented internally as a mental representation. There are four subphases of the separation-individuation phase: the differentiation subphase, from about five to nine months; the practicing subphase, from 10 to 15 months; the rapprochement subphase, from 16 to 24 months; and the fourth subphase, the attainment of object constancy, from 25 to 36 months.

In the symbiotic phase, the mother had been the one to determine both the degree and the rhythm of closeness and separateness between herself and her baby. From about six months on, once the infant's coordination enables him to do so, and particularly when he becomes able to crawl, he begins to determine the degree of closeness with and separateness from his mother by means of his active distancing and approach behaviors. Only the beginning of these distancing behaviors is seen during the differentiating period. They will become more evident during the practicing period.

The development of the infant's mental and motor apparatus brings about a widening of his horizons. He begins to turn more actively to the outside world—to other people, to the use of his body, and to play with toys—for pleasure and stimulation, as well as for the relief of tension. At the same time, he actively wards off tendencies to return to the symbiotic undifferentiated relation with the mother.

The infant may push the mother away or wriggle out of her arms when some other object or activity interests him more. He may refuse her attention or her food by keeping his mouth closed or by turning his head away. His striving to outgrow the enveloping symbiotic relation can be seen in such behaviors as stiffening rather than molding of his body when held, by turning, and looking away from the mother, and pushing himself away from her body. These behaviors may be accompanied by expressions of unpleasure, as well as by an increased interest in events occurring at a distance from his mother and himself.

As will be seen, these developments are accompanied by the infant's beginning ability to differentiate his own body from that of his mother. It is not too long after he has established a specific attachment to his mother that he starts to have an awareness of his own body as separate and distinct from his mother's body.

With this turning away from his mother he becomes interested in other people. He develops a specific attachment to and a special relationship with his father, who from now on becomes increasingly important in his life. He also turns to other familiar people if his apprehension or stranger anxiety is not too strong. He even engages in a prolonged visual and tactile exploration and study of the faces of other people at close range, as if he is comparing and checking the features—the appearance, feel, contour—of the face of the other person with his mother's face and with his beginning mental image of her.

In this way the infant builds up a differentiated sensorimotor and affective picture of his world: other people come to be recognized as different from, even though similar to, his mother. Toward the end of the first year, this picture includes a much wider variety of familiar and less familiar animate and inanimate objects, which are more or less related to the mother and to his sensory and motor experiences with them. It may be that in children in whom confidence and basic trust are maximal, interest and curiosity constitute the predominant reactions to less familiar people. By contrast, in children whose basic trust is minimal there may be prolonged periods of stranger anxiety.

During the period from five to 10 months, the baby sits comfortably and without effort, pulls himself to a standing position, and begins to creep on his hands and knees. He makes further progress in the coordination of hand, mouth, and eye movements. Sitting, standing, and crawling provide him with a new approach to the world and a new perspective on it. The greater variety of his experiences enables him to learn more about his immediate environment. Any object can be used as a toy, to be picked up, manipulated, mouthed, looked at, or banged. Just as he is using his body more actively and assertively, so, too, there is more aggressive expression of his oral drive. The infant derives pleasure from biting (this begins at about the same time as the onset of teething). There is in general a more active taking in of the environment by means of all the sensory modalities.

Among the infant's earliest playthings are parts of his own body and parts of his mother's body. He plays with his hands and his feet, as well as with toys. He also develops strong preference for one toy over another, and he may object strenuously if a toy he wants to hold onto is taken away from him. He begins to initiate such imitative games as peek-a-boo, pattycake, and bye-bye.

In all these ways, the infant begins to express active pleasure in the use of his entire body, shows interest in objects and in the pursuit of goals, and turns actively to the outside world for pleasure and stimulation. He has become interested in his immediate environment, and he explores it. Moreover, he repeats those actions that accidentally produce interesting changes in this environment. If he sets a hanging toy in motion by accidentally striking it with his hand, he will repeat the action over and over for his own pleasure. He may even try to influence in a magical way events that happen accidentally and at a distance from him, by similar movements of his hands. In his painstaking exploration of toys and objects, he begins to distinguish one from another and to recognize that there is an objective reality that must be learned about and mastered, rather than simply acted on.

At this time the baby's developing functions and activities are expressed mainly in close proximity to the mother. Up to the age of 10 months, he prefers to play in the vicinity of her feet. If, however, his mother happens to be absent or not immediately available, the infant can now comfort himself at least to a limited extent with his thumb or a favorite toy, thereby indicating that he is starting to develop resources for coping actively with stress and tension. A soft toy animal, a blanket, or a doll may serve as a substitute for the mother. Such an object is called a "transitional object." It becomes a beloved and important possession. The infant enjoys the way it feels—its sensuous character—because it reproduces some of the sensations of his contact with his mother. It is during the first year that one generally sees the beginnings of this attachment, which becomes more prominent in the second year.

These ways of comforting himself make the baby somewhat less dependent on his mother when he is not unduly overwhelmed; they also serve to protect him against the tendency to regress to the previous undifferentiated symbiotic relationship with the mother, permit the discharge of tension, and provide pleasure. In adult life a number of similar activities ranging from hobbies to addictions may serve similar purposes.

During the symbiotic phase, the infant had not been noticeably bothered by brief separations from his mother, so long as his needs were appropriately cared for. After about seven months of age, however, whenever the mother leaves him for even a brief period of time, the infant looks sad. He misses her and longs for her. If this reaction is intense, he loses interest in his surroundings and appears to be preoccupied with regaining an inner feeling of the previous state of closeness with the mother, seemingly in an effort to maintain his equilibrium during her absence. At such times, self-comforting does not help much, and there is little the infant can do apart from accepting comforting. When this reaction is marked, it looks rather like the withdrawal and the accompanying total inability to do anything about it that is seen in some depressive conditions later in life.

Even though the infant's needs may be gratified while the mother is absent, he still misses her and is distressed. The persistence of this distress over longer periods of separation indicates that a specific libidinal attachment to the mother has been established. The infant is now capable of maintaining his tie to the mother, irrespective of frustration or satisfaction or of whether she is present or absent. At this age the object cathexis is, however, still too fragile to be sustained over very long absences. The infant's sense of well-being is now dependent upon the presence of the mother or of a suitable familiar substitute for her, to whom he has also become attached.

Just as the infant now recognizes that his mother and other family members are distinct from other people, so he also begins to be dimly aware of the boundaries of his own body. This is a slow process, based on the perception of sensations inside his body, along with the visual perception and feel of his own body as compared with his mother's body and other objects. He looks at parts of his body and touches them; he plays with his hands and sucks his thumb and toes. In these ways he begins to learn about his body and its boundaries.

When these experiences in self-stimulation occur side by side with the experiences of being touched, moved, and handled by the mother, he slowly becomes aware that the experiences themselves are different. The experience of touching his own body is not the same as the experience of being touched by his mother or touching his mother. Similarly, the experience of moving part of his own body is not the same as having that part moved by his mother. In addition to these ways of learning about the boundaries of his own body, the infant begins to perceive dimly the difference between the relief of inner tension by his mother and his own efforts to comfort himself. At this time he is beginning to become aware only of his body self; later he will start to become aware of his mental self.

How well the infant develops during the differentiation subphase will depend on the mother's ability to respond appropriately to his initiative in his bids for attention, for social exchange, for motor and exploratory activities, as well as to the indications of his special preferences. This calls for a certain keenness in reading and appreciating the infant's cues and in responding to them in a way that takes into account his specific individuality. If the mother is insensitive to or ambivalent about the infant's newly emerging capacities and preferences, she may respond inappropriately. She may, for example, interfere with activities that are directed away from her or are engaged in independently of her wishes, whereas those that are directed toward her may be fostered and encouraged. An overprotective mother may hamper her child's developing initiative; an overly intrusive mother may force her infant to ignore her or to ward her off; a mother who pushes her child too rapidly in the direction of independent functioning may cause the child to cling to her. If the mother places her own wishes in these matters above the infant's inclinations, she is laying the groundwork for future conflict between herself and her child.

Although maturational factors are necessary for successful development in the first 10 months of life, equally essential ingredients are the care and stimulation provided by the mother in the setting of the family. Infants in institutions do not show the same pleasure and variety of feelings. They are subdued, apathetic, and irritable, more preoccupied with their own body needs and comforts than they are with other people. They do not vigorously enter into or initiate playful interchanges with their caretakers, nor do they communicate by signaling their needs to the adult with their voices. Most important, they show little or no reaction when the person who is caring for them leaves them: their attachments are not sufficiently strong.

The Practicing Subphase

During the period from approximately 10 to 15 months there is a considerable change in the infant's behavior as a result of the advances that take place in his motor, intellectual, and emotional development. There is a steadily increasing investment in practicing motor skills and exploring the expanding environment, both human and inanimate. The infant's love for his mother seems to have become transformed into a love for the objects and objectives of his immediate world. His urge for discovery and for sensory experience is like an insatiable hunger, incessantly driving him on. Energy that was once centered exclusively on the satisfaction of body needs in close proximity to the mother is now released for the pursuit of goals outside the body in the objective world.

It is the infant's confidence in his mother's physical and emotional availability that allows him to feel secure in creeping and toddling further and further away from her in order to explore his new-found world. A secure mother—secure in her confidence in the ultimate separateness and integrity of her child—acts as a stable base of operations for her infant as his growing motility and curiosity carry him away from her. He no longer needs to, nor does he prefer to, play close by her feet. In fact, he is often so absorbed in his activities that he seems to be oblivious of his mother's presence. Usually he is so involved with himself and his pleasures that he shows a remarkable tolerance for knocks and falls, as well as for other minor frustrations such as having a toy taken away from him by another child. Periodically, and especially when he is tired or upset, he crawls or walks to his mother for a brief period of physical closeness to her. He rights himself on her leg, leans against her or touches her, and this brief contact seems sufficient to refuel him emotionally, so that he can resume his explorations.

Those children who have had the most gratifying relations with their mothers show greater curiosity about their surroundings, move away from her more freely, and explore at greater distances from her. Toward the end of the first year and the beginning of the second, while children are seemingly unaware of mother's whereabouts, at the same time they appear to be secure in their awareness that mother is somewhere at hand and available. Mother seems to have become a secure fixed base: she is taken for granted, and not thought about except when the need for her arises.

While he is engaged in practicing his newly emerging motor skills and in exploring his widening horizons, the infant's mood is usually cheerful. In fact, he is often elated, particularly when he attains the upright position and begins to walk. A powerful biological urge—largely independent of environmental influence—propels him to stand erect and compels him to practice and to attain mastery of his emerging locomotor skills, as well as to cope with the feeling of anxiety that moving away from his mother is at first likely to bring on. His pleasures in his new-found world are so great that his mood is now usually independent of his mother's mood. As a matter of fact, he seems to be quite delighted with his new achievements and quite in love with himself.

The urge toward activity and upright posture is so strong that it is no longer easy to change the baby's diapers. He struggles against being kept flat on his back and lying passive. He dislikes naptime and bedtime, for they have now come to mean separation from loved ones and from the things he loves to do. Frustration of his wishes or interference with his activity may bring on protest and anger, but at this time these are usually short-lived.

The same paradox that was manifest during the five- to 10-month period is now more strikingly evident. At that time, when the baby first became strongly attached to his mother and could hardly bear to be separated from her, he had nevertheless already begun to leave her. Now that he has entered upon his love affair with the world and with himself, his ties to the mother are even further loosened; he is now less dependent on her than he was earlier. He is able to initiate more complex goal-directed activities, both by making more specific demands on his mother and by moving away from her, physically and emotionally, in order to seek pleasure elsewhere. His mother is a secure base to move away from, not only in order to practice and to explore, but also to develop meaningful attachments to other people.

As the infant's stranger anxiety diminishes toward the end of the first year, his curiosity about and interest in familiar people increases. His play, his laughter, his first words become part of a playful interchange with these people. He wants to share with them both his discoveries and his play, and he even begins to show some understanding of their feelings. The capacity for empathy begins. The infant can now accept and trust familiar persons without having his main attachment—to his mother—disturbed. This is based in part on the trust and confidence that he has developed in her, which has by now spread to other people and to the world around him. The world of people, as well as the inanimate world in which he feels comfortable and secure, has expanded. The father becomes a very exciting and special person, associated with the baby's excitement in exploration and discovery, while the mother is taken for granted as a safe refuge for care and comfort.

As a result of his explorations, there is a tremendous spurt in the infant's learning. He examines objects and people from every possible angle, and slowly a more coherent picture of his limited world takes shape in his mind. As he creeps and walks, his world becomes larger, and he comes into contact with many more things and people. He is able to go to something he wants or away from something he does not want. He begins to insist on his "rights," and he now has a greater ability to satisfy his wishes as well as to defend himself. These are the precursors of the important ability to cope actively—by either fighting or fleeing—with ensuing developmental tasks and, later on, with difficulties both in his inner (mental) life and in the outside world. He is not only learning by way of his experiences; he is also beginning to learn by imitating his mother's tone of voice, her manner, and her attitude.

Late in the first year the infant begins to associate the "ma" and "da" sounds with his parents, because they have responded to and repeated these sounds with great pleasure. By the end of the first year, the infant can make all the basic sounds he will need for speaking, and he also has two or three words in his vocabulary. He can recognize many objects that are named for him and can understand much that is said to him. He begins to use a delightful jargon, in which he speaks in long "sentences," with much expression but in an unknown tongue. Because of his incessant activities, he often hears the word "no." At first he ignores this word, or it frightens him if it has been associated with punishment, but soon it stops him from continuing what he is doing, because he recognizes its meaning. To a limited extent, he can now be controlled through verbal communication from a distance.

As the infant progresses from the differentiation subphase to the practicing subphase, he becomes more consciously aware of the relation between his mother's absence and his own distress. He begins to anticipate anxiously the possibility of her leaving, and tries to keep her from doing so by protesting in advance. When the mother does leave the room, the infant is likely to creep or toddle to the door in an attempt to follow her; while she is absent he may repeatedly go to the door, and at around one year of age or a little later, he may say, "mama." These behaviors suggest that by the end of the first year the infant has developed a more differentiated image of his mother. To some degree, he is now able to cope with separation distress by means of active mastery, as contrasted with his previous passive helplessness.

The more positive the child's feelings are for his mother, the more trust and confidence he has gained in his relationship with her, the better will his memory of her serve to sustain him during her brief absences. One indication that the child feels secure in his relationship with the mother is a characteristically cheerful reunion with her, in contrast to that experienced by children who, for example, typically fret, cry, or avoid their mother on her return.

Just as "recognition memory" has become sufficiently stable toward the end of the first year so that stranger anxiety diminished markedly, so the memory of the absent mother, activated by the stimulus of inner need, becomes sufficiently stable to sustain the child to a certain extent during her absence a few months later, from roughly 12 to 16 months. This memory has gained some degree of autonomy from the stimulus of need; at the same time, the need for the mother has become less urgent, mainly as a result of advances in ego development. The child's pleasure in practicing his recently acquired motor skills, in exploring his expanding environment, as well as the emergence of new capacities, resources, and interests, enables him to use play and substitute adults in order to tolerate and to cope actively with separation distress.

Concomitantly with the establishment of a mental image of his mother, the infant continues to build up a mental image of his own body. He also begins to develop an awareness of his mental self. This awareness depends on his ability to move toward and away from his mother; his distress at his mother's disappearance, coupled with his realization that she will return, especially when he calls; and his mother's response or lack of response to his feelings, wishes, and activities. In addition, he learns the specific names for his parents, sometimes for himself and body parts such as eyes, nose and mouth, and for objects. He matches his own feelings with a dawning awareness of the feelings of other people and tries to get them to share his pleasures and even to join in them.

How well the child will develop during the practicing period (from 10 to 15 months) will depend on the extent of his mother's continued emotional availability. His confidence in her has already enabled him to transfer experiences of gratification in his relationship with her to gratification in experiences in his immediate world. If she encourages this development and fosters his growing independence, he will be able more easily to tackle the problems that await him in the months ahead.

Some mothers, unfortunately, react adversely to the infant's growing independence: they may attempt to maintain the earlier symbiotic tie by "infantilizing" the child, thereby hampering his growing autonomy. Other mothers may push the infant too rapidly in the direction of independent functioning. This may create doubts in the infant's mind about his mother's emotional availability and make him apprehensive about his ability to cope with his expanding environment, thus also hampering his striving for independence.

It is important for the mother to be able to respond appropriately to the increasingly specific wishes, feelings, and demands of the child. If the mother's availability is certain, then the infant is able to turn to greater novelties; but if the mother ignores him, he may become absorbed in making demands on her or he may ignore her in turn. If the mother is uncertain and ambivalent, his demands may provoke either excessive anger or surrender on her part.

During the first 15 months, the infant has learned an amazing amount. He began life as a helpless, sleeping neonate, aroused only periodically by hunger or discomfort, and without either awareness or memory of himself or others. By 15 months he has become an active, walking, and talking toddler, with strong feelings, attachments, wishes, and interests. He has established a love relationship with his mother, whom he trusts, and this relationship has spread to include both other people and the world about him. He has progressed a long way in differentiating inner from outer and self from object. He has developed mental images of his mother and other familiar people, of himself, and of a variety of inanimate objects, as well as some practical sense of the permanent existence of objects, of space, and causality. He exhibits some empathy for the feelings of others; he has learned the beginnings of patience and tolerance; and he is able to anticipate many events. His mood is usually cheerful and often elated.

REFERENCES

Ainsworth, M. S. (1969), Object Relations, Dependency and Attachment: A Theoretical Review of the Infant-mother Relationship. *Child Development,* Vol. 40, No. 4.

——— & Wittig, B. A. (1969), Attachment and Exploratory Behaviour of One-Year-Olds in a Strange Situation. In: *Determinants of Infant Behaviour,* ed. B. M. Foss. London: Methuen, New York: Barnes & Noble.

Alpert, A., Neubauer, P. B., & Weil, A. P. (1956), Unusual Variations in Drive Endowment. *The Psychoanalytic Study of the Child,* 11:125-163. New York: International Universities Press.

Bell, S. M. (1970), The Development of the Concept of Object as Related to Infant-Mother Attachment. *Child Development,* Vol. 41, No. 2.

Benedek, T. (1938), Adaptation to Reality in Early Infancy. *Psychoanalytic Quarterly,* 7:200-214.

——— (1956), Psychological Aspects of Mothering. *American Journal of Orthopsychiatry,* 26:272-278.

Benjamin, J. (1961), Some Developmental Observations Relating to the Theory of Anxiety. *Journal of the American Psychiatric Association,* 9:652-658.

Bergman, P. & Escalona, S. K. (1949), Unusual Sensitivities in Very Young Children. *The Psychoanalytic Study of the Child,* 3/4:333-352. New York: International Universities Press.

Bibring, G. L., Some Considerations of the Psychological Process in Pregnancy. *The Psychoanalytic Study of the Child,* 14:113-121. New York: International Universities Press.

Brody, S. (1956), *Patterns of Mothering: Maternal Influences During Infancy.* New York: International Universities Press.

Coleman, R. W., Kris, E., & Provence, S. (1953), The Study of Variations of Early Parental Attitudes: A Preliminary Report. *The Psychoanalytic Study of the Child,* 8:20-47. New York: International Universities Press.

Erikson, E. H. (1950), *Childhood and Society.* New York: W. W. Norton.

Escalona, S. K. (1963), Patterns of Infantile Experience and the Developmental Process. *The Psychoanalytic Study of the Child,* 8:197-244. New York: International Universities Press.

Greenacre, P. (1958), Early Physical Determinants in the Development of the Sense of Identity. In: *Emotional Growth.* New York: International Universities Press, pp. 113-127.

——— (1960), Considerations Regarding the Parent-Infant Relationship. In: *Emotional Growth.* New York: International Universities Press, pp. 199-224.

Hoffer, W. (1950), Development of the Body Ego. *The Psychoanalytic Study of the Child,* 5:18-23. New York: International Universities Press.

Kessler, J. (1966), *Psychopathology of Childhood.* New Jersey: Prentice-Hall, pp. 18-43.

Korner, A. F. (1964), Some Hypotheses Regarding the Significance of Individual Differences at Birth for Later Development. *The Psychoanalytic Study of the Child,* 19:58-72. New York: International Universities Press.

Lidz, T. (1968), *The Person.* New York: Basic Books, pp. 93-158.

Mahler, M. S. (1965), On the Significance of the Normal Separation-Individuation Phase, With Reference to Research in Symbiotic Child Psychosis. In: *Drives, Affects, Behavior,* Vol. 2, ed. M. Schur. New York: International Universities Press.

Murphy, L. (1964), Some Aspects of the First Relationship. *International Journal of Psychoanalysis,* 45: 31-43.

Piaget, J. (1962), The Stages of the Intellectual Development of the Child. *Bulletin of the Menninger Clinic,* 26:120-129.

Sander, L. W. (1962), Issues in Early Mother-Child Interaction. *Journal of the American Academy of Child Psychiatry,* 1: 141-166.

Schaffer, H. R. & Emerson, P. E. (1964), The Development of Social Attachments in Infancy. *Monograph of the Society for Research in Child Development,* Vol. 29, No. 3.

Spitz, R. A. (1950), Anxiety in Infancy: A Study of Its Manifestations in the First Year of Life. *International Journal of Psychiatry,* 31: 128-143, or *Bulletin of the American Psychiatric Association,* 6: 66-68.

Tennes, K. H. & Lampl, E. E. (1964), Stranger and Separation Anxiety in Infancy. *Journal of Nervous & Mental Diseases,* 139: 247-254.

Thomas, A. (1963), *Behavioral Individuality in Early Childhood.* New York University Press, 1964.

Weil, A. P. (1970), The Basic Core. *The Psychoanalytic Study of the Child,* 25: 442-460. New York: International Universities Press.

Winnicott, D. W. (1958), Transitional Objects and Transitional Phenomena. In: *Collected Papers: Through Paediatrics to Psychoanalysis.* New York: Basic Books, pp. 229-242.

Wolff, P. H. (1966), *The Causes, Controls, and Organization of Behavior in the Neonate* [*Psychological Issues,* Monograph 17]. New York: International Universities Press.

SUGGESTED READING

Fraiberg, S. H. (1959), The New-Born. In: *The Magic Years.* New York: Scribner, pp. 35-102.

Mahler, M. S. (1963), Thoughts About Development and Individuation. *The Psychoanalytic Study of the Child.* 18: 307-324. New York: International Universities Press.

Provence, S. (1967), *Guide for the Care of Infants in Groups.* New York: Child Welfare League of America, Inc.

Spitz, R. A. (1965), *The First Year of Life.* New York: International Universities Press.

Winnicott, D. W. (1957), *Mother and Child, Primer of First Relationships.* New York: Basic Books.

CHAPTER FIVE

The Toddler: From Sixteen to Thirty-Six Months

JOHN B. McDEVITT, M.D.

Between the ages of 16 and 36 months, the child is a toddler. A central issue of development during this time arises out of his powerful striving to become aware of himself as a person among other persons and his wanting to do things for himself without help or hindrance and, at the same time, without coercion.

The toddler gradually becomes aware of who and what he is, what he can do, and what he feels and thinks. He likes to "show off," and he is determined to get his way. When he succeeds, he is full of fun and joy. But he discovers that he cannot always get his way, that the person who generally interferes, disappointing and angering him, is his mother, the very same person he loves and wants to please.

The realization thus dawns on him that there are forces over which he has no control, that he and his mother are separate persons, each of them with wishes and wills of his own. As he comes to recognize his separateness and the limitations of his powers, he begins to feel alone, helpless and sad in a confusing and uncertain world.

The Rapprochement Subphase

Between the ages of 16 and 24 months the child is a junior toddler. This is a difficult and vulnerable time, both for him and for his mother. At one moment he is loving and giving, at another he is angry and demanding. He may shift from appearing to be proud and independent to being in actuality helpless and forlorn, particularly at times when fatigue, disappointment, or anxiety overtake him. He is often at the mercy of his impulses and his rapid mood swings. The relative obliviousness to his mother's presence, characteristic of the 10- to 15-month period has waned.

Although the junior toddler knows very little of the real dangers in the physical world and must be restricted for his own safety, he has a greater awareness of the dangers in his emotional world. His mother has long since let him know that she disapproves of aggressive acts on his part—pulling her hair, pinching her cheek, biting, hitting, or throwing. He now not only knows that it is possible for his mother to leave him physically, but that there is reason for him to fear the loss of her love, her disapproval, and her punishment.

The junior toddler is therefore in a dilemma. On the one hand, he wants to assert to the limit his initiative, his independence, his autonomy; yet, on the other hand, he feels insecure in his separateness and doubtful of his mother's acceptance of him. Although minor conflicts between mother and child may have been present earlier, they now reach the point of outspoken struggle. Whereas the mother previously took pains to gratify his wishes and to encourage his expanding activities, she must now limit them. This therefore becomes a time of decisive encounter. The junior toddler is struggling for an adequate assurance of his mother's love and acceptance at the very same time that he is struggling to assert himself against her limitations and restrictions. This struggle is similar to the infant's struggle to detach himself from his mother at the very time when his attachment to her was growing stronger.

The junior toddler tends to become angry, stubborn, and negativistic when his mother interferes with his activities, frustrates his wishes, pays attention to a sibling, or attempts to impose her will in teaching him proper eating or bowel habits. He says "no" to practically everything—to what he wants as well as to what he does not want. What he is trying to say by his "no" is that he protests emphatically and vigorously against any attempts by his mother to interfere in any way with his activities and his pleasures. At the same time he wishes to please his mother and to win her approval because of his love for her and his awareness of her importance to him in providing comfort, protection, and pleasure.

This is therefore a period of marked ambivalence on the junior toddler's part. Because he cannot easily manage opposite feelings of love and hate he vacillates from one to the other, often to the bewilderment of his parents. He tends to look upon the gratifying mother as the "good mother" and the frustrating mother as quite another person—the "bad mother." Similarly, he may look upon himself as two children: a good, pleasing child and a naughty, unpleasant one. In short, his struggles are not only with opposing feelings, but also with conflicting tendencies within himself—namely, to get his own way as opposed to pleasing his mother.

At one moment, he can be affectionate and loving; at another he can be demanding and angry. He is both a delightful and an exasperating child: delightful because of the many things he does to communicate and share his feelings and because of his increasingly more complex achievements; exasperating because it is difficult to understand his moods and feelings and because he is often less cooperative than he was.

Between the ages of 16 and 24 months, the relative obliviousness to the mother's presence that was characteristic only a few months earlier is now replaced by active approach behavior and a constant concern with her whereabouts. The growing realization of his separateness leads him to wish to share with her every new acquisition of skill and every new experience. He approaches her actively and seeks her involvement in his activities; as a result, his explorations and his mastery of motor skills become less important to him when he is forced to be preoccupied with concern for his mother. Generally, he reassures himself about her presence with a glance in her direction; if he is overly concerned, however, he will need once again to go to her for comforting.

He bridges the gap created by the realization of his separateness by frequently taking toys or other objects to his mother and by trying to play games with her. As he grows older, he will be able to bridge this gap in other ways, such as by talking and sharing his thoughts and feelings with her. He will also make her part of himself, in a sense, by imitating and identifying with her behavior and attitudes.

The junior toddler is no longer impervious to knocks and falls or other frustrations. He can even be surprised by sudden realizations of his separateness. This can be seen, for example, when he hurts himself and discovers, to his perplexity, that his mother is not automatically at hand. Separation anxiety is once again more marked, because he is not able to tolerate his mother's brief absences as well as he could during the practicing subphase. Nor does he accept substitutes for his mother as easily as previously. The junior toddler is no longer characteristically cheerful or elated. His realization of his separateness and his limitations has the effect of bringing about a collapse of his love for himself, his self-esteem, and his sense of magical powers, resulting in periods of inexplicable crankiness and disgruntlement.

In order to understand the changes in the toddler's personality and behavior between the ages of 16 and 24 months certain aspects of his mental and emotional development will now be examined in greater detail.

Cognitive Development and Mental Representation

The infant, when in the preverbal sensorimotor period of cognitive development, does not have the capacity to evoke or bring to his mind objects in their absence (the symbolic function) nor does he have the mental representations with which to do so. He does develop a practical intelligence, however, between the eighth and twelfth month of age. This intelligence, which is oriented toward getting results, succeeds in eventually solving a number of problems—such as locating distant or hidden objects—by way of his constructing a complex system of mental action schemes that organize reality in terms of space, time, and causality. In the absence of language or the symbolic function, however, these schemes are constructed with the sole support of perceptions and movements—that is to say, by means of the sensorimotor coordination of actions, without the intervention of mental representations or thoughts.

Similarly, the infant only remembered the mother at those times when he recognized her or perceived or experienced something that reminded him of her or when he felt an inner need for her. His memory of her was bound to these stimuli and experiences, both external and internal. When they were not present, the image of the mother presumably did not come to his mind.

Toward the end of the practicing subphase, we see the beginnings of deferred imitation and of symbolic play, as well as the verbal evocation of the mother in her absence. The child may go to the door and say "bye bye" or "mama" in anticipation of or during the mother's absence; or the junior toddler, especially the little girl, may mother a doll in symbolic or imaginary play, using this play to comfort herself while her mother is away. She may be heard to say "mama" and "baba" while cradling and rocking her doll.

These behaviors are significant for several reasons. First, they indicate that the junior toddler is now able to effect mental representations of behavior patterns, thereby making possible the evocation of the mother at a time when she is neither present nor perceived. Action has now become detached from its previous motoric context and rests instead on representation in thought. Second, this is the beginning of identifications that are based on a representational model. By recreating in play an actual experience with the mother, the junior toddler is able to function better during her absence, at least prior to the ambivalence and the conflicts of the rapprochement subphase. Third, symbolic play based on identification serves as an intermediate step between the actual mother-child relationship and the transfer of that relationship to the toddler's inner world. It is impressive how often play, such as mothering a doll, exactly replicates features of an actual mother-child relation.

At first, deferred imitation, symbolic play, and verbal evocation of the absent mother seem to be brought about by an inner need for the mother. As a further step in cognitive development, beginning at 16 to 18 months of age, behaviors (primarily verbal) occur that indicate a beginning capacity to evoke a mental image of the mother with relative autonomy from the stimuli of external experience and inner need. With this capacity, the child is on the verge of representational thought.

Partly as a result of these cognitive developments, objects and people, such as the mother and the self, are now capable of being evoked in the mind by means of an image memory. They are permanently fixed in the mind, their physical and emotional attributes can be recalled, and their movements in space can be imaginatively reconstructed.

The toddler now regards himself as one person among others in a world that is made up of people who have a permanent existence in his mind and who can therefore be evoked in his memory. He not only recognizes that he and his mother are separate human beings, he also recognizes that there are causes that exist outside himself, quite independent of his needs and his wishes. He can no longer attribute everything that happens to his own feelings and actions; he is no longer the sole initiator of all activity around him.

When mental images evolve from mental schemes of sensorimotor actions, we see the beginnings of the establishment of more complex and more differentiated mental representations of the love object and the self, of identification, and of thought and language. However, this is only the beginning. The junior toddler's mental image or representation of his mother and of himself is still unstable. He is repeatedly perplexed by the awareness of his separateness and uncertain about his ability to function "under his own steam." His mental representation of the mother requires reinforcement through repeated contacts with her. This is all the more true in view of the junior toddler's ambivalence, conflicts, and primitive way of thinking.

This is a critical period, during which profound changes occur in the child's mental and emotional development. These include the achievement of independent walking; the capacity for evocative memory and representational thought; the more precise demarcation of the self- and object representation; and the shift to the anal-sadistic and early genital phases of psychosexual development. The mother, body parts, feelings and wishes, prohibitions, etc., as well as the complex relations between all these, start to become capable of representation in mental terms. Thoughts and feelings persist beyond the immediate situation in which they have their origin. Conflicts with the mother continue in the child's mind for longer periods of time.

The existence and persistence of intense conflicts between mother and child, as well as within the child between opposing feelings and tendencies, place a considerable strain on the junior toddler. At such times the mental representation of the mother is so buffeted by violent and angry feelings that the stability of her image is disrupted, and the junior toddler may experience severe separation anxiety. During the mother's brief absence, he will not infrequently displace his anger onto his caretaker (who as a consequence becomes the "bad object"), in an attempt to maintain a good image of the absent mother. Also, at such times he is most likely to cling to his mother and to follow her. There seems to be, roughly speaking, an inverse relation between the child's ability to assert himself pleasurably in independent play and the hostile aggression against the mother that causes him to cling anxiously to her.

In the earlier differentiation subphase (five to 10 months), fear of object loss was related to the differentiation of mother and not-mother (stranger anxiety) and to the beginning differentiation of self and mother (grief reactions in response to mother's absence). Now, in the rapprochement subphase, the fear of object loss is determined by the more complex intrapsychic differentiation of the self representation and the maternal representation which contributes to the toddler's sense of separateness and also by the conflicts characteristic of this subphase.

When aggressive forces outweigh libidinal forces, as they often do during the rapprochement subphase, the mental representation of the mother is rendered unstable. It cannot sustain the junior toddler during her absence; maintenance of its stability requires reinforcement through repeated contact with her, and that interferes with his play and with his relation with other adults and children. Furthermore, at these times, identification with the mother seems to be temporarily disrupted by the child's intense ambivalence and his need to cling to her.

Identification

Identification is based in part on deferred or internalized imitation. As the little boy plays with his truck and his tools and the little girl with her dolls, it is possible to observe their identification with the father or the mother. The toddler not only plays that he is his parents, he literally attempts to behave as if he were his parents. He imitates such household tasks as sweeping and cleaning, and often re-enacts what is done to and for him. He also begins to copy his mother's or father's tone of voice and, at times, their attitudes—disgust at messiness, for example, shame at misbehavior, or sympathy for a child who has been hurt.

These attitudes are still in their nascent state; they come and go in accordance with the toddler's inclinations. They nevertheless illustrate one of the processes through which the toddler takes into himself or incorporates the models provided by his parents, and they also show how these models gradually become part of his own personality. He participates in the adults' feelings and reactions and emulates their methods of solving problems and coping with both external and internal conflicts.

Identification with parental attitudes and behavior slowly enables the toddler to learn how to do new and more complex things, how to channel his impulses constructively, and how to function separately and independently. At the same time, identification also enables him to continue his close relation with his parents, inasmuch as this relation has been moved from the external world to the inner world, that is, has become internalized. In this sense, the parents become a part of and enrich the toddler's mental life, enabling him to cope with external tasks, with conflicts, and with feelings of longing and anxiety.

Language

Learning to talk and to think are achievements unique to man. Although thinking can take place without language, it is immeasurably facilitated through the use of language. The toddler communicates not only with others, but also with himself. He develops an inner language that is part of his ability to think. Even though the capacity to develop speech is an innate human aptitude, to be able to speak meaningfully and with feeling requires a close relation with an adult. The parents' speech helps to stimulate and organize the toddler's language and thought. He hears much about himself and his world: people and things are named for him; feelings and actions are talked about with approval or disapproval; events are explained.

During the first half of the second year, the toddler emits a continual stream of jargon in which he verbalizes many of his simple wishes, designates objects, and imitates adult speech. His first words are global expressions. Only slowly, as it comes to designate the unity and identity of an object as perceived from different perspectives and in differing situations, does the word gain a distinct and specific meaning and become a symbol. When at 18 months of age the toddler says "mama," he is symbolizing his mother's identity as he has experienced it under various conditions. By 18 months he is able to recognize and to name familiar objects in pictures, including his mother's photograph, and, several months later, his own photograph. This shows that he is able to make a connection between a real object or person and a picture of that object or person, thus indicating further growth in his mental ability.

There is a marked push forward in the use of speech during the second half of the second year. By forming a sentence out of one or two words the toddler says, the mother helps him to elaborate his own sentences and to stabilize his pronunciation. By the age of two, the toddler can speak in short sentences, using pronouns. He knows the names of people and things, and he can ask and answer simple questions. He can use speech for a variety of purposes: to ask for what he wants; to express his joy; to register a protest; to state his fears; or to commend himself for good or bad behavior.

The toddler begins to realize that everything has a name. He discovers that he needs the names of things in order to learn through talking and to be able to internalize his environment symbolically so as to make possible its imaginative manipulation. By his third birthday he has acquired hundreds, even thousands, of words, and he uses nearly all the syntactical forms of the language in sentences of 12 to 15 words. He can now begin to reason, play more imaginatively, and have more complex fantasies.

The development of the toddler's language ability, however, can be deceiving. The junior toddler is egocentric: he lacks both self-perception and objectivity, and he is unable to conceive of anything beyond his own experience and his own feelings. He attributes to his first words and thoughts a magical power to make things happen and this primitive sense of power also carries with it some frightening possibilities. As the toddler becomes aware that he has hostile thoughts about his mother, whom he also loves and wants to please, he fears that these thoughts might come true and that some harm might occur to her as a result. He is trapped in an inner conflict between his feelings of love and his feelings of rage. He is likewise trapped between his hostile wishes and his memory of his mother's disapproval of such wishes. For the toddler, anything is possible. Whatever is felt or imagined can also be real: both good things and bad things can happen, depending on his feelings and his thoughts. Wishes, thoughts, dreams, make-believe stories or television programs are treated as is reality.

Feelings of Helplessness

Because the junior toddler experiences repeated disappointments in the carrying out of his own magical and realistic efforts, he is forced to conclude that his powers are limited. But since there must be an explanation of events in keeping with his primitive thinking, he attributes to his parents the magical powers he earlier thought were his own. No doubt some of his anger against his mother stems from the mistaken belief that it is she who is responsible for all his disappointments and frustrations. When experience then demands that he question this belief in his parents' omnipotence, he is left with a truly helpless feeling. It is this feeling, along with the infant's feeling of separateness, of no longer being "one" with his mother and thus sharing in her omnipotence, that contributes to making 16 to 24 months of age such a vulnerable period.

The junior toddler is poorly equipped to cope with the conflicts he experiences. It seems that his emotional and mental development brings about a turmoil in both his inner and outer life that does not begin to abate until he has become a senior toddler. His helpless feelings stimulate the desire to regress to the earlier undifferentiated symbiotic relation with his mother. To ward off such regressive tendencies, he fights against nap time and bedtime, and against being placed passively on his back in order to be diapered. This same helpless feeling often leads the toddler to insist on sameness, and even ritual, in order to make life more predictable and thus bearable for him. Routines must be the same from day to day—stories, for example, must be read to him again and again in exactly the same way.

Aggression and the Anal Phase

When the child was an infant, nonhostile aggression (self-assertion) accompanied his practice of motor skills and his exploration of the world around him. He had begun to learn that his mother disapproved of hostile aggressive impulses, which were as a rule poorly focused and diffusely expressed. By the time the child becomes a junior toddler, his aggression takes on a different quality.

It is more intentional, focused and object-directed because of the advances in his mental development. Its difference lies in the frustrations and disappointments that the toddler experiences and, what is more important, in the fact that he is now entering the anal phase of psychosexual development. The dominant role in drive activity passes at this time from the oral zone to the anal zone as a result of maturational advances.

The toddler gains pleasure from passing or withholding bowel movements, which stimulates the eroticized anal mucosa; he also values highly his body products, which have become invested with both libido and aggression. At the time of toilet training, feces may be treated either as precious gifts, which are surrendered to the mother as a sign of love, or as weapons by means of which disappointment, anger, and rage can be expressed. When he is angry, the toddler may smear, soil, or withhold his feces.

In a more general sense, many of the toddler's activities during the anal phase express opposing tendencies—to hold on to and to let go. This is in contrast to the tendencies during the oral phase of taking in and ejecting. These anal tendencies may be seen in activities such as giving and taking, filling and emptying, collecting and hoarding. The toddler enjoys placing toys in a box and then retrieving them, or repeatedly removing toys from a shelf and then returning them.

Corresponding to this double investment of his body products, the junior toddler's entire attitude toward people and things is dominated by ambivalence—that is, by violent swings between love and hate. He experiences urges to possess and dominate, to harm and destroy, and to make sadistic attacks on loved persons or their substitutes, such as pets. The toddler enjoys touching the anal area and playing with his feces. When his training prevents him from doing so, he still retains this pleasure by playing with clay, sand, water, and paints. He distinguishes a wide variety of smells with pleasure; he also destroys objects because of the sheer joy he experiences in their destruction.

It is important for the toddler to realize that aggressive behavior and angry feelings are not per se bad. Rather, it is their form of expression and the conflicts they bring about that create the problem. Aggression as such is essential for survival, learning, and adaptation. Aggression makes it possible for the toddler to assert his rights, to compete with a rival, to satisfy his curiosity, and to display his body and his abilities.

What becomes increasingly necessary, however, is the control of aggressive behavior and the channeling of aggressive energy into constructive activity. Such control is, in part, brought about by identification. As a result of these changes, aggression can be used not only to master tasks in the external world, but also, in time, to cope actively with and to master internal conflicts and anxieties. If the toddler's aggressive expressions are stifled, his activity may be replaced by passivity and the constructive function of his aggression inhibited.

Conflict and Anxiety

As a consequence of the toddler's mental development, the memory of both his mother and her prohibitions, as well as of his feelings of anger, are able to persist in his mind for longer periods of time, making internal conflict possible. If memory did not persist, there would be no internal conflict, any more than an external conflict could exist between the toddler and his mother if she were not present. It is not only the wish for his mother's love that causes the toddler to seek her attention; because of his hostile feelings, he must also continually reassure himself by her presence. Conflicts with the mother no longer simply flare up and disappear. Anger at the mother continues beyond the situation that brought it on.

A 17-month-old was angry with his mother. He peeked at her from the other side of a partially closed door, then he shut the door—in effect, shutting his mother out of his sight. Because he could not tolerate this for very long, he soon opened the door once again, entered the room, fussed, and crawled onto her lap. In a nursery-like setting, it was typical of this toddler, as it was of other toddlers, to leave his play suddenly in order to go to his mother for reassurance. Although this occurred when the mother was in the same room as the child, it was especially noticeable on those occasions when she happened to be in a nearby room. After a brief greeting, a hug, or an exchange of toys, he could then return to his play. How frequently and how strongly the need for reassurance came to the toddler's mind depended on many things, one of the most important of which was the nature of his relation with his mother at the time. If it happened to be particularly ambivalent, he had to seek her out more often. Only later, in the third year, is the senior toddler able to speak of his wish for the absent mother and then go on with his play without having to seek her out.

The toddler usually feels both distress and rage as he watches his mother preparing to leave him. His wishes to hurt or to destroy may bring on the fear that his mother will retaliate—will show her disapproval by punishing him, by not returning. If he is actually punished at such times, this will lend some justification to his apprehension. Beginning as early as the eighteenth month, the toddler may develop fears of such things as Halloween masks, monsters, or vacuum cleaners. It seems likely that by this age these are imaginary or symbolic fears, possibly representing punishment by the mother for hostile feelings and thoughts. They are simple, transitory fears. Although they soon disappear, they may nevertheless be the beginnings of more complex fears and of symptom formation later on.

Bowel training is usually completed between the ages of 15 and 30 months. But the toddler resents this intrusion into his rights and pleasures. The conflict of giving or withholding in conformity with the mother's expectations may become quite intense; if so, it epitomizes the child's resistance to all the demands made on him to control himself. In contrast to infancy, when needs are usually satisified, the toddler is expected to give up important pleasures—and without understanding the reason. He eventually does so, but solely in order to gain his mother's love and approval. The fact that he finally does comply illustrates with particular clarity his identification with his mother's demand for cleanliness; this indicates that a mental representation of this demand continues to be remembered, and that he is capable of fulfilling it, independently of the mother's presence or absence. In this case, both the external conflicts with his mother and the internal conflicts become resolved. It is only slowly, however, that similar conflicts between the toddler's wishes and feelings of rage and his remembered fear of his mother's disapproval become resolved.

As the anal phase wanes and is overlapped by the phallic phase, during the third year, the intensity and nature of the toddler's destructive urges diminishes. Because aggression is counterbalanced by the increasing strength of the senior toddler's love feelings, it can be more easily controlled and channeled into constructive outlets. The senior toddler is no longer impelled to act on the impulse of the moment.

The Self and Identity

The development of the sense of self and of personal identity progresses rapidly in the toddler. He distinguishes other people from himself by name, understands the pronouns "me" and "you," assigns ownership to various objects, and becomes conscious of himself as a person, as an "I." He begins to speak of himself in the first person or by using his own name. His evolving sense of self includes his growing perceptions, his feelings and experiences, his capacities, and his awareness of his body and its functions. He likes to show off, to draw attention to himself, to seek admiration.

How the junior toddler feels about himself is much more dependent on his relations with his mother than was true in the 10 to 15-month period. At that time the relations were more or less taken for granted; now they have become more complex. Positive feelings for the mother increase his sense of well-being; angry feelings against her cause him to feel less well about himself. If his parents are pleased with his behavior, his self-esteem is heightened; if he feels he is strongly disapproved of, he thinks of himself as undesirable. Not only does the toddler see himself through his parents' eyes; he also identifies with their attitudes, which slowly become part of himself. If a toddler feels that he is a failure because he is unable to live up either to his parents' expectations or to his mental representations of these expectations, he will not be pleased with himself.

The junior toddler's vulnerability to loss of self-esteem is further complicated by his dawning realization that he and his mother are two separate human beings. That realization seems to bring on feelings of loss and sadness similar to feelings he had earlier, on occasions of actual physical separation from the mother. These changes in the child's development are the result of an internal psychological process; they are part of the process of intrapsychic separation from the mother, as opposed to actual physical separation. The vulnerability to loss of self-esteem is further compounded by the toddler's aggression against his mother, which causes him to feel that she disapproves of him.

The toddler's vulnerability to loss of self-esteem as well as his sense of helplessness are counteracted by his realistic achievements and by his identification with his parents. Only gradually can his previous unrealistic love for himself, his belief in his magical powers, and his belief in his parents' omnipotence be replaced by a realistic recognition of, belief in, and enjoyment of his individual autonomy. For this to take place, he needs his mother's understanding of his moods and his ambivalence. A significant lack of acceptance and understanding by the mother can perpetuate his vulnerability to lowered self-esteem and create a predisposition to a basic depressive mood later in life. Excessive disapproval and restrictions can bring about feelings of shame in the toddler and undermine his developing sense of self-confidence as well as his initiative and autonomy.

Father's Role

At this time, the relation with the father becomes even more significant. The father seems to be associated with external reality and successful autonomous functioning, rather than being a source of constraint and frustration or a source of maternal comforting—both of which may threaten the development of the child's initiative. The junior toddler's intense ambivalence and regressive tendencies seem to be specifically linked to the mother, whereas the father appears to be experienced as a powerful, "uncontaminated," helpful ally. He serves to dilute the ambivalence of the mother-child relation and helps the toddler to fight against regressive tendencies by encouraging autonomous development and serving as an important person with whom to identify. It may be that a satisfactory relation with the father is of major importance for the resolution of the ambivalent tie to the mother and for the achievement of individuation.

Siblings

The relations with a sibling are one of the most significant influences in the toddler's early development. The arrival of a new baby may provoke intense jealousy, disappointment, and rage. It may also bring on regression to more infantile ways of behaving. The toddler's angry outbursts against the baby create severe conflicts with his mother, who must protect the younger child and thus can no longer practice her customary tolerance of the elder child. In time the toddler learns to control his behavior in order to maintain his mother's approval.

The toddler is likely to have feelings of both love and envy for an older sibling, who has more perogatives. His envy may cause him to emulate and to compete with his sibling. If his attempts are beyond his capacities, however, he will feel frustrated, defeated, and resentful. How conflicts resulting from sibling rivalry are resolved will have an important bearing on later personality development. The child may become unduly aggressive and competitive or he may turn out to be overly kind and timid in his relations with his peers.

Play

The child's earliest play is with his own body and his mother's body, and with familiar toys and objects. During the second year of life, he enjoys simple games involving running, chasing, and hiding. After the middle of the second year, fantasy or imaginary play begins. This play frequently reflects the toddler's relations with his mother. He plays the role of the mother with himself, with small children, animals, toys, and even with the mother. He hugs the doll or the teddy bear and feeds it, puts it to bed, talks to it lovingly, or spanks it. By 18 months of age, the toddler's play is quite complex, already revealing subtle qualities and characteristics of his past and present relations with the mother or the father. The beginnings of the process through which the toddler identifies himself with his parents can be seen in much of his play, as can the increasing complexity of his fantasy life.

In his fantasy play, the toddler restructures reality to suit his wishes: he re-enacts events that were fun, assumes grown-up roles, "bosses" his toys and imaginary helpers to make them obey his every wish. In his re-enacting of painful experiences, he actively reverses the roles. This playful repetition helps him to gain mastery over these experiences, as well as over the anxiety or humiliation that accompanied them.

Although the child's play brings about wish-fulfillment, pleasure, and a sense of well-being, it is not simply a direct manifestation of the urge for immediate gratification. Instead, it is frequently an effort to deal with dangers in his external or internal world in accordance with the developmental tendency to become active, to master problems, and to deny or cope with anxiety or other painful feelings.

The junior toddler is capable only of "parallel play." This consists of toddlers engaging in *similar* activities, but not yet playing *with* one another. The presence of other children, particularly of the same age, begins to become important to the senior toddler. He plays with them, imitates them, becomes attached to them, and in this way gains a new perspective of himself. Confidence in himself and others provides a foundation for relating to children, including the freedom to assert himself, on the assumption that other children will be friendly.

Defense and Adaptation

The toddler's external conflicts (between his desires and his mother's prohibitions) and his internal conflicts (between love and hate, between his hostile wishes and his fear of his mother's disapproval or punishment) give rise to feelings of fear and anxiety. At this early age, he has only limited means other than play for dealing with anxiety. If he experiences his hostility for his mother as too dangerous, he may displace it either onto other people or onto himself in an attempt to keep the relation with his mother intact. If he has an urge to hit or bite his mother, he may instead hit or bite a doll, a smaller child, or himself. The wish to hit his mother in the face may be turned into a playful game; or the toddler may whine and cling to his mother instead of hitting her. He may surrender unhappily a toy he has snatched from another child, or fretfully hand over to his mother a figurine he knew he should not have picked up. When he is doing something he knows is forbidden, he may at the same time say to himself "no" or "bad boy." He may also express his fear of punishment verbally, or he may disown his naughtiness and maintain that it was another child or an animal who committed the wrongdoing. He is the "good child"; it was the "bad boy" or the "bad dog" who pushed the plate off the table.

Of the infant, it is possible to speak only of prototypes or precursors of defense mechanisms. Closing the eyes for example, may be considered a prototype for denial. In the toddler, by contrast, it is possible to see the primitive beginnings of some of the typical mechanisms of defense. These mechanisms are relatively unstable, however; they come and go. Many of them serve the purpose of learning and adaptation more than the purpose of defense. Which mechanisms the toddler will choose depends upon his inner characteristics and his parents' behavior, both in terms of their responding selectively to his behavior and as models for identification.

Identification is a normal developmental device, which brings pleasure and security to the toddler by causing him to feel closer to his mother and father. By means of identification, the toddler takes over his parents' attitudes, makes them part of himself, and employs them for learning and for self-control. The toddler may also identify with the parent who frustrates or punishes: he does to his doll or to a smaller child what has been done to him; he may leave them or spank them. One two-and-one-half-year-old was afraid of monsters, for example. He dealt with this fear by acting like a monster. The toddler who insisted that it was not he but the "bad boy" or "bad dog" who pushed his plate off the table was using the defense mechanism of *projection*—by attributing forbidden wishes or thoughts to someone or something else.

The mechanism of *denial* is related to magical thinking: the toddler acts as if he can alter reality by ignoring it. He may deny the painful feelings brought on by physical separation from his mother by simply turning his head so that he no longer sees her preparations to leave or her actual leave-taking.

By using the mechanism of *repression,* the toddler makes unconscious a painful feeling, memory, or thought along with its accompanying affect; *reaction formation* turns the feeling or thought into its opposite. A 16-month-old was angry when his sister was born. By the time he was 21 months old, however, he showed consideration for her, often petting her. He no longer seemed aware of his anger; his aggression had been changed into affection. As a consequence of toilet training, the toddler's pleasure in dirt and messiness is often repressed and turned into the opposite. He may give up playing with clay or engaging in water play for a while and become fastidious, concerned that he might dirty his hands or his clothes.

The toddler uses the mechanism of *displacement* in order to shift his feelings from the person toward whom they are directed onto someone or something else. If he is frightened by his rage against his mother when she leaves him, he may displace these feelings onto the adult who is caring for him. *She* will then become the "bad mother" who is frustrating and leaving him. In this way he can keep a "good" image of his mother in his mind, since her image is no longer burdened with his anger.

Superego Precursors

Although the toddler reaches his third birthday with greatly improved self-control, it cannot be said that he has as yet developed a conscience or a superego. Conscience, strictly speaking, consists of standards and prohibitions that have been taken over by the child from others and govern his behavior from within. This does not emerge before the fifth or sixth year.

In the toddler, it is possible to speak only of precursors of conscience development. The toddler gradually learns to comply automatically with his parents' prohibitions. He no longer needs constant reminders;

he has already begun to establish habits of cleanliness and obedience. However, he still treats the moral demands made upon him as part of his external environment. If he is alone or angry, he may either deliberately displease his mother or do as he wishes, restrained only by the anticipated fear of loss of love or punishment.

The toddler's good behavior is concrete and specific; it is based primarily on prohibitions—that is, activities that one must not do rather than activities that one should do—rather than on general ethical principles. The toddler does not suffer the pangs of guilt feelings; he suffers only from the fear of immediate or anticipated punishment. Nevertheless, these patterns of parental control are established within the ego and become merged later on with the conscience or superego.

The Fourth Subphase

During the course of his third year the toddler's mental and emotional development gradually brings about a change in his behavior. He becomes more consistently loving, friendly and cooperative; he is better able to withstand frustration, to delay gratification and to accept substitute satisfactions. His feelings for other people and toward himself are less at the mercy of mood swings. There is a shift from self-centered, demanding, clinging behaviors to more mature ego-determined object relationships. The senior toddler shows more regard for the interests and feelings of others; plays more cooperatively, by sharing and taking turns; and has the ability to be concerned, to make small sacrifices, to offer gifts. There is more complex fantasy play, role play, and make-believe. At the same time, play becomes more purposeful and constructive; it also includes many detailed observations about the real world.

The senior toddler's previous concern about his mother's constant presence diminishes, and he is able to tolerate her absence for longer periods of time. He displays a greater interest in adults other than the mother, as well as in playmates. He can accept familiar substitutes for his mother during her absence and is able to accept separation more easily, just as he had been able to toward the end of the 10 to 15-month period. His sense of comfort seems to rest on the existence of a more secure and stable mental representation of the mother. The mother, who had in the practicing subphase served as a secure base from which to explore, now begins to take the form of a secure mental representation.

The senior toddler's ability to tolerate better his mother's brief absences indicates the beginning attainment of *libidinal object constancy.* The concept "libidinal object constancy" refers both to a stage in the development of object relations and to the contributions of the ego to the gradual development of object relations throughout childhood. The development of object constancy is determined by the changing nature of the libidinal and aggressive cathexis of the love object; the progressively more complex levels of memory organization and mental representation; and the emergence of such aspects of ego development as anticipation, intentionality, frustration tolerance, identification, neutralization, reality-testing, etc. The meaning of object constancy and the criteria for its attainment therefore change as the child progresses from one phase in development to the next.

Most psychoanalytic writers place the attainment of object constancy within an age range of the sixth to the eighteenth month, using as their criteria degrees of libidinal attachment to the love object and some form of mental representation. From the viewpoint expressed in this and the previous chapter, only during the course of the third year does a stable mental representation of the mother become predominantly invested with libidinal as opposed to aggressive cathexis; only then is it capable of persisting in this same form, regardless of frustration, instinctual need, or the mother's temporary absence. The ambivalence that is characteristic of the rapprochement subphase does not begin to be resolved until well into, or even toward the end of, the third year of life. At the same time that this ambivalence is subsiding, the quality of the mental representation of the mother conveys to the child a sense of security and comfort, just as the actual mother had.

It is partly on the basis of these advances in the development of object relations that the senior toddler is ready to enter nursery school, and can even benefit by doing so, when he is around three years of age. His readiness however, also depends upon comparable progress in other areas of development, such as his ability to care for his physical needs, to wait and take his turn, to communicate verbally, and to play constructively and cooperatively with other children.

The extent to which the toddler has arrived at the stage of libidinal object constancy will influence, not only his ability to cope with the problems that he will encounter in succeeding developmental phases, but also the nature of his relations with loved ones later in life.

Personal and Gender Identity

The changes in the senior toddler's behavior also reflect the emergence of a more stable sense of personal identity. His self-representation comes to be invested predominantly with love feelings as opposed to feelings of dissatisfaction and rage. Self-esteem is heightened: he feels more confident and more desirable, and he is once again pleased with his own accomplishments.

The development of a sense of the self as an individual starts with the infant's awareness of his body and proceeds from there to the adult's sense of self-esteem and of personal sexual and social identity. "Identity" refers to one's knowledge of one's sameness and continuity in the midst of change. The toddler has come only part way in this complex developmental line; he must also achieve a firm sense of identity as male or female.

Although the child's sex is genetically determined, biological factors play only a partial role in the determination of his gender identity. The sense of being male and feeling masculine, or of being female and feeling feminine is primarily dependent on the way in which parents relate to the child, how they interact with each other, and their own sense of sexual identity. The gender assigned—the one in which the child is reared—usually outweighs chromosomal and hormonal influences and even the appearance of the genitals in determining the child's gender identity. In addition, the toddler's basic attitudes of activity or passivity, of sadism or masochism, also enter into the development of male or female traits, as does his identification with the personalities of his parents and their own success or failure in their sexual roles.

In the process of learning about the body, the child usually discovers the genital area by the end of the first year. During the second half of the second year, he further discovers that there are pleasurable sensations in that part of the body. Hence the genitals take on a very special importance for the child: they become a source of erotic pleasure and of comfort. Masturbation is accompanied by fantasies about the parents, their content being derived either from oral wishes, such as being cuddled or nursed, or from anal wishes, such as defiance and hostility, or being beaten and punished. By 24 to 30 months, the gender identity of the toddler is well ingrained in his awareness and behavior. At this time (although it may be as early as 16 months), the discovery of the anatomical differences between the sexes comes as quite a surprise. That discovery can serve as a critical turning point in the lives of many toddlers.

On the basis of the toddler's aggressive and destructive feelings and behavior, as well as his knowledge that some objects, such as toys, wear out and break, he (or she) is likely to deduce that the absent penis in the girl can be accounted for only in terms of some unfortunate mishap. The impact of this discovery is apt to be more severe on the girl, who tends to feel hurt and deprived. She assumes either that she was born without a penis or that her penis has been removed, and she is more than likely to hold her mother responsible for this unhappy state of affairs. Anger may once again disturb her relations with her mother. She may become babyish, demanding, and possessive, and once again find it difficult to separate from her mother. Although the little boy takes pride in the penis that he possesses, he may assume that girls have had their penises cut off, and he may thus be led to fear for his own intactness and male identity.

These concerns—termed "castration anxiety"—may cause the senior toddler to go through a stage of excessive worry over minor injuries, such as scratches, cuts, and bruises; to become cautious about climbing and jumping; and to stay closer to his mother for reassurance. Toilet training introduced at this time may be frightening, since the loss of the feces can represent for the toddler the loss of the actual or imaginary penis—imaginary for the little girl, who, in order to bolster her self-esteem, may persist in believing that she has a penis hidden somewhere in her body.

The manner in which the toddler assumes his gender identity and reacts to the anatomical differences between the sexes leads to variations in the stability of his gender identity. These variations will have considerable bearing on the toddler's sense of self-esteem and personal identity, as well as on his or her future role as a husband and a father or as a wife and a mother.

Summary

When the child was an infant, his mother protected him from excessive external and internal stimuli that might otherwise have produced undue tension and anxiety. By the time he has become a senior toddler, his ego has developed limited capacities to tolerate frustration, to deal with conflicts, and to master anxiety. He has his own unique methods of defending against and coping with the dangers in his life. He has learned to manage better the conflicting tendencies between moving toward and away from his mother, between love and hate, between his wish to please his mother and his wish to get his own way. Love feelings gain dominance over aggressive feelings; self-control improves, and there is more sublimation and neutralization. Anxiety is mastered, to some degree at least, by imaginary play and fantasy, by identification with parental attitudes, by defense mechanisms, and by a better sense of reality. To a greater extent, the reality principle replaces the pleasure principle, the secondary process takes the place of the primary process.

As a result of drive maturation and progress in ego development, of the beginning attainment of libidinal object constancy, and a more stable sense of self-identity, the senior toddler is able to achieve better relations with his parents and the external world, as well as to find solutions for bringing about a more stable harmony between his own wishes and the requirements of the human family, where a strong tie between parents and child exists. The relative success or failure of these achievements will influence the toddler's ability to cope with the danger situations, conflicts, and anxieties in ensuing phases of development: it will be the foundation on which is built adaptation to external and internal problems later in life.

REFERENCES

Abelin, E. (1971), The Role of the Father in the Separation-Individuation Process. In: *Separation-Individuation, Essays in Honor of Margaret S. Mahler,* ed. J. B. McDevitt, & C. F. Settlage. New York: International Universities Press, pp. 229-252.

Erikson, E. H. (1959), *Identity and the Life Cycle* [*Psychological Issues* Monograph 1]. New York: International Universities Press.

Fraiberg, S. H. (1969), Libidinal Object Constancy and Mental Representation. *The Psychoanalytic Study of the Child,* 14:9-47. New York: International Universities Press.

Freud, A. (1948), Notes on Aggression. *The Writings of Anna Freud,* Vol. 4. New York: International Universities Press, 1968, pp. 60-74.

——— (1951), Observations on Child Development. *The Writings of Anna Freud,* Vol. 4. New York: International Universities Press, pp. 143-162.

Greenacre, P. (1958), Early Physical Determinants in the Development of the Sense of Identity. In: *Emotional Growth.* New York: International Universities Press, pp. 113-127.

Hartmann, H., Kris, E. & Loewenstein, R. M. (1947), Comments on the Formation of Psychic Structure. In: *Papers on Psychoanalytic Psychology* [*Psychological Issues,* Monograph 14]. New York: International Universities Press, pp. 27-55.

Kessler, J. (1966), *Psychopathology of Childhood.* Englewood Cliffs, N.J.: Prentice-Hall, pp. 44-67.

Kris, E. (1955), Neutralization and Sublimation. Observations on Young Children. *The Psychoanalytic Study of the Child,* 10:30-46. New York: International Universities Press.

Lewis, M. M. (1957), *How Children Learn to Speak.* New York: Basic Books, 1959.

Lidz, T. (1968), *The Person.* New York: Basic Books, pp. 159-188.

Mahler, M. S. (1963), Certain Aspects of the Separation-Individuation Phase. *The Psychoanalytic Quarterly,* 32:1-141.

——— & McDevitt, J. B. (1968), Observations on Adaptation and Defense in *Statu Nascendi. The Psychoanalytic Quarterly,* 37:1-21.

Peller, L. E. (1954), Libidinal Phases, Ego Development, and Play. *The Psychoanalytic Study of the Child,* 9:178-198. New York: International Universities Press.

Ritvo, S. & Solnit, A. J. (1958), Influences of Early Mother-Child Interaction on Identification Processes. *The Psychoanalytic Study of the Child,* 13:64-91. New York: International Universities Press.

——— ——— (1960), The Relationship of Early Ego Identifications to Superego Formation. *International Journal of Psycho-Analysis,* 41:295-300.

Sander, L. W. (1962), Issues in Early Mother-Child Interaction. *Journal of the American Academy of Child Psychiatry,* 1:141-166.

Stoller, R. M. (1964), A Contribution to the Study of Gender Identity. *International Journal of Psychoanalysis,* 45:220-226.

Stone, J. & Church, J. (1957), *Childhood and Adolescence: Psychology of the Growing Person.* New York: Random House, 1966, pp. 105-135.

Wolff, P. H., (1967), *Cognitive Considerations for a Psychoanalytic Theory of Language Acquisition.* [*Psychological Issues,* Monograph 18/19]. Pp. 300-343.

SUGGESTED READING

Fraiberg, S. H. (1959), *The Magic Years.* New York: Scribner, pp. 107-168.

Freud, A. (1963), The Concept of Developmental Lines. *The Writings of Anna Freud.* Vol. 6. New York: International Universities Press, pp. 62-92.

Freud, S. (1905), Three Essays on the Theory of Sexuality. *Standard Edition,* 7:135-200. London: Hogarth Press, 1953.

Mahler, M.S. (1966), Notes on the Development of Basic Moods: The Depressive Affect. In: *Psychoanalysis—A General Psychology: Essays in Honor of Heinz Hartmann,* ed. R. M. Loewenstein, L. M. Newman, M. Schur, & A. J. Solnit. New York: International Universities Press, pp. 152-168.

Piaget, J. & Inhelder, B. (1969), *The Psychology of the Child.* New York: Basic Books, pp. 3-27, 51-63, 80-96.

CHAPTER SIX

Psychological Disturbances During the First Three Years of Life

JOHN B. McDEVITT, M.D.

Constitutional or environmental conditions that depart too far from the "average" are likely to interfere with development by disturbing the typical unfolding of the drives, the ego, the superego precursors, and object relations. Preventive or therapeutic intervention early in life should be aimed at modifying such conditions. At present, however, too little is known about the nature or range of "average" or even "optimal" conditions for development, as well as about the natural history of normal or pathological development to be able to lay down hard and fast rules.

Prediction and Outcome

It is possible to trace a patient's psychological disturbance to its origins in early childhood, but it is not so easy to recognize conditions that will create difficulties in the future. Although events do have an impact on behavior and development at the time they take place, their long-range effects cannot be consistently demonstrated. It is not yet possible to say with certainty what kinds of early experiences will yield what sorts of personality make-up. Similar disruptive family settings can produce individuals with different kinds of emotional disturbances and also persons who function normally.

At the age of three, the toddler's personality has not taken permanent form. Disturbances that are specific to the infant and toddler phases of development usually disappear when those phases are outgrown. The young child, furthermore, has a remarkable capacity to adapt and to change. As long as this flexibility exists, one cannot predict the future effects on development of either current personality make-up or of a wide range of anticipated, much less unanticipated, future events. It is possible to think only in terms of probabilities and alternative possibilities. The toddler's personality will undergo continuous changes throughout the years of childhood. Such a trait as overaggressiveness may become permanent in the personality structure or it may be reversed in the direction of passivity or it may be tamed and used constructively for growth and development. This last outcome will, of course, be favored should the toddler make age-adequate progress in all areas of development.

Our present inability to predict consistently the long-range effects of early events does not, to be sure, mean that these events are not of vital importance. We do know that the experiences of early childhood provide the foundations of future emotional stability and basic character traits and intellectual development. At no other time will the individual's experiences become so irrevocably a part of him. If, during these early years, essential intrinsic or extrinsic ingredients for satisfactory development are missing, the result will be an interference of one sort or another with the progressive forces inherent in development.

Children who are born into families marked by poverty, neglect, and family disintegration tend to suffer losses in cognitive skills and to run a greater risk of psychological impairment than do children from stable and nurturing backgrounds. This is seen most dramatically in the development of motherless children reared in institutions, as well as among those unwanted infants and toddlers who are shifted from home to home.

The Effects of Prolonged Institutionalization and Separation

Children who spend their infancy in institutions show impoverishment in their relations to people, as well as retardation in most aspects of their development. In one of the most thorough direct studies (Provence, S. & Lipton, R., 1962), the development of 75 babies who had been placed in an institution when they were less than three weeks old was compared with that of 75 infants who had remained with their families. At the end of the first year, the institutionalized infants were dull and uninterested in the world around them: there was minimal play with adults, toys, or with their own bodies. Their repertoire of emotions was limited and constricted, and they rarely turned to an adult for help, comfort, or pleasure. They showed no signs of strong attachment to any one person, nor was there any evidence of the development of trust or confidence in the adults who cared for them. Although the maturation of motor skills was normal, these skills were not used for seeking pleasure or avoiding unpleasure, for initiating a social interchange or exploiting the environment for learning, nor were they used for expressing feelings. The retardation in speech was striking, as was the meagerness of all forms of communication. The infants used no words, had no names for people or objects, and made use of very few vocal sounds in order to express their feelings or to indicate a need. Activities of the sort that both reflect and facilitate the development of the awareness of the body self were few in number. They showed significant impairment in the ability to anticipate the future, to delay immediate gratification, and to integrate multiple stimuli, indicating that later on there would be difficulties with problem-solving and with thinking.

These infants were developmentally retarded despite their good endowment, normal maturational progress, and the adequacy of their physical care. Their basic deficiency was the absence of a specific maternal person who could provide consistent and predictable individualized care and who would be able to respond selectively to the expressions of needs. The grouping of a number of babies under the supervision of several different caretakers led to a poverty and infrequency of personal contact. This arrangement could not provide rich and appropriate stimulation, nor could it create the conditions that are necessary for attachment between an infant and an adult.

Follow-up studies of some of these children, who had been placed in families when they were about one-and-one-half years old, showed that from two to five years of age they improved considerably. The adaptability they demonstrated, their resilience and capacity for improvement, were impressive. Nevertheless, residual impairments of a mild to severe degree persisted: emotional relations were shallow and undiscriminating; play and imagination were impoverished; thinking was unduly concrete; and language development and learning were impaired.

The long-range effects of enlightened group care in model institutions is not yet known. The evidence to date, indicates, however, that some degree of retardation is still to be expected in those areas of development—language, social behavior, and learning, for example—that are dependent upon strong emotional ties to a parent or parent substitute. It is not likely that an institutional caretaker will be able to love or interact with the infant as a parent would. The turnover of caretakers in institutions is unpredictable, and it is rare for the infant to have a permanent mother substitute.

Because retardation in development increases in severity as deprivation is prolonged, it is advisable to place infants in suitable adoptive or foster homes as soon as possible. These homes should be selected with care, in view of the harmful effects of recurrent separation associated with repeated changes in foster homes.

In contrast to babies who have never known a home and who have grown up in institutions are those young children who were separated from their homes as the result of institutionalization or hospitalization. Here it is difficult to distinguish between the effects of separation from the mother and the effects of institutionalization. Although the immediate consequences of separation from the mother are known, the severity and duration of these effects depend on such factors as the child's age, the level of ego maturity and object constancy, the previous mother-child relation, the environmental setting, the kind of substitute maternal care provided, the duration of the separation, and events following separation.

The Effects of Brief Separation

The child may experience temporary separation from his mother as the result of a number of circumstances, such as his own or his mother's illness. He reacts most intensely to separation between the ages of seven and 36 months—the period that corresponds to the interval between the specific attachment to the mother and the beginning attainment of object constancy.

The immediate reaction of toddlers when confronted with the combined trauma of separation and institutional care is crying, grief, and strong protest. The protest probably represents an active effort to regain the lost mother. This may be followed by sleeplessness, refusal of food, resistance to toileting, and avoidance of adults. After a few days, the child's crying becomes monotonous and intermittent. He appears apathetic and withdrawn from the environment and from people. A return to more babyish ways of behaving may be manifested by greediness, loss of bowel and bladder control, a reduced use of words, and diminished control of aggression. This regressive behavior may express the toddler's wish to retrieve a relation with the mother, similar to that which existed when he was a baby.

After about two weeks, the toddler no longer seems able to tolerate the intensity of his suffering. He stops crying for the mother and ignores the favorite toy he had brought with him from home. He seems to be trying to make the most of his desperate situation by denying, repressing, or detaching his strong feelings of longing for his mother, and by trying to adopt a caretaker, if one is available for this purpose, as a mother substitute, as well as by increased oral intake and aggressive greediness for material goods.

When the toddler returns home after a few weeks or months, he may appear not to recognize his mother, and he may ignore her. He shows a variety of behavior disturbances; for example, hostility to the mother intermingled with excessive dependence and pervasive anxiety over losing her. How soon he is able to resume an affectionate relation with his mother seems to depend largely on the length of the separation. It is only when this relation is resumed that sleep improves, sphincter control returns, language use increases, and identification with the parents progresses.

The results of follow-up studies several years later are inconclusive. Although no obvious or overt effects of the separation and deprivation may be apparent, it is possible that the experience may have created a vulnerability to disturbances in relation to subsequent separations or other traumatic experiences.

When toddlers who have been separated from their mothers for several weeks are cared for adequately in their own homes or in a suitable foster home, they do not show the same picture of protest, despair, and detachment. Although the experience is a strain, the relation to the substitute or foster mother in a more or less familiar environment is able to keep the children in a state of manageable anxiety with relatively little regression. Variations in children's reactions to this experience are related to age, level of ego maturity and object constancy, and previous relation with the parents.

The long-range effect of separation can be inferred only from retrospective studies. These studies, however, do not permit the establishment of a clear-cut distinction between the effects of institutionalization, separation, and other variables. Nevertheless, the variety of disturbances found later in life in children who suffered repeated separations and depriving environments does emphasize the harmful effects of these experiences. It would appear that favorable experiences later on are able to modify the impact of separations and deprivations, whereas repeated separations and deprivations, as in the case of frequent changes in foster homes or recurrent institutionalization, lead to a greater impairment in development.

Even though separations for several weeks under favorable circumstances do not appear to be traumatic, prolonged separations should be avoided if at all possible. If they do become necessary, as in the case of acute illness or surgery, it is advisable to minimize the emotional trauma as much as possible. Every effort should be made to maintain the contact between mother and child, to foster the child's memory of the mother, and to help him cope actively with separation anxiety.

Developmental Disturbances Occurring in the Family Setting

Developmental retardations and personality disturbances similar to those observed in institutionalized children may also be seen in infants and toddlers who live in environments characterized by emotional deprivation, intellectual poverty, and family instability, or who are cared for by mentally or emotionally disabled parents. Depressed or apathetic mothers may be able to do little for or with their children beyond providing food and physical care; selfish and neglectful mothers may ignore the child's needs; hostile mothers may not only deprive and neglect, but also grossly mistreat the child. Occasionally infants are beaten or battered for crying or in other ways disturbing immature and unstable parents. As a rule, abuses such as these take place in early infancy, when the child is unable to escape or to complain.

Interference with development may be even more marked when constitutional vulnerability, organic disorders, and socioeconomic deprivation are combined with unfavorable parental attitudes and emotional deprivation. Children with limited mental endowment, minimal brain damage, physical handicaps, or sensory defects require special care. This places an added burden on the mother, and makes childrearing more difficult.

It is hoped that the intellectual and personality damage seen in many deprived children can be mitigated by providing advice and support to parents, good day-care programs and health supervision for children, and, whenever it becomes necessary, model residential care. The accomplishment of these goals is of the utmost social significance, for it appears that the handicaps suffered become established during the first years of life and are not readily amenable to amelioration later on.

The effect of the mother's employment on the child depends on many variables, such as the mother's personality, how she feels about her work role and her maternal role, the care the child receives while she is away. Even for the youngest child, the fact that the mother is employed is not likely to be the most relevant factor in the mother-child relation. Except for the very young baby, the *quality* of the mother's emotional availability to her child is more important than the quantity of her care.

Absence of the father has a primarily indirect effect on the child's development during infancy, by way of its effect on the mother and her care of the baby. The toddler, on the other hand, may suffer when the father is not available to dilute the ambivalent relation with the mother, or to serve as a model for identification. The father's absence may also increase the possibility of a disturbance in the development of gender identity.

Transitory Disturbances in Development

Less serious disturbances are often encountered in normally endowed children growing up in "average" family settings. Although these disturbances are usually transitory, they may represent the early stages of later emotional problems. They occur when the child's needs are not met appropriately, when demands are made on him that are neither reasonable nor age-adequate, or when development is disturbed by internal stresses.

Because infants and toddlers are unable to care for themselves, they must put up with whatever care they receive. If satisfaction is denied them, or if unreasonable demands are made upon them, tension increases; it may be expressed through crying, fretfulness, clinging, or through disturbances in eating, elimination, or sleep. There is a strong tendency in early childhood for the body to provide expression for problems that involve the emotions.

Each child has his own natural inclinations, rhythms, and idiosyncracies: his own sleep rhythm, his own methods of comforting himself, his own food preferences, and his own time of readiness for training. The baby's stomach contracts with its own rhythm, not according to a timing imposed from without. These inclinations should be respected. Child rearing should be based on a responsiveness to and an understanding of the individual child and not on whim, preconceived notions, superstition, or dogma.

In contrast to stresses brought on by the environment, many of which are avoidable, internal stresses become inevitable as the child grows older. It is as natural for the toddler to seek immediate gratification of his wishes as it is inevitable for the mother to impose restrictions on him. Conflicts between the mother and the child are therefore bound to occur. Conflicts also occur within the toddler when he is torn between feelings of love and hate, or between his wish to get his own way and his anticipation of disapproval or punishment. If development proceeds satisfactorily, the toddler, in order to resolve these conflicts, will begin to impose the same restrictions and demands on himself.

Disturbances brought on by external stress generally respond to appropriate child care; those caused by internal stress usually disappear once the developmental phase in which they occurred has passed and once the relevant drive- and ego positions have been outgrown. Both types of disturbances, particularly when they are combined, however, may lay the groundwork for later emotional difficulties.

Feeding Difficulties

The first conflicts between the infant's needs and the mother's requirements usually occur around feeding. These conflicts center around quantity, quality, frequency, and procedure of eating; they may occur during nursing, weaning, the introduction of solid foods, self-feeding, etc.

The young child's attitude to food is inseparably connected with his emotional tie to his mother. The early equation of love for food and love for the mother inclines the child to treat food provided by the mother as he treats the mother herself, which means that all disturbances in the mother-child relation may enter into the feeding situation. Conflicting emotions about the mother are transferred onto the food, which has now become a symbol for her. When biting and chewing solid foods become important, eating may symbolize an aggressive action against food and therefore against the mother. The toddler may hence develop inhibitions over eating; he may refuse to bite, chew, or swallow his food, or he may refuse to eat anything that reminds him of a living animal.

Battles around eating the mother's food are an expression of the toddler's ambivalent relationship to her. If the mother experiences the toddler's refusal of food as a personal rejection, this will contribute to the battle from her side. Under these circumstances, feeding ceases to be a pleasure and becomes instead a struggle between mother and child.

As a result of toilet training, some children become anxious when their fingers are sticky or dirty; they may also show disgust and dislike for any foods that by their sight, touch, or smell remind them of fecal matter. As a consequence, children's "food fads" are at their peak between the second and third years of life.

Considerate handling of the toddler's feeding, along with a reasonable amount of self-determination, makes the function of eating less vulnerable to disturbances later in life. Pleasure in eating is enhanced when young children are allowed to play with their food and to feed themselves. Oral pleasures, such as thumb-sucking or a craving for sweets, should not be treated harshly at this young age. The symbolic connection between mother-love and food can best be undone by encouraging the toddler to handle food independently, rather than by giving him the impression that he eats "for mother's sake." It is only after the age of three that eating becomes either a completely independent and pleasurable activity or an unpleasurable experience caused by internal conflicts that persist irrespective of the mother's presence or absence.

Fears and Disturbances of Sleep

Once the developmental phase of object constancy has been attained, at around the beginning of the third year, temporary separations, such as holidays for the parents, hospitalization for the child, or entry into nursery school can be lengthened. The more ambivalent the mother-child relation, the longer this achievement is delayed and the more intense are the child's separation reactions.

Every effort should be made to help the child learn to tolerate separation in small doses and to encourage his own active efforts to overcome separation anxiety. These efforts will be hampered, however, if he is subjected to traumatic separation experiences, if the threat of separation is used as a form of punishment, or if overly anxious parents convey their attitudes about separation to him.

The infant's fears of darkness, thunder, strange places, and unfamiliar faces are to be expected. They soon disappear. The toddler's fears are probably symbolic; they are simple and usually transitory and resemble later, more complex fears.

Unless there has been some significant disruption in his life, a healthy infant drops off to sleep at a moment's notice if he is tired. The toddler, however, often has difficulty in going to sleep or in remaining asleep. He will protest when he is put to bed, he will toss and turn and insist on company. These difficulties can usually be accounted for by his reluctance to relinquish contact with loved ones; by his fear of regressing to the symbiotic state; by overexciting or frightening experiences, such as a recent separation from the mother or a visit to the doctor's office; and by inner conflicts, such as the conflict between the desire to soil and the fear of mother's disapproval.

The toddler's control over his anal and urethral sphincters is uncertain. He also has limited capacities for controlling angry impulses or coping with anxiety. This is especially true when he is asleep or falling asleep. The fear of soiling or wetting and thereby losing his mother's love—a fear that may occur particularly when training is too harsh—may cause the toddler to fear sleep; it may also bring about anxiety dreams that interrupt sleep.

Sleep disturbances ordinarily disappear as soon as the senior toddler attains libidinal object constancy, better sphincter control, and greater ego mastery over impulses and anxiety.

Bowel and Bladder Control

Toilet training can proceed gradually and uneventfully if it is undertaken when the toddler has already indicated his physical and psychological readiness to comply with his mother's requests, and if, during the training, he is treated with consideration. Toddlers are usually ready to be trained some time between 18 and 30 months of age.

If the mother—because of her early training or her reaction formation of disgust or orderliness—starts the training too early, however, or if she expresses her demand for control in a harsh and uncompromising manner, a major battle is likely to ensue. The toddler will become rebellious and stubborn: he will not move his bowels in the toilet, he will withhold bowel movements, he may even become constipated; or, if obedience is won with respect to training, he may express defiant feelings in some other way; he may develop eating problems, sleep disturbances, and temper tantrums; or he may become generally disobedient, cruel, and destructive.

Occasional accidents are to be expected insofar as the toddler's ability to control his bowel movements or his urination is largely dependent on the stability of his relations with his mother. It is only later, when the child's concern with cleanliness is disconnected from this relationship and instead attains the status of an autonomous ego and superego concern, that bowel and bladder control become secure.

Behavior Disorders

The toddler's behavior difficulties express themselves either directly through destructiveness, messiness, and restlessness, or reactively through clinging, whining, and temper tantrums. These usually disappear when his love for his mother outweighs his aggression and when he learns to control himself in order to please her.

There may be a transitory obsessional phase characterized by excessive orderliness, ritualistic behavior, and bedtime ceremonials. Such behavior is the result of defenses set up in order to counteract aggression against the mother or the wish to soil. Later on, however, it can lead to such valuable assets as punctuality, conscientiousness, and reliability.

The destructive tendencies in the toddler may be quite marked where love for the mother has become disrupted as the result of severe disappointments, separations, rejections, and the like. These traumas do not permit love feelings to develop sufficiently to counteract and tame aggression. The toddler neither wishes to please the mother, nor is he inclined to identify with the parents. This is a special danger during the second and third year, because aggression reaches a normal peak during that time. As a result, the playful, provoking stubbornness of the toddler may become fixed in the personality in the form of quarrelsomeness, ruthlessness, acquisitiveness, and destructiveness.

Disturbances in Communication

In the second half of the first year, the infant should be able to indicate his needs by producing many different sounds with his voice. Failure to begin to communicate in this way or an inability to imitate may be due to an organic disorder or may reflect a deficiency in the mother-child relation. The timetable of speech development in the toddler is highly variable. If the two- to two-and-one-half-year- old, however, has no words with which to communicate his wishes, this may be due to organic causes, to developmental interferences, or to conflicts. The mother may be depressed or neglectful, or she may be infantilizing her child. Oral and anal aggression may interfere with the development of speech, as it may with eating. Toddlers occasionally stammer at the height of toilet training—in part an indication of the conflicting tendencies of holding in and letting go. Once the conflict over toilet training has been resolved, there is often a spurt in speech.

Failure to speak is often multidetermined. It may reflect at one and the same time anal stubbornness, the wish to remain a baby—a wish that is often shared and reinforced by the mother—and a way of forcing attention from the parents. The toddler's beginning ability to use words can easily be lost during periods of stress. Separations, the birth of a sibling, or hospitalization may bring about a regression to earlier forms of communication or speech.

The fact that a young child has more than the usual amount of emotional problems should not automatically be taken as a reflection of his mother's care of him. Not only are many circumstances beyond the parent's control; some severe disturbances in early childhood, such as infantile psychoses and atypical development, seem to be the result of the absence of vital inner experiences, whether this absence is the result of inadequate mothering or of an inborn deficit in the child. This is all the more so in such situations as minimal brain damage, mental retardation, or organic brain conditions. Under these circumstances, maternal care is difficult, and all the more so if the mother has been blamed and made to feel guilty. In contrast, well-endowed infants have a remarkable ability to extract the emotional supplies that are necessary for adequate growth and development from the most adverse environmental settings.

The immediate effect of traumatic environmental influences—whether resulting from inherent disturbances in the mother-child relation, or unforeseen and unfortunate events of an accidental character—can be observed in the wide variety of developmental retardations and disturbances that have been described. These early disturbances may result in retarded, defective, and infantile personalities; or, on the other hand, with ego and superego growth, they may contribute to the development of neurotic illnesses in later stages of development.

A child's development can be evaluated at any time by examining the various aspects of his personality for signs of age-adequacy, precocity, or retardation. Fixations in drive maturation, arrests in ego development, and disturbances in object relations, if severe enough, indicate the need for therapeutic intervention. This can be illustrated by describing briefly the retardations and disturbances in the early development of two children observed during the course of a longitudinal research study (Kris, 1962; Ritvo, et al, 1963).

By the time Ann was eight months old, she showed a retardation in development similar to that seen in institutionalized children. This retardation took place despite the fact that she was a well-endowed, attractive baby, easy to comfort, and cared for solely by her mother. The interference in her development was created both by a deficit in the quantity of maternal care and in the quality of that care.

The mother, as a result of her own personality disturbance, experienced the baby as a rival, a competitor, and an intruder into her life. She regarded Ann as unattractive, and she rarely cuddled her or picked her up. The lack of contact between mother and child was striking: the mother could not easily perceive cues indicating Ann's needs, nor was she able to respond appropriately to them. While she carried out the correct procedures of child care, she gave little of herself to the child in doing so.

When Ann fussed or cried, the mother's ambivalence was expressed in mounting aggressive excitement. If attempts to calm the baby by feeding her or picking her up failed, the mother then adopted punitive measures, ranging from leaving the infant to her own resources to shouting at her and spanking her. By the time Ann was eight months old, the mother reported the existence of prolonged crying spells, which seemed to be more frequent on those days when the mother herself felt particularly lonely and depressed. The more intense the child's crying grew, the stronger became the mother's urge to hit her. The mother's guilt feelings were turned against the "naughty" child, whom she held responsible for her own distress.

Assessment of Ann's development at 15 and 26 weeks of age revealed signs that were suggestive of insufficient social and physical stimulation. By the time she was eight months old, the developmental picture gave rise to serious concern. Ann could not yet sit alone, except momentarily, nor could she support her full weight on her feet when held. All gross motor functions were significantly retarded. Her interest in toys was considerably less than expected for her age. There was also a delay in the ability to communicate.

Although Ann's retarded development was the consequence of a marked lack of stimulation, her frantic crying, her nutritional deficiency, and her marked fear of strangers were not in keeping with the developmental pattern usually seen in institutionalized children. They were not the result of lack of stimulation, but rather of periodic provocative overstimulation that produced mounting tension in the child without offering appropriate avenues of discharge.

Because the situation was regarded as critical, therapeutic aims were directed toward providing psychological help for the mother as well as outside help with the child's care. An effort was also made to help the mother increase the amount of physical handling and stimulation given the child. By the time Ann was 13 months of age, all areas of her development appeared to be up to her age level—possibly because the mother had followed some of the advice given her, possibly because of changes in the family that led to a greater acceptance of Ann on the mother's part and a closer relation between Ann and her father. The mother began to take pleasure in Ann's developmental progress and to enjoy teaching her. She was able to respond more positively to the child as a toddler than she had when Ann was an infant. By the time Ann reached the age of three, she had receovered from the developmental retardation, was a friendly and smiling child, and her physical status was satisfactory.

Jerry was an active, hypertonic, jittery newborn who reacted to any stimulation with massive discharge movements. During the course of his early development, this innate predisposition to motor activity was reinforced by sexual and aggressive overstimulation from the environment. This, in time, interfered with his ability to postpone discharge and to sublimate, and thus promoted impulsivity to an abnormal degree.

His mother was emotionally labile and volatile, a woman of shifting and tempestuous moods, who frequently gave evidence of a poor capacity for impulse control. She became preoccupied with Jerry's bowel functioning, massaging the anus with a suppository and manipulating a thermometer in the rectum for the purpose of helping Jerry defecate and expel gas. At 15 months of age, Jerry was a thin, wiry child, almost constantly in motion and always "getting into things." The mother seemed to invite him to touch or to break objects, after which she reacted as if his behavior were a provocation on his part, to be met with retaliation and punishment—followed by reconciliations.

The father, an unstable man, also handled Jerry in an exciting, stimulating, seductive manner. Jerry was not only drawn into repeated family arguments and crises, he was also employed by the parents to an unusual degree as an object through whom they gratified their instinctual strivings in a direct and relatively unmodified way.

Jerry's developmental progress was otherwise excellent up to the age of nine months. Between nine and 12 months, however, developmental assessment revealed a persistent disturbance in integrative functioning, failure to use language as a means of communication, difficulty in inhibiting the immediate discharge of impulse, easy distractibility, and a lack of interest in toys and objects, as well as a failure to use them in an adaptive way. Because these problems were felt to be related primarily to the disturbed mother-child interaction and to foreshadow a later disturbance in thinking, learning and sublimation, every possible effort was made to help the mother in her care of the child.

Jerry's pediatrician recommenced early entrance into nursery school, hoping that the child's general development might benefit from his being in a supportive but neutral educational atmosphere. In nursery school, Jerry proved to be hyperactive, impulsive, negativistic, and aggressive. He showed little judgment, caution, or control. His play was poorly organized, and he rarely used speech for communication. There was little in the way of a recognizable learning pattern that could be counted on for the prediction of later school achievement.

It was evident that Jerry needed the combined efforts of nursery school teacher and child analyst to help him with his impulse disorder. As a result of the nursery school experience, some increase in ego strength was achieved; by means of analytic treatment, there was some reduction of anxiety and resolution of inner conflicts. Jerry did make gains in the areas of control and organization, concept formation, communication, and social behavior. Probably as a result of these therapeutic interventions, as well as of subsequent external and internal changes in his life, Jerry's impulsivity and acting out had diminished considerably by the time he was 15 years old. By then his family life was more settled, he was managing to get along fairly well in school, and his energies were more constructively channeled.

Conflict and Anxiety

Although a great deal can be done to protect the child against the most severe psychological disturbances of early childhood and later, less can be done to protect him from mental conflict and anxiety, which are, after all, essential ingredients in normal human development. Without them the child would become neither socialized nor civilized. The fear of disapproval and the desire to be loved slowly bring about the acquisition of a conscience. It is the fear of one's own conscience that lies at the base of moral conduct. Conflicts between the biological drives and the moral conscience and its precursors are inevitable. Under unfavorable circumstances, these conflicts may produce a neurotic illness. What is important is the child's ability to master anxiety and to find healthy, as opposed to neurotic, solutions to conflicts. These abilities are to a considerable extent determined by the child's development during the first three years of life.

If the child does not acquire the means for dealing with the dangers inevitable in his early life, he will be reduced to chornic helplessness and panic. The baby's innate reaction to danger is anxiety. At the beginning of his life, he behaves as if any unexpected event—such as a sudden loud noise or a sudden exposure to strong light—were a danger to him. Later, when his attachment to his mother increases, he reacts with sadness and anxiety to her disappearance from sight. Still later, he becomes anxious when he loses or anticipates the loss of his mother's love, or when she disapproves of his behavior or punishes him.

The toddler and his mother are often in conflict with each other. One way in which the toddler manages to reduce the anxiety brought on by these conflicts is to move the conflict from the external world to the internal world. When this occurs, opposite tendencies exist in the child himself, one of which represents drive or id tendencies, while the other represents previously experienced external prohibitions, in the form of internal prohibitions stemming from the ego and the superego precursors. One part of the toddler's personality seeks gratification of his wishes, another part opposes that gratification. The forces opposing the toddler's tendencies are no longer only external; they now begin to exist in the form of internalized demands that represent externalized prohibitions. A wish that earlier gave rise to anxiety because it was disapproved of by the mother now brings on anxiety because it is disapproved of by the ego and the superego precursors. Anxiety begins to be generated internally, just as it was formerly generated externally.

When mental conflicts are active in the toddler, he may experience anxiety or temporary symptom formation in such areas as feeding, elimination, or sleep. These usually disappear as soon as adaptation to the developmental level in which they emerged has been achieved, or when the peak of that level has passed. These symptomatic manifestations of underlying difficulties, however, may reveal the vulnerability of the child. They often prepare the way for new disorders, which arise at the next developmental level (the phallic-oedipal phase) and usually do not disappear without leaving some weakness in one or another area of development—a weakness that becomes significant for neurotic symptom formation and character disorders in later life.

When the toddler becomes a preschool child, a more complex personality structure comes into existence as the consequence of a higher level of drive- and ego development. The division of the personality into the drives and the id on the one side, and the ego and superego on the other, leads to conflict between the psychic agencies. These conflicts are more complex than those that existed during the toddler period. If a satisfactory solution is not found, intolerable anxiety, regression, and neurotic symptom formation may follow in the form of an infantile neurosis. Adverse influences and pathological development during the preoedipal and separation-individuation phase may therefore not only lead to psychological disturbances at that time; they may also have a significant effect in determining the child's ability to cope with the danger situations and anxieties of the phallic-oedipal phase. Moreover, they may lay the groundwork on which complex mental conflicts will develop in the phallic-oedipal phase, as well as play a role in determining the nature of these conflicts, their forms of expression, their severity, and the child's ability to deal with them.

There is no simple way of preventing the onset of neurotic symptoms or the formation of neurotic character structure, in view of the inevitability of anxiety and mental conflict in the child's development. A neurosis is not necessarily an indictment of the parent-child relation; a neurotic child is not necessarily an unloved or a rejected child. At best it can only be said that, although the child who is well endowed, who has strong ties to his parents, and who develops well during the early years is not thereby insured against the onset of neurotic illness later on, he will, for these reasons, have the best possible inner resources to deal with conflict—resources that may then provide greater resistance to neurotic illnesses.

Each child not only reacts to danger in ways that are specific to him; he also employs specific ways of defending and protecting himself against danger, mastering anxiety, and finding solutions to mental conflicts. His ability to tolerate tension and to cope actively with anxiety and mental conflict is determined by innate tendencies, by the experiences of the early years, and by current events. When he was an infant, the child was dependent upon his parents to relieve his tensions, to anticipate dangers for him, and to remove the sources of his anxiety. If, at that time, however, he experienced undue tension and anxiety, a predisposition may have been created to develop excessive anxiety later on at times of stress.

Early in life the child acquires certain stabilizing ego characteristics that are of particular importance for his ability to deal with stress and mental conflict later on. These include a high tolerance for frustration, a good potential for sublimation, effective ways of dealing with anxiety, and a strong urge toward the completion of development.

Toddlers between the ages of 18 and 30 months are often afraid of such things as monsters or the vacuum cleaner with its deafening roar. One toddler may attempt to overcome his fear by anticipating the presence of the monster or guessing when the vacuum cleaner will be used; another may do so by learning to control the switch or the imaginary monster, thereby putting himself in command of the situation; still others may "make a study" of monsters, or investigate to find out why the noise occurs; and, finally, some children may transform themselves into a monster or a vacuum cleaner and prowl around the floor, making loud noises in pretend play.

Summary

In this chapter an attempt has been made to examine some of the wide variety of psychological disturbances that may occur during the first three years of life. These disturbances range from the *severe developmental retardations and personality defects* that result from massive and multiple deprivations and repeated separations, to the *transitory symptomatic disorders* of eating, elimination, and sleep that may occur during the course of normal development as a consequence of external and internal stress. Although the future outcome of these disturbances cannot be predicted accurately, they may interfere with the child's ability to cope successfully with the stresses and strains of later developmental phases; if so, they will thereby later on contribute to symptom formation and personality disturbances.

REFERENCES

Beres, D. & Obers, S. J. (1950), The Effects of Extreme Deprivation in Infancy on Psychic Structure in Adolescence: A Study in Ego Development. *The Psychoanalytic Study of the Child,* 5:212-235. New York: International Universities Press.

Bowlby, J. (1951), *Maternal Care and Mental Health:* A report prepared on behalf of WHO as a contribution to the United National Programme for the welfare of homeless children. Geneva: WHO.

——— Robertson, J. & Rosenbluth, D. (1952), A Two-Year-Old Goes to the Hospital. *The Psychoanalytic Study of the Child,* 7:82-94. New York: International Universities Press.

Freud, A. & Burlingham, D. (1944), *Infants Without Families: The Case for and Against Residential Nurseries.* Medical War Books. New York: International Universities Press.

Heinicke, C. M. & Westheimer, I. J. (1965), *Brief Separations.* New York: International Universities Press.

Kris, E. (1962), Decline and Recovery in the Life of a Three-Year-Old; or: Data in Psychoanalytic Perspective on the Mother-Child Relationship. *The Psychoanalytic Study of the Child,* 18:175-215. New York: International Universities Press.

McDevitt, J. B. (1971), Preoedipal Determinants of an Infantile Neurosis. In: *Separation-Individuation, Essays in Honor of Margaret S. Mahler,* ed. J. B. McDevitt & C. F. Settlage. New York: International Universities Press, pp. 201-226.

Nagera, H. (1966), *Early Childhood Disturbances, The Infantile Neurosis, and the Adulthood Disturbances—Problems of a Developmental Psychoanalytical Psychology.* New York: International Universities Press.

Provence, S. & Lipton, R.C. (1962), *Infants in Institutions: A Comparison of Their Development with Family-Reared Infants During the First Year of Life.* New York: International Universities Press.

——— & Ritvo, S. (1961), Effects of Deprivation on Institutionalized Infants. Disturbances in Development of Relationship to Inanimate Objects. *The Psychoanalytic Study of the Child,* 16:189-205. New York: International Universities Press.

Ritvo, S., McCollum, A. T., Omwake, E., Provence, S. A. & Solnit, A. J. (1963), Some Relations of Constitution, Environment, and Personality as Observed in a Longitudinal Study of Child Development: Case Report. In: *Modern Perspectives in Child Development,* eds. A. J. Solnit & S. A. Provence. New York: International Universities Press, pp. 107-143.

Schaffer, H. R. & Callender, W. M. (1959), Psychological Effects of Hospitalization in Infancy. *Pediatrics,* 24:528-539,

Spitz, R. A. (1945), Hospitalism: An Inquiry into the Genesis of Psychiatric Conditions in Early Childhood. *The Psychoanalytic Study of the Child,* 1:53-74. New York: International Universities Press.

——— with the assistance of Wolf, K. M., (1947), Anaclitic Depression: An Inquiry into the Genesis of Psychiatric Conditions in Early Childhood. *The Psychoanalytic Study of the Child,* 2:313-342. New York: International Universities Press.

SUGGESTED READING

Fraiberg, S. (1950), On the Sleep Disturbances of Early Childhood. *The Psychoanalytic Study of the Child,* 5:285-309. New York: International Universities Press.

Freud, A. (1947), The Psychoanalytic Study of Infantile Feeding Disturbances. *The Writings of Anna Freud,* Vol. 4. New York: International Universities Press, pp. 39-59.

——— (1965), *Normality and Pathology in Childhood. The Writings of Anna Freud,* New York: International Universities Press, pp. 108-164.

Robertson, J. & Robertson, J. (1972), Young Children in Brief Separation: A Fresh Look. *The Psychoanalytic Study of the Child,* 26:264-315. New York: Quadrangle Books.

Yarrow, L. J. (1964), Separation from Parents During Early Childhood. In: *Review of Child Development Research,* 1:89-136, ed. M. L. Hoffman & L. W. Hoffman. New York: Russell Sage Foundation.

CHAPTER SEVEN
The Oedipal Period

HENRY F. MARASSE, M.D.
and MARION G. HART, M.D.

Brave Jack chopped down the beanstalk, killed the wicked giant, having robbed him of his riches, and lived with his mother happily ever after.

Snow White and Cinderella managed to overcome the thwartings of their wicked, jealous stepmothers and marry their handsome princes, to live happily ever after.

For generations, these fairy tales have delighted the imaginations (and gratified the wishes) of children between the ages of three and six. Through these stories, children vicariously experience the dangers and emotions of the oedipal period. "Jack and the Beanstalk" is a variation on the oedipal tragedy. Both Oedipus and Jack killed their fathers; but whereas Jack, somewhat ambiguously, lived with his mother, Oedipus married Jocasta and could not live happily ever after.

According to the Greek myth, Oedipus, son of the King of Thebes, was exposed on a mountainside, his feet pierced (hence his name: swollen foot) because an oracle had prophesied that he would one day kill his father and marry his mother. A local shepherd rescued the baby, who grew to manhood totally ignorant of his heritage. After killing his father, whose identity he did not know, he liberated the city of Thebes from the dreadful Sphinx by being the first to answer the riddle: "What, when young, walks on four feet, when grown, walks on two feet, and finally walks on three feet?" Oedipus understood that the riddle described the stages of man's development. His answer caused the Sphinx to commit suicide, and the grateful city gave him the hand of the widowed Queen, unwittingly fulfilling the ancient prophecy.

Although it is customary to use the term Oedipus complex in connection with both boys and girls, the expression "Electra complex" is sometimes applied to the female version. Electra, "child of the wretchedest of mothers," Clytemnestra, remained loyal to her beloved father and to her equally beloved brother, Orestes. There are differences between the two tragedies, which correspond to some of the different problems that confront boys and girls of this age. Values of love and loyalty are stressed in the one story; the sinfulness of incest in the other. The Electra myth begins with the feeling of deprivation; Electra was sinned against and allowed her revenge. The Oedipus legend ends with deprivation, the mutilation Oedipus inflicted on himself to atone for his incest—he tears out his eyes and thus renders himself helpless. Feelings of deprivation usher in the oedipal complex in girls; castration anxiety is paramount in the oedipal complex in boys. The focus of the child's emotional life during these years is on the drama of the parents-child triangle: incestuous love of the son for his mother (or daughter for her father) and rivalry between the son and his father (or daughter and her mother).

General Description

The oral, anal, and phallic phases of development as described by Freud refer strictly to phases in the development of the instinctual drives. The terms preoedipal, oedipal, latency, adolescence, are broader in that they embrace total development—of drives, ego, and superego as these become crystallized in the child's relations to the important members of his environment, usually his parents and siblings. The child enters the oedipal period still very much a baby (although he is considered a "senior toddler"), and he leaves it a school child. How he evolves through these three years, three to six, is crucial to his achievement of independence and self-confidence.

During this period the child's play activities show a progressive enrichment of his capacities. At three, socialization is still tenuous, and his activities with peers can still be described as largely parallel play. But by four, he is already playing with, rather than alongside, his playmates. The same development characterizes his use of language. By the age of four it is relatively uncommon to observe what has been called "dual monologue"—analogous to parallel play—in which the participants preserve their own trends of thought, essentially uninfluenced by replies from their partners.

Imagination in play reaches its apogee during these years because of the confluence of two factors: increasing social awareness and language skills combined with an as yet very limited knowledge of the real world. At four, a block can be a train, an engine, an animal, whereas, by the time a child is six, his growing store of knowledge results in his requiring more sophisticated toys.

Bowel control at age three, although established, is still shaky. Regression to earlier, more infantile modes of response is frequent. By the age of six, self-control has been much more firmly established, and the child's egocentricity has become diluted by an awareness of the needs of others. His capacity to love others has matured. Often, an imaginary playmate helps him to bridge the gap between his egocentric past and his social future. It is during this period that the concept of self arises and the basis for the sense of identity that is consolidated in late adolescence.

As a child's verbal facility increases, he learns to rely on it as an instrument for dealing with his environment. This helps him to distinguish between fantasy and reality, a process that extends over many years and is never really completed. The capacity for abstract thinking, the rudiments of which are necessary in school, also develops during these years. And, last but not least, this is the time when the differences between the sexes become increasingly important to the child and affect his development.

Psychosexual Development

Freud described oral and anal primacy in 1905 in his "Three Essays on the Theory of Sexuality," which laid the foundations of the theory of infantile sexuality. In 1923 Freud, recognizing that somewhere between the ages of three and six libidinal investment shifts from the anal to the genital zone, particularly to the phallus, made an addendum to his theory and introduced the term *phallic phase.* Of course the genital area plays an erogenous role from birth onward, even though it does not become the leading erogenous zone until the oedipal phase. When the primacy shifts to the genital zone at about the age of three, it results in a gradual sharpening of the conflicts surrounding the triangle situation between the child and his parents, whom the child sees as a couple rather than as individuals. The phallic phase of libidinal development, together with the development of object relations, usher in the oedipal period.

Prior to the oedipal period, the little boy cannot conceive that girls do not also have a penis. When he discovers they do not, he first denies it, then consoles himself with the fantasy that they will grow one later on. He refuses to believe that those who do not have a penis have been intentionally deprived of it. To the four-year-old the world becomes divided into those who do and those who do not possess a phallus. As his interest in his phallus grows and, with this interest, the realization of its absence in girls and women, the boy develops anxiety about retaining his most prized possession. This anxiety is referred to as *castration anxiety.* Sometimes the little boy is subjected to actual castration threats; sometimes these threats are expressed only indirectly or symbolically in relation to a prohibition against masturbation or exhibition. But even with only relatively minor stimulation, the little boy develops castration anxiety because he expects talionic retribution for his phallic wishes—wishes involving the most significant person in his environment: his mother. Just as his mother has been the principal satisfier of his oral and anal needs, so is she the first object of his sexual strivings.

What are these sexual strivings? They have to do with phallic sensations, with erections; they involve showing off this prized organ; and as the child's interest in the function of the penis and in the creation of babies grows, his aim is to experience some kind of dimly imagined sexual penetration of mother or to possess mother through holding on to her. Here he runs headlong into competition with his father, whose possession of his mother he envies and whom he begins to see as a rival. The wish to eliminate his rival makes the boy extremely vulnerable to castration anxiety, inasmuch as he is so little and his father is so big and powerful. Castration, then, the loss of the offending organ, is the fitting punishment for wanting father out of the way.

Because the little boy also loves his father, a state of inner conflict arises. The result of this conflict may lead in one of two directions. Normally he relinquishes his mother as a sexual object. He identifies with father and expects to find a girl "like mother" when he grows up. If, however, the castration anxiety is too severe, he may seek refuge in passively submitting to the powerful father and totally give up interest in mother and her sex. This may later on lead to sexual symptomatology varying from premature ejaculation to impotence or homosexuality.

The capacity for self-control is directly related to the formation of the superego, which results from identification with the authoritative role of the parents, particularly the parent of the same sex. It is in this process that the Oedipus complex plays such an important role. Initially, it is castration anxiety that restrains the boy from acting on his oedipal wishes. With increasing identification with his father, however, guilt feelings related to unacceptable wishes, including the wish to eliminate the rival, begin to appear. These guilt feelings are the expression of the developing superego. The internalized prohibitions are frequently much more severe than the prohibitions expressed by the parents. Their Draconian quality is related to the intensity of the wishes that must be warded off. By the formation of an inner authority that helps the child to control his behavior as well as his fantasies, it becomes possible for him to resolve his Oedipus complex and to accept a postponement and displacement of those wishes that seemed so overwhelming only a short while before. This resolution of the Oedipus complex—its complete resolution takes place years later during adolescence—results in a marked diminution of oedipal fantasies and wishes, a diminution characteristic of the next developmental phase, that of latency.

The Oedipus complex, as we have said, develops differently in girls. Whereas the boy's conflict drives him to protect his penis, the girl must cope with the fact that she lacks one. Her primary love-object is the same as the little boy's, and it is the mother whom she blames for her anatomical deficiency. When she realized that mother, too, does not have a penis, the little girl turns from mother to father, from whom she then expects a penis, or its substitute, a baby.

Like castration anxiety, penis envy is a normal phenomenon. The little girl, upon observing the anatomical differences between the sexes, reacts with mortification. The little boy has something she does not have, he can urinate standing majestically, setting up jets and the like (as he is only too pleased to demonstrate). Many small girls try desperately to urinate in imitation.

A class of three-to-four-year-olds, exposed to coeducational bathroom facilities, was sent into a turmoil. The mothers reported their daughters were experimenting with the standing position. One little girl wailed that she wished she had a pony tail like the little boys. Another became depressed, openly expressed her wish for a penis, and grew increasingly abusive of her baby brother, calling him "Peter Penis." Many of the girls took to hanging ornaments around their waists that dangled in the manner of a penis; a few, even more insistent, took to hiding bulky articles in their underpants.

The psychological reaction of the girl to the anatomical differences between the sexes, however dimly or clearly these may be perceived, is what we designate penis envy. This concept sums up observations of childhood behavior and data gained from the psychoanalysis of adults. Penis envy has been under attack as if it were an ideological product of "male chauvinist" Freudians, and *not* part and parcel of observable facts. In adulthood, penis envy is normally buried in the unconscious and becomes manifest only through its derivatives—in some women, for example, by low self-esteem, lack of self-assertiveness, or, through reaction formation, by qualities the very reverse of these. The social position of women in a male-dominated society may reinforce attitudes having their origin in the oedipal period, especially if the conflicts of this period have not been resolved.

The little girl develops theories to account for her lack of a penis. Perhaps she once had one, but it was taken from her because she had been naughty, because she masturbated. Or perhaps it was not taken from her at all—perhaps it is invisible. The outcome of such conclusions can have dramatic and long-lasting effects on character. The little girl who continues to fantasy herself castrated may develop into an intelligent and attractive woman, but will feel stupid and ugly. On the other hand, the little girl who clings to the fantasy of the hidden phallus may never be willing to accept her feminine role, lest it be a sign of weakness.

The manner in which the girl resolves her phallic and oedipal conflicts has far-reaching effects on her sense of identity and her self-esteem.

> Carol, age five, who was brought in for treatment because of her inability to get along with her mother, temper tantrums, and enuresis, had a wish for an invisible penis. "I think Mommy knows where my penis is, but she is not telling me. If I could have a penis I would be big. I could control everyone. I could push Mommy around, tell her she can't have any supper, make her cry all the time. I would yell. Then I would take off with Daddy and leave her out."

One might find it odd that Carol conceived of having a penis as a way of wooing Daddy away from mother. The meaning of penis envy need not be exclusively the wish to have a penis; it can also represent the magic that will get the little girl all she desires.

The girl has a twofold task. She must shift her sexual interest from her primary mother-attachment to father; whereas the boy need not change love object.

The girl's hostility against her mother results in guilt feelings, just as does the boy's oedipal hostility against the father, but the danger for the girl is not that of castration as punishment for incestuous feelings. She already feels deprived of the penis—that is, castrated. The girl is threatened by fears of being penetrated and injured, and by the supposed dangers of childbirth. These fantasies, even when they succumb to repression and become unconscious, may be the source of powerful inhibitions and a refusal to become pregnant later on in life.

Just as with the boy, the girl can turn to a heterosexual or a homosexual resolution of the conflict. Overt homosexuality, however, is much less frequent in women than in men, despite the greater complexity of the oedipal development in the girl. Because the mother is the primary object, the little girl tends to preserve a greater amount of affectionate attachment to her mother than is generally true in the case of the boy's feelings for his father. This may explain the more open display of affectionate behavior between women than men. This behavior, of course, is also determined by the general attitudes and mores prevailing in a specific society or social class.

There has been considerable discussion whether the formation of the superego shows essential differences in the two sexes. One of the main problems is how to differentiate the basic aspects of personality formation from time-bound sociocultural influences which may, for example, emphasize passivity in girls and aggressivity in boys.

Even prior to the oedipal period, the girl displays a wish to have a penis and concomitant resentments against the mother for not having provided her one. This is slowly replaced by the wish to have a baby from the father. The little girl feels angry at the mother for making this impossible. As a consequence of her anger, the little girl fears the loss of her mother's love. This anxiety plays an important role in the eventual resolution of the oedipal conflicts and the establishment of the superego by way of identification with the mother.

Ego Development

The three-year-old has already developed a degree of object constancy which allows him to separate from mother without overwhelming anxiety. The capacity for object constancy increases during this period and is less and less subject to regression under stress. The maintenance of the mental representation of the object is essential to the development of the Oedipus conflict. The conflict could not exist unless the inner representation of the parent remained constant.

During the oedipal phase, the child is fiercely possessive of his parents. His curiosity, growing out of his wish for sexual knowledge, is boundless. He explores endlessly—both his own body and, to the extent he is permitted, those of his parents and others. The child of this age also takes great pleasure in exhibiting the body of which he has only recently become acutely aware. Exhibitionism and extreme ambition have their roots in this phase of development. Freud's case of Little Hans (1909) affords a vivid example.

With the development of object constancy is a concurrent development of the sense of self. As the perceptual and motor functions become increasingly precise, the self- and object representations become increasingly differentiated. Whereas the three-year-old is still quite "egocentric" by the time he reaches the age of six he has usually developed a reasonably adequate sense of self in a social setting of adults and peers. There is, during this three-year period, a remarkable development of secondary-process thinking which makes use of the rapidly increasing store of information accumulated during this time. The result is better reality testing, which leads to better self-control, and by the time the child is six, he usually is able to satisfy the demands of ordinary schooling.

Pathology and Treatment

Pathology related specifically to the oedipal period might assume a variety of forms, and, of course, is always related to the child's prior development and areas of fixation. There might be manifestations of faulty sexual identification, evidence pointing to a negative oedipal resolution, such as cross-dressing in the little boy, persistent mother attachment or unusually intense penis envy in the little girl. The causes are complex and multiple; they may include faulty objects for identifications, too severe castration anxiety in the boy, strong narcissistic mortification in the girl. In families where the father is absent for one reason or another, the resolution of the Oedipus complex is impeded. The father's absence invariably leads to some degree of developmental disturbance. The oedipal closeness to the mother often becomes exaggerated in the boy, although the castration anxiety is frequently displaced onto other men in the child's life—uncles, grandfathers, or the mother's male friends. The girl's relations with men may be seriously affected if the father is absent during the oedipal phase, but the girl's feminine identification—her feminity—suffers less than the boy's masculinity.

If the father's absence is the result of recent divorce, the child, whether boy or girl, may assume responsibility for the marital discord, and this may lead to intense feelings of guilt. Similar guilt may be experienced if the father's death or prolonged absence occurs during this period, because of the child's ambivalent feelings about him.

At about the time three-and-a-half-year-old Robby's father was hospitalized for spinal surgery, Robby announced he was now a big boy and would like to be transferred from a crib to a bed. Soon after, although toilet-trained since the age of two, he became enuretic. He also developed uncontrollable night fears, awakening and screaming for hours. His stuttering, present since the onset of speech, worsened.

Robbie delighted in playing house with his therapist. He was the daddy, she the mommy. He told his therapist he was frightened when he went to the doctor. He was so frightened of the big needles. Then followed a denial in fantasy. Didn't she think he was the strongest, biggest, bravest boy there was? He spent the rest of that session picking up heavy objects in the room, demonstrating his physical prowess to her.

Robby seemed to be acting out the exciting, sexual relationship he experienced with mother, intensified with father away in the hospital. The doctor with the needle was father with his menacing, prohibiting phallus. Short-term psychotherapeutic intervention made it possible for Robby's development to proceed in a normal manner.

The child might react to the sexual and aggressive pressures of this stage by regressing to an earlier developmental stage. He might manifest immature behavior, aggressive outbursts, hyperactivity, enuresis, encopresis, clinging behavior. With such children, it is most important to consider the possibility of a brain dysfunction, the differential diagnosis sometimes being made after therapeutic investigation.

The presenting symptoms might resemble neurotic symptoms, phobias being an almost ubiquitous manifestation of this stage. The child's phallic drives, so paramount during this period, lead inevitably to a confrontration with reality. This compels the child to recognize how small he is in relation to his big, powerful, feared rival, which, in turn, contributes to castration anxiety and fear of separation. This, in general terms, underlies the development of phobia, the classical neurosis of this period.

The principal phobias of the oedipal phase are animal phobias, fear of the dark, and fear of being alone. Anxiety at bedtime and nightmares are common. Our understanding of the structure of a typical phobia during the oedipal phase dates back to Freud's well-known clinical study of Little Hans (1909). Hans, a five-year-old boy, developed a fear of horses which prevented him from leaving his house. This phobic symptom not only kept him near his mother, toward whom he manifested a wish for physical closeness, but it also allowed him to maintain a good relation with his father by displacing his fear of the father onto the horse. He was thus able to resolve his ambivalence to his father, whom he also loved very deeply. In Freud's case report, we see the genesis of Hans's symptoms in his discovery of the difference between the sexes, his intuitive understanding of the birth process at the time of his sister's arrival, and his mother's castration threat when he masturbated; we then follow the resolution of the phobia and its understanding by the child during a three-month period of treatment.

Regression or symptom formation are modes of coping with the anxieties of this period—castration anxiety, fear of loss of love and of separation. Treatment would then be directed to helping the child deal with the fear of his projected aggression (phobias) and guilt stemming from masturbation. The aim of treatment would be to enable normal development to occur.

A therapeutic approach must always include the family. Sometimes, counseling of the parents may be enough to effect a change in family attitudes, and the child need not come into direct contact with the therapist or counselor. An exploration frequently reveals that the family is either having trouble tolerating the child's aggressive manifestations, encouraging earlier modes of functioning, or unconsciously seducing the child sexually by excessive nudity, continuing to bathe and dress him, bringing him into the parental bed, or exposing him inadvertently to sexual intercourse between adults. Treatment that did not involve an alteration of such practices would be ineffective.

Therapeutic Considerations

The oedipal period is a favorable one for therapeutic intervention, although many children who show neurotic disturbances at this time are not referred for help until the symptom picture is in sharper focus, when the child starts school. If trouble is recognized while the child is still in the process of dealing with his oedipal conflicts and repression is relatively weak, treatment is frequently of shorter duration than later and tends to offer a better prognosis.

Intervention at this time tends to prevent pathological resolution of the oedipal complex. It also helps the child to come to grips with the oedipal situation instead of regressing to preoedipal modes of coping and relating, which, of course, interferes markedly with his capacity to socialize and leads to learning and behavior problems in school.

In fatherless and underprivileged families, exposure of the child to adults other than mother or grandmother can help prevent the development of psychopathology. Regular contact with a "father substitute" may help the child to resolve his Oedipus complex as well as to overcome the effects of emotional deprivation and lack of intellectual stimulation.

REFERENCES

Buxbaum, E. (1954), Techniques of Child Therapy. *The Psychoanalytic Study of the Child,* 9:297-333. New York: International Universities Press.

Deutsch, H. (1944), *Psychology of Women.* Vol. I, New York: Grune & Stratton.

Erikson, E. H. (1950), *Childhood and Society.* New York: Norton.

Freud, A. (1936), *The Ego and Mechanisms of Defense. The Writings of Anna Freud,* Vol. 2, New York: International Universities Press, 1966.

——— (1965), *Normality and Pathology in Childhood. The Writings of Anna Freud,* Vol. 6. New York: International Universities Press.

Freud S. (1905), Three Essays on the Theory of Sexuality. *Standard Edition,* 7:125-243. London: Hogarth Press, 1953.

——— (1907). The Sexual Enlightenment of Children. *Standard Edition,* 9:130, 139. London: Hogarth Press, 1959.

——— (1907), On the Sexual Theories of Children. *Standard Edition,* 9:207-226. London: Hogarth Press, 1959.

——— (1909), Analysis of a Phobia in a Five-Year-Old Boy. *Standard Edition,* 10:3-150. London: Hogarth Press, 1959.

——— (1923a), The Ego and the Id. *Standard Edition,* 19:3-66. London: Hogarth Press, 1961.

——— (1923b), The Infantile Genital Organization. *Standard Edition,* 19:141-153. London: Hogarth Press, 1961.

——— (1924), The Dissolution of the Oedipus Complex. *Standard Edition,* 19:173-179. London: Hogarth Press, 1961.

——— (1925), Some Psychical Consequences of the Anatomical Distinction between the Sexes. *Standard Edition,* 19:242-258. London: Hogarth Press, 1961.

——— (1931), Female Sexuality. *Standard Edition,* 21:223-243. London: Hogarth Press, 1961.

Greenacre, P. (1952), The Prepuberty Trauma in Young Girls. In: *Trauma, Growth, and Personality.* New York: International Universities Press, 1969, pp. 204-223.

Lidz, T. (1968), *The Person,* New York. Basic Books, pp. 189-236.

Piaget, J. (1954), *The Construction of Reality in the Child.* New York: Basic Books.

——— (1962), *Play Dreams and Imitation in Childhood.* New York: Norton.

Senn, M. & Soln, T.A. (1968), *Problems in Child Behavior and Development.* Philadelphia: Lea & Febiger, pp. 61-89.

Sophocles, *The Complete Greek Tragedies.* The University of Chicago Press, 1959.

Stone, L. & Church, J. (1965), *Childhood and Adolescence.* New York: Random House, pp. 274-360.

Wolman, B.B. (1972), *Handbook of Child Analysis.* New York: Van Nostrand Reinhold.

SUGGESTED READING

Erikson, E. (1959), Growth of the Healthy Personality In: *Identity and the Life Cycle,* New York: International Universities Press.

Fraiberg, S. (1959), *The Magic Years.* New York: Scribners, pp. 179-282.

Harrison, S. & McDermott, J., eds. (1972); *Childhood Psychopathology.* New York: International Universities Press.

Kessler, J. (1966), *Psychopathology of Childhood.* New York: Prentice Hall.

Neubauer, P. (1960), The One-Parent Child and his Oedipal Development. *The Psychoanalytic Study of the Child,* 15:286-309. New York: International Universities Press.

O'Connor, F. (1952), *My Oedipus Complex. Stories of Frank O'Connor.* New York: Knopf.

Peller, L. (1954), Libidinal Phases, Ego Development and Play. *The Psychoanalytic Study of the Child,* 9:178-199. New York: International Universities Press.

Robertson, J. & Freud, A. (1956). A Mother's Observations on the Tonsillectomy of her Four-Year-Old Daughter. *The Psychoanalytic Study of the Child,* 11:410-433. New York: International Universities Press.

CHAPTER EIGHT

The Latency Period

AARON H. ESMAN, M.D.

"The Latency Period" is the term coined by Freud that has come into general use to refer to the years from five or six—the close of the oedipal phase—to 11 or 12—the onset of puberty. It roughly corresponds with the elementary school years in Western society.

In his "Three Essays on the Theory of Sexuality," Freud (1905) described the biphasic pattern of human sexual development with its peaks in early childhood and at adolescence. The valley between, characterized by a relative subsidence of libidinal drive energy and of manifestations of overt sexual (e.g., masturbatory) behavior, he referred to as "the period of sexual latency." It was conceived of as the consequence of the defensive struggles instituted by the ego against the unacceptable and ungratifiable incestuous urges of the oedipal phase. Obliged by the danger of castration or the anguish of penis envy to renounce these urges, the child diverts his libidinal energies into channels assessed as socially acceptable and consistent with the standards of the superego, newly consolidated by internalization of parental values and prohibitions. He thus achieves discharge by way of a process Freud termed sublimation.

It is under these dynamic conditions that the child becomes educable; that is, that he becomes capable of directing his attention and energies toward objects outside the family and toward issues of an abstract nature. In Piaget's terms, the child, having solved the problems of family relations, turns his interests and energies to problems in the larger world outside the family. Thus, in almost all cultures we know of, the formal education of children begins at about age six. It is during these early latency years that, as Piaget has shown, the child experiences a major advance in his cognitive capacities, in the development of stabilized logical thought based on concrete and formal operations.

In Freud's view, latency is a biologically determined state inherent in the innate pattern of unfolding of the sexual drive. It is, therefore, universal and only secondarily dependent on educational influences. Anthropological investigations have shown, however, that in some primitive societies, overt sexual activity, including intercourse, goes on throughout these years. What is universally forbidden in every culture that has been described, is overt incestuous sexuality. The incest taboo is so ubiquitous that it may represent the biological bedrock of latency.

Freud emphasized that his description of latency represented an ideal; that latency was actually a relative rather than an absolute state, and that some residues of infantile sexuality were likely to be seen in all children, however well established latency might be. It is in this sense that latency must be understood today—as a period of relative quiescence of erotic activity and fantasy, seen most typically in industrialized Western societies where the demands for formal academic learning and instinctual renunciation go hand in hand. Indeed, as we shall see, pathology in many instances can be understood in terms of deviation from the state of latency, or survival into this period of major overt manifestations or derivatives of infantile sexuality.

The principal developmental task of the latency-age child can be defined as that of acquiring the capacity for sustained, effective work at activities that serve his adaptive needs and make sense within his environmental framework ("sublimations"). This is normally accomplished through learning certain culturally defined skills; the child's mastery of these skills promotes his growing sense of competence and purpose. Erikson (1950) has epitomized the outcome of this process as the establishment of a sense of *industry* and the prevention of lasting feelings of *inferiority*.

Phenomenology

It should be understood that the latency period is not a uniform state. The child is, of course, undergoing constant developmental and maturational change during these years, and it is hardly to be expected that the six-year-old and the 11-year-old will behave similarly or show identical psychic organizations. A clearer picture will be gained if we adopt Bornstein's (1951) division of this period into two subphases—the first, early latency, extending from five to about eight; the second, late latency, from eight or nine to pubescence.

Early latency is dominated by the persistence of intense inner pressure of the masturbatory impulses and incestuous fantasies which the child has only recently and shakily succeeded in repressing. The newly formed superego is importunate in its demands for renunciation, and the sense of danger of eruption of the forbidden urges is constant.

Consequently, in early latency, alongside the expected investment in learning, expansion of ego functions, and deepening and broadening of object relations, one typically sees behavior reflecting regressive defensive efforts at maintaining mastery of the oedipal conflict. Characteristically, these efforts will take the form of anal preoccupations and anal language in boys, while little girls, responding to the cultural expectation for conformity and propriety ("sugar and spice and all things nice"), will show exaggerated disgust and fastidiousness—i.e., reaction formations against similar anal regression. At the same time, there is typically a great concern for and adherence to rules and ritualized modes of conduct. The typical rituals of latency—avoiding cracks in sidewalks, counting fence posts, etc.—have their origin in this period as part of the defensive effort to erect a rigid system of controls against regressive anal-sadistic fantasies ("step on a crack—break your mother's back"). Or, as A.A. Milne put it in "When We Were Very Young"

They try to pretend that nobody cares
Whether you walk on the lines or squares
But only the sillies believe their talk,
It's ever so 'portant how you walk.

As a further buttress to the defensive efforts to renounce sexual impulses, a more or less rigid sexual segregation appears. No longer do little boys and girls share play activities and engage in common make-believe; each sex groups together in a mutually exclusive band, reinforcing the separation with expressions of scorn and contempt for the other. This tendency will increase as latency progresses, until prepubertal stirrings (especially in girls) begin to direct the pattern toward adolescent commingling.

During this early period, it is not unusual for some of the anxieties of the preoedipal period to persist and even to intensify. Nightmares and mild phobic symptoms, on the one hand, and mild obsessive-compulsive traits, on the other, may, as transient phenomena, be part of the normative experience of early latency.

As the child develops, as his defenses become consolidated and more refined, as he acquires a wider range of competence in ego functioning—as, that is, he matures and passes into later latency—the picture shows substantial change. No longer are the external evidences of conflict so sharp. The consolidation of reaction formation as a major defense leads to the diminution of the regressive anality and its replacement by socially approved modes of behavior, while at the same time, the superego strictures seem less rigid and arbitrary. There is great expansion in motor and cognitive skills, particularly in the capacity for logical, causally directed thinking. There are varied indications of anticipation of and preparation for adolescent and adult roles; Peller (1958) has described the manner in which this is reflected in the reading preferences of latency boys and girls.

The child in late latency is typically a collector par excellence. Everything from rocks and bottlecaps to plane models and postage stamps may become treasured objects, and pockets are usually filled with endless items seemingly useless to adult eyes but of utmost importance to the child. One might account for this behavior as a "sublimated" anal-retentive phenomenon, but it is at least as true that it reflects the child's growing curiosity about his environment and his efforts to structure and organize its bewildering complexity. Such collecting is often transitory, but it may become the basis for life-long hobbies or even vocational interests.

A striking characteristic of late latency is the "best friend" phenomenon. Though most typical of girls, it is also found in boys, who may characterize their friends as "my best friend, my second-best friend, my third-best friend," etc. Such friendships usually exist within the context of peer groups or cliques, which may in themselves be exclusionary and structured ("clubs"), with rules of organization, secret codes, handshakes, and the like. Much concern may be shown about inclusion or exclusion from such cliques, and the shifting sands of peer group loyalties may be poignant indeed to the child who feels temporarily or permanently left out.

At the same time, the latency child becomes aware of the realities of ethnic and class distinctions. Children who have in earlier years seemed "color blind" and indifferent to distinctions of religion and wealth may show acute consciousness of these issues, and the early manifestations of prejudice and discrimination are often evident during these years.

Capitalizing on the tendency of latency-age children to form groups and maintain stable peer relations, institutionalized groups, such as Cub Scouts, Little League Teams, play groups, and church groups, serve to direct energies and aims into channels prescribed or favored by the society. Trained group workers are frequently utilized in such programs, which represent a major instrument of socialization and inculcation of cultural values as well as affording opportunities for planned recreation.

Many of the early stirrings of puberty are felt in what was formerly regarded as late latency, particularly in girls, who characteristically mature from one to three years earlier than boys. Typically, the 10- or 11-year-old boy clusters with his male peers, preoccupied with masculine interests, such as sports and "making things," while girls are typically seen gossiping and giggling together, intensely aware of the boys they ostensibly still avoid and depreciate, but whom some are already pursuing, at least in fantasy. Children in this phase are particularly attuned to adolescent mores and often seek to ape their adolescent brothers and sisters in such matters as clothing, musical tastes, and, occasionally and unfortunately, drug use.

Pathology

As will be evident from the nature of the developmental issues characteristic of this phase, the typical pathological patterns reflect one side or the other of the struggle to control the eruption of phallic or preoedipal impulses into overt behavior or consciousness. Thus, whereas the prototypic neurosis of the oedipal period is the phobia in which, as described in the previous chapter, the fear of castration or punishment for forbidden incestuous wishes is dealt with by displacement, the phase-specific neurosis of latency is the obsessive-compulsive neurosis.

Chris, a 7-year-old boy of mixed Italian and Jewish parentage, came for psychiatric evaluation because of the intense anxiety he had been experiencing for the past year. When crossing streets with members of his family, he was terrified by the thought that one of them—stepmother, father or brother—would be hit by a car and be killed. No amount of reassurance could assuage his concern. In addition, he was obsessed by worries about his parents' safety when they went out at night and when they went away on trips. While he was at school, he was fearful that something was going wrong at home. He was usually able to concede intellectually that these concerns were unreasonable; nonetheless, he was oppressed by anxiety.

Despite these recurrent thoughts, Chris did well in school. He was usually a sweet, agreeable child who had, however, occasional violent tantrums when frustrated, and who tended to be tyrannical at times. Significant in the history was the fact that his mother had died of cancer when he was four and that his father was with her in the hospital much of the time during her last few months of life. His stepmother was sure that Chris felt guilty about his mother's death, though she had no idea why. When seen, Chris expressed great distress about his obsessional thoughts and the anxiety associated with them. He related well, was friendly and open, and was eager for help.

Chris showed the typical descriptive and dynamic features of the obsessive-compulsive child—recurrent uncontrollable irrational anxieties revealing, behind the reaction formation of concern for others, a latent unconscious hostility which the symptom seeks to control. Occasionally the rage broke through the defensive system in tantrum-like uncontrolled outbursts usually followed by intense guilt and efforts at making up. It seemed that his mother's illness and death were critical factors in reinforcing Chris' ideas about the destructive quality of his angry feelings and fantasies. That Chris, despite his symptoms, was able to function adequately in school and relate appropriately to others was crucial to establishing the diagnosis and in differentiating his condition from a more severe borderline or psychotic one in which these essential ego capacities would be impaired.

In many instances, of course, the pathology is more subtle and less alien to the self-image than that of Chris. Many latency children show compulsive behavioral features, such as exaggeratedly ritualistic behavior, especially at bedtime or in relation to meals and other routines, and are emotionally constricted, unimaginative, somewhat authoritarian and superior in manner, intellectualistic and argumentative. These are typical characteristics of an incipient obsessive-compulsive character. These children do not experience overt anxiety and are generally reluctant to acknowledge illness or involve themselves in treatment despite the extreme limitations in the freedom of play, object relationships, and school performance imposed on them by their rigid defensive structure organized, as with the neurotic child, against the danger of breakthrough of anal-sadistic impulses and fantasies.

As mentioned above, the phobic disorders typical of the oedipal phase may be seen in latency as well. Specific to the latency period, however, is one type of phobic symptom—the so-called "school phobia." Typically, the child who has gone to nursery school and/or kindergarten for one or more years, suddenly begins to resist going to school in the morning, complaining either of overt anxiety or, more often, stomachache, headache or vague distress, which vanishes when he is allowed to remain at home. If compelled to go to school, he will manifest his anxiety either in panic-like distress or, defensively, in violent physical resistance. Tears and pathetic clinging to the parent are frequent, as are nausea and vomiting. On weekends and holidays, and if allowed to remain at home, the child may be entirely free of anxiety, though he may show similar distress reactions if the parents go out at night.

It must be remembered that, like any phobia, "school phobia" is a symptom that may occur in a number of pathological states. It is often mingled with obsessional features in which the child's concern about leaving the parent is tinged with apprehension that some disaster may befall the parent in his absence. The common thread that runs through most cases, however, is that of *separation anxiety.* Where actual disturbing elements in the school situation are ruled out, one is almost always dealing with the fear of separation from the parent, most often the mother (see Johnson et al., 1941).

This separation anxiety is typically the consequence of intense unresolved ambivalence, with the child feeling unconsciously that the parent will be destroyed by his hostile impulses if he is not in constant reassuring contact. In some instances, this may be intensified or precipitated by the birth of a younger sibling; the child may wish to see to it that all the parents' attention is not lavished on its rival. In other cases, the child may wish unconsciously to prevent the parents from having sexual relations in his absence. Diagnosis of "school phobia" requires, first of all, elimination of the question of actual sources of anxiety in school itself, such as a frightening teacher, conflict with peers, self-esteem problems due to learning difficulties, etc. As in all clinical diagnosis, the symptom must be assessed in the context of a thorough study of the total personality; particularly in late latency and adolescence, careful evaluation of ego functioning is necessary to exclude the possibility of a psychotic disorder. The child's relationship to the parents must be carefully assessed. In many cases it has been shown that the mother unconsciously fosters the child's reluctance to go to school because of her own unresolved dependency needs and her wish to keep the child close to her.

In all the situations described above, the child's conflicts are essentially internal ones, with symptoms generated by anxiety over the eruption of unacceptable, unconscious wishes. Under other circumstances, however, the child's impulses may achieve discharge with little or no apparent conflict or anxiety; this maladaptation is characterized by unacceptable behavior rather than by symptom formation. Such children are aggressive, impulsive, and at times antisocial, even in latency. They may engage in various perverse sexual activities or may show highly deviant sexual identification in such forms as transvestitism. Such children are said to suffer from *behavior or conduct disorders.* These are of two types: (1) those that are *secondary* to or complicated by organic brain damage, and (2) those that are based primarily on pathological relationships with parents and other authority figures, or an identification with pathological models, the so-called *primary* behavior disorders.

Organic brain pathology can take many forms, ranging from profound mental retardation and cerebral palsy to almost undetectable deviations in perceptual motor functioning ("minimal brain dysfunction"). In the latter, there is often found a syndrome characterized by hyperactivity, distractability, and poor impulse control that may lead to serious difficulty in the child who is expected in school to be able to concentrate, attend, restrain impulse, and limit activity to prescribed periods. Where, in addition to the organic disorder, significant intrapsychic conflicts or difficulties with parents are present, the child's capacity to tolerate the frustrations of school life and peer relationships may be overwhelmed and serious behavioral difficulties may ensue.

More common, however, is the problem of the child who, because of faulty resolution of oedipal conflict or severe preoedipal difficulties, has failed to develop adequate ego controls or to internalize superego standards. Frequently the products of broken homes with one absent or inadequate parent, exposed to excessive stimulation of sexual drives or subjected to cruel aggression by adults, such children may *identify with the aggressor,* taking on the characteristics of the deviant adult world to which they are expected to adapt. Indeed, these children may show, alongside the ego and superego defects that characterize them, remarkable capacities for perception of their disordered social world and highly effective techniques for survival in it. Their "ego weakness" is balanced by certain "ego strengths" that are not, unfortunately, suited to adaptation to the larger social framework.

A frequent finding in the histories of such children is that of maternal deprivation in the early months or years of life. Indeed, many studies have shown that children who suffer from severe deprivation syndromes in infancy regularly manifest behavior disorders in latency and early adolescence, characterized by impulsivity, shallow object relations modeled on need satisfaction, poor frustration tolerance, and learning difficulties.

Similar but less severe pictures may be seen in those children who, reared at home, have been subtly deprived by emotionally absent or unavailable mothers. This may be seen particularly in the matriarchal family structure of the black ghetto where the father is absent from the home and the mother leaves her children to the care of the maternal grandmother. The latter, often overtaxed and overwhelmed, will oscillate between intense overindulgent affection and violent corporal punishment, while the mother herself is often a shadowy, uncertain, and inconsistent figure in the child's life. Deprived of a male model with whom to identify, and lacking consistent warmth and acceptance, such a child will move into the culture of the street, where he receives an intense exposure to antisocial influences and may be absorbed into the drug and criminal culture well before adolescence.

Of course, in many cases, a clear-cut difference between neurosis and behavior disorder will not prevail. Children who have only partially internalized parental values and have significant but defective superego formation may develop transient guilt feelings or even neurotic symptoms, but the deficiency in ego controls makes it impossible for them to adequately regulate their impulses. These transitional states are referred to as "behavior disorders with neurotic features," and are the precursors of certain types of character neurosis of later life.

Learning disorders and psychotic disturbances of latency will be discussed in later chapters.

Treatment Considerations

Latency is the period during which the greatest number of children are brought for treatment. Disorders that have passed unnoticed in the preschool years reveal themselves beyond the possibility of denial under the impact of school demands and peer interaction. The ratio of boys to girls is almost universally reported as about 3 to 1; this does not mean that girls are less likely to be disturbed, but that their problems are less likely to disturb the environment. Girls tend to be less aggressive and troublesome than boys of the same age, and their pathology tends to be more autoplastic than alloplastic at this age—i.e., they are more likely to show symptoms and inhibitions than to behave in anti-social or disruptive ways.

The neuroses of early latency are generally considered to be the optimum field for the operation of child analysis and analytic child therapy. In these situations, where both anxiety and accessibility are relatively high, prognosis is excellent. In later latency, where the defenses are better consolidated and the therapist is looked on as a threat to the rigid defensive structure, the task is more difficult and in many cases is best left until puberty has reactivated earlier anxieties. In the case of the severe behavior disorders, particularly where family disorganization is an etiological factor, residential treatment may be needed.

Close collaboration with the school and the use of ancillary resources, such as special teaching, remedial education, remedial recreational facilities, and so forth, are in most instances of great value in the treatment of emotional disorders of latency.

In cases where individual therapy is too threatening, or where major difficulties in peer relationships exist, the technique of activity group therapy (Slavson, 1947) is frequently useful, and is a field in which social workers most frequently serve as therapists. The social worker is also of major value in maintaining liaison with schools and other social institutions involved in the care of latency children; indeed, as mental health consultant to schools, the social worker may play a crucial role in case finding, parent/teacher education, and program development.

REFERENCES

Bornstein, B. (1951), On Latency. *The Psychoanalytic Study of the Child,* 6: 279-285. New York: International Universities Press.

Erikson, E. H. (1950), *Childhood and Society.* New York: Norton.

Freud, S. (1905), Three Essays on the Theory of Sexuality. *Standard Edition,* 7:125-243. London: Hogarth Press, 1953.

Johnson, A., Falstein, E., Szurek, S. & Svensen, M. (1941), School Phobia. *American Journal of Orthopsychiatry,* 11: 702-711.

Peller, L. (1958), Reading and Daydreaming. *Journal of the American Psychoanalytic Association,* 6:57-70.

Redl, F. & Wineman, D. (1951), *Children Who Hate.* Glencoe, Illinois: Free Press.

Slavson, S. R. (1947), *The Practice of Group Therapy.* New York: International Universities Press.

SUGGESTED READING

Cramer, J. (1959), Common Neuroses in Childhood. In: *American Handbook of Psychiatry,* ed. S. Arieti. New York: Basic Books, p. 797.

Hawkes, G. R. & Pease, D. (1962), *Behavior and Development from Five to Twelve.* New York: Harper.

Lidz, T. (1968), *The Person.* New York: Basic Books, Chapter 9, The Juvenile.

CHAPTER NINE

Psychoses and Psychotic-like Reactions of Childhood

AARON H. ESMAN, M.D.

In every phase of childhood one sees a relatively small but significant number of children who show severe and at times extreme deviations from the expected norms of behavior and personality development. In general, these children are characterized by extensive disturbance in their relations with other people, in their control and modulation of impulse and drive expression, in their thinking and learning processes, and in their relationship with the commonly conceived reality of the world around them. These children have been variously described as "schizophrenic," "atypical," "autistic," "ego-deviant." In this discussion they will be referred to as psychotic, a general descriptive term which does not imply a specific disease with a unitary etiology.

The recognition of such severe psychotic conditions in children is relatively recent. It awaited the development of the discipline of child psychiatry to the point where such extreme disorders could be distinguished from the normal range of deviation, on the one hand, and mental defect, on the other, and their fixity differentiated from transient developmental-phase phenomena. Hence, although de

Sanctis described cases of early psychosis as early as 1908, it was not until 1933 that Potter presented the earliest systematic discussion of "childhood schizophrenia" in the American literature. This was rapidly followed by the work of Despert (1938), Bradley (1941), and others, so that by 1947 Bender was able to present a detailed description of the syndrome based on the study of over a hundred cases.

Bender described, in addition to the psychological manifestations referred to above, a wide range of physiological symptoms and signs that, in her view, were integral to the syndrome of "childhood schizophrenia" as she conceived it. These include instability of peripheral circulatory and gastrointestinal systems, muscular flabbiness or rigidity, excessive sweating, hyperventilation, etc. Her observations led her to the conception of "childhood schizophrenia" as a type of "encephelopathy" (i.e., brain pathology) based on "a maturational lag at the embryonic level of development," affecting all systems of the organism but, most particularly, the central nervous system. Bender considered the behavioral manifestations of the disorder to be a consequence of a basically organic, probably genetically determined deviation in the organism's capacity for integrated patterned behavior on all levels.

Most of the early reports of psychotic disorders of children concerned themselves with children who had been apparently well in their early childhood and had shown the onset of their psychosis at the oedipal period or the early school years. Kanner (1942), however, described a group of children whose disorder appeared to be present virtually from birth and who had never shown a capacity to relate to other people. Previous to his reports, such children had usually been considered mentally deficient. Kanner referred to these as cases of "early infantile autism" and distinguished them from those children whose illness seemed to begin later in childhood. Kanner suggested that the disorder in his cases might be the consequence of severe affect deprivation by cold, narcissistic, obsessional, overintellectual mothers.

Rank (1949) also described a group of preschool-age children with extensive disturbances whom she referred to as "atypical" children. The "atypical development" from which these children suffered was, she indicated, the consequence of serious pathology in the mothers, with marked narcissistic patterns resulting in an incapacity for adequate mothering.

Mahler (1952, 1954, 1968; Mahler and Elkisch, 1953; Mahler et al., 1959) has in the past 20 years contributed extensively to the understanding of clinical aspects of childhood psychosis and has elucidated the phases of normal infant development. She has delineated two basic subtypes of psychosis—the "autistic" and the "symbiotic"—which differ not only in their clinical manifestations but in their pathogenesis. The "autistic" subtype can be observed virtually from birth: the child makes no contact with human objects, shows little or no development of communicative speech and has many bizarre characteristics, including some of the somatic phenomena Bender has described. This, Mahler suggests, represents a fixation at the developmental phase usually observed during the first two to three months when the mental representations of self and object are undifferentiated and the child lacks any conception of the mother as an object capable of emotional investment.

The "symbiotic" type, on the other hand, does not typically show itself until the second year of life when the infant, immersed in an intense symbiotic relation with the mother, is faced with developmental pressures toward separation and individuation. The child may show intense clinging attachment to the mother and/or other persons, with little discrimination between one object and another and with dire panic reactions when threatened with separation. The unconscious wish to engulf, or the fear of being merged with, the partially differentiated object may be secondarily defended against by means of intense warding off maneuvers so that a "secondary autism" may complicate the diagnostic picture. Mahler suggests that a careful history will serve to differentiate many such cases from those of true primary autism, but in clinical practice such differentiations are often difficult.

Clinical Picture

The range of the clinically observed phenomena in childhood psychosis is protean. The picture will differ extensively, depending on such constitutional factors as inherent sensitivity and response patterns, as well as age of onset, degree of "organic" contamination, family dynamics and parental behavior, favored defenses, etc. A few illustrative cases will indicate some of the more commonly seen patterns.

At age five, Matthew T. was incapable of any but the most primitive efforts at communication. When seen in the playroom he played listlessly with toys, focusing his attention on the dollhouse, which he arranged and rearranged repetitively in a compulsive fashion. He did not respond when addressed, but occasionally muttered largely incomprehensible phrases in a private monologue. His mother complained that he was unmanageable at home, reacting to the slightest frustration with violent tantrums. His bowel training was highly unstable. He was fascinated by the phonograph, which he would sit and watch for hours, seemingly more interested in the movement of the turntable than in the music. At times he would parrot TV commercials, though without any sense of comprehension and without any relevance to what was going on around him.

Mrs. T. first dated the onset of Matthew's troubles from one-and-a-half years of age when he fell through a cellar window, suffering a scalp wound. Yet there had never been any indication of significant injury or neurological damage, and careful exploration brought out the fact that even before the accident Matthew had been an unresponsive infant who showed little interest in people. Although his motor development had been normal, he had not shown the usual prelanguage sounds typical of the one- to one-and-a-half-year old. It was of significance that the parents' marriage was a most unsatisfactory one and that the mother was a very disturbed woman who had been highly ambivalent about having this child.

Matthew showed, in short, the typical features of a child with an autistic type of psychosis—the absence of relatedness to people, the absorption in mechanical objects, failure of speech development, and lack of frustration tolerance and impulse control. When seen several years later, after extensive residential treatment, he was still a bizarre, detached boy, who, though he had developed fair verbal capacities, was mask-like and mechanical in his responses. He was essentially unrelated, although he retained an extraordinary recollection of his previous examination.

Larry L., just short of seven, was referred to a child guidance clinic by a psychiatrist who had seen him briefly in consultation. His mother, an obese, lethargic woman with inappropriate affect and slow hesitant speech, complained that Larry was slow in learning to speak. He had not really communicated in words before age four and a half and still did not express himself well. In addition, he was enuretic nightly, had many fears and nightmares, and clung to his mother. In his sleep he rolled his head and ground his teeth. He had many food fads and avoidances. He was able to go to school by himself, but once there lost himself in fantasy and rarely finished his work. He was, his mother said, "sex conscious," was preoccupied with his mother's breasts, and on at least one recent occasion had climbed on top of her and made coital motions.

Mrs. L. confided that for the first two years of Larry's life she had never spoken to him because, "I knew he couldn't answer me." Their contact had been largely physical, and Larry had been slow in almost all aspects of self-care. He had slept in the parents' bedroom until he was two, when he was displaced by his younger brother and reacted with intense resentment.

Larry was a slim, blond, vacant-looking boy who left his mother easily and related very quickly to a strange examiner. Speech was scanty. He was guarded and unrevealing, but when he did talk there was a good deal of incoherence. He denied all problems. His free drawing was of a vaguely constructed airplane which was connected by a rope ladder to a boat; the ladder actually penetrated the boat and as Larry elaborated it, it became a solid band connecting the two.

Mr. and Mrs. L. had been involved in intense marital conflict for years. Mr. L. was a chronic paranoid schizophrenic, generally withdrawn from the family except for sporadic outbursts of rage. Mrs. L. was a vague, disorganized woman who clung to Larry in his early years as a source of gratifications she craved but did not obtain from her husband. As Larry improved gradually in the course of his treatment, Mrs. L. deteriorated so that she ultimately had to be hospitalized because of an acute psychotic breakdown. This, along with Larry's separation anxiety and the symbiotic bond between them in his drawing, betokened the symbiotic nature of his psychosis.

Peter was brought for help when he was six and a half. His parents complained that he was retarded in social and verbal development, although quite advanced in other areas. He was negativistic at home, had severe tantrums and could not play with children other than his siblings. His speech development was markedly retarded. He had spoken words at age two, but did not really communicate until three and a half. At the time of referral, his speech consisted largely of naming things, expressing his wants in repetitive compulsive questioning. He was unable to converse. His sentences were fragmented and disconnected, and he was often unresponsive when addressed. Peter's early development was not particularly unusual. He was the fourth child of parents with an RH incompatibility, but he showed no apparent abnormalities at birth. Early motor development was unremarkable, except that he did not walk until 16 months, which his mother thought unusual in comparison with his siblings. Mr. and Mrs. F. were bright, agreeable, devoted parents who showed no detectable marital discord or individual maladjustment, although the mother was somewhat rigid and emotionally cool. The three older siblings appeared at the time to be essentially normal.

At referral, Peter was an odd-looking boy, with a fixed inappropriate smile. There was no detectable separation anxiety. His gait was often sloping, and he had peculiar grunting respirations at times. Contact was tenuous, conversation virtually impossible. His play was scattered, but he was able to concentrate on things that interested him. It was impossible to elicit any fantasy material. Neurological examination at age five had been essentially nonspecific, resulting in an impression of "cerebral dysgenesis," i.e., failure of brain development. Extensive and repeated psychological testing revealed no organic impairment, but did suggest a picture of "schizoid" development in a boy with exceptionally high intellectual potential but with markedly uneven functioning.

Nevertheless, this boy was considered a psychotic child with a significant component of diffuse nonspecific organic pathology, resulting perhaps from the RH incompatibility of his parents. His disorder in speech development was similar in many respects to that seen in organic conditions. Six years' follow-up essentially confirmed this impression. Though he showed substantial improvement in his intellectual development and to some degree in his social performance, there were still considerable verbal difficulties, including a great deal of uncertainty in word-finding and occasional inappropriate and apparently incongruous verbalizations.

Steven was an eight-year-old boy brought to the clinic by his mother because of his withdrawal, isolation, absorption in fantasy, and lack of emotional reactivity. Though she dated her concern about him from her separation from the father a few months before, the school had suggested some time earlier that she seek help for Steven because of his withdrawal. She spoke of Steven's "absentmindedness" (forgetting to zip his fly and tie his shoes) and his clumsiness and poor coordination. On the other hand, she described him as a warm, happy, pleasant child with an infectious laugh, who was extraordinarily gifted intellectually and showed great creative capacities.

Steven's parents were both Bohemian types. The father was a marginally successful painter, outspokenly nonconforming, intensely intellectual, and notoriously bizarre in his behavior. He had had a number of psychiatric hospitalizations. He left his wife when he felt she was becoming too bourgeois for him. She, in turn, was a chronically depressed woman with a history of two hospitalizations. She had formed a liaison with her husband out of loneliness and despair. After seven years of psychotherapy, however, she felt strong enough to get along without him, and had recently, in addition to her own artistic pursuits, been taking graduate studies at a local university.

Steven had been wanted by his mother but not by his father. Pregnancy and delivery were normal. Mrs. J. described an intense early involvement on her part, with much emphasis on real or fancied "communication" between her and the infant. On the other hand she was afraid to handle him and concerned lest she "impose" herself on him. No limits were ever set for him: he was always free to walk around nude in the presence of guests and to urinate and defecate on the floor. His intellectual precocity had been much encouraged by both parents. On examination, Steven was a slovenly, unkempt little boy in ill fitting and filthy clothes. His fly was unzipped, his shoelaces untied. He came willingly to the interview, spoke clearly and responsively, but was unable to stay in one place for more than an instant. He was obviously of extraordinarily high intelligence (I.Q. 143 minimal), but spoke little about personal concerns. He described with considerable relish, however, the imaginary country he had conceived of, mapped out, and populated with imaginary people and animals. He had no friends and spent all his free time spinning out such stories. He drew a bizarre, Martian figure; his human figure was crude, primitive, and unorganized.

The impression was that of a psychotic child with marked intellectualization and with incipient paranoid character organization. Object relations were tenuous and maintained largely through intellectual contact and isolation of affect. Intense unconscious hostility was dealt with by denial and projection. Both parents were borderline psychotic personalities, neither of whom was able to provide stable reality orientation or foster appropriate ego growth. Nonetheless, Steven's remarkable intellectual endowment and his creative capacities made it possible for him to function in school and ward off feelings of isolation and depression.

Psychodynamics of Childhood Psychosis

As will have been seen, the outstanding feature of all the cases described is the abnormality of ego development. In all instances there are obvious defects in a wide range of ego functions, most particularly those which serve survival needs, e.g., communication, object relations, reality testing, thought processes, and impulse regulation. These developmental defects represent the core of the disorder in the psychoses of childhood; unlike the neuroses, intrapsychic conflict appears to be a secondary aspect in the genesis of the pathology.

This is not to suggest that intrapsychic conflict does not exist in the psychotic child. It is common indeed to find neurotic symptomatology derived from such conflict in these children, but what is characteristic of the psychotic child is precisely the fact that his adaptive devices are not adequate to maintain his conflicts within the bounds of neurotic personality organization. The defense equipment of the child is insufficient to prevent either massive breakthroughs of anxiety or primitive unneutralized drives, or massive withdrawal from involvement with other human beings.

Mahler and Elkisch (1953) have described the deanimation of the world of the psychotic child, his preoccupation with inanimate, or at least nonhuman objects (see also the case of Matthew, above). It is precisely because of the sense of danger he experiences in situations with human object involvement that the ego-deviant or psychotic child withdraws into a fantasy world of machines and other nonhuman objects. Unlike the neurotic child who fears the danger of castration, or the preoedipal, preneurotic child who fears loss of object love, the psychotic child fears the loss of a sense of self, loss of the fragmentary unformed sense of autonomy, or total loss of ego function with the breakthrough of unneutralized instinctual, primarily aggressive impulses.

It will be apparent that these children have not attained autonomy of the ego. Not only such secondary functions as reality testing and defense, but even certain of such primarily autonomous functions as perception and motility frequently show impairment. This defect is not like that of a neurotic, in which an inhibition of the function exists as a result of anxiety in the face of instinctual impulse, but is a fundamental developmental defect. Indications of such a defect may be found very early in the child's life.

This is one of the facts that makes the nature-nurture controversy such an active one in the study of childhood psychosis. The field is split between those who maintain a primarily organic etiology, and those who regard these disorders as the consequence of disturbances in the early mother-child relationship, especially in the sphere of affective communication. As is so often the case in the controversies, the weight of evidence suggests that neither position is exclusively correct. Insistence on one or the other alternative ignores the fact that childhood psychosis is not a unitary disease, but a syndrome or group of syndromes covering a wide range of clinical variations and deriving from multiple sources. Mahler has suggested and most other investigators agree that a basic constitutional deficiency is necessary for the interpersonal, genetic, and dynamic processes they have described to result in a psychotic disorder. Goldfarb (1961) has delineated at least two subtypes manifesting a predominance respectively of "organic" and psychosocial factors in their etiology. Further investigations are clearly required to elucidate more fully the relative roles of endowment and experience in the origin of the various subtypes of clinical psychosis or "childhood schizophrenia." It is clear, however, that Freud's assertion that all mental disorder is a result of interaction of constitution and environment applies here again.

The Borderline Problem

In recent years, the diagnosis of "borderline" psychosis or borderline condition has been much in vogue (Kut-Rosenfeld & Sprince, 1963). Like the conditions to which it refers, it is a loosely defined and nonspecific term. Most frequently it has been applied to the child who, though not manifestly psychotic, shows occasional psychotic-like outbursts or is eccentric in certain significant respects. He may suffer from a great number of phobic and/or compulsive symptoms with shifting patterns. He may have some shallow social relationships, but no deep or lasting friendships; those he has may be largely founded on interlocking pathology (a shared preoccupation, for example, with weird science fiction). His capacity to communicate with others may show no gross impairment; this may also be true of his ability to deal with the demands of traditional academic learning as experienced in school.

The salient feature of such children is the fragility and instability of ego structure: a readiness of basic functions superficially intact to fail under minimal stress. At first resembling a severe neurotic or a particularly aggravated behavior disorder, such a child may, upon extensive study, be seen to have a severe degree of ego weakness. It is of the utmost importance to make the distinction as early as possible because therapeutic aims and techniques will differ accordingly, to a substantial degree.

Differential Diagnosis

As suggested earlier, the severe ego disturbances of childhood with their wide range of manifestations must be carefully distinguished from a variety of other conditions, normal and pathological. Particularly in early childhood it is necessary (and often difficult) to distinguish the earliest signs of abnormal development from normal variations of developmental rate and rhythm. An early sign of disturbed ego development, for instance, is retarded speech. It is not easy to tell at age two whether the nonverbal toddler is a normal child late in maturing, is intellectually retarded, or is deviant in the development of this critical ego function. The head-banger of the same age may be expressing transient frustration or may be involved in a highly deviant autoaggressive pattern that portends severe developmental pathology. Similarly the hyperactive, distractible, impulsive five-year-old may be suffering, on the one hand, from organic brain damage or, on the other, from a psychotic deficit in the regulating functions of the ego. Only careful scrutiny can distinguish between these alternatives. The fearful, nightmare-ridden, ritualistic, latency child may be a severe neurotic, but he may just as likely be suffering from a developmental defect in his defensive capacities, in his ability to neutralize aggressive wishes, and in his capacity to distinguish fantasy from reality.

The definitive differential diagnosis in such situations requires the skill of a child psychiatrist who will utilize information from a variety of sources. Of particular value will be psychological-test findings, neurological evaluation, and the detailed history of the child's early development. It is necessary to note particularly the development of the child's object relations, their range, plasticity, and stability. It is also important to look for the presence of bizarre, unrealistic or deviant fantasies, or persistent incapacity to discriminate the "real" from the imaginary, i.e., a severe impairment of reality testing.

In infancy and early childhood, the distinction must at times be made between infantile autism and "anaclitic depression" or deprivation syndrome. In this condition, delineated by Spitz (1946), the infant shows developmental retardations and severe affective disturbances resulting from massive deprivation of emotional and sensory stimulation. Most often, these are infants reared in institutions or in very deviant homes. This fact alone is a salient differentiating point, since the typical psychotic child does not experience such blatant deprivation. The infants who suffer from deprivation syndromes do not typically develop into psychotic children, but acquire impulsive character disorders, with limited capacity for emotional relations with others and sharply restricted affective range.

The differentiation of the severely psychotic or autistic child from the child with mental retardation is another issue of major individual and social significance in early childhood. The training schools for the mentally retarded, due to faulty diagnosis, admit many young children who have potentially normal intellectual functioning but who suffer from autistic psychosis. The primary criterion for differentiation in such cases is the pattern of object involvement, which, in uncomplicated cases of mental retardation, will be far less deviant than in the autistic child. In addition, the autistic child will show unevenness in ego functioning, which is not characteristic of the child with mental retardation.

Young children (under three years) who have suffered severe physical abuse (Battered Child Syndrome) may present a picture approximating that of early autism (Galdston, 1965). They may be unresponsive, mute, and apathetic or intensely fearful to the point of withdrawal. Often they do not eat and seem totally unrelated to adult caretakers. Their behavior is not, however, bizarre, and with careful, warm, substitute mothering, their panic subsides and they become responsive and active. Diagnosis is founded, of course, on the associated physical signs of injury and/or malnutrition. Parents typically show gross distortions in their own perceptions of the child, experiencing him as a hostile, willful adult toward whom they are intensely and violently ambivalent.

Above all, the diagnostic judgment must be based, not on the impression created by single symptoms, signs, or characteristics, but rather on an over-all assessment of the child's total behavior, thought, and affects, and their relation to the established norms of development.

Prognosis

Traditionally based on the unitary concept of childhood ego disorders reflected in the term "childhood schizophrenia," the prognosis of children suffering from such illness has been considered rather grave. Bender's study indicated that 70 to 80 per cent of children diagnosed as "childhood schizophrenics" showed psychotic pathology after five or more years' follow-up, regardless of therapy (1947). Among those who had not acquired the capacity of speech by the age of five, the prognosis was uniformly bad.

There is no question that the psychotic disorders carry with them an extremely guarded prognosis. It is certainly true, as Bender pointed out, that a child whose ability to relate to people has not by age five developed to the point at which verbal communication is possible is highly unlikely to progress to adequate adaptive functioning. But as we seek to establish a typology of childhood psychosis and to concern ourselves with the multiplicity of etiological factors in the genesis of these severe disorders, it becomes apparent that no categorical judgment about prognosis will stand up. Certainly a rigid attitude of therapeutic nihilism in the face of the diagnosis of childhood psychosis cannot be justified. Many psychotic children have benefited profoundly from intensive therapeutic regimes, particularly those that add to psychotherapy the enhancement and fortification of ego function through special education and well-timed socialization programs (Goldfarb et al., 1969). Very long-term treatment with timely interruptions and resumptions may frequently be necessary to keep the child functioning at an adequate level; even then, one can rarely expect totally "normal" adjustment, but an open approach to the treatment of the psychotic child will frequently yield highly beneficial results. Drug therapy is also of considerable benefit, especially with the agitated hyperactive child. The social worker can contribute to the treatment program through concurrent work with parents. This is essential both to help them to understand the nature and implications of the child's disorder and to explore the role of family pathology in contributing to it. To sum up, we are only on the threshold of our understanding of the possibilities of treatment of childhood psychosis.

REFERENCES

Bender, L. (1947), Childhood Schizophrenia. *American Journal of Orthopsychiatry,* 17:40-56.

Bradley, C. (1941), *Schizophrenia in Childhood.* New York: MacMillan.

de Sanctis, S. (1908), Dementia Praecoccisima Catatonica. *Folio Neurobiol.*, 2:9-12.

Despert, J. L. (1938), Schizophrenia in Children. *Psychiatric Quarterly,* 12:366-367.

Galdston, R. (1965), Observations on Children Who Have Been Physically Abused and Their Parents. *American Journal of Psychiatry,* 122:440-443.

Goldfarb, W. (1961), *Childhood Schizophrenia.* Cambridge: Harvard University Press.

——— Mintz, I. & Strooek, K.W. (1969), *A Time to Heal.* New York: International Universities Press.

Kanner, L. (1942), Autistic Disturbances of Affective Contact. *Nervous Child,* 2:217-250.

Kut-Rosenfeld, S. & Sprince, M. P. (1963), An Attempt to Formulate the Meaning of the Concept "Borderline." *The Psychoanalytic Study of the Child,* 18:603-635. New York: International Universities Press.

Mahler, M. (1952), On Child Psychosis and Schizophrenia: Autistic and Symbiotic Infantile Psychoses. *The Psychoanalytic Study of the Child,* 7:286-305. New York: International Universities Press.

——— (1954), Childhood Schizophrenia. *American Journal of Orthopsychiatry,* 24:523-526.

———(1968), *On Human Symbiosis and the Vicissitudes of Individuation.* New York: International Universities Press.

——— & Elkisch, P. (1953), Some Observations on Disturbances of the Ego in a Case of Infantile Psychosis. *The Psychoanalytic Study of the Child,* 8:252-261. New York: International Universities Press.

——— Furer, M. & Settlage, C. (1959), Severe Emotional Disturbance in Childhood: Psychosis. In: *American Handbook of Psychiatry,* ed. S. Arieti. New York: Basic Books, 1:816-839.

Potter, H. (1933), Schizophrenia in Children. *American Journal of Psychiatry,* 12:1253-1270.

Rank, B. (1949), Adaptation of the Psychoanalytic Technique for the Treatment of Young Children with Atypical Development. *American Journal of Orthopsychiatry,* 19:130-139.

Spitz, R.A. (1946), Anaclitic Depression. *The Psychoanalytic Study of the Child,* 2:313-342. New York: International Universities Press.

CHAPTER TEN
Learning Disturbances
JOHN B. McDEVITT, M.D.

The existence of severe reading disabilities in at least 10 per cent of the elementary school population is one of our major social problems. The problem becomes even more serious when we also consider the large number of potentially capable older students who "underachieve" in school. Disabilities and failures in academic learning both arise from and in turn create disturbances in the child's intellectual and emotional development.

Inability to learn brings on feelings of despair, discouragement, and frustration in the child who in the classroom is daily faced with the proof of his inadequacies. The disapppointment and criticism of his parents and his teachers only add to his distress. Although the child has no means of physical escape from the classroom, he often finds an emotional one. He denies the existence of his disability, avoids the disagreeable task of academic learning, and as a consequence will forever be handicapped and a liability to society.

It is essential that children who show potential or beginning learning disturbances be identified early so that pieventive and remedial help can be provided promptly. Too many such children do not receive help before the third grade or later, a delay based on the assumption that the child may be a "late bloomer" and will outgrow his disability. By that time, however, the situation may have become irreversible.

Compared with the lower animals, who function chiefly through instinct, the human baby spends years completing his intellectual structures and capacities, which at birth are present only as possibilities. This does not occur automatically or in a vacuum. The potentialities for perception, motility, memory, thought, and language can mature and develop only when they are stimulated by appropriate experiences and when opportunities exist for practice. The first five to seven years of life are the most significant years, not only for the child's emotional and social life, but also for his intellectual development. Unless his potentialities are developed during that time, they may remain forever unrealized.

The infant first learns how to solve problems by means of sensorimotor actions; later he learns to represent actions, things, people and feelings symbolically. His first symbols are images, which allow him to recall reality briefly. A word is then learned; soon words are put together to form larger units. Between the twelfth and eighteenth months, the child begins to grasp the shorthand that will enable him to hold in his mind his immediate reality and to manipulate it symbolically. During the next five years, one of the child's chief intellectual tasks is the creation of a symbolic vocabulary made up primarily of words, but also including numbers, pictures, musical notes, etc.

Language development is a continuum, embracing all aspects of communication: speaking, reading, writing, spelling, and composition. The ability to handle the spoken language is basic to reading. By the age of six, children are expected to have mastered the use of oral symbols. One of the most intricate learning experiences the child will ever have occurs during the span of time between his initial ability to comprehend the first simple words and the emergence of an ability to receive and meaningfullly decode the infinitely complex set of discrete auditory stimuli that is characteristic of each of the three thousand or more words he brings with him to school. Once he has reached the first grade, he is expected to cope with a secondary symbolic system, with visual signs that must be correlated with meaning. He must begin to read.

The terms "cognitive development," "cognitive process," and "cognition" refer to the higher mental processes—perception, learning, thinking, problem solving, intelligence, and concept formation. Oral language, reading, and concept formation are interrelated facets of the cognitive process, each contributing its share to the growing development of thought during childhood. Whereas concepts are nurtured and developed through oral language, it is only when the child acquires the ability to learn through the printed word that he acquires the means for greater abstraction.

Learning Disabilities

Academic difficulty is the most common reason for the referral to child guidance clinics and social agencies of children between the ages of seven and 14. This difficulty may result from a disturbance in any of a wide variety of factors and, as such, resembles a symptom. In contrast to symptoms, however, for which the underlying pathology is known, the descriptive term "learning disorder" is not a discrete diagnostic entity, nor does it provide any indication of the nature of past or current interferences with the learning process.

The child responds with all aspects of his personality to the task set for him by the school. The extent to which a child is ready to learn and the eventual level of learning he will attain do not depend solely on general intelligence, neurological maturation, and the development of perceptual-motor and language skills; they also depend on motivation and educational opportunity, as well as on personality characteristics and such psychological factors as the degree to which learning is an autonomous ego function, relatively free of anxiety, conflict, inhibition, or restriction.

By far the commonest area of learning difficulty is reading. Reading disability or retardation exists when there is a discrepancy of one or more years between the child's current level of reading achievement and his intellectual potential. A learning disorder exists when a child is unable to conform to a currently acceptable academic norm.

There have been two methods of studying learning disorders: group and individual. Group studies are heterogeneous, often inconclusive and superficial: they are also descriptive rather than explanatory. The individual case study provides a better understanding of learning disorders in a few individuals, but whether the findings are representative of the large number of children with learning problems is questionable. Both approaches must be used in order to understand learning disorders.

No matter which approach is used, however, any understanding of learning disabilities should be based on developmental, structural, and dynamic considerations that distinguish between those disturbances caused by a failure or delay early in life to attain those skills and functions necessary for learning to occur, and those caused by a breakdown in or interference with the use of already attained functions, later on, during the school years. Although many factors may create a disturbance in the learning experience and although they operate in an integrated manner, for purposes of clarity they will be discussed separately and chronologically.

Intelligence and Learning

An evaluation of a child's level of academic achievement must be considered in relation to his intellectual potential. Estimates of intelligence or achievement, however, are never completely valid or reliable. The testing instruments themselves are always subject to a degree of error: the child's physical and emotional condition also affect test results. Quantitative scores are therefore useful only as rough measures. Generally speaking, difficulties in evaluation are created by the following considerations: (1) it is not easy to distinguish between intellectual potential and actual functioning as measured on specific tests; (2) school achievement is more closely related to the capacity to deal with language symbols than to general intelligence; and (3) retardation in intelligence is determined not only by constitutional factors, but also by adverse environmental and psychological factors. If intelligence is high and achievement low, some other factor is interfering with the ability to learn. If both are low it may be that both have been affected by the same adverse influences.

BIOLOGICAL AND NEUROLOGICAL INFLUENCES ON LEARNING

For the child to learn to his full potential, he needs, in addition to intelligence, adequate vision and hearing, the absence of serious speech impediments, and, particularly, intact neurological integration. The brain-injured child may have difficulty learning to read; he may or may not, in addition, be restless and hyperactive and unable to pay attention or concentrate.

Just as children show different rates of biological maturation in physical growth, so irregularities and delays in neurophysiological maturation are found in differing degrees. The more severe delays (maturational lag) are thought to constitute a specific genetically determined syndrome that occurs about five time as often in boys as in girls, rather like color blindness. Several names have been given to this syndrome: primary or specific reading disability, developmental dyslexia, minimal brain dysfunction. Dyslexia is considered specific in the sense that it is not a manifestation of a general learning retardation as might be seen in deprived children. Dyslexic children may also be hyperactive, but not necessarily so; and many hyperactive children do not have a specific language disability.

These children show difficulty forming words and expressing themselves orally, have a poor ear for words and a marked difficulty with reading and spelling and are often clumsy in writing or in other movements. Immature visual functioning does not allow for the distinction between letters like "b" and "d" or such words as "went" and "want" or "was" and "saw." Children with this problem will persist in misreading, guessing, and substituting extraneous words. Delayed auditory discrimination causes difficulty in detecting differences in the sounds of letters, or between such words as "beg" and "bag."

Deficiency in the visual area will lead to problems in learning through the sight or "look-see" method. Difficulties in the auditory sphere will interfere with the use of the phonic or sounding method. Confusion in directionality and in blending different sounds adds further to the handicap: letters and words are reversed, unknown words cannot easily be deciphered.

Environmental Influences on Learning

Children may also be at a disadvantage with respect to acquiring academic skills and knowledge long before they enter school through a variety of adverse environmental influences. Constitutional defects, and emotional deprivation act together to impede normal intellectual and personality development. This can be understood in terms of a series of complex interactions between poverty, poor nutrition, and inadequate medical care, as well as greater susceptibility to damage of the child during pregnancy, on the one hand, and the psychological consequences of socioeconomic, sensory, intellectual, and maternal deprivation, on the other. A large number of these children show impulse disorders early in life. These disorders represent a disturbance in ego organization and object relations that will later on contribute to learning problems.

The fact that children born to poverty, neglect, and family disorganization tend to be less able intellectually and to achieve less well in school than do children from stable, nurturing backgrounds becomes apparent early in life—as early as nine months of age. Delays in communication, in control and modulation of impulse, in capacity to anticipate, and in ability to integrate numerous stimuli foreshadow later difficulties with problem solving, abstract thinking, and language development.

It is no longer a question of whether maternal deprivation, together with social and cultural disadvantage, depresses academic ability; the basic problem, still unresolved, is to learn more about those specific aspects of early experience that can be proven (rather than inferred) to hinder intellectual development and academic achievement. The outcome is well known: children from deprived backgrounds score well below middle-class children on standard individual and group measures of intelligence (the gap increases with age); they come to school without the tools necessary for coping with first-grade work; their language development, both written and spoken, is relatively poor; auditory and visual discrimination skills are not well developed; in scholastic achievement, they are retarded an average of two years by grade six, and almost three years by grade eight; they are more likely to drop out of school before completing their secondary education; and, even when they have adequate ability, they are considerably less likely to go on to college. By contrast, children from more favorable home environments tend to be intellectually curious; they usually learn to read easily and with joy and delight.

Certain specific early experiences may hamper the child's academic ability. Coercive early training, for example, may leave a residue of resentment against the authority of the teacher. Conflicts with the parents over such activities as feeding or toileting may lead to conflicts with the teacher over learning. The absence of a suitable model for identification can disturb the child's attitude to the teacher and to learning. Curiosity, the desire to master the environment actively, the wish to grow up—all these may be hindered rather than encouraged. Some parents make no demands on their children. While they succeed in avoiding all possible frustrations, they also thereby hamper the development of independence and self-assertion. These qualities are important, for learning is work and, as such, requires an expenditure of energy; the child cannot be simply an inert, passive recipient of information.

The effect of parental ambition for the child varies. If it is wholesome and if the child is capable of fulfilling it, it will be beneficial. If it stems primarily from the parents' needs rather than those of the child, and especially if it pushes the child beyond his actual capacities, he may passively resist and become a nonlearner.

Psychological Readiness to Learn

At the time of school entry, the child must, in addition to being biologically and intellectually ready to learn, also be psychologically ready. This usually occurs with the successful passing from the phallic-oedipal phase of development to the latency phase, when ego control comes to be more stable and the superego is established. As a result, controls over impulses and behavior are more fully internalized and the child becomes more responsible for his own behavior. He no longer needs to struggle with the teacher as he did with his parents; instead, the struggle begins to occur within himself. His superego—the successor to his parents—is now on the side of the teacher and of learning.

When the phallic-oedipal phase is prolonged, however, the child may transfer fears and hates, envy and jealousy, needs and frustrations, from his home to his school, his teachers, and his fellow students. This will make it difficult for him to become fully integrated into group life; it will interfere with learning and may lead to homesickness and school phobias. He becomes so preoccupied with personal difficulties that he has little interest or energy left over for learning.

The psychological readiness to learn also requires age-adequate progress in many other areas of ego development. These include the ability to control, inhibit, or modify impulses in order to use the learning experience constructively; to sit still, as well as to pay attention and to resist distractions; to carry out preconceived plans with minimal regard for the lack of immediate pleasure gain and for intervening frustration; and to attain satisfaction in active mastery and task completion.

In addition to those factors already mentioned, the child's reactions to and his identification with his parent's conscious and unconscious attitudes to learning are certainly significant in shaping his attitude and motivation toward academic learning. Learning involves a teacher-pupil relation, which requires the pupil's acceptance of the teacher's authority and, in exchange, the teacher's encouragement of his curiosity and his ambition to succeed. The child responds to the teacher in accordance with his past and present relations with his parents, who have conveyed to him not only their own personal attitudes to learning but also the more general attitudes of the culture.

Neurotic Interferences with Learning

Irrespective of previously acquired capacities, during the school years, the child, in order to participate optimally in the learning process, must be free to invest neutralized and sublimated psychic energy in the schooling experience. Emotional problems of any type may interfere with this freedom to learn. More specifically, a learning disorder may be due to a neurotic learning inhibition. This inhibition may be general, or it may be restricted to certain specific academic skills, subject matter, or developmental phases, such as those which coincide with starting school or the beginning of puberty. Learning, both in terms of the process of learning and of the content learned, is ordinarily an autonomous ego function. If it becomes associated with unconscious wishes and fantasies, however, it can become involved in an internal mental conflict between these wishes and the forces that oppose them. Because learning now represents these fantasies, it becomes the object of the ego's defensive operations. The forbidden instinctual impulse becomes so closely connected with the wish to read, to calculate, or to speak in class, that the ego prevents or at least mars the execution of this wish. If the active looking that is required for reading, for example, represents forbidden unconscious voyeuristic wishes, reading will be experienced as a dangerous activity and will be inhibited in order to ward off anxiety. It may be that reading and learning lend themselves to involvement in neurotic conflict precisely because they are such complex tasks.

Conflicts over oral impulses, which in the past may have created eating disturbances, may also be displaced onto the area of learning and interfere with the intake of knowledge. Similarly, conflicts over anal impulses may interfere with the production of what has been learned: the child may be unable to talk in class or to express himself in writing. Conflicts over exhibitionistic urges may inhibit the child from "displaying" his knowledge in class, just as he may be anxious about displaying his body. Such conflicts as these may give rise to the common experience of "stage fright."

Inhibitions of ego functions that are used in learning should be distinguished from restrictions of their use, insofar as inhibitions and restrictions operate in different ways. A child who suffers from a neurotic inhibition is defending himself against the painful feeling of anxiety that may be brought on by the translation into action of some forbidden instinctual impulse. A child who has an ego restriction avoids certain activities or events because they may reactivate painful feelings that were associated with similar activities or events in the past. For example, competition may be avoided because it revives the hopeless feeling of rivalry with the father in the oedipal phase; a child may turn away from activities that involve a comparison of his own performance with that of others either because these activities may arouse feelings of envy or discouragement that the child experienced in comparing himself with his sibling when he was younger, or because they may arouse the disagreeable reminder of the difference between the sexes. The essential difference between inhibition and ego restriction is that in the former the ego is defending itself against its own inner processes; in the latter, it is defending itself against external stimuli and impressions. In one, the activity of learning is inhibited; in the other, it is the mental pain brought on by that activity that is avoided. When ego restrictions are extensive, whole fields of interest are abandoned and learning suffers.

External factors, too, may interfere with the child's ability to learn during the school years. A child may find it difficult to concentrate or pay attention for reasons of poor health, family stress or divorce, frequent moves to new homes and new schools, or inadequate knowledge of the language. Furthermore, the condition under which the child learns is an important factor. Many learning problems have their origins in unfavorable circumstances at school—overcrowded classrooms, ineffective and unstimulating teaching, inappropriate reading material, lack of equipment, and the like.

Remedies

An adequate explanation of why disturbances in the learning process are so prevalent is not yet available. Perhaps because the learning process is so complex, it is particularly vulnerable to a large number of influences. Because there are so many etiologic components, any approach to learning problems must be multidisciplinary.

There is also as yet no adequate answer to the question of how learning disturbances can be prevented or how remedial help can best be provided. This reflects both the complexity of the problem and our ignorance. The issues of family background, cultural and parental attitudes, and early experience are so complex that preventive and remedial action must proceed on a broad sociological, economic, educational, and mental health front. With groups of susceptible or "high-risk" children, such as those from "disadvantaged neighborhoods," enriched preschool programs can probably contribute to cognitive and ego development—if they are undertaken when the child is very young. It also may be possible in other ways, to build programs designed to amplify the world of the biologically, environmentally, and emotionally vulnerable child. For example, assistance can be provided for the overburdened mother in the home in order to create sensory and intellectual stimulation similar to that which the more fortunate child receives. Or, programs in which the same nursery school teacher stays with the same "disadvantaged" children in small classes for several years may reduce the number of children with impulse disorders. A positive attachment to the teacher over a long period of time can lead to a stable identification with her, and in that way diminish the number and severity of impulse disorders, in addition to promoting ego and personality development. Small-group special-education schoolrooms can help emotionally disturbed and biologically impaired children, who are unable to function in the larger, competitive school setting. The availability of such facilities frequently means the difference between a learning opportunity for the disturbed child and total educational neglect.

It may become possible on the basis of relatively simple tests, used in combination with the subjective impression of the kindergarten teacher, to predict with reasonable accuracy which children will have difficulty learning to read in the first grade. If so, small transition classes could be provided between kindergarten and the first grade. Intensive training, along with psychological help, if indicated, tailored to the child's individual needs, could be provided while he remains in this class and until he is biologically, intellectually, and psychologically ready for the first grade.

Remedial techniques should be undertaken in the school, soon after a reading or learning disturbance is detected. Most children with reading disabilities can improve their reading through proper help and guidance in school. If this fails, however, then there is reason to assume that an internal resistance to learning exists; this warrants a thorough investigation, and, as a rule, a specialized remedial program. If therapy is also indicated, it is not wise to forgo remedial help—at least in those children who can profit from such help—for these children are usually behind in their academic skills, and this places an additional emotional burden on them. If a reading or learning disturbance has existed for some years, the approach depends on its nature and severity and on the facilities available. If remedial help within the school system is not sufficient, a combined approach of skilled individual tutoring and therapy may be indicated.

REFERENCES

Blanchard, P. (1947), Psychoanalytic Contributions to the Problems of Reading Disabilities. *The Psychoanalytic Study of the Child,* 2:163-187. New York: International Universities Press.

Bruner, J. S. (1966), *Toward a Theory of Instruction.* Mass: The Belkap Press of Harvard University Press.

Buxbaum, E. (1964), The Parents' Role in the Etiology of Learning Disabilities. In: *Troubled Children in a Troubled World.* New York: International Universities Press, pp. 60-87.

Durkin, D. (1966), *Children Who Read Early, Two Longitudinal Studies.* New York: Teachers College Press, Teachers College, Columbia University.

Ekstein, R. & Motto, R. (1969), *From Learning for Love to Love of Learning.* New York: Brunner & Mazel.

Freud, A. (1931), Introduction to: *Psychoanalysis for Teachers.* London: Allen & Unwin.

——— (1936), Restriction of the Ego. *The Ego and the Mechanisms of Defense. The Writings of Anna Freud,* Vol. 2. New York: International Universities Press, 1966, 100-113.

——— (1946), Freedom from Want in Early Education. *The Writings of Anna Freud,* Vol. 4. New York: International Universities Press, 1968.

Hellman, I. (1964), Some Observations on Mothers of Children with Intellectual Inhibitions. *The Psychoanalytic Study of the Child,* 9:259-273. New York: International Universities Press.

Hunt, J. McV. (1961), *Intelligence and Experience.* New York: The Ronald Press.

Jarvis, V. (1958), Clinical Observations on the Visual Problem in Reading Disability. *The Psychoanalytic Study of the Child,* 13:451-470. New York: International Universities Press.

Myklebust, H. R. (1965), *Development and Disorders of Written Language, Picture Story Language Test,* 1:1-68. New York: Grune & Stratton.

Pearson, G. (1954), *Psychoanalysis and the Education of the Child.* New York: Norton.

Peller, L. E. (1946), Incentives to Development and Means of Early Education. *The Psychoanalytic Study of the Child,* 2:397-415. New York: International Universities Press.

——— (1956), The School's Role in Promoting Sublimation. *The Psychoanalytic Study of the Child,* 11:437-449. New York: International Universities Press.

Pringle, M. L. K. (1963), *Deprivation and Education.* London: Longmans.

Roswell, F. & Natchez, G. (1964), *Reading Disability, Diagnosis and Treatment.* New York: Basic Books.

SUGGESTED READING

de Hirsch, K., Jansky, J. J., & Langford, W. S. (1968), *Predicting Reading Failure.* New York: Harper & Row, pp. 33-39, 45-47, 70-73, 84-92.

Lustman, S. L. (1966), Impulse Control, Structure, and the Synthetic Function. In: *Psychoanalysis—A General Psychology, Essays in Honor of Heinz Hartmann,* ed. R. M. Loewenstein, L.M. Newman, M. Schur, & A. J. Solnit. New York: International Universities Press, pp. 190-221.

Mahler, M. S. (1942), Pseudoimbecility: A Magic Cap of Invisibility. *Psychoanalytic Quarterly,* 11:149-164.

Pearson, G. H. J. (1952), A Survey of Learning Difficulties in Children. *The Psychoanalytic Study of the Child,* 7:322-386. New York: International Universities Press.

Rabinovitch, R. D. (1959), Reading and Learning Disabilities. In: *American Handbook of Psychiatry,* ed. S. Arieti, Vol. 1 New York: Basic Books, pp. 857-869.

CHAPTER ELEVEN
Mental Retardation
LEONARD HOLLANDER, M.D.

Throughout history, attitudes toward the mentally retarded and the mentally ill have reflected the dominant social, religious, philosophical, and scientific trends of the times. Kindly treatment or cruel persecution depended on whether these afflicted people were "children of God" or evil and "possessed by the Devil." Shifting views of mankind meant changes in the way the mentally retarded were regarded and treated. The boundaries of the field were set, first by the conventions and needs of society, and only later by biological and psychological findings.

Occasional references related to issues of protection and responsibility are found in Roman, Jewish, and Old English Law. Several attempts at definition in the sixteenth century preceded the classification system devised by Willis in 1672.

In the first half of the nineteenth century, increased interest in the investigation and humane treatment of the mentally retarded paralleled similar efforts with the insane, the blind and the deaf. An outstanding example was the attempt of the French physician, Itard to treat the "Wild Boy of Aveyron." The educational principles underlying his treatment were based on the philosophy that environment could accomplish everything, i.e., that sensory input could make a major change in Victor's intellectual development. Itard's pioneering work was carried on by his disciple, Seguin, who later became the first president (1876) of the predecessor of the American Association on Mental Deficiency.

Samuel Gridley Howe (1801-1876), who continued the tradition of educational training of Itard and Seguin in the United States, is known as the founder of institutional care of retarded children in this country.

The growth of mass education made it necessary to devise more precise instruments to sort out those who needed special programs. In France, Binet and Simon constructed graduated scales for the objective measurement of intelligence beginning in 1905. An American Standardization by Goddard in 1910 was followed by a 1916 Terman Revision, usually called the Stanford-Binet test. The Stanford-Binet has since been revised in 1937 and 1960. It has been less frequently used in recent years for wide-scale testing of general intelligence than the Wechsler Adult Intelligence Scale (WAIS) and the Wechsler Intelligence Scale for Children (WISC), although it is still widely used in the field of mental retardation.

When the original hopes for cure through environmental means were not realized, institutional emphasis shifted from rehabilitative training and discharge to institutional care for the protection of society. The differences between the Environmentalists and the Hereditarians widened in the early part of the twentieth century. An alarmist movement at that time led to sterilization laws for the retarded in many states, starting in 1907.

Advances in medical research in the last half of the nineteenth century were rapid, once the basic assumption of a unitary cause for mental retardation was refuted. Tay and Sachs in the 1880's made one of the first discoveries of a structural abnormality of the nervous system associated with mental deficiency, known as amaurotic familial idiocy.

In 1908, Von Reuss reported a new entity, galactosemia, due to a metabolic fault. Folling's 1934 report on phenylketonuria, a reversible enzyme deficiency, sparked new interest in the organic roots of mental retardation. Landsteiner and Weiner's landmark findings (1940) that fetal and maternal blood incompatabilities (Rh factors) may result in mentally retarded infants introduced a new era in etiology and diagnosis related to prenatal conditions. In 1959, Lejeune, Gautier, and Turpin discovered a chromosomal aberration in Mongolism (Down's Syndrome). This was the first proved connection between specific organic changes in the chromosomes transmitting hereditary information and mental retardation. President Kennedy initiated governmental support in the sixties, sparking renewed interest in exploring the potentials in this field. Research and treatment activities have expanded rapidly since.

What Is Mental Retardation?

Mental retardation as a label has many different connotations, not only for those who use it, but also for the retardates and their relatives. Too often, a lack of knowledge or misinformation leads to a hopeless or defensive reaction to this diagnostic category and limits what is planned or attempted. An understanding of the definition and its ramifications will help avoid such errors.

Mental retardation is a condition characterized by significantly subaverage general intellectual functioning and inadequate adaptation to the demands of the social environment. It originates during the developmental period, from conception to 18 years of age. This means that the condition has usually existed from birth or early childhood. It is manifested by a slow rate of physical and/or psychological maturation, together with limited learning capacity.

An individual cannot be considered mentally retarded *now* on the basis of *past* findings of social and intellectual inadequacy. Current measures must be taken, for the dimensions of performance are not fixed—they change over time. Performance on an intelligence test that falls within the mentally retarded range is a necessary but not a sufficient criterion of mental retardation. Tradition and the availability of objective, calibrated test materials have led to the erroneous concept that the test score alone represents enough about a person to classify him. The quantitative appearance of I.Q., expressed as it is by points, is convenient for definition, but tends to overemphasize one kind of performance, and neglect other areas of functioning.

Subaverage intellectual functioning is statistically defined by the American Association on Mental Deficiency to include the lowest 3 per cent of the population on which the intelligence test was standardized (67 I.Q. or less on the Stanford-Binet, 69 I.Q. or less on the Wechsler-Bellevue). In a change from previous official classifications, the borderline intelligence group (Stanford-Binet I.Q. 83-68, Wechsler-Bellevue I.Q. 79-70) is no longer included among the mentally retarded.

Impairment in adaptive behavior is relative to age and social requirements. As the child grows, more is expected of him. During the preschool years, an important measure of adaptive behavior is the rate of development of motor skills, such as walking and talking. In the school years, learning is a major dimension of adaptive behavior. Adult standards are set in terms of culturally imposed demands for personal independence and vocational and social responsibilities. Subcultures differ in the level of performance needed for successful functioning within them. The intellectually limited individual who can adapt within a simpler rural economy may have major difficulties in a more complex urban setting. Standard measures of adaptive behavior will be discussed later under the heading of instruments for evaluation.

Categories of Mental Retardation

It has been estimated that about five and a half million Americans (3 per cent) show some degree of mental retardation. Important to note is that 89 per cent of these are only mildly retarded. The remainder fall into the moderate (6 per cent), and severe (3.5 per cent), or profound (1.5 per cent) classifications. Of 126,000 infants born yearly who are or will be mentally retarded, 4,200 (0.1 per cent of all births) will be unable to earn a living, and 12,000 (0.3 per cent of all births) will remain below the seven-year-old intellectual level. The remaining 110,000 (2.6 per cent of all births) will be mildly retarded, and represent those who can acquire limited job skills and attain a measure of independence.

The ability to function in the open society is related to the degree of retardation. In mild cases of retardation, the person may be practically independent. At the profound extreme, nursing care is necessary. The characteristics described within each section of the accompanying chart are generalizations which do not necessarily hold true to the same extent for all persons within each I.Q. range. I.Q. is only one factor in mental functioning. Other determinants are social adaptability and emotional control.

The multiple etiologic factors resulting in mental retardation fall into three groups: organic, sociocultural, and psychological. Organic components play a much larger role among moderately and severely retarded cases than they do among the borderline and mildly retarded. In the latter, early cultural influences, social environment, and psychological problems predominate as causative elements. The presence of organic features does not exclude the possibility that retardation will be mild, and, in some instances, psychosocial and cultural determinants may be associated with moderate or severe retardation.

Genetic factors (as in mongolism) and genetic disorders of metabolism (as in phenylketonuria) affect the central nervous system to varying degrees. Prenatal events, such as German measles during the first three months of pregnancy, or carbon monoxide poisoning, may result in brain damage. Major causes of retardation dating from birth are lack of oxygen, blood incompatibilities between mother and child (relating to Rh factor differences), and injuries due to difficult delivery. After birth, the child's brain may be damaged in a number of ways: by infections such as meningitis and encephalitis; by accidental and "battered child" injuries; by poor nutrition; by brain tumors, and by disorders of metabolism.

A large percentage of the more severely retarded have organic defects and physical handicaps. Many are multiply handicapped. Not only may any of the senses be impaired, but physical deformities and poor muscular coordination may also be present. The most common physical problems among the retarded include cerebral palsy, epilepsy, speech and hearing disorders, a variety of ophthalmologic disorders, congenital malformations, and dental defects.

Of the specific disease entities, a few will be discussed in more

Developmental Characteristics of the Mentally Retarded Classified According To Psychological Test Results And Chronological Age*

Degree of Mental Retardation	*IQ Range* Stanford-Binet	Wechsler	*Pre-school* Maturation & Development	*School Age* Training and Education	*Adult* Social and Vocational Adequacy
			0-5 Years of Age	6-20 Years of Age	21 Years of Age and Over
Mild	69-52	69-55	Slower to talk, walk, and feed self than most children; may appear normal	Can acquire practical and academic skills to 3rd-6th grade level; can be guided toward social conformity	Can usually achieve adequate social and vocational skills to allow minimum self-support; may need guidance and aid when under unusual social or economic stress
Moderate	51-36	54-40	Noticeable delays in motor development, particularly speech; responds to training in various self-help activities	Can learn simple communication, health, and safety habits, and manual skills; unlikely to progress beyond 2nd grade academic level	Can perform simple tasks under sheltered conditions, participates in simple recreation; travels alone in familiar places; usually incapable of self-maintenance

Severe	35-20	39-25	Marked delay in motor development; little or no communication skill; may respond to training in elementary self-help	Has some understanding of speech and some response; can profit from systematic habit training.	Can conform to daily routines and repetitive activities; needs continued direction and supervision in protective environment
Profound	19 and below	24 and below	Gross retardation; minimal capacity for functioning in motor areas; needs nursing care	Delays in all areas of development; shows basic emotional responses; may respond to training; needs supervision	May walk and have primitive speech development; usually benefits from regular physical activity; incapable of self-maintenance; needs nursing care

* We wish to thank Parke, Davis & Company for their permission to reproduce with minor modifications the chart on the developmental characteristics of the mentally retarded, originally published in Patterns of Disease, March 1964.

detail. Down's Syndrome (more popularly known as Mongolism because of an "Oriental" slant to the eyes) was first described in 1866 by Langdon Down. Extensive investigations to discover its etiology have been undertaken since then. Lejeune's discovery (1959) of 47 chromosomes instead of the usual 46 was a major breakthrough, leading the way to further revelations of other chromosomal syndromes. Older mothers are more likely to give birth to a child with Down's Syndrome. The diagnosis is made in approximately one out of every 700 births.

Mental retardation is the primary feature of this condition, and it may be moderate or severe, with few having an I.Q. over 50. Some clinicians have pointed out a significant incidence of cases having mild to severe emotional disturbances. However, those children showing a cheerful and placid disposition are easy to keep at home. Of the over 100 signs of Down's Syndrome, the most frequently encountered are poor muscle tone, small flattened skull, a protruding (fissured) tongue, "Oriental" eye shape, shortness of body, strabismus, and lax ligaments. Nervous system abnormalities include a number of alterations in the development of the brain. Cardiac defects and hypogonadism are frequent. In some of the variations, the individual has few obvious features of the condition and may have normal intelligence. No treatment of Down's Syndrome has proved effective.

Phenylketonuria (more familiarly called P.K.U.) is another entity on which extensive work has been done. Folling (1934) found that the large amounts of phenylketones in the urine of some retardates resulted from a missing or inactive liver enzyme. If untreated, the majority of patients became severely retarded. Such cases have frequent temper tantrums and often show weird movements similar to those of schizophrenic children. Eczema and convulsions are present in a third of these youngsters. Early diagnosis is crucial so that a diet low in substances converted to phenylketones in the urine can be used to prevent these damaging effects. If the diet is started before three months of age and continued for five or six years, normal intelligence is likely to develop and be maintained.

The Rh factor, or other blood incompatibilities between mother and child, lead to the breakdown of immature blood cells and anemia. The result may be stillbirth or cerebral palsy, mental retardation, or hearing deficiency. Exchange transfusion of compatible blood to replace the child's blood is the treatment of choice.

The mildly retarded category contains up to 90 per cent of all retardates. In many respects, the mild retardate may be more like the normal than like other retardates. His deficiency is likely to be first discovered in the school years. He may understand what is going on, but may have trouble using good judgment or making the right decisions. In many situations, it will be difficult to identify him as different. As a result, he may function in society without coming to anyone's notice, though his functioning may be marginal, or he may occasionally break the law. He is less likely than the more severely retarded to show evidence of physical or organic causes or defects. In fact, a valid question arises as to whether the mildly retarded may not belong to a distinctly different population than the more severely retarded. Some investigators have called the more severely retarded (presumably organic) mentally defective, grouping them separately from the mildly retarded. Terms applied to the group of mild retardates have included subcultural, familial, or environmentally deprived. The mild retardate is considered to be a variation of the general population, not sharply distinguished from the rest. As elaborated in the chart, an arbitrary, statistically determined line divides him from the borderline and normal.

Environmental Factors

Where there is no discernible organic etiology, retardation is presumed to be linked to environmental and psychosocial factors. One cause is environmental deprivation, stemming from severe sensory impairments (deafness, blindness, etc.) or extreme environmental restrictions of social interaction. Prolonged and very severe neurotic disturbance from an early age, and major personality disorders or childhood schizophrenia are other causes of impaired mental functioning manifested by low I.Q. scores. The vast majority of retarded individuals are the unfortunate victims of social and educational deprivation.

The frequency of retardation in the lowest socioeconomic classes is estimated to be between 10 and 30 per cent as compared to a three per cent frequency in the total population. In a series of studies, Pasamanick and his colleagues showed that low socioeconomic status is associated with premature births, complications ,of pregnancy, and mental retardation. Factors contributing to fetal risk include the quality of nutrition of the mother, her prenatal care, her infections and illnesses. After birth, the child may suffer from poor diet, or inadequate medical care for serious illnesses. Some data indicate that severe malnutrition in the first year of life results in the development of fewer than the usual number of brain cells. A number of comparative studies suggest that early malnutrition during the period of rapid brain growth may produce permanent mental deficits. Infections or nutritional deficiencies may lead to brain damage. Additional causes of impaired cerebral functioning are poisoning by lead or other toxic substances, accidents, burns, and the battered-child syndrome.

Any discussion of cultural background must include the caution that what is described as a general condition may not hold for an individual child, nor for all families in a specific subculture. Adequate planning for any one youngster requires consideration of the interrelationship of individual, familial, and cultural factors. Inclusion in a broad socioeconomic group does not explain a particular retardation. The presence or absence of specific stimuli will, of course, be the pertinent information on which to base an understanding of a particular individual's retarded intellectual functioning.

Keeping such considerations in mind, certain patterns seem to recur among the deprived. The family is more likely to be broken, with the mother working and the child frequently left alone or in the care of multiple and changing mother substitutes. In an often disorganized and haphazard household, the child is thrown prematurely on his own, learning early to attend to survival needs in an unpredictable environment. The lack of proper controls, as well as the models of sudden impulsive violence he often sees, are likely to lead to an action-orientation which interferes with the development of attitudes necessary for intellectual growth. Either under- or overstimulation from the environment is a harmful influence on the retarded individual. Verbal communication and language usage, the basis for learning in school, are often deficient. The emphasis on the concrete and immediate will probably interfere with long-term planning, patience, and higher-level thinking.

The mother or other caretaker can be a key person in giving the youngster a sense of stability, a "knowing what to expect" that is so important a precondition for learning. She is the infant's principal teacher. By appropriate play and interplay, by furnishing suitable toys and other materials, by encouragement of his imaginative behavior, and by giving attention to his inner experiences, she and the child's other caretakers can facilitate his growth. The absence of such influences leads to failures in capacities of imaginative play and thought. Lack of such capacities will most likely mean that the ability to plan ahead and stick to a goal or to perceive fully the consequences of his actions, will be limited. The child's capacity for fantasy play makes possible multiple solutions to problems and alternate outlets for exploration, curiosity, and mastery. The exercising of imagination is an essential preparation for the use of school materials and the development of verbal and cognitive skills. Deprivation in these areas may seriously limit thinking ability and interfere with intellectual functioning.

Those aspects of the deprived family environment which affect cognitive functioning and academic readiness have been selected for discussion. Variations in these patterns within a subculture, as well as differences between cultures, influence the child's development. The emotionally, socially, and materially deprived family does not possess the resources within itself to help enrich the life of a child whose developmental handicaps arose from the background of those very deprivations. Consideration of these points has led to vigorous efforts to establish good health through the use of public health measures, regular medical care of families, and close attention to prenatal and early developmental years through obstetrical clinics and well-baby clinics. Project Head Start is a community-based, federally-sponsored educational venture designed to stimulate learning, help the parents foster learning in their children, and assist in getting adequate medical attention. However, if such early childhood programs are not followed-up in a sustained fashion, I.Q. levels may drop back and nullify their short-term effects.

The Mentally Retarded Child and His Family

The caution about stereotyped perceptions of the mentally retarded child holds for his personality development as well. In the absence of careful studies, vague impressions and generalizations are rife. A wide range of personality patterns and psychopathological features arising from a multiplicity of etiologic conditions are found among these youngsters. Confusion arises when contradictory descriptive statements are made. Clear distinctions identifying different populations will help clarify these situations. No universal picture can be expected to hold true. At the present stage of our knowledge, statements must be linked closely to individual case experience. The major thrust of longitudinal case studies of normals has not yet extended to retarded children. Hopefully, recently renewed interest in the field will result in more research in this area.

In view of the lack of hard facts, the material presented here—based on clinical findings—is tentative and subject to revision. The more limited in intellect the person is, the more likely he will need the supporting framework of his family. The mother, so central a figure in normal development, plays a vital role in the development of the retardate. He needs her to function as his auxiliary ego over a longer period of time than does the normal child. Because the interplay between them is so important, both child and mother, individually as well as together, should be considered. A previous history of mental retardation, a pregnancy complicated by infection or known Rh sensitivity, or obvious physical stigmata of retardation in the newborn will arouse anxiety in the mother and often distorts the mother-child relation. If the mother has no suspicion of something wrong, and if the retardation is mild, no question about deficiencies in intellect may arise in the first few years of life. Of course, the striving mother, pressing for achievement, may worry early about discrepancies from inflated standards, or compare this child with siblings or neighbor's children. Similar situations are found in mothers of normal children and are not unique for the retarded. Worry is less likely to occur in families without such aspirations for their children, particularly where there are no marked differences from others.

Defects in sensory apparatus, perceptual distortions, poorly established object constancy, or lack of differentiation of the mother from others, may interfere with the formation of the primary bond with the mother. The lack of responsiveness of her child and the difficulty she has in satisfying and comforting him may cause the mother to lessen her efforts and the child in turn to withdraw. Initial delays and distortions affect the timetable of change from an early symbiotic stage to a stage of separation-individuation. Separation-individuation may start later than normal or remain incomplete. Under such circumstances, the mother and her child are likely to encounter difficulties in progressing to more independent stages. Shared patterns of pathology may then continue, with the mother's ego substituting for and interfering with continued development of the child's ego. As a phase of ego maturation, negativism may start later in the retarded child and continue, rather than develop toward further autonomy and self-sufficiency. Difficulties may persist in making distinctions between the familiar and nonfamiliar, persons and places, or persons and inanimate objects. The relationship between the father and the child must also be kept in mind. The father can play a major role, starting his direct contacts and sharing of care when the child is very young, and indirectly influencing the child through his effect on the mother and her state of well-being. If the mother continues exclusive care, and the father remains uninvolved as the child grows older, the imbalance between them becomes another source of potential trouble.

The retarded child does not inevitably experience a distorted relation with his mother and others. Given optimal conditions, he is capable of healthy bonds and normal personality development. The more severe the retardation, the greater will be his vulnerability to adverse conditions in the family and in the community.

In comparison to his brighter peers, the retarded child experiences more hazards. He is less able to carry on satisfying and meaningful interactions with others. Communication may be limited. Poor differentiation of ego functions may continue in a number of areas: reality orientation, object relations, modification of instinctual impulses, and the attainment of autonomy. The retarded child often has limited ability to displace drives to new goals. He has difficulty finding alternate solutions to his conflicts. His efforts at coping tend to be repetitive and inflexible. His curiosity about his world may be limited or absent. His emotional life is often simple, and the defense mechanisms he uses primitive.

The adaptive mastery of the ego in mediating inner and outer demands is likely to be compromised by limitations in intellectual resources. As the child becomes aware of his weakness, he becomes anxious, and a degree of withdrawal and isolation from others may occur. Where anxiety is strong and persistent, and the child withholds his attention from the external environment, perceptual distortion, narrowed conceptualization, and impaired abstract thinking result and may increase. Personal and social functioning is thus rendered even more ineffectual. The retarded child may have trouble accepting what is available, in terms of compromises or alternate possibilities of equivalent satisfactions. His strong reactions to frustration of short-term immediate gratification may disconcert him further and disrupt his activities. In other words, the child's self-image may be incomplete and negative. His standards for himself may be higher than he can attain and result in a constant sense of failure and unworthiness. He may respond to his familial and social role-assignment as the slow child by acting the part he has been given, even though capable of a higher level of behavior. He may feel that he can never be effective or influence his environment favorably. His conclusions may well be that the locus of control of his life lies outside of himself and his own actions. When, however, the retarded child can be taught to play and use his imagination, he, like the culturally deprived child, may add a mediating factor between impulse and action to his repertoire, thus increasing his frustration tolerance.

The focus up to this point has been on the retarded child as a person, with less emphasis on the family and its importance. The mild retardate in the culturally deprived family often does not pose problems for the parents, who have their own intellectual limitations and expect only modest achievement from their children. Emotional problems are more apt to be present for those families in which the retardation is more severe, the disparity from the family level of intellectual functioning is marked, and environmental deprivation is not involved. Parents, noting a slowness in development and a lack of alertness, seek reassurance for their uneasy feelings that something is wrong. The situation develops into a family crisis. The parents are often unwilling to believe the diagnosis of mental retardation at first and prefer to search for a more acceptable explanation. Grief, anger, resentment, a sense of failure, denial, and projection of the blame on to someone else (the marital partner, obstetrician, or pediatrician) are not unusual. As denial and projection diminish, guilt feelings begin to emerge and magical cures are sought. This is the point at which the realities of etiology and therapeutic possibilies should be discussed.

The parents' unconscious wish to be rid of the defective child is a powerful operating force, too, insofar as it may lead to overprotectiveness and the fostering of overdependence, which after a time becomes unbearable for the parent. On the other hand, parents may require more from the child than he can possibly achieve and then overtly or covertly reject him. After the initial turmoil, parents may be more ready to work out suitable plans for the child and themselves.

Treatment Modalities

The process of helping a family with such problems is best accomplished by an interdisciplinary approach, utilizing the skills of the social worker, the nurse, the pediatrician, the psychiatrist, the psychologist, and the educator. A workup will be most expeditiously accomplished in a center where the skills of these professionals are available, and there is also access to other medical specialists and laboratory studies.

A good medical-social history will cover the family history of the parents, hereditary factors, sociocultural background, developmental landmarks, and emotional relationships of child and family. When and how parents first became aware of the problem, their efforts to get help, their knowledge of and attitudes to mental retardation are important areas to explore. Reports should be obtained from agencies, hospitals, schools, physicians, and psychologists. In some situations, the worker or the public health nurse may make home visits.

Physical and neurological examinations, along with necessary laboratory procedures, contribute to an understanding of organic bases and lead to the treatment of remediable physical defects and dental care. Impaired hearing may contribute to the picture of retardation. Speech levels should be accurately assessed as part of any evaluation of the degree of retardation.

Psychological examination is an important phase of evaluation. The Gesell, Cattell, and Bayley tests are often useful for infants, although they are considered to be of less predictive value than tests used at later ages. The Stanford-Binet and the Wechsler Intelligence Scale for Children are widely used beyond the early years. The more recently devised Wechsler Pre-School and Primary Scale of Intelligence is appropriate for young children. A measure of adaptive behavior may be obtained by rating on the well-known Vineland Social Maturity Scale or the American Association on Mental Deficiency Adaptive Behavior Scale. Items in these scales are related to competence in dealing with the environment and meeting various life situations.

The psychiatrist focuses on the child's major modes of coping, his strengths, and his deficits. He attempts to estimate such factors as object relations, affect, flexibility, level of maturity, reality testing, skills at handling materials, motor functions, speech, drive control, distractibility, distortions in perception and memory, ability to learn from experience, sublimation potential, and frustration tolerance. Self-image, self-confidence, and sense of adventure are other important points to ascertain.

Particularly puzzling to differentiate are those cases where the child is severely retarded and at the same time shows features of autism (or childhood schizophrenia) and brain damage. It is frequently impossible to sort out the antecedent from the consequent conditions by the time the child is seen. The reason for attempting such a heroic task is to devise a treatment plan. Which came first, however, has little significance, in the sense that contact with the child must first be established before any treatment can be successfully applied. The fixity of the symptomatology has overriding importance in deciding the approach to use for such a severe state.

In other conditions, a knowledge of etiology is essential in the making of recommendations for treatment. Depressed intellect related to cultural deprivation may improve in the presence of a stimulating, enriched environment. Specific chronic brain dysfunction may affect reading, writing, and communication skills even among children with normal intellect. The adverse influence of a sensory handicap on test scores may result in an inaccurate classification of mental retardation.

In seeking an understanding of the factors underlying the below normal performance of the emotionally disturbed child, one important clue is a history of prior functioning. A finding of higher competence up to the time of a traumatic event, and subsequent emotional disturbance and diminution of intellect is one possibility. An alternate possibility is that an examination of the past will reveal intellectual retardation similar to the present, with no indication of greater potential. Determination of these points has bearing on expectations of therapeutic success, and therefore on planning and disposition. Treatment might be recommended for both situations, but in one the treatment will be that of a mentally retarded individual with the object of relieving emotional or behavioral distress. In the other situation, where the emotional problem is primary, treatment may reverse the intellectual deficit to some extent. Sorting out the primarily intellectually retarded from the primarily emotionally disturbed has implications for the kind of referral to be made as well as for the type and goal of treatment. The intellectually retarded may be more suitably referred to resources specializing in problems of retardation; whereas, for the emotionally disturbed, a different referral may be more appropriate.

These and other issues arising from the assembled information should be discussed at a staff meeting which may include representatives from the agencies most likely to be involved in working with the child and family. Often, the findings and recommendations of the conference will then be given to the parents at a joint meeting with the pediatrician and social worker. Additional interviews with the social worker are necessary to help the parents understand the findings and the recommendations, to answer any questions they may have, and to offer them more support and help with their guilt and anxiety. This has to be done over an extended period and, consequently, limiting contacts to a one-session summary for the parents falls far short of what they need.

Where the evaluation-center staff can function in an ongoing counseling role, parents often make repeated visits for advice about handling and training the child, or help in dealing with developmental deviations and educational, emotional, and vocational problems. Where available, the public health nurse is often a valuable source of help and guidance, particularly in regard to practical everyday care and habit training. After working out some of their feelings in continuing contacts with the social worker, parents are better able to judge the feasibility of continued care at home or placement away from home. With normal siblings at home requiring attention, with the retarded child suffering from isolation or even being made a scapegoat by his peers, with pressure from relatives and neighbors, parents may find their strong resolve to keep the child within the family weakening. The most difficult decision to make is whether to keep the child or to place him. Parents often need lots of time to arrive at a solution, since criteria for either choice are not clear cut. When they have resolved some of their own neurotic conflicts centering around the retarded child, parents can examine the pros and cons of placement and living at home more realistically. They can be more aware of their own motivations, guilt feelings, strengths, and limitations. Their own needs and those of their other children can then be taken into account in trying to meet the special needs of the retarded. Otherwise, retardation problems may result in neglect of the rest of the family.

Several assumptions parents have must be kept in mind in working with families of the retarded. One is that all placements away from home are bad and that no thoughts in this direction should be allowed to emerge. The parents' unspoken questions about the future may need to be verbalized by the social worker to start a discussion of alternate possibilities. The worker may, for example, ask what the parents anticipate as the child becomes older, and may then help them clarify practical difficulties and sort out realistic from unrealistic concerns. Another assumption often held by parents is that what is good for the child is bad for the family, and that what is good for the family is bad for the child. A fresh look, with the help of the social worker, will lead from an identification of compatible as well as discordant aspects in the living together of the retardate and his family to a search for various solutions within and outside the family and home. The introduction of factual material on available treatment and custodial public and private residential facilities must be synchronized with their readiness to consider positive aspects as well as drawbacks of placement. Viewing the process not only as a separation and deprivation, but also as the appropriate addition of a number of resource services to the child's life helps the family keep a more balanced perspective. A visit to the residential facility will give the parents first-hand information on the available services and living conditions. Because waiting lists are large, early applications are recommended. These can always be withdrawn, or the child can be removed from placement if the parents change their minds.

Parents have a strong need to feel they are effective and successful, particularly inasmuch as they experience a blow to their self-esteem on learning the child is retarded. An understanding of the child's personality and problems and the knowledge of practical approaches in relating to him enable the parents to feel more competent in coping with different situations. The National Association for Retarded Children and its local chapters are active parent groups where mothers and fathers can further their interests in retardation and also help establish resources for their children. Becoming part of such a group has its therapeutic effects. It is a major step toward acceptance of the situation of retardation. Sharing a common concern with others makes the problems more tolerable. In addition, participating in efforts aimed at the improvement of facilities for the care and treatment of the retarded can alleviate the parents' sense of guilt and helplessness.

When the parents decide that the child will live at home, specialized educational facilities need to be found. At earlier ages, preschool and kindergarten programs are important as preparations for mental retardation classes at the grade-school level. Reference to the chart of developmental characteristics reveals that the mildly retarded can be predicted to progress academically as high as the sixth grade in school. The moderately retarded can usually go no higher than the second grade. It is customary to place the lower limit for the educable retardate at an I.Q. of 50, and to regard a child as trainable within an I.Q. range of 25 to 50.

Some preschool and school programs are designed with specific therapeutic goals in mind. In these, individual remedial tutoring and speech therapy, and group and individual therapy may be offered, in addition to learning in small classes. Parents are also seen individually and in groups in such settings. The clinical team consisting of pediatrician, psychiatrist, social worker, and psychologist is often part of the day treatment program. Dental and medical care and physical rehabilitation are more likely to be found in a hospital setting. Vocational guidance facilities and sheltered workshops are useful for the older retarded.

In dealing with the retarded, stress has been placed on the use of multiple treatment modalities, including counseling, correction of somatic handicaps, recreational and vocational services, perceptual training, educational programs, community resources, psychotropic medication, and psychotherapy. Several lengthy reviews of psychotherapy and other adjustment techniques have been published, the most recent by Bialer (1967). The present discussion is devoted mainly to psychotherapeutic techniques. While there are some reports of a rise in intellectual level following psychotherapy, behavioral and emotional change are the usual emphases in therapeutic efforts. Where emotional maladjustment is the major etiologic agent of the retardation, chances for improvement of intellect by means of psychotherapy are considered better than if the primary cause is neurological deficit or cultural deprivation.

This does not mean that the child with neurological deficit or cultural deprivation will not benefit from psychotherapy. Regardless of etiology, feelings of failure and inadequacy, low self-esteem, emotional conflicts, and maladaptive defense mechanisms are frequently present. A planned therapeutic relation may have a major effect on the fate of the retardate, allowing him to function outside of the institution. This can be most effective when the parents are getting help as part of a total approach which encompasses individual physical, emotional, educational, social, and family needs. The expertise of the social worker is especially important in referring to appropriate services or meeting family needs in a continuing casework relation. If treatment efforts are devoted to the child alone, the chances for change are poor.

The stereotype that all retarded children are the same led to the automatic exclusion of psychotherapy, particularly because intellectual brightness has been thought of as a key asset in treatment potential. Dispelling such prejudice allows more objective decisions based on a total evaluation of the child and family rather than on intellectual level alone. No specific lower limit of intelligence can be set to bar the retarded child from consideration for psychotherapy until enough results are gathered about attempts at psychotherapeutic procedures extended to low ranges of intelligence. However, the severely or profoundly retarded youngster is not likely to be aware of his incapacity and therefore probably will not develop emotional problems related to this awareness.

Decisions about psychotherapy and other ways in which to help the retarded child must be based on the same considerations used for populations with normal intelligence. Goals need to be set relating to specific aspects of behavior and emotional life. Intellectual level affects ability to grasp concepts and therefore the degree of insight of which the child is capable. Imagination may be simple in nature and difficult to stimulate among those with low intellect. No one-to-one correlation has been established between level of intellect and the ability to fantasize. Imagination probably drops off sharply at some point that has not yet been established.

Supportive, relationship, and play therapy have been recommended and utilized. Group psychotherapy is another approach that has often produced results. Psychologists have reported success with behavior-modification techniques. In measuring outcome from any of these techniques, the degree of success will depend on the definition of goals as well as the appropriateness of techniques. Goals and techniques devised to reach these goals vary, depending not only on the individual child and family but also on the theoretical stance of the therapist. For example, where a child's behavior is disruptive in school, the study of the total situation (family, child, school) may lead to a recommendation for a trial period of psychotherapy. In treatment, the establishment of a child-therapist relation is primary in the pursuit of intervening goals toward the ultimate objective of change of behavior. Hypotheses concerning reasons for the behavior lead to a choice of sequences, such as release of anxiety, expression of aggression in treatment, and direction into socially acceptable channels.

The genetic-dynamic formulations of psychotherapy are considered of little relevance in behavior modification approaches. Relinquishing unwanted current behavior and establishing desirable behavior in its place is attempted by the application of such techniques as positive and negative reinforcement (reward and punishment) and the use of a token economy. Behavior modification programs have become popular in treating retarded populations, particularly for the low-level retardate in institutions where little or no psychotherapy is available.

In psychotherapy, the therapist must keep in mind that expression of feeling has the potential for further disturbances of behavior. Therefore, where the ego is relatively immature, the risks of the spread of disruptive action outside the treatment session must be offset by clear definition of what is appropriate and allowed under which circumstances.

Play techniques are emphasized in psychotherapy because of the limits in speech and abstract thinking of most retarded children. They may also be unable to engage in imaginative play, or will simply repeat sequences, such as cuddling or feeding a doll or rolling a truck.

Leland and Smith (1965) developed a series of important concepts and techniques around play therapy through the use of learning theory and behavior principles. They attempt to make the child think by applying selective reinforcement (through rewards and punishment), using appropriate play materials and techniques. The child is also alerted to socially acceptable standards of behavior which require modification of his actions. To fulfill these purposes, Leland and Smith devised four different kinds of play therapy patterns, differentiating degrees of structure and play materials and therapist's role. These variations follow: (1) Unstructured materials (such as sand, water, clay) with an unstructured approach (U-U) is most appropriate for the emotionally disturbed, brain-damaged, and severely retarded child with very poor adaptive behavior. Goals are self-recognition and control of impulses within acceptable social limits. (2) Unstructured materials with a structured approach (U-S), typical of occupational, recreational, and music therapy, is for the child who, at a higher level than (1) is aware of his responsibility for his actions but not sufficiently cognizant of the meanings of this responsibility. The child with central nervous system pathology underlying his emotional disturbances and retardation will often improve his self-concept, impulse control, and social acceptability through the development of fantasy, imagination, and social reality in a U-S setting. (3) Structured materials with an unstructured therapeutic approach (S-U) is traditional play therapy for the child who has an adequate self-concept and impulse control but needs help in handling social and cultural realities and developing realistic personal goals in the presence of feelings of aggression, hostility, and anxiety in relating to people and objects. (4) Structured materials in a structured therapeutic approach (S-S), as in special educational settings, fits the child who is at a more advanced level of psychological and social functioning but still needs help in specific problem areas leading to improved social maturity through improved cognition, greater understanding of his worth and place in the world, and more realistic levels of aspiration.

In addition to individual and group psychotherapy and behavior modification techniques, social casework and social group work have helped the retarded child and his family. A casework approach to the retarded may in many ways resemble psychotherapy. In fact, caseworkers in day treatment and residential centers often learn and use play therapy and related techniques. The caseworker may place more emphasis on a supportive relation involving reassurance, advice, guidance, discussion, ventilation, and environmental manipulation. Adjunctive treatment includes art, music, occupational, and recreational therapy.

Adulthood

The major emphasis in the discussion up to this point has been on the child as he develops. The general principles that apply to his health and welfare apply also to the adolescent and adult. Viewing the retarded as one who can grow through learning leads to more favorable teaching and training attitudes and an open-mindedness that emphasizes those aspects which can change. Such an approach avoids the self-fulfilling prophecy of pejorative labeling in which a constricting definition leads to feelings of hopelessness in the retarded and those with whom he comes in contact. A closely related major goal is an existence as near to the normal as possible. These two major concepts in no sense preclude consideration of handicaps and deficits. They allow for realistic attempts to plan situations of optimal advantage to the retarded person and to the society in which he lives. He can then extend himself to reach a higher level, provided that the standards of accomplishment are not out of his reach. Creative and imaginative efforts in recent years have aimed at normalization, i.e. everyday living approximating patterns of the main stream of society. This is in contrast to isolation and segregation where the retarded might only associate with each other and feelings of difference, inferiority, and powerlessness abound, reinforced by social stereotypes of them en masse.

The 1967 Stockholm Symposium of the International League of Societies for the Mentally Handicapped declared that the rights of the mentally retarded are the same as the rights of other human beings: to preserve the physical and psychological integrity of his person, to privacy and dignity, to have a place to live, free education, leisure time activities, vote, marry, have children, to be given a fair trial for his legal offenses, to strengthen his ability to exercise these rights with a minimum of abridgment through specialized training, rehabilitation, guidance and counseling, and to have unhampered access to services. These are his rights unless it can be shown that his own interests or those of others are placed in jeopardy if he exercises these rights. If he does show a general inability to manage his life and to protect his welfare, then a guardian should be appointed for him.

A number of innovative ideas have evolved to augment the limited resourcefulness and balance the handicaps of the mentally retarded. The aims are to help the individual function more adequately and as independently as possible.

One of the newer concepts envisions the citizen advocate, an interested volunteer, to help the retarded person obtain those benefits to which he is entitled for further changes in his life, such as vocational guidance and training, schooling, housing, legal rights and benefits, etc.

A series of residences and foster homes and graded degrees of supervision and independence have been proposed as alternatives to institutions, when parents can no longer take care of a retarded member of the family. Short term, "respite" care accommodations are also available in some communities at times of family crises or parent vacations.

More institutions are abandoning their traditional isolation, and are facilitating relationships with the community. The shift in focus is to preparation for life outside the institution whenever possible. One outstanding example is the Elwyn Institute which changed from a custodial emphasis to innovative programs of vocational and social rehabilitation providing services for all levels of handicap. The area of work was approached in a graded series of classes which included occupational therapy, vocational training, sheltered workshops, and an adult education program. The latter stressed proper work habits, money management, dress, and how to find and keep a job. Community adjustment covered a range from coping with emergencies to voting. One hundred and thirty residents averaging over 15 years at Elwyn were discharged to independent community living in the four years following the initiation of the new program. Their I.Q.'s ranged from 45 to 80, and they all had severe educational deficits. The majority were below the fourth-grade reading level. Many were multiply handicapped, often with gross physical defects. A follow-up study on 65 graduates six months to three years after discharging to the community revealed that 75 per cent were working steadily; 91 per cent were employed at the time of the interview. Work was primarily in unskilled and semi-skilled occupations involving personal service, food, and building service fields. They were operators, laborers, stock and factory workers. Many were dissatisfied with their low salaries, and low status, and were sensitive to the lower prestige of the positions they held. They had avoided serious legal difficulties, coped with everyday living problems and tended to be responsible citizens. Less than one-third had married and those who had children seemed adequate as parents. The Elwyn Project experience is evidence that a traditional custodial institution can shift its emphasis to rehabilitation and discharge large numbers of educable retardates to independent living. In the rehabilitation programs, concrete, practical, manual training and work experience within the institution established vocational skills which prepared these mentally subnormal people for competitive community employment. An extension to the original project was the establishment of a community-based facility providing a transition for the mentally handicapped individual who needs more community experience to function independently, vocationally, and socially. This facility allows for a trial run preliminary to living independently, and the resident here is responsible for paying rent, shopping for food and clothing, using public transportation to and from work, cooking, and engaging in leisure-time activities.

Some communities are much more advanced than others in the number and kinds of facilities and services they offer to the handicapped, and more specifically to the retarded. Many ways to minimize the handicaps and maximize the possibilities for independent living have now been tested and proved. Where a community lacks facilities and services of the type described here, the parents of the handicapped, the professionals, the citizen-advocates, the legislators, and the politicians must work together to guarantee their availability.

The goal is appropriate help for the individual (and his family) rather than a limited choice of ill-suited alternatives. Our ever-growing knowledge can be applied to all degrees of handicap. The educable mentally retarded person has the potential for satisfactory independent functioning, and, given sufficient preparation, he can realize that potential without the necessity for institutional placement.

REFERENCES

Bayley, N. (1969), *Bayley Scales of Infant Development.* New York: Psychological Corporation.

Bialer, I. (1967), Psychotherapy and Other Adjustment Techniques with the Mentally Retarded. In: *Mental Retardation,* ed. A. A. Baumeister. Chicago: Aldine Publishing Co., pp. 138-180.

Binet, A. & Simon, T. (1905), Methodes Nouvelles pour le Diagnostic du Niveau Intellectuel des Anormaux. *L'Annee Psychologique,* 11: 191-336.

Cattell, P. (1949), *Cattell Infant Intelligence Scale.* New York: Psychological Corporation.

Cranefield, P. F. (1961), A Seventeenth Century View of Mental Deficiency and Schizophrenia: Thomas Willis on Stupidity or Foolishness. *Bulletin of the History of Medicine,* 35: 291-316.

——— & Federn, W. (1967), The Begetting of Fools: An Annotated Translation of Paracelsus' *De Generatione Stultorum. Bulletin of the History of Medicine,* 41:56-74, 161-174.

Doll, E. A. (1953), *The Measurement of Social Competence: A Manual for the Vineland Social Maturity Scale.* Minneapolis: Educational Test Bureau.

Down, J. L. H. (1867), Observations on an Ethnic Classification of Idiots. *Mental Science,* 13:121-128.

Folling, A. (1934) The Excretion of Phenylpyruvic Acid (ppa) in the Urine—an Anomaly of Metabolism in Connection with Imbecility. In: *Papers on Human Genetics,* ed. S. H. Boyer. Englewood Cliffs, New Jersey: Prentice Hall, 1963.

Gesell, A., et al. (1925, 1949), *Gesell Developmental Schedules.* New York: Psychological Corporation.

Goddard, H. H. (1910), A Measuring Scale for Intelligence. *The Training School,* 6:146-155.

Itard, J. M. G. (1801), De l'Education d'un Homme Sauvage. Paris: Gougon. [*The Wild Boy of Aveyron.* New York: Appleton-Century-Crofts, 1932].

Johnson, R. & Fraser, M. (1972), Right to Treatment. *Mental Hygiene,* 56:13-19.

Kanner, L. (1960), Itard, Seguin, Howe—Three Pioneers in the Education of Retarded Children. *American Journal of Mental Deficiency,* 65: 2-10.

Kivitz, M. S., Rosen, M., & Clark, G. R. (1972), From Research to Community Living. *Human Needs,* 1:25-28.

Knobloch, H., Rider, R., Harper, P., & Pasamanick, B. (1956), Neuropsychiatric Sequelae of Prematurity, a Longitudinal Study. *Journal of the American Medical Association,* 161:581-585.

Kugel, R. B., & Wolfensberger, W., ed. (1969), *Changing Patterns in Residential Services for the Mentally Retarded.* Washington: President's Committee on Mental Retardation.

Landsteiner, K., & Weiner, A. S. (1940), An Agglutinable Factor in Human Blood Recognized by Immune Sera for Rhesus Blood. *Proceedings of the Society for Experimental Biology and Medicine,* 43:223.

Lejeune, J., Gautier, M., & Turpin, R. (1959), Study of the Somatic Chromosomes of Nine Mongoloid Idiot Children. In: *Papers on Human Genetics,* ed. S. H. Boyer. Englewood Cliffs, New Jersey: Prentice-Hall, 1963.

Leland, H., Shellhaas, M., Nihira, K., & Foster, R. (1967), Adaptive Behavior: A New Dimension in the Classification of the Mentally Retarded. *Mental Retardation Abstracts,* 4:359-387.

——— & Smith, D. (1965), *Play Therapy with Mentally Subnormal Children.* New York: Grune & Stratton.

Nihira, K., Foster, R., Shellhaas, M., & Leland, H. (1969, 1970), *Adaptive Behavior Scale.* Washington, D.C.: American Association on Mental Deficiency.

Pasamanick, B. & Lilienfeld, A. M. (1955), Association of Maternal and Fetal Factors with Development of Mental Deficiency. *Journal of the American Medical Association,* 159:155-160.

Pintner, R. (1931), *Intelligence Testing: Methods and Results* (New Edition). New York: Holt, Rhinehart & Winston.

Sachs, B. (1887), On Arrested Cerebral Development, with Special Reference to its Cortical Pathology. *Journal of Nervous and Mental Diseases,* 14:541.

Talbot, M. (1967), Edouard Seguin. *American Journal of Mental Deficiency,* 72:184-189.

Tay, W. (1881), Symmetrical Changes in the Region of the Yellow Spot in Each Eye of an Infant. *Transactions of the Optholmological Society of the United Kingdom,* 1:155.

Terman, L. M., (1916), *The Measurement of Intelligence.* Boston: Houghton Mifflin.

——— & Merrill, M. A. (1937), *Measuring Intelligence.* Boston: Houghton Mifflin.

——— ——— (1960), *Stanford-Binet Intelligence Scale.* Boston: Houghton Mifflin.

Von Reuss, A. (1908), Zuckerausscheidung im Saüglingsalter. *Wiener Medizinische Wochenschrift,* 58:799.

Wechsler, D. (1949), *Wechsler Intelligence Scale for Children.* New York: Psychological Corporation.

——— (1958), *The Measurement and Appraisal of Adult Intelligence, Fourth Edition.* Baltimore: Williams & Wilkins.

——— (1963, 1967), *Wechsler Preschool and Primary Scale of Intelligence.* New York: Psychological Corporation.

Wolfensberger, W. (1972) *Citizen Advocacy for the Handicapped, Impaired, and Disadvantaged: An Overview.* Washington: President's Committee on Mental Retardation.

SUGGESTED READING

Adams, M. (1971), *Mental Retardation and its Social Dimensions.* New York: Columbia University Press.

Baumeister, A. A., ed. (1967), *Mental Retardation.* Chicago: Aldine Publishing Co.

Gardner, W. I. (1971), *Behavior Modification in Mental Retardation.* Chicago: Aldine-Atherton.

Grossman, H. J., ed. (1973), *Manual on Terminology and Classification in Mental Retardation.* Washington: American Association on Mental Deficiency.

Group for the Advancement of Psychiatry (1959), *Basic Considerations in Mental Retardation: A Preliminary Report,* No. 43. New York: Group for the Advancement of Psychiatry.

——— (1963), *Mental Retardation: A Family Crisis— The Therapeutic Role of the Physician,* No. 56. New York: Group for the Advancement of Psychiatry.

——— (1967), *Mild Mental Retardation: A Growing Challenge to the Physician,* No. 66. New York: Group for the Advancement of Psychiatry.

Haywood, H. C. (1970), *Social-Cultural Aspects of Mental Retardation.* New York: Appleton-Century-Crofts.

Jacobs, J. (1969), *The Search for Help.* New York: Brunner/Mazel.

Kanner, L. (1964), *A History of the Care and Study of the Mentally Retarded.* Springfield, Illinois: Charles C. Thomas.

Menolascino, F. J., ed. (1970), *Psychiatric Approaches to Mental Retardation.* New York: Basic Books.

Sarason, S. B., & Doris, J. (1969), *Psychological Problems in Mental Deficiency* (Fourth Edition). New York: Harper & Row.

Schreiber, M., ed. (1970), *Social Work and Mental Retardation.* New York: John Day.

Smith, R. M. (1971), *An Introduction to Mental Retardation.* New York: McGraw-Hill.

CHAPTER TWELVE

Adolescence

EVERETT P. DULIT, M.D.

Adolescence has a well-defined beginning, marked by the biological event of puberty, and a rather ill-defined ending, shading off gradually into young adulthood. The study of adolescence clearly shows us the interweaving of biological, psychological, and sociocultural forces: puberty is a biological event with profound psychological repurcussions, and these psychological developments are themselves markedly influenced by sociocultural forces, indirectly through the family and directly as the adolescent moves out of the family into his peer group and the world at large. My goal in this chapter is to highlight some of the central trends in adolescent development, to offer some perspectives on the wide range of normal variation, and to outline some of the more important pathological entities.

Depending upon the combined influence of the sociocultural context, family dynamics, and intrapsychic determinants, one can see an adolescence ranging in duration and complexity from one extreme—in those "primitive" societies where the transition from childhood to adult status is condensed virtually into a single brief ritual-ofpassage—all the way over to the prolonged adolescence (lasting a decade or more) characteristic of cultures like our own. Richly flavored soup generally requires long slow simmering. Fine wines generally require a long time in the bottle. And more richly developed kinds of adulthood are generally preceded by a decade or more of psychological "simmering" and "ripening" in adolescence.

Puberty

The age of onset of puberty is distributed over a bell-shaped curve, 11 being early onset, 12 to 13 average for girls, 13 to 14 average for boys, and 15 or 16 getting to be late onset. Girls mature approximately a year earlier than boys, a fact usually strikingly apparent in the 7th-grade classes, where some of the girls have begun to blossom into young womanhood and where the boys still look like children—and seem still to be more interested in baseball cards than in the girls. Some of the major physical developments in the order in which they usually appear are: for girls, breast budding, straight pigmented pubic hair, maximum physical growth, kinky pubic hair, menstruation, axillary (armpit) hair; for boys, beginning testicular growth, straight pigmented pubic hair, enlargement of penis, early voice changes, first ejaculation, kinky pubic hair, maximum growth, axillary hair, marked voice change, development of beard. It takes about two years from the beginning to the end of this process. When the question arises whether or not a youngster has completed puberty, the presence of lush axillary hair—a late development about which one can ask perhaps more easily than about genital developments, tends to clinch the point. Fertility in girls tends not to be established at all until a year or two after menstruation begins, and maximum fertility usually not until late adolescence or the early twenties. It follows that an adolescent girl who begins sexual activity early without bothering about birth control can be lulled into a false sense of security about the possibility of impregnation—until fertility catches up.

Sometimes puberty begins late as a direct consequence of endocrine abnormality. Where that is suspected, the patient should be referred to a physician who specializes in making such assessments. But most young people with delayed puberty are simply on the tail end of the normal distribution curve. No long-range physical consequences ensue; such youngsters can be reassured that by the time they complete puberty they will be "the same as anyone else." But to be the "last on your block" to develop a properly adolescent body is a very real psychological hazard with effects on self-esteem often lingering well past adolescence.

Feelings in adolescence run especially strong, and there are few things about which adolescents feel more strongly than they do about their developing bodies. Boys are concerned about genital size, height, and muscularity; girls about breasts and hips, and figure in general. Both are concerned about facial features and hair, sometimes becoming greatly exercised about what seem to parents (and others) to be minutia. Shortness is a psychological hazard for boys, excessive height for girls (also vice versa, but to a lesser degree, given "the rule" that men are supposed to be taller than women). Obesity is a major psychological hazard for both.

Two features of pathological physical development sufficiently common to be included here are acne and gynecomastia. *Acne,* still only partially understood, tends to begin in the adolescent years. Patients with a marked acne that does not respond to the usual home remedies deserve referral to a dermatologist, because neglected acne can lead to irreversible scarring. *Gynecomastia* is a temporary enlargement and tenderness of the breast tissue in boys, giving an appearance suggestive of the female breast, naturally very distressing to young men at a time when the issue of developing masculinity is so highly charged. Some degree of gynecomastia occurs in about 20 per cent of young men, which is high enough for cases to be far from rare, but low enough so that a young man who suffers from *prominent* gynecomastia is likely never to see or hear of anyone so afflicted as himself and to suffer silently while making mysterious excuses to absent himself from the beach. Gynecomastia has no implications whatsoever with regard to masculinity or femininity; it is nothing more than a transient response of the body during a time of rapid change in the level of circulating sex hormones. When the hormone levels stabilize, the gynecomastia disappears. The feelings and fantasies about having had it disappear rather more slowly.

Psychological Development

Adolescence can be divided into three principal stages: early adolescence beginning with puberty, shading off into middle adolescence by 15 or 16, and into late adolescence by 18 or 19. These subdivisions tend to overlap, but they are useful because each tends to have a fairly characteristic cluster of behavioral features.

Early adolescence is a time of emotional lability. For most youngsters, the relative calm of the latency years is shattered by the impact of puberty and replaced typically by the much more edgy quality of inner turmoil barely held in check. The vitality of childhood, laced through with good feelings bubbling up, changes its character, the same vigor now coming to be rather more frantic, more frenetic, more shot through with anxiety and tension. These are the years of breaking into tears for no apparent reason, of mysterious moods, of walking off in a huff. Emotions run rampant, unpredictability is the rule, and neither parents nor teachers nor the youngsters themselves know quite what to expect from moment to moment. Because these are youngsters past the easy charm, the relative compliance, and greater openness of the childhood years and not yet into the appreciably greater sense and sensibility of the high school years, this is the age range probably most difficult to work with. In many ways the young adolescent is the quintessential adolescent: very much betwixt and between, very much in turmoil.

Middle adolescence sees a distinct settling down, a greater capacity for composure and compromise, and a way of relating to adults (parents and therapists included) that is noticeably more "civilized" and complex. Self-absorption begins to give way to a greater capacity to again become absorbed in work. The defensively supercharged total commitment to peer group so typical of early adolescence begins to give way to a more differentiated response and to a greater capacity to cope with pressures from within the peer group, including the all important capacity to stand separate from the group when necessary. It becomes easier to "work things out" with middle adolescents—in the family, in school, and in therapy (not *easy,* but easier).

Standing on the more secure platform attained in the years of middle adolescence, the young person reaches, as he moves through the years of late adolescence, for progressively more complex levels of "getting himself together," a phrase nicely expressive of a central psychological task of the age. This is the time when major life choices concerning work and career begin to be made. The exploratory, experimental, "as if" quality normally present (even necessary) to some degree in middle adolescence begins to give way to more definitive "choices" and to the increasingly irreversible emergence by late adolescence and young adulthood of the kind of person one is going to be. This pertains not only to choice of career and to choice of companions, but perhaps most important of all, to "choice" of identity, as defined by Erikson (1959), that synthesis into one relatively unique, relatively coherent psychological "self" of all the diverse strands of character, individual inclinations, and partial identifications that have been at work through the years of childhood and adolescence, an outcome partially achieved by many and fully attained only by some.

The developmental trends outlined above can be expressed and understood in terms of shifting interactions among the major structural subdivisions of the psychic apparatus. In latency, the pressure of id forces is relatively quiescent, and ego dominates. With the advent of puberty, things become unstuck. There is a surge of hormonal events, and riding the crest are the sexual and aggressive drives. The balance between ego and id shifts. To use Freud's metaphor of id as horse and ego as rider, the horse bolts and the rider is left running behind, a poor second. In some ways, these years after puberty recapitulate the situation that prevailed in "the magic years" of early childhood, to use Selma Fraiberg's felicitous phrase. Sometimes one even sees an exquisitely specific reactivation in a given youngster of precisely those individual conflicts which were "front stage center" just before they were set aside at the onset of latency now again coming to the fore in virtually the same form, perhaps slightly updated. This reactivation of old conflicts previously quiescent in a state of partial resolution, is associated often enough with the emergence of symptoms and anxiety. But the relative melting of defensive structures also affords a kind of second chance in adolescence for reshaping childhood resolutions of centrally significant early conflict issues, faulty resolutions of which we know to be at the heart of neurotic conflict and symptom formation in adult life. Working with the more mature ego of adolescence, there is at least the potential for making a more satisfactory resolution this second time around.

Some degree of id dominance and ego regression is normally characteristic of early adolescence, but of course there are degrees of regression and disorganization so extreme that they have to be regarded as pathological even at this "normally pathological" age. The distinction between normal abnormality and abnormal abnormality in early adolescence is not an easy one to make. Experience helps. But often the best strategy for beginner and expert alike is to postpone definitive diagnosis, to counsel moderation and to play for the time one needs in order to see which way things will go.

By middle adolescence the ego once again vaults into the saddle and brings the horse under some appreciable measure of control. One sees a characteristic settling down, a process deepened and carried forward through the years of late adolescence. Successful defensive maneuvers, conflict resolutions, and coping mechanisms become relatively firm, practiced, and shaped into a more or less stable pattern that will serve for better and/or for worse throughout the remainder of life.

Now let's follow superego through the same years of development. Established in a major way in the aftermath of the phallic stage, the superego is further consolidated and exercised through the years of latency. Then comes the surge of sexual and aggressive feelings in puberty and the associated reactivation of forbidden unconscious oedipal fantasies, this time in a body more nearly approximating an adult body. Intensely threatening to ego and superego, this provokes a proportionately intense counterreaction of the defensive forces, contributing to the sense of inner strain so characteristic of this time of life. The adolescent now seeks distance, defensively, from the parents, who have become too highly charged with the newly reactivated forbidden unconscious oedipal feelings and fantasies. They become labeled old fashioned and impossible, a process notoriously hard on parents, but a normal process, and one that tends to simmer down (to everyone's relief) by middle and late adolescence. But at the peak of that outbreak of defensive hostility to parents, all those superego standards, values, and restraints which the child learned and internalized out of love for the parents become fair game for scornful questioning and, often enough, for precipitous abandonment, subject to the same defensively motivated depreciation (in a process of "guilt by association") as the parents, and typically replaced for a time by the standards of the peer group.

The intense shake-up of superego in early adolescence is a normal development process, even necessary insofar as some superego standards learned in childhood—notably the prohibitions against sexuality and against some forms of aggression—apply only to childhood and require gradual replacement through the adolescent years to admit of a full rich adulthood. At the same time, there is the very real risk that the influence of peer group and culture at this time of life will work to the disadvantage of the best of what parental standards represent. (Although the phrase may be overused by parents, there is such a thing as bad company.) When things go well, youngsters tend to preserve the best of what the parents represent, to be reasonably prudent and self-protective in their choice of peer group and its influences, sometimes changing nothing more than superficial forms and matters of style, and using those to needle parents and to get distance. But when things go badly, owing to some combination of intrapsychic and social forces, one may see a major disintegration of standards.

Of the many possible pathological outcomes of the interplay of psychic forces, three deserve special mention. Sometimes the counterreaction of ego and superego against the perceived upsurge of sexual and aggressive instincts is so great that one sees a virtual blocking of psychological adolescence. These are the terribly overcontrolled youngsters who hang on to latency, stiffly and under strain, against increasing pressure from within. Clearly, the therapeutic task with such youngsters is to help them to be less afraid of the changes they are experiencing and to help them to develop more flexible controls. Sometimes the balance swings all the way over in the other direction, especially when from the outset there have been serious flaws rooted either in individual or family pathology, or in the destructive effect on family and child of disastrous social circumstance. Here one can see a virtual abandonment of latency superego standards, replaced either by "anything goes" or by the other-directed standards of the peer group, in both instances often with a heavy undercurrent of self-destructiveness. Helping such youngsters requires trying to set up in adolescence (a far from favorable time for beginning) some version between therapist and adolescent of the deep human involvement that ought to have prevailed with the parents, out of which can grow a late-blooming version of self-restraint by identification. Finally, special mention should be made of the highly specific patterns of persistent and misplaced superego interference with normal ego and id function which we recognize as the familiar neurotic inhibitions. The foundations of such pathology are laid down in early childhood, but crucial and major reorganizations can take place in adolescence. When such potentially beneficial reorganizations of superego do not take place, one sees the consolidation of the kind of neurotic illness that can be so destructive of a full, rich adult life.

Another important psychoanalytic perspective on development in adolescence is carried by the concept of genital dominance. The last in the sequence of successively unfolding psychosexual stages organized around the erogenous zones is the genital stage, with its onset in early adolescence and its consolidation through adolescence and young adulthood. The basic concept here is that the pregenital impulses (oral, anal, phallic) find expression and gratification in adulthood within a context predominantly organized around and under the dominance of genital activity, pleasure, and function. Forging that optimal final outcome is psychological work done in the years of adolescence.

Finally let us sketch, in broad outline some features of the object-relations line of development through the years of adolescence. Emotionally, the latency-age child, despite involvement in school and with friends, is still firmly rooted within the family. But in early adolescence this pattern is disrupted by the normal distancing from parents and the corresponding turn to the peer group. At this time, deeply significant ties can develop with the group and especially with one or two friends of the same sex, the all important close chum of the early adolescent years. The sharing of feelings and experiences within the protective intimacy of this special relationship have an enormous potential for personal growth and can foreshadow and facilitate subsequent capacities for the development of closeness and intimacy with others. Typically, peer-group and chum involvement is followed by mixed peer group, then double dating, and finally by pairing off. When all goes well, the strident commitment to peer group mellows, the relation with parents moves from clash and distancing toward some kind of adult-adult relation, and the anxious testing of the waters of intimacy (too hot?, too cold?), so prominent a feature of adolescence, gives way to a more confident capacity to immerse oneself and to swim in those tricky currents and undercurrents with increasing ease and fulfillment.

As the turmoil of early adolescence gives way to the relative settling down of middle adolescence, and as some partial mastery of psychosexual issues is achieved, the psychological task that comes to the fore in later adolescence is identity formation. Identity is the private and public answer that each young person makes to the question so characteristic of adolescence: "Who am I?" Partially expressed in words and ideas but most significantly expressed in the way that they "are," including elements of conscious and deliberate choice, but at the same time including deeply unconscious trends and working with all that has gone before, identity formation is a process "gradually integrating constitutional givens, idiosyncratic libidinal needs, favored capacities, significant identifications, effective defenses, successful sublimations, and consistent roles." That omnibus quotation, which bears rereading and reflection, is from Erikson who with his colleagues, notably Keniston and Friedenberg, have made major contributions to our understanding of the process of identity formation in late adolescence. A fully realized and stable identity, like most of later development and like most aspects of psychological maturity, is partially achieved by many, fully achieved only by some.

All of adolescent development can also be looked at from the point of view of the family. That can be done strictly from "the parents'-eye view" or, more in keeping with modern perspectives on systems theory, by conceptualizing the family itself as a complex unit of interacting parts with its own system of internal regulations. One theme, recurrent in clinical practice, can serve nicely as illustration: the reaction of parents to the flowering of sexuality and the surge of aggressive independence in their adolescent offspring. Invariably that confronts father and mother in middle life with a challenge to their own personal resolutions of those universal issues and their own versions of "how to live the good life." Just as adolescence reactivates earlier conflicts in the adolescent, the interaction between adolescent and parent reactivates earlier conflicts in the parent. Much of the clash of generations is played out around these issues, and, as with conflict in general, it has potential for both pathology and growth. Spinning out some of the infinite range of interactional possibilities is left as an exercise for the reader. Some measure of conflict, in the family as within the adolescent himself, is a part of normal development. One of the challenges for the therapist is to become sensitive to the "sound" of normal conflict, and to learn to distinguish it from the "sound" of pathological conflict. There are many shades of gray.

Cognitive Development in Adolescence

The years of adolescence also bring the potential for a vast expansion in the capacity for abstract thinking. We are indebted to Jean Piaget, the Swiss psychologist, for much of our modern understanding of the development of intelligence. The "great leap forward" in the capacity for abstract thought taken by some adolescents is conceptualized by Piaget, within the systematic framework of the sequence of cognitive stages he has elucidated, as a shift from the concrete stage to the formal stage of thought. The concrete stage, roughly overlapping with the years of latency, is characterized by thought in terms of categories and graded series. Beginning in early adolescence, there is a shift to the formal stage where the basic elements of the thought process are identified by Piaget as an ordered "matrix" of all the possibilities inherent in the system (arrived at by identifying and grouping into some ordered structure all possible combinations of all possible values of all the variables inherent in the situation at hand) plus all the mental operations needed to "move around" in that structure. Closer to the descriptive level, one sees a shift from thought about "things" to a vastly expanded capacity for thought about words, concepts, thoughts, hypotheses, ideas. In childhood, problem solving (as distinguished from fantasy, reverie and dream which are something else again) is organized almost entirely around concrete actualities. Possibilities not previously actualized play an exceedingly subsidiary role, if they are present at all. In the formal stage the full range of possibilities comes to the foreground, now generated by combination and recombination *within the mind* of variables abstracted from the problem at hand, and actuality can come to be treated as "merely an interesting special case."

Clearly this provides a cognitive underpinning for the characteristic full flowering in adolescence of an intense commitment to systems of thought, and for the surge of thinking about "things which could be but are not" (the valedictory address would be a classic example). The passion and the fervor are rooted elsewhere than in the cognitive sphere, but the capacity to generate that vastly expanded set of possibilities is the defining characteristic of the formal stage, the cognitive acquisition of adolescence.

For some youngsters, this opening up of the horizons of thought is truly a heady experience. But unlike the earlier cognitive stages outlined by Piaget, the formal stage becomes fully developed in only about a third of the population. A large proportion of adolescents develop partial access to formal stage modes, and the characteristic "sound" of hypothetical-deductive efforts is commonly to be heard in discussions through these years even where the substance may leave something to be desired. Many of these youngsters, who master formal stage modes only partially, develop other strategies of problem solving, most notably reliance on a "repertoire" of standard methods for standard problems, and a strategy of seeking to match new problems to that repertoire. Clearly such a method lacks the power of full formal stage function for attacking new problems, but can be quite adequate within some "average expectable environment."

Getzels and Jackson (1962) and Hudson (1966) have contributed an essential dimension to our understanding of adolescent (and adult) thinking. They emphasize the emergence in adolescence of two different styles of thinking: convergent and divergent. Convergers tend to think in terms of zeroing in on one correct answer; divergers tend to be good at spinning off multiple related possibilities from any given starting point. Convergent youngsters tend to gravitate to careers such as mathamatics, science, and engineering; divergent youngsters to the arts and letters. Good thinking includes an interplay between the two modes, but commonly one predominates. Because the school system and conventional intelligence tests tend to favor convergent modes, divergers can have a hard time in conventional schools. The ghetto experience tends to favor the development of divergent modes. The concept of convergence versus divergence adds to our understanding of cognitive development—its stress on style rather than degree of development.

Cognition inevitably gets caught up in the process of identity formation. As a consequence, late adolescence sees a wide range of vicissitudes in the handling of abstract capacities. Some choose to set them aside as "high flown kid stuff" and settle down to the concrete actualities of adult life. Some—those who aspire to be mind workers—seek to weave those capacities for abstraction together with reality rooted perspectives into a whole that will combine the power and freedom of the former with the substance of the latter.

The many vicissitudes of the cognitive line of development, and the fact that full formal function is achieved by only a modest percentage of the population can be used as an illustration of a very general principle of development in adolescence: adolescence is the time when the principle of development by stages begins to lose its overriding power and takes its place as one among many organizing principles as an explanatory principle for the complexity of human behavior. Through childhood, the concept of development by stages is an excellent first approximation. By early adolescence, to begin to cover the increasing range of variation at a given age, it becomes increasingly necessary to weave in such organizing principles as diagnosis, favored defensive patterns, character formation, educational level, sociocultural categories. By late adolescence and adulthood, the stage of development is only a part of the over-all picture, and a wide range of individual variation is the rule.

Two pathological outcomes deserve special emphasis. The special quality of abstraction is a prominent feature of thought disorder in schizophrenia. Because flights and excesses are so commonly seen among normal adolescents greatly caught up in but not yet adequately in control of this new cognitive capacity, one of the recurrent challenges for the therapist is to try to distinguish normal adolescent "irregularities" of thought from seriously pathological thought disorder. This can be a difficult distinction even for the expert. A diametrically opposite trend can be seen in delinquent adolescents where the capacity for abstraction is commonly greatly underdeveloped, in large measure a casualty of their overinvestment in direct concrete action: Thought is something one does while counting to ten. Delinquent adolescents rarely take that much time before acting on their impulses. As a consequence, they rarely find themselves troubled by second thoughts—usually not even by first thoughts about the probable consequences of that next move they're about to make. Therapy with such patients may very well be directed, in part, at trying to reverse that trend.

Sexual Development

For girls, the onset of menstruation is a physical and psychological event of paramount importance. Within recent decades the average age of menarche in most Western countries studied has been dropping at the rate of about four months per decade. As a consequence, a girl is likely to have her first menstrual period almost a year earlier than her mother did. The current average age in the United States is about 12.5 years. The reasons for this trend are not altogether established, but probably improved health and diet play a major role. For most middle-class educated women in our time, the first menstrual period rarely comes as a surprise and seems to be taken in stride more often than some of the older literature would suggest. But that is not to say that the same matter-of-factness prevails at deeper levels; generally not. Menarche invariably is an event with profound psychological implications. There are the pitfalls inherent in the troublesome fantasies inevitably associated with blood, and with uncontrolled discharge from one's bottom. Above all there is the enormous range of both universal and exquisitely individual fantasies and feelings about the transition from girlhood to womanhood and the advent of the possibility of having a baby.

For boys, first ejaculation plays a somewhat similar role, also marking the transition from boyhood to young manhood with a dramatic genital event. According to Kinsey's data, this takes place about two-thirds of the time in masturbation and about one third of the time in the form of a nocturnal emission (a wet dream). Parents do not forewarn their sons about first nocturnal emission as regularly as they do their daughters about first menstruation. But because the first ejaculation is either deliberately sought in masturbation or occurs during sleep only to be discovered as "something starchy on the bedclothes" the next morning, it is not commonly experienced as seriously unsettling, though it can be where conflicts about sexuality are intense or if the nocturnal emission touches off previously intense conflicts around bedwetting.

According to the most recent data on adolescent sexuality, it is not until late adolescence that 50 per cent of young people begin to have intercourse. As a consequence, most adolescent sexual activity is masturbatory. For boys, masturbation to orgasm usually begins by early or middle adolescence. By late adolescence over 90 per cent have begun, according to Kinsey's data. For a young man, failure to have begun masturbating by late adolescence is highly associated with sexual inhibition and fairly intense conflicts about the body. Based on that information alone, such a young man deserves the opportunity for referral for therapy or, at least, for a consultation. Average frequencies of masturbation for adolescent males are in the range of one to three times a week, although there is a wide range of normal variation. Unusually high frequencies are associated with the syndrome of compulsive masturbation, but a criterion more psychologically meaningful than frequency is that compulsive masturbation is done and experienced virtually without pleasure, driven more by pervasive anxiety (and the search for relief of that anxiety) than by sexual impulse and the experience of gratification. Among adolescent girls, the Kinsey data shows only about 20 per cent have begun to masturbate by age 15, that percentage leveling off at about 60 per cent by the twenties. The data on frequency of masturbation for those girls who do begin also shows a lower level of activity than the range for boys, the average being in the range of once every other week. This data tends to support the general impression that the impulse to seek sexual gratification through masturbation is rather less pressing for girls than for boys, although there is wide variation for both boys and girls, and unquestionably sociocultural forces also play a major role in facilitating or inhibiting this behavior. For a girl never or rarely to have masturbated to orgasm during adolescence and yet to go on to experience a full unimpaired capacity for sexual responsiveness in intercourse would not be rare. The same would be rare for a boy.

Most middle-class youngsters have ample exposure to the information that masturbation is normal and causes neither mental or physical damage. There is nonetheless considerable guilt and anxiety connected with it, deriving largely from the fantasies and conflicts—both conscious and unconscious—that are almost universally associated with masturbation.

A recurrent situation in clinical work with adolescents is the young man of high school or college age who comes in greatly distressed that he may be a homosexual. Adolescence is indeed the time of life when true homosexuality tends to become overt. But the vast majority of adolescents who come in with this complaint turn out to be youngsters who are suffering from the same fears and anxieties about heterosexuality as their peers, only doing less well with progressive mastery of those fears. The more strongly those fears block gratification and expression of heterosexual impulses, the more strongly the homosexual component of the inherent relatively universal bisexuality emerges as the only available alternative. It is some sudden awareness of that emergent homosexual component that usually triggers the intense distress reaction that brings these youngsters to the therapist. Some may be but most are not on the foreordained path to homosexuality that they fear. When there are social supports for bisexuality the picture is further complicated both for the diagnostician and for the young people themselves.

Adolescence in the Ghetto

Ghetto adolescents present one of the most pressing and challenging issues of our time. The violence, the destructiveness, the self-destructiveness, and the aimlessness of adolescent lives gone awry in a setting of pervasive social and family pathology rightly engages the lion's share of the time and energy of those who work in the inner city, especially in the large public and private institutions. All the basic principles of adolescent development apply to this group of young people, as they do to every other; but there are also the special characteristics of ghetto adolescents deriving from their special social circumstances and life experiences, and it is to these that we turn our attention.

Communication between ghetto adolescents and middle-class professionals is complicated by unfamiliarity and stereotyped expectations on both sides. Guardedness and expecting the worst is the rule among all adolescents brought unwillingly to some adult authority figure. But it is all the more severe when the age and authority gap is compounded by racial difference, by major class difference, and by the language difference that can present such an enormous obstacle to communication—all the more so when the influence of that language difference is obscured by the assumption that both middle-class interviewer and ghetto adolescent share a common standard English. Sometimes they do; more often they do not. To work well with ghetto adolescents it is necessary to be able to understand ghetto language when one hears it, especially in a group setting where youngsters will be talking among themselves. The problem is partly vocabulary, partly cadence, style, sound, and implicit understandings. As with any new language, the more one listens, the clearer it becomes.

Ghetto adolescents commonly have had a fragmented educational experience which, compounded by a host of influences within the family affecting cognitive development, can give even the best and the brightest difficulty when placed in educational competition with middle-class youngsters. This has to be taken into account in all efforts to get ghetto youngsters the education they need. Whereas it might be enough simply to get a middle-class youngster back into school after some crisis, the ghetto adolescent usually requires much more attention. He needs to be placed at a level he can manage, to be taught by teachers alert to the special issues involved and given ongoing psychological support.

Sexual experience, for both boys and girls in the ghetto, commonly begins much earlier and is probably much more frequent in the context of a passing or frankly exploitative relation. Experiences with intercourse in very early adolescence are far from rare. At the same time, there is no shortage of shy, inhibited, or inexperienced youngsters in the ghetto. Among the experienced as well as among the inexperienced, one will find a veritable hodgepodge of misconceptions, fears, and illusions about sexuality, pregnancy, and childbirth. The need for good sex education for ghetto adolescents is loud and clear.

Street-wise youngsters can have a curious mixture (curious, that is, by middle-class standards) of remarkably early independence and unfulfilled dependency needs, of hardened maturity covering tender immaturity. It is important to be mindful of *both* sides of that contrast. The tough youngster who breaks down and virtually melts into parent-child closeness with a youth worker and then snaps out of it to be angry at himself as well as at the adult who, perhaps unwittingly, precipitated the emergence of those long repressed yearnings, is usually greatly unsettled by the experience of such intense and conflicting feelings. It's better if at least the worker understands.

The gang ethos plays a supremely important role in the life experience of young men growing up in the ghetto. For mere survival, it can be essential to know that one can call "one's boys"—and for others to know that. The price is loyalty to the gang. Before the importance of "not being a punk," all other considerations can pale, including Thou Shalt Not Kill. The ethic of "not being a punk" is a double-edged sword. It is perhaps first and foremost among the potential sources of pride and self-respect and, at the same time, one of the most recurrent sources of serious difficulty. It makes these youngsters vulnerable to challenges flung at them by the most disturbed and violent members of their peer group. It works against their capacity to tolerate the inevitable "feeling like a punk" that goes with trying to make it in school or with trying to make it on the job (where even under the best of circumstances one has to have some degree of tolerance for taking gaff from the boss, from other workers, and even from the customers).

Orientation toward the future (deferring immediate gratification in the service of long-range goals) is understandably much less developed among ghetto youngsters who live in an environment where the future (as seen in the lives of parents and neighbors) looks bleak. When young people can see that even mere survival is a matter of real uncertainty, understandably enough, it seems best to live in the here and now.

The exposure to violence, to death, and to the harsher side of life, so commonplace in the ghetto, can lead to hardness, callousness, indifference, and a blunting of the finer feelings. That is so manifestly adaptive and responsive to external events in the ghetto as to be virtually a necessity. However, it can work against the development of the empathic response to the pain of others which serves as such an important restraint against doing violence to others. The foregoing shouldn't be overstated; even in a gang fight it happens not infrequently that someone is judged to be "going too far" and is stopped by his peers.

Identity formation is obviously greatly complicated for the black adolescent by the harsh facts of racism. The powerful movement in the direction of expanded black consciousness and pride has been of enormous advantage to young blacks seeking a group identity to which they could relate. The grim realities of ghetto life nonetheless remain, and even the improvements in recent years which provide long overdue opportunities to black adolescents to move increasingly to middle-class schools and careers bring with them the special problems of being "between two worlds."

Work with ghetto adolescents calls for a balance between an appreciation of the ways in which they are influenced by the special circumstances of ghetto life, and an equally deep appreciation of the fact that they share with all young people the universals of the experience and the conflicts characteristic of the years of adolescence.

Principles of Treatment

Good therapy, adolescent therapy included, is always better the more it is informed by a broad and deep acquaintance with the phenomenology of normal and pathological development. The wider the background of knowledge and experience (first *and* second hand) the more likely that a wide range of possibilities will come to mind for consideration, and the more likely that things will go well in evaluation and in treatment.

In therapy, honesty is always the best policy (in fact the only policy—it is our stock in trade) but especially so in therapy with adolescents. Adolescents are remarkably effective detectors of hypocrisy and are not yet of an age at which they might be disposed to forgive you your trespasses.

Actively building a working alliance must have top priority from the outset with adolescent patients, who are so commonly brought against their will with an age-specific readiness to assume, not without reason, that the therapist is basically one of "them" (adults, parents, school, agency, "establishment"). The best way to begin is to try to find something with which the adolescent himself is truly dissatisfied and to organize the work from the beginning as much as possible around that issue. This is not always possible, but it is always worth a serious try. Where the adolescent is forced to meet with the therapist, at least that should be freely acknowledged. In any event, most adolescents, especially those in trouble, experience it as an agreeable surprise to encounter an "official adult" who is absolutely on the level, who listens, and who is genuinely interested in their life, their feelings, their wishes, and their experiences. That can come as a breadth of fresh air, and can get things off to a roaring good start despite the most adverse of circumstances.

Silence is poorly tolerated by most adolescents, especially from an adult in a position of authority. The skillful adolescent therapist manages to fill the silences, even with a bit of chatting, before they get too lengthy. He spends a fair amount of time "thinking out loud" about the material. That keeps things moving along at a pace sufficient to keep the adolescent interested and engaged, and tends to elicit all sorts of reactions. The "thinking out loud" should always be expressed in a way that leaves plenty of room for disagreement and for, "What do you think about that?"

Young adolescents commonly take it for granted that the parents will have private conversations with the therapist. But with adolescents of any age in the throes of rebellion, it is crucial to avoid even the appearance of being in league with the parents. From the outset the primary bond should be to the adolescent patient; and confidentiality, if it is promised, should be firmly respected. It may not always be possible to maintain an absolutely pure confidential relation; some adolescent therapists prefer to deal with that difficulty by openly accepting some measure of identification with the *best* intentions of the parents and/or social agency, coping as best they can with the extra difficulties those commitments and contacts create in their relation with the adolescent. Others (the author included) prefer to lean in the opposite direction, especially in outpatient work, giving top priority to forging a bond with the adolescent and coping with the difficulties such a strategy can create in maintaining a responsible and trusting relation with parents and agencies, who unquestionably have their legitimate stake in the process. There are no easy answers here, and cases do differ.

In office work, one approach that works well for the first session is to see everyone (adolescent plus parents), to listen to whomever begins the explanation of the problem (usually a parent), to turn every so often to the adolescent for clarifications and objections, and then, after the broad outline and some details of the situation have been set down, to ask the parents to step out, and take it from there with the adolescent alone. This constitutes a powerful nonverbal communication (which should be a valid one, and not a sham) that it is the adolescent who really counts in the treatment relation you are trying to set up. The parents may have a very understandable wish to talk with the therapist privately, but in general it is probably better to wait. If things go well, it is almost always possible to talk with the parents later on without rocking the boat. However, in a confidential treatment relation with the adolescent, it is essential to tell the adolescent what was said, and to inform the parents that you will do so beforehand.

In therapy with adults, a legitimate working stance for the therapist can be to work on only what the patient wants to work on. With adolescent patients, this can be seriously unsatisfactory. Young people are often closing off very real potentialities in their life at an age when many options are still wide open and many choices still reversible. It behooves the therapist to point this out in a way that will catch the adolescent's attention and interest. At times this can get perilously close to a kind of evangelism, but not doing it at all leaves untouched too much of the heart of the matter in adolescent psychopathology.

SCHIZOPHRENIA

In this as in so many other respects, adolescence is a time of transition between two other somewhat more stable states: childhood schizophrenia and adult schizophrenia.

Where adolescence has been preceded by a distinctly atypical childhood (bizarre behavior, extreme withdrawal), schizophrenia in adolescence is likely to be a continuation of a lifelong insidious and progressive "process schizophrenia" with a relatively poor prognosis. Where childhood seems to have been reasonably within normal range, one is more likely to be dealing with the early onset of adult schizophrenia (or, in late adolescence, with a quite common age of onset). In such cases, one is more likely to see the initial episode take the form of an acute break, and the prognosis is statistically somewhat better, with some of the acute breaks resolving back to a relatively intact state (although of course others do not, but resolve instead to some degree of chronic schizophrenia, especially if there are recurrent episodes).

Schizophrenia in adolescence tends to be somewhat more ambiguous in its manifestations than schizophrenia in either childhood or adulthood. When there are clear-cut delusions, hallucinations, or grossly disordered thinking, the diagnosis is made readily enough. But more commonly, one sees a blurred picture which raises suspicions, but leaves lots of doubts. The criteria that should tend to raise suspicions are: a quality of illogic or vagueness in thinking that seems different from or well beyond the more ordinary kind of illogic or vagueness that one has to learn to recognize from experience with normal adolescents; pervasivensss of pathology (many aspects of functioning affected); persistence of ordinarily transient pathology; behavior that doesn't make sense even when looked at from the point of view of the motivations and values of the adolescent himself; extreme philosophical preoccupation expressed in terms exceedingly difficult to follow; inappropriate suspiciousness, withdrawal, guardedness, hostility; incapacity to relate to others and a feeling of unrelatedness experienced by the interviewer; flattened affect. Any of the items on the foregoing list can be present in normal adolescence to some degree, but the more they are pronounced, persistent, pervasive, and inexplicable, the more one should consider the possibility of an underlying schizophrenic process. Acute schizophrenia has to be distinguished from acute psychotic states brought about by hallucinogens or stimulants. Of course, the information that someone has just recently taken pills makes "tripping" the most likely explanation, but even without such information, a history of past drug-taking plus a predominance of visual hallucinations makes hallucinogens a likely possibility, and "high" manic behavior should certainly lead one to consider the possibility of "ups." Such patients almost always require medication and hospitalization, although it is possible for experienced people to "talk down" such patients without either. Sometimes patients have recurrences ("flashbacks") long after having used the drug. Some proportion of "flashbacks" are undoubtedly related to an independent underlying schizophrenic process. As a consequence, isolated "bad trips" have to be *distinguished from* schizophrenia, whereas recurrent "flashbacks" may be *associated with* schizophrenia.

Acute psychotic episodes usually require hospitalization and medication. Subsequent outpatient psychotherapy tends to be long term and supportive, encouraging socialization, helping the patient to restrain inappropriate behavior and to build ego functions and adaptive mechanisms (in a way that can come very close to teaching), and, occasionally, relieving by supportive interpretation the stress that conflict can impose on an already fragile ego.

Depression, "Emptiness," Hypochondriasis, and Suicide

Reactive depression, which is an immediate reaction to events in real life, can be severe at any age, adolescence certainly included. Endogenous depression, i.e., depression not *primarily* responsive to external events is associated more with later life, but it commonly emerges out of a background of lifelong depressive inclination which is not uncommonly already present by adolescence.

Depression in the adolescent years tends to have its own characteristic forms. It is not rare to see the usual mood of heavy sadness, with a loss of vitality and capacity for enjoyment similar to depression in adulthood. But especially characteristic of the adolescent years would be depression manifest in the form of "emptiness" and boredom covered over by overt and even dramatic efforts defensively to fill the emptiness and to counter the boredom with drugs, delinquency, thrill-seeking, and risk-taking of all sorts. Energy, daring, and intense activity are unquestionably age-specific characteristics of the years of youth, but where they seem driven and self-destructive, look for underlying depressive pathology.

Another characteristic manifestation of depression in adolescence is hypochondriasis. Preoccupation with the body is such a prominent feature of normal adolescent development, it is little wonder that depression in these years should become focused on those normal concerns, exaggerating and distorting them into the forms we recognize as hypochondriasis. These can range from mild and transient fears all the way to severely incapacitating convictions of illness, injury, inadequacy, and deformity. At the more severe end of the spectrum, a note of bizarreness should raise suspicion of compensated or incipient psychotic illness underlying the depression. Being relieved of unwelcome demands and securing an extra measure of dependency gratification are secondary gains of hypochondriasis that can make it all the more difficult to help these young people. At a more intrapsychic level, the defensive advantage that accrues from being able to displace onto the body depression and anxiety originating elsewhere in conflicts that they would prefer not to think about can create essentially the same difficulties.

Suicide is not a frequent occurrence in adolescence, but suicidal thoughts, fantasies, impulses, and even preoccupations are quite common, as are suicide attempts and gestures, particularly among late adolescent girls and young women as part of an intense reactive depression in the aftermath of some loss, most typically, the loss of a boy friend. In such cases, the prognosis for the adolescent is strongly dependent on the degree to which the suicide attempt marshalls concern and support from within the family. Where the family responds, the prognosis is much more favorable than when it does not. One of my colleagues is fond of saying that when an adolescent makes a serious suicide attempt there is someone in the family who would just as soon they were dead. That's worth looking for in a family with a seriously self-destructive adolescent and, if present, can provide a most useful place to start working on the pathological relations within the family as they are affecting the adolescent.

Among adolescent boys, the self-destructive trends tend to merge with dynamic issues having to do with proving one's masculinity. Gang warfare, "not being a punk," accepting and even provoking challenge, drug abuse, recklessly and adventurously risking one's life, especially with cars—all have social and group dimensions ("I'm not the only one") and are distorted near-neighbors to some potentially positive dynamics which come dramatically to the fore in adolescence (trial by ordeal, testing and proving oneself). But a careful look at the inner dynamics of those young people who get hurt repeatedly and who are recurrently involved in self-destructive behavior will reveal, again and again, frankly self-destructive motivations based partially on "not caring that much" anymore, and partially on a kind of testing to see if the powers-that-be really care. In Polynesia, one time-honored means of coping with the feelings of depression, shame, and self-destructiveness stimulated by having suffered a loss, including loss of face, is to set out to sea in an outrigger without provisions. If favorable winds and currents bring one to safety, one feels that the Gods have smiled and one is judged worthy of surviving. This can also be conceptualized partly as providing an opportunity for unconscious inner forces to operate from behind the scenes subtly but powerfully to tip the balance one way or the other. There's a lot of that kind of thing going on in adolescence, not only in Polynesia. Reckless driving provides a perfect vehicle for self-destructive impulses. An unknown but sizeable proportion of all accident fatalities, particularly in adolescence, are deliberate or unconsciously intended suicides.

Finally, it seems worth emphasizing that one of the most important clinical features of a disturbed adolescence, closely related to depression, is a kind of profound emptiness. This can reflect depression, blocked feelings, impoverishment of experience, schizoid or schizophrenic difficulty with object relations, deprivation of affection and human relations throughout childhood—any or all of these. But the final outcome is commonplace among disturbed adolescents. And the word itself suggests the most common defensive mechanism they use to counter it (when they do): they attempt to fill that emptiness with action and its consequences, with drugs, and sometimes with food. Usually to no avail. The task for the therapist is to try to understand the roots of that emptiness. And to try to help the patient fill it with more solid fare: more genuinely satisfying action and mental life, meaningful work, and meaningful human relations.

Delinquency

Delinquency is perhaps most simply defined as antisocial action. For most young people, adolescence is a time of action and activity, a developmental characteristic rooted in the psychobiology of adolescence. Little wonder that the form of psychopathology perhaps most closely associated with adolescence should be delinquency. Also little wonder that it should be the form of adolescent psychopathology perhaps most fully studied, since society has such a direct stake in trying to do something about it.

Insofar as delinquency is defined as *antisocial* action, the pathology is defined "from the outside." (Of course this is true for all psychiatric diagnoses to *some* degree, but for none other perhaps quite so directly). However, some students of the subject prefer to emphasize the internal roots of delinquency, stressing the impulsiveness and the failure of controls from within. For a good over-all understanding of delinquency, it is best to combine both points of view.

Early studies in the field have concentrated on the hereditary biological element, noting the tendency for delinquency to "run in the family." As we have come to understand more about how great a role can be played by learning and identification (not to mention the influence on successive generations of the same social forces), much of that early work seems dated. Distinguished work on delinquency from a psychodynamic point of view was done early in this century in Vienna by Aichhorn (1948). The perspectives on delinquency and on its treatment developed by this wise and canny man remain a model for work done to this day. Psychoanalytic perspectives on delinquency have concerned themselves with failures in the development of superego, and with the constellation of causes behind that failure. The studies of Johnson (1949) on "superego lacunae"—resulting from the subtle ways in which parents can encourage their children to act out the parent's own impulses—deserve special mention. So does a more recent contribution by Anderson (1968), which statistically substantiates the importance of the father's active presence during the years of latency in the prevention of subsequent delinquency in adolescence. Within recent decades, sociological perspectives have been richly developed, emphasizing the background of poverty and inner-city street life that tends to generate delinquent behavior. There is also the well-known study by the Gluecks (1950) tabulating a whole compendium of factors statistically associated with the eventual development of delinquency.

It might be helpful to list a few of the recognizably different kinds of adolescent patients one might see and identify as delinquents. They can differ rather widely in the clinical picture they present and in implications for treatment:

For some adolescents, impulsive antisocial action is closely tied to active neurotic conflict. Antisocial action can be a final common pathway for any of a variety of conflict areas, including conflicts around masculinity and feminity (various forms of aggression and sexual acting-out behavior), independence (running away), "negative identity" (better to be a bad somebody than a well-behaved nobody), the dynamics of depression and self-destructiveness (when life feels hardly worth living and when one feels that one has nothing to lose, exciting and dangerous activity can serve as an active defense against depression), or any of the virtually infinite variety of psychodynamic issues that can characterize the human condition in adolescence. Where the neurotic conflict that underlies the delinquent behavior is still alive and accessible, insight-oriented psychotherapy makes excellent sense as a treatment of choice.

For some adolescents, impaired in their capacities to "make it" in the peer group and in school by virtue of serious adaptive deficiencies (intellectual and otherwise), the temptation to band together into a group of "outsiders" to seek a kind of distinction, excitement and success through illegal, antisocial, and destructive activities can be very powerful indeed. I am speaking here not so much of ghetto youngsters where external factors play such a powerful role, but mostly of the kind of working-class or middle-class adolescent whose *internal* limitations interfere with his "making it" in a setting that is *not* particularly stacked against him. Therapy here must find some way to help these youngsters feel more hopeful about themselves, must help them find some way to achieve, and must provide some equally engaging equivalent for the powerful lure of the delinquent group process.

For ghetto youngsters, the context of social forces within which they come to adolescence and through which they move as adolescents is of enormous importance. Behavior regarded as delinquent by middle-class standards is commonplace, accepted, and even valued "on the street," especially within the social structure of the gang. This must be taken into account in assessing anti-social behavior among ghetto adolescents. Worthy of special mention here—only part of the larger picture, but an important part—is the ghetto youngster with impressive ego capacities who gets caught up in delinquent activity, not uncommonly as the leader. In the ghetto, delinquent activity can be conceptualized as one established route to success and prestige within the subculture. Youngsters who emerge as leaders or who "succeed" as delinquents are often youngsters who have a lot going for them. If one can help such inherently able youngsters turn those capacities to productive ends, obviously the advantages to them and to society can be enormous. Such people are not rare. But helping them to turn themselves around probably is.

Some delinquents are primarily narcissistic characters who, out of grandiosity, refuse to play the game by anyone else's rules. The treatment of narcissistic characters is one of the major emerging themes in the psychoanalytic work of our time (see Kohut, 1971; Kernberg, 1967, 1968, 1970).

Some delinquents, perhaps the most seriously disturbed of all, are people with a pervasively disturbed capacity for object relations, "empty," incapable of feelings for others, the drifters, virtually without conscience, what one might call the archetypal psychopath. Some of them are adolescents. Such patients are, to say the very least, difficult to engage in therapy—of any sort.

A perspective on the psychotherapeutic approaches to delinquency that is both useful and amusing is offered by Noshpitz (1969), who groups therapists into four categories: (a) reality hammerers, (b) dissimulators, (c) interpreters, and (d) gratifiers. The *reality hammerers* patiently and repeatedly address themselves to the islands of healthy adaptive functioning in the sea of delinquent pathology, repeatedly pointing out to delinquent youngsters how they create their own difficulties and how they might do otherwise. Noshpitz likes to emphasize "I just cannot understand how somebody of your intelligence can get himself into so much trouble," pointing to concrete details of what they did and how it predictably led to trouble. Reality hammerers try to avoid moralizing. Although moral issues are involved and certainly can get mentioned, delinquent adolescents have usually heard more than enough moralizing and are experts at blocking it out. Instead, the emphasis is on the realities of life and on alternative modes of adapting.

The *dissimulators* attempt to bore from within, becoming so knowledgeable about the world of the delinquent as to be able to beat the patient at his own game: "deceiving the deceiver." Aichhorn was apparently a master of this approach. If the therapist, who comes across as a master manipulator, chooses not to play the game of crime, the delinquent may well come to wonder: "Whom am I to try?"

The *interpreters* use a fairly standard, insight-oriented approach, listening for the dynamics that underly the acting-out behavior and trying to alter the patient's internal equilibrium by making him aware, even against his will, of what his behavior means and what he is trying to accomplish with it in term of his own intrapsychic economy. The hope is that interpretation will alter that equilibrium, with the assumption that acting-out behavior thrives best in an atmosphere of unawareness. Of course, delinquent patients have ample capacity for "not hearing" interpretations. But sometimes a correct depth interpretation can be remarkably effective. The interpreters would say: "At least it is worth a try."

The *gratifiers* concentrate on trying to be the good parent the delinquent never had, trying to generate some facsimile of that loving relation which is at the core of the process of normal superego development, during which children accept self-restraint and "proper" standards of behavior out of love for the parent to retain that love.

Each of the foregoing has its pitfalls and failures. Each has its successes. Most therapists use them all.

REFERENCES

Aichhorn, A. (1948), *Wayward Youth.* New York: Viking.

Anderson, R. (1968), Where's Dad: Paternal Deprivation in Delinquency. *Archives of General Psychiatry,* 18: 641-649.

Erikson, E. (1959), *Identity and the Life Cycle* [Psychological Issues, Monograph 1, pp. 101-164]. New York: International Universities Press.

Freidenberg, E. (1962), *The Vanishing Adolescent.* New York: Dell.

——— (1965), *The Dignity of Youth,* Boston: Beacon Press.

——— (1966), *Coming of Age in America.* New York: Random House.

Getzels, J. & Jackson, P. (1962), *Creativity and Intelligence.* New York: John Wiley.

Glueck, S. & Glueck, E. T. (1950), *Unravelling Juvenile Delinquency.* Boston: Harvard University Press.

Hudson, L. (1966), *Contrary Imaginations.* New York: Schocken Books.

Johnson, A. (1949), Sanctions for Superego Lacunae of Adolescents. In: *Searchlights on Delinquency,* ed. K. R. Eissler, New York: International Universities Press, pp. 225-245.

Keniston, K. (1967), *The Uncommitted: Alienated Youth in American Society.* New York: Dell.

——— (1968), *Young Radicals: Notes on Committed Youth.* New York: Harcourt Brace Janovich.

——— (1971), *Youth as a Stage of Life.* In: *Adolescent Psychiatry,* Vol. 1. New York: Basic Books.

Noshpitz, J., (1969), Psychotherapy vs. Delinquency. Unpublished address given at Department of Psychiatry, Albert Einstein College of Medicine, Bronx, New York.

SUGGESTED READING

Blos, P. (1962), *On Adolescence,* New York: Free Press.

Caplan, G. & Lebovici, S. (1969), *Adolescence: Psychological Perspectives.* New York: Basic Books.

Feinstein, S., Giovacchini, P. & Miller, A. (1971), *Adolescent Psychiatry.* New York: Basic Books.

Freud, A. (1936), *The Ego and the Mechanisms of Defense.* The Writings of Anna Freud, Vol. 2. New York: International Universities Press, 1966, pp. 137-151.

——— (1958), Adolescence. In: *Research at the Hampstead Child-Therapy Clinic, and Other Papers.* The Writings of Anna Freud, Vol. 5. New York: International Universities Press, pp. 136-166.

Group for the Advancement of Psychiatry (1968), Report No. 68, *Normal Adolescence.* Washington, D.C.: Group for the Advancement of Psychiatry.

Holmes, D. (1964), *The Adolescent in Psychotherapy.* New York: Little Brown.

Meeks, J. (1971), *The Fragile Alliance.* Baltimore: Williams & Wilkins, Co.

Tanner, J. M. (1962), *Growth at Adolescence.* Springfield, Ill.: Charles C Thomas.

CHAPTER THIRTEEN
Adulthood

RICHARD BURNETT, M.D.

As the tumult of the adolescent process subsides, the rate of intrapsychic change slows down markedly. A certain "crystallization" occurs, giving the personality its permanent cast, a sharper definition of character. The young adult becomes more predictable in his behavior, reacting to situations in characteristic ways. Less self-centered and dependent, he is more dependable and responsible in his relations with others. His emotions are more stable, and there is greater constancy in his loves and hates. His interests are less diffuse, more focused. He is more aware of who he is and how he fits into society. One might say he has "settled down" or "found himself."

These phenomena are manifestations of a new intrapsychic organization—the final and permanent one of maturity.[1] It is a balanced and stable organization due to the hierarchical arrangement of elements that have been carried forward through the various stages. It thus contains a complete record of the individual's development.

[1]The terms *adulthood* and *maturity* are used interchangeably in this chapter. Both refer to the (relative) completion of the developmental process that follows the innate maturational ground plan.

Established within the total personality is a rank order of the psychic institutions (the ego being dominant), as well as of the elements within each institution. This was described first by Freud, in 1905—who emphasized its instinctual-drive aspects—as the establishment of *genital primacy,* and, more recently, in the broader context of ego psychology, as *identity* formation (Erikson, 1950), and *consolidations leading to the final formation of the self* (Blos, 1962).

The Instinctual Drives

The process of unfolding psychosexual phases that Freud described comes to a close. The final loud and clear assertion of the innate maturational force is in the pubertal gift of the adult sexual organs and functions—the last of the constitutional "givens." Now, elements of the earlier phases that are not sublimated or integrated into the character structure find direct expression under the primacy of the genital zone, which has become the bearer of the mainstream of the instinctual currents. No longer pressing for independent satiation, the pregenital strivings become tributaries that feed into and swell the mainstream, contributing the forepleasure that builds toward, and subserves, the climactic end-pleasure—the orgasm. In the female, the clitoris relinquishes primacy to the vagina, although retaining an important initiatory role in foreplay. The genital organization is completed by the joining of this newly acquired orgastic capacity to the developed capacity for mature object love (more fully described below). Full, direct, genital drive gratification, if not an absolute necessity, facilitates the maintenance of the equilibrium of the adult intrapsychic organization.

In the normal adult, much of the aggressive drive has been tamed by neutralization and is expressed largely as constructive activity toward adaptive goals, e.g., in finding an occupation, pursuing it, and advancing in it; in finding a love object, pursuing it, and developing and sustaining the relationship. The healthy adult has learned how to cooperate as well as compete—and with whom to do each. He has more friendly rivalries and fewer hostile ones. But he is not incapable of passionate anger, constancy in hate, or counteraggressive action in the service of self-preservation. He is consequently not prone to self-hate and self-destructive actions.

The Ego

In the mature ego, as in the drive organization, we find hierarchical arrangements—of its functions, interests and attitudes, and defense mechanisms. Primary autonomous functions have remained intact. There has been a marked increase in secondary autonomy, with expansion of the conflict-free sphere of the ego and large increments of neutralized energy available for adaptive use. This reduces vulnerability to severe regression—another important factor in stabilizing the mature organization.

At the top, the higher ego functions of synthesis and integration, in conjunction with judgment and the intellectual functions, may be said to constitute a "primacy of intelligence" (Hartmann, 1939), which organizes and regulates all—even irrationality, and controlled, limited temporary regressions in the service of the ego. Although secondary process predominates, there is still a place for primary process in dreams, humor, and creative imagination; there is still a place for illusion in art, in the state of being in love, or in religion; and in the altered state of consciousness at the height of orgasm, the early ego state of fusion with the object is momentarily restored. These provisions for dynamic equilibrium also contribute to the stability of the mature organization.

The higher functions have an executive role in ordering the personality—in the processes of identity, or self-formation. They are responsible for such higher defense mechanisms as reaction-formation and sublimation predominating over such primitive ones as denial and projection. Experience of actual coital sensations and their affective reverberations puts the final and definite stamp on the heterosexual identity and the permanent direction of object choice. As the feeling of having unlimited choices contracts, emerging preferences in love needs and ego interests gradually lead to firm commitments in the choice of object and vocation (Blos, 1962).

The higher functions also insure the possibility of further development. Despite the decline of the maturational push and the reduced plasticity that consolidations bring, a healthy mature organization retains sufficient flexibility for a long time to come for development to proceed by learning from experience—the integrative function of the ego taking over where maturation left off. Important events such as marriage, pregnancy, parenthood, illness, death of loved ones, divorce, job loss, and climacterium present adaptive challenges that may overtax the stabilizing mechanisms and lead to regression. But they may also stimulate the reworking of residues of conflict, which may eventuate in fresh consolidations and increments to maturity. This development does not, of course, proceed in orderly, sequential phases reaching new levels of organization.

The Superego

At maturity the superego has lost some of its harsh and punitive quality and become more tolerant—it is now more a guide, less a prosecutor. Its core contents—the taboos against incest and parenticide—remain unalterable moral imperatives in every culture. Thus, although it now permits heterosexual object choice, it still imposes the requirement that it may not be a (too) incestuous one. Some of its elements are reprojected onto the environment, facilitating adaptation by helping to knit the individual into the community, as, for example, when we join with others behind a leader to "clean up City Hall."

The ego ideal, subjected to the ego's more accurate perception of the self in relation to the environment, is also modified. Renouncing the aspiration to omnipotence, it sets more realistic goals based on achievement and gratification. Independence and responsibility are increased as the regulation of self-esteem from within is stabilized, and self-consciousness and social anxiety are mitigated. We cannot, of course, say what the specific content of the ego ideal should be. Collaborating with the ego's synthetic function, it integrates certain of the ideals, values, and social roles the culture offers into hierarchies that emerge as personal, ego-syntonic value systems, standards, ideologies and world views—modulating the rampant idealism of adolescence (Blos, 1962). Although the superego did not exist at the beginning of life, it was in the ground plan; and although much modified, it does not wither away at maturity, but remains as much a part of "natural" man as his instinctual life.

Concepts of Normality and Mental Health

The innate ground plan has guided development to the achievement of the mature psychic organization. No further developmental phases sparked by maturation will occur, and regulation, instead of coming from within, will henceforth consist predominantly of fitting together the developed capacities with the environment, i.e., adaptation.

Once, when Freud was asked, "What does a normal adult do well?," his off-the-cuff response was, "*lieben und arbeiten*" (loving and working) (Erikson, 1950). Man must work to survive, and though there is pleasure in the successful struggle, he must love to make it worthwhile—and if he cannot, he must fall ill (Freud, 1914).

What avenues does the environment make available for the exercise of man's developed capacities? All societies offer certain social roles and institutions, e.g., marriage for the need "loving," and an occupation for the need "working." They are as imperfect as the individual's developed capacities, and the difficulties in articulation are manifold and well known, both as individual problems of marital and occupational maladjustment and as social problems, such as the care of neglected children, the population explosion, crime, or unemployment. To the extent that one can reconcile individual needs and social demands, adaptation is successful and health is maintained. It may be accomplished through changing the self, changing the environment, or both. The mentally ill cannot adapt well in even the most favorable environment. And even the healthy cannot adapt well when societies fail to provide such average expectations as job opportunities.

Hartmann, tracing the development of our concepts of normality and mental health, tells us that although each formulation contributes to our understanding, none is complete, and we must ultimately rely upon studying how people adapt. When adult psychopathology was the focus of interest, mental health was thought of as the antithesis, i.e., as lack of symptoms. With the discovery of the role of conflict in the production of symptoms, health appeared to be lack of conflict.

But increasing knowledge of the ego and its defenses, and the study of character, have obscured the sharp line between health and illness. Instead, they seem to be points on a continuum, with the pathological an exaggeration of the normal, as, for example, when orderliness—a useful, adaptive trait—is carried to absurd lengths as a symptom in compulsive neurosis; or an optimistic disposition is inflated to elation in mania; or distrust becomes suspicion and then delusion of persecution (in paranoia). From a slightly different point of view, normality appears to be the happy medium between pathological extremes—e.g., normal moods can be viewed as midway between depression and mania. But to draw clear lines between health and illness is still difficult and unsatisfactory.

Conflicts are found in healthy people as well as neurotics—in everyone, in fact—and their omnipresence is recognized as the human condition. Their pathogenicity, or lack of it, depends upon quantitative factors such as the relative strength of the drives and the ego and the time of their occurrence in the sequence of developmental stages. Certain conflicts and types of anxiety are seen to be typical of certain phases of development. With intensive study of children, developmental norms have been established and we have come to rely upon age and phase-adequacy as the standard for the child, correlating *normality* with the level of development attained, and *health* with sustained progress through the phases toward maturity, with only limited, temporary, reversible regression at times of stress. Severe and irreversible regression leads to deviant development or illness (A. Freud, 1965).

So far as regression is concerned, this holds true for the adult as well. But progression has become elusive. Without further sequences of phases by which to measure it, we may substitute reliance upon external evidences of "happiness" or "success" to prove progress. In simpler societies, it might be simply an accumulation of years or children. In ours, it may tend to be excessive or exclusive striving for power, fame, wealth, or social status. Or ideals colored by moral, ethical, or other value systems may be set up as standards of health. There is a tendency in this psychological era to make normality the new morality (Reider, 1950). We are exhorted, for instance, toward the ideal of "natural" or "instinctual" man, with such slogans as "express yourself," "get rid of your inhibitions," "be spontaneous—outgoing," or toward an aesthetic ideal of "be creative"—whether you are talented or not.

It is not possible to be precise and statistical with regard to health concepts. We cannot call the exceptional ("abnormal") achievements of a genius pathological. Nor would we call a person ill because he has a few cavities in his teeth—most people do. So do most people have a few quirks in their minds, and our concept of health must be broad enough to include deviations compatible with a generally satisfactory and productive life if we are not to regard everyone as ill. Those who find imperfection only in others, who can never themselves feel anxiety or depression, are suffering from what Hartmann calls a "health neurosis."

The many failures to achieve a stable mature organization attest to the magnitude of the integrative task of the ego at this phase. Pathological tendencies become more manifest and fixed if early fixations remain unrectified. Their regressive pull sometimes overcomes the urge to complete development, now weakened by the decline of the maturational push. But when the urge for the satisfactions of maturity remains strong, the further consolidations necessary to the achievement of this goal may be reached through therapy.

Sometimes there is a prolonged stalemate between progressive and regressive forces, and although the struggle may go either way, pathological outcomes are frequent. Some, fearing success or failure in mature responsibilities and the narrowed options of consolidation, cling to what they view as the "last chance" for dependency—or "freedom." Familiar examples are those who are unable to choose a mate or a vocation, finish college or a Ph.D. thesis. Others accept the trappings of maturity in its institutionalized forms of marriage and career, but merely go through the motions, without zest for the challenges or pleasure in their activities and achievements. The urge to complete development, failing to articulate with the environment through a formed identity, has become blocked or delayed. Without therapeutic intervention it may be locked into an adult organization, crystallizing in a pathological form until its force dwindles away.

It is apparent that, when we come to the clinical assessment of normality in the adult, we can no longer rely on developmental criteria alone. Instead of progression through phases, we scrutinize carefully the functioning of the mature organization in adapting to the environment. We look for intactness of primary autonomous functions of the ego, without invasion by drive derivatives. Perceptual avenues are open, not blocked, colored, or distorted. There is a continuous thread of memory from age five or six, with no major gaps (except the universal amnesia for the infantile period). Action is controlled by the ego, not the id—the normal adult acts constructively to attain realistic goals, and is not given to impulsive acting-out. He has a full range of affects, without severe anxiety or symptoms. He uses speech for communication with others, not for exhibitionistic purposes. His defense organization is flexible, mechanisms of a higher order predominating. Reality testing is adequate—sensation from inside is not confused with perception from the outside, and the external world is seen clearly as it is, not as it is wished or feared to be. We examine the functioning of the total personality in specific life situations, looking for the ability to persevere; to delay gratification; to tolerate frustration and suffering where necessary; to stand disappointments, losses, misfortunes, and failures; and the ability to enjoy the ordinary pleasures of life—love in all its aspects, social, sexual, parental—and work (A. Freud et al., 1965).

Loving—Object Relationships

Freud (1905, footnote of 1910) pointed out that in the erotic life of antiquity the instinct itself was glorified, while little account was taken of the object. With the rise of Judeo-Christian morality, and particularly of romanticism with the troubadors of the twelfth century, there was a shift toward the opposite extreme, with devaluation of love's sensual aim and exaltation of the object. Now it appears that, in the antiromanticism of the sexual revolution, the pendulum is swinging back toward the ancients' valuation with a quest for all joy and no pangs in love. Actually, in civilization, both elements are always present, in varying amounts, in the universal longing for exclusive, unrivaled tender and passionate love with an idealized object—ungratified since its inception in the oedipal phase of childhood.

Freud succeeded—where the philosophers had failed—in explaining how love's sexual aim and the idealized object are integrated. Observing the regular decline in the value placed upon the love object following each early satisfaction of the sexual aim and a corresponding increase in that value when the aim is temporarily frustrated by internal or external obstacles, he concluded that temporary obstacles are necessary to dam up libido to the proportions of falling in love. An overvaluation of the object is produced by the summation of these sensual currents not discharged, with affectionate currents from childhood and tender feelings from the pregenital phases. In addition, idealization of the object occurs as the narcissistic cathexis of the self is shifted to it, putting it in the place of the ego ideal. Normally, the wish for sexual gratification will sooner or later be fulfilled, and the dammed-up libido is discharged. The feeling state of "being in love" can shift to ordinary "loving" as its ecstasy is shifted to the orgasm.

With growing knowledge of early ego development, echoes of the intimate communications between mother and child have been found in adult object love. Those fortunate enough to have had good mothering, developing from narcissism to object love through the steps from basic trust to attainment of object constancy, will have the potential to traverse this path again later in life. For example, residua of the infant's stranger reaction of shyness will not permit immediate, all-out emotional and sexual surrender of the adult to every stranger who smiles and nods his head. But this normal reserve may be overcome by the patient wooing of intimacy—just as the mother attracted to herself the infant's narcissistic investment during its first year. In the narcissistic adult who had been less fortunate in this early relationship, we find continuing difficulty in retracing the path to the love object. In severe cases, there may be an inability to leave the narcissistic position at all—a feeling of fear, distrust, prejudice or hatred for the unfamiliar object—or simply an insurmountable obstacle to feeling close to anyone. Others may respond totally to simple need-gratification without discrimination between objects—like the infant of three months who does not yet distinguish mother from others.

Bak (1973) has shown that the poets were right in their allusions to a fusion of self and object—that the feeling state of "being in love" indeed aims to undo separation, not only from primary objects, finally nearing completion in the adolescent process, but of later object losses as well. The regression thus initiated is facilitated by flooding of the ego and sexualization of its functions of perception, judgment, and anticipation, which makes overvaluation and its containment of ambivalence possible.

In pathological instances that caricature romantic love, exaltation of the object goes so far that the joys and pangs of love resemble manic-depressive psychosis, the alternations of omnipotence and ecstasy with suffering submission and despondency depending as much upon the vicissitudes of narcissistic cathexis and ambivalence as upon the behavior of the object. Often such people are said to be "in love with love" as they pursue it fanatically, but the inflated ideal they project usually cannot adhere to any object very long, and they may not have faith in the love if the object returns it, and only hate—of the object, the self, or the object within the self (by identification)—if the object does not. Uncontrolled regression may end in suicide or psychosis.

In others, the regression may not go so far, and the relationship becomes established on the basis of unconscious gratification of regressive needs, forging a bond as strong as that of normal love. They may live in this bondage until death does them part—usually with benefit of matrimony to magically reinforce the bond and contain the potentially explosive tensions. Although their storehouse of shared experiences seems to contain more suffering and bitter grievances than pleasures, the relationship always affords unconscious gratifications based on equations of spouse with the need-gratifying or preoedipal mother, the breast, or the penis. For such people, marriage may mean permanent symbiosis, a guarantee of eternal unearned love, or it may be experienced as a feeling of being restored to wholeness, undamaged, with nothing missing—the spouse being manipulated and exhibited as if part of the self rather than loved as a separate person (Stein, 1956). With divorce, the magic is gone—all is "loss"—and they are re-exposed to the dangers for which the relationship had provided relief. Anxiety or depression is often the result, unless a new substitute promptly appears.

In the healthier, who make the shift to ordinary loving, separate identities are firmly re-established and the decline of the object from overvaluation is compensated for by the increase in real value due to ongoing sexual gratification and appreciation of the real qualities of the object. Unburdened by infantile demands for unearned love, willing efforts are made to please and gratify the other, to allay anxiety, to meet the needs of the partner—verbally expressed or empathically understood—even if, at times, they conflict with one's own. But self-interest and interests of the object coincide more than conflict when the partner is cared for as much as the self. In the interdependence that has replaced infantile dependence, masculinity and femininity complement each other, facilitating cooperation rather than competition. They make an effective team. Such a relationship provides the matrix for continuing development of each personality, and their separate and mutual experiences—especially parenthood—add new dimensions to the life of each.

Normal Sexual Functioning

The differences between masculine and feminine sexual feelings, attitudes, and behavior are the logical, ultimate psychological consequences of the anatomical differences between the sexes, as modified by maturational and environmental—including cultural—forces. In their most central aspect—the desire for gratification in genital union—feelings must conform harmoniously to the behavior required by the anatomically determined, different coital roles. Differences in anatomy become acceptable as a part of one who is loved, and fully appreciated as a result of satisfying coital experience—dissipating the anxiety that these differences formerly aroused.

In every sexual encounter, the history of individual psychosexual development is recapitulated in condensed form, following an inner "script" which obviates the necessity for handbooks on sex technique. In foreplay, a variety of active and passive expressions of impulses from earlier phases—e.g., to look, touch, hear, smell, and mouth—are gratified by both partners. Erection of the penis and lubrication of the vagina, objective manifestations of arousal, make genital union possible, and as the accumulated pleasurable tensions become focused in the genital mold, the respective organs become the vehicles of the characteristic masculine desire to penetrate, occupy and take over, and the feminine desire to be penetrated and filled—to yield in spirit as in flesh. With control of himself and, thus, of the situation, the man may then bring both to orgasm, at the height of which the desire of both for blissful fusion with the object is fulfilled. In genital union the highly differentiated organs, desires, and persons are fully complemented, making it possible for the ego to tolerate without fear the momentary return in orgasm to the undifferentiated state, the simultaneous extinction of the self and powerful affirmation of its existence with the simultaneous discharge of fused libido and aggression (Bak, 1973).

When this kind of integrated functioning is the happy denouement of the developmental process, the stability of the adult psychic organization is powerfully protected. With fusion in its place, separateness, like sexual difference, may be appreciated rather than feared. The battle of the sexes loses its venom, and shifting cultural dictates about sexual roles lose their immediate relevance.

Impaired Sexual Functioning

But human relationships are seldom ideal, and frailties that may not show in social intercourse, work, and other areas of functioning may appear in situations of greater intimacy. Sexual functions, too, respond sensitively, with variations in degree of desire, control, and pleasure, to the everyday vicissitudes of the relationship and fluctuations of intrapsychic equilibrium. Such mild or occasional limitations must be regarded as within the normal.

More severe or persistent inhibition of function, manifestly pathological, is known as impotence in the male, and frigidity in the female. The former is manifested in failure to attain or sustain erection, control (eventuating in premature ejaculation), or orgasm. The latter is manifested objectively by failure to produce sufficient lubrication of the vagina, maintain its patency (due to tight spasm of the muscles around the entrance), or, subjectively, by pain, absence of sensation, or, most often, incomplete satisfaction. It is apparent that the presence of any of these conditions must interfere with either penetration or gratification.

Impotence and frigidity are very common in Western civilization. In 1912, Freud recognized the importance of cultural factors, pointing to the strong prohibitions against premarital sexuality, especially for women, and the difficulty, among cultivated men, of combining sensual and affectionate currents of the libido toward an idealized object. It must be understood that this cultural influence is exerted mostly through internalization during individual development. Superego prohibitions thus formed do not change as easily as mores with relaxation of external restraints, and we should not be surprised that we do not find a prompt reduction in the incidence of sexual dysfunction in the wake of the sexual revolution. The only real freedom comes from within—through the successful struggle with developmental tasks, i.e., with ego victories over id and archaic elements of the superego.

Sexual dysfunction appears regularly as one of many symptoms in any of the symptom neuroses, and has the same genetic determinants, dynamics, and prognosis as the neurosis. In some, impotence or frigidity is the only symptom. Although it may be expressed in regressive forms, the Oedipus complex, with its incestuous wishes and typical dangers, especially genital injury, but also loss of love is usually at the center. The symptom, an inhibition of function, is the ego's defense to prevent the anticipated danger, and, often, the superego's prohibitions and threats are attached. Sometimes, however, the symptom expresses the unconscious wish itself. Thus, for example, vaginal muscle spasm after penetration may express unconscious envy, hostile desire for revenge, and the wish to take the penis from the man, whereas its occurrence before penetration may be directed against guilt or the fear of retaliation associated with this wish. In other cases, this symptom may operate to prevent the damage, however exciting, associated with the little girl's fantasy of penetration by the father's large penis.

The vicissitudes of the aggressive drive are also, of course, important in masculine sexual functioning. For example, if, instead of the normal aggressive cathexis of the phallus that contributes the active, probing quality to its aim and function, there is too much sadism—giving penetration the quality of a destructive, painful piercing, or defilement—the man must lose his erection or have a "hit and run" premature ejaculation to avoid the anticipated guilt or retaliation.

The incest taboo inhibits sexual functioning in various ways and degrees. There may be simply a limitation of desire with infrequent performance and little passion. If every member of the opposite sex is unconsciously equated with the oedipal object, performance with any must be impaired. In both sexes, especially men, the taboo can sometimes be compromised by separating sensual from affectionate currents of the libido, or loved and idealized from little known, or degraded, objects. Thus, we find the man who is impotent in the marital bed, but potent with pick-ups and prostitutes—or even with his wife if he takes her to a motel feeling that he is treating her "like a whore." And there are women who are frigid with their husbands but orgastic when nearly raped by a near stranger.

If both desire and penetration escape inhibition, control may be disturbed. Premature ejaculation aborts the man's own orgasm, which may be its primary purpose. But it can also prevent the woman's, to which end it may be directed out of fear of guilt or castration for being responsible for her fulfillment, or, out of revenge, to frustrate the woman who depends on him as his mother frustrated him when he depended on her. In the woman, inhibition may prevent her from yielding control to the man and, thus, bearing the guilt or anxiety associated with taking responsibility for her own wish for feminine fulfillment, i.e., to let him give her an orgasm in coitus. In both sexes, orgasm may be impaired by fear that the loss of self at its height may be more than momentary.

Although most men achieve orgasm in some degree, vitiation of genital power by pregenital aims, manifested in premature ejaculation of little force and pleasure, is common. Mild impairments often go unrecognized unless, as sometimes happens, an increment of pleasure is experienced during the course of treatment undertaken for other reasons. Among women, failure to achieve orgasm is very common and not fully understood. More often than generally recognized, it is due to limitations of male potency, but most instances must be attributed to the greater number of hazards her more complex development subjects her to. Some women, who seem to be normal in every other way, report full satisfaction in coitus without a definite, circumscribed climax. It may be that a special quality of object relatedness, due to a spreading of the experience of fusion with the object over a longer interval than the moment at the height of orgasm, can make the lesser intensity fully satisfying.

The sexually promiscuous usually suffer from character disorders of the impulsive type. It is their characteristic to seek in quantity what they lack in quality, but it is a hopeless quest, for pregenital aims cannot be fully gratified genitally, and the reassurances of love are not for the inconstant. Some are impulse-ridden "love addicts" who seek to ward off depression with the elation of new love as some people do with alcohol, drugs, rich foods, or a spending spree. For them, the sexual embrace is not an end in itself, but the means to the end of trying to feel again—or for the first time—the physical closeness and security of a well-mothered nursling. Others are "bargain hunters" who compulsively repeat the disappointment of buying the glamorous, "nationally advertised" sex package only to find its contents as cheap as their own investment.

The aggressive element is important in promiscuity. The Don Juan collects "notches on his belt," marking each triumph in overcoming a new victim—a safer outlet for hostile aggression than combat and competition with men, which he has avoided since his infantile confrontation with the oedipal father or the dominant preoedipal mother. The nymphomaniac is often a kleptomaniac who does not use the mechanism of displacement from the phallus to other objects. In her unconscious fantasy, she collects as trophies the penises she steals from her victims, achieving each time a moment of relief from the painful feelings of inferiority as a "castrate," which otherwise beset her.

Sometimes, as in counterphobic mechanisms, the Don Juans are bound to their promiscuous pattern by the heady exhilaration of being daredevils who can perform the feared act (coitus) always escaping the feared penalty (castration). They may even contrive to increase the peril, and thus the pleasure, by their seemingly careless provocations of irate fathers or jealous lovers or husbands. This "flirting with danger" is also a form of flirting with the man, a near breakthrough of unconscious feminine wishes. Strong unconscious homosexuality is usually a significant feature in the psychopathology of heterosexual promiscuity. It is denied in acting out the proof that "I do not love *him;* I love *her,*" or, in women, "I do not love *her;* I love *him.*"

Marriage

Woman's freedom has always been limited by nature. Her biological role as servant of the species imposes on her a greater dependency and, therefore, greater concern with security. In her development, a tighter bond between love and sex was forged. Until recent times there was strong cultural reinforcement of the inner restrictions of her sexual freedom, in return for which her longer and stronger claim to romantic fulfillment and security was recognized. These were conferred in marriage ceremonies and contracts guaranteeing exclusiveness and permanence. Male dominance and exclusive sexual rights were guaranteed in return for acceptance of family responsibility and partial renunciation of freedom.

But with the emancipation of women came greater economic independence, and with the advance in contraceptive technology came freedom from fear of pregnancy. The need for external protective control of her sexuality was correspondingly lessened, and the double standard has collapsed. Some women, who have the developed feminine potential to keep their priorities straight, are able to use this new freedom to find fulfillment in love and marriage as well as in motherhood and satisfying careers. To achieve such a synthesis of sexual, maternal, and occupational identities is a formidable task, requiring the developmental potential of a solidly integrated psychic organization. Such a woman will also need a husband of similar strength to support her effort with constant love and sexual gratification—without competing for any of her shifting roles, or regressing to infantile dependence upon her.

Others, poorly integrated and of persisting bisexual disposition, misapprehend the opportunity, taking it as freedom to repudiate their biological role and all of femininity. Taking stands on their equal rights and capacity for independence and sexual satisfaction, they may enter into a driving, narcissistic pursuit of career ambitions or a demand for orgasm which takes priority over romance, marriage, motherhood, and love itself—dooming all their relationships to failure. For them, liberation proves to be a new trap as they pursue to its dead end the illusion of equality without difference that takes them further from feminine fulfillment along the route of masculinization.

Many young women, temporarily preoccupied by the search for separate identity, forego their old prerogative to seek marital commitment from the men they live with, often deferring it until they feel ready for parenthood. Sometimes they find only then that the man had been taking advantage of the protection she had given up and is not really mature enough to assume the responsibility of marriage.

Parenthood

Parenthood is still frequently the accidental by-product of lust—nature's way of insuring the preservation of the species. But sometimes it is the result of a conscious decision made under pressure of pathological needs, as, for example, to save a failing marriage. Fortunately, it is often the result of a decision growing out of psychological readiness in a successful relationship.

The desire to become a father is rooted in the man's need to survive—to live on in his offspring—which may only show clearly at the threat of death, such as going off to war, or in his pleasure in a child of his later years. More apparent is the need for an outlet of his developed parental feelings. As in the woman, these are derived ultimately from the early identification with the nurturing mother, and may still show clearly as motherliness in some, even normal, men. But usually the man's feelings have for the most part been transformed into the more specifically fatherly desire to provide for and protect—by way of later identifications with his own father and others. This limits the father's interest in the infant, delaying development of a fuller relationship until the child is more capable of it.

For the woman, parenthood is much more. The wish to bear and nurture a child is biologically anchored in her uterus and breasts, and its fulfillment normally brings a sense of well-being, wholeness, and completion that may dispel lingering feelings of inferiority (to her mother as well as to the opposite sex). Because it is such a prolonged and intensive creative process, it occupies much of her body and preoccupies her mind, requiring some shift of cathexis from the outside world to the self, the foetus, and the baby. Many complexes and regressive trends are stirred during pregnancy, causing at least mild and temporary disturbances of psychic equilibrium in many, and more serious ones in some. Fears of bodily injury in the birth process and fears of having a defective child may be exaggerated by castration anxiety. At parturition, the physical separation stirs separation anxiety if pregnancy was experienced as another fusion with mother by overidentification with the foetus, and castration anxiety if the fantasy was of growing a penis. The latter is sometimes obviated by having a boy. The mother's empathic sensitivity to her baby's needs, essential to her management of the symbiotic and separation-individuation phases, will be disturbed by excessive separation anxiety in herself, causing more anxiety in the child.

Throughout the child's development there will be continuing juxtapositions of his developmental phases with those reactivated in the parent. If these are severe neurotic fixation points in the latter, empathy will be disturbed, parental behavior and guidance inappropriate, and the development of the child adversely affected. If they are less severe and the crises are successfully negotiated, the parent may, in the process, rework the residues of old conflict and take a developmental step forward with the child. The possibility of such further consolidations diminishes with age and increasing rigidity of the psychic structure—one of the reasons for the generation gap and the great distress both middle-aged parents and their adolescent experience.

Working

Although the suckling infant is often envied for the opportunity to get "something for nothing," he does, in fact, work for a living, expending energy for the reward necessary to his survival. Attempts to emulate the fantasy about the infant are seldom very successful. The thief, the gambler, the addict, the prostitute, and the beggar spend their time and energy often for meager rewards.

In modern urban industrial society, specialization and the

interposition of many middlemen between producer and consumer obscure the relationship between effort and reward, and it is easy to lose sight of the fact that pleasure still adheres to the successful struggle for survival. Most adults survive through socially useful occupation; feelings of belonging to the community support their self-esteem and emotional security. Getting up at the same hour and going to work at the same place, or, as among professionals who work alone, "talking shop" when they get together, strengthens the ego by way of identification with the peer group. Work helps to define one's place in society, contributes to a sense of identity, and binds one more securely to reality. Without work there is a feeling of loss and deprivation, often leading to defensive assertiveness or resignation and passivity, an important problem of aging in our society.

There is pleasure in the functioning of muscles and mind, first manifest in the autoerotic play of the infant with his own body. Play always retains its instinctual quality, its pleasures immediate and ongoing through the occupation itself, and the means and the end are the same. In work, the pleasure is often deferred until the completion of the task and is greater if the task is well done in conformity with the ego ideal. In the adult, larger quantities of neutralized energy are available to sustain the effort to the end. Where skill is required, there is ongoing pleasure in the increasing mastery of it, although mixed with frustration stemming from failure to achieve the standards set by the ego ideal. The modern factory assembly line provides few narcissistic gratifications, although the worker may still identify himself in a positive way with co-workers, the organization, or the product.

Feelings of obligation, unpleasantness, or of submitting to punishment, often attached to work, are derived from the superego and early object relationships requiring repression or regulation of drive activity. It is the constant expenditure of energy to counter this that makes ordinary work so exhausting for some.

Laziness, indifference, and overwork patterns are derived from the need to fulfill or reject or use masochistically the attitudes and ideals of the family and community. For example, when the assignment of work as a punishment is used in the home and school during childhood, this attitude is then incorporated into the superego.

When one works out of fear of loss of love—or for success as proof of being loved—one will have an unconscious wish to lose or fail to spite the demanding parent or superego, or one will regress to a more infantile level where one can please with a more purely playful effort (Oberndorf, 1951).

Vocational choices have many determinants. Accidents of fate sometimes play a role, e.g., in inherited talents, or existing opportunities such as a family business. More frequently, identifications with parents, teachers, and other idealized figures, or rebellion against them, influence these decisions. Sometimes the choice is made to fulfill a parent's wish. Unconscious instinctual needs, usually pregenital, are a powerful force, turning interest in the direction of vocations which offer better opportunity for sublimation of specific drive expressions, as, for example, painting and sculpture for fecal play; surgery or soldiering for sadism; photography, astronomy, or psychoanalysis for voyeurism; or the performing arts for exhibitionism.

Throughout history, in addition to work roles determined by each particular culture, woman's position has been determined by her biological role. Modern contraception offers her released time and energy from her biological role, and socioeconomic pressures force her out of this job to an increasing degree. The more adaptable of the sexes, her complex needs must be met by an adaptable society's consideration of these multiple roles. As society faces the task of limiting rather than fostering reproduction, the biological determinants of woman's role will seem less important. Smaller families and increased availability of social institutions for child-care assistance will probably mean that even those women who do have children will be able to pursue their own individual development and careers more and more on a par with men, a not unmixed blessing so far as the children are concerned.

REFERENCES

Bak, R. C. (1973), Being in Love and Object Loss. *International Journal of Psycho-Analysis,* 54:1-7.

Blos, P. (1962), *On Adolescence.* New York: Free Press of Glencoe.

Erikson, E. H. (1950), *Childhood and Society.* New York: W. W. Norton.

Freud, A. (1965), *Normality and Pathology in Childhood. The Writings of Anna Freud,* Vol. 6. New York: International Universities Press.
——— Nagera, H. & Freud, W. E. (1965), The Metapsychological Assessment of the Adult Personality—The Adult Profile. *The Psychoanalytic Study of the Child,* 20:10-41. New York: International Universities Press.
Freud, S. (1905), Three Essays on the Theory of Sexuality. *Standard Edition,* 7:125-243. London: Hogarth Press, 1953.
——— (1912), On the Universal Tendency to Debasement in the Sphere of Love (Contributions to the Psychology of Love, II). *Standard Edition,* 11:178-190. London: Hogarth Press, 1957.
——— (1914), On Narcissism. *Standard Edition,* 14:69-102. London: Hogarth Press, 1957.
——— (1921), Group Psychology and the Analysis of the Ego. *Standard Edition,* 18:64-143. London: Hogarth Press, 1955.
——— (1930), Civilization and its Discontents. *Standard Edition,* 21:59-145. London: Hogarth Press, 1961.
Hartmann, H. (1939), Psychoanalysis and the Concept of Health. In: *Essays on Ego Psychology.* New York: International Universities Press, pp. 3.18.
Oberndorf, C. (1951), Psychopathology of Work. *Bulletin of the Menninger Clinic,* 15:77-84.
Reider, N. (1950), The Concept of Normality. *Psychoanalytic Quarterly,* 19:43-51.
Stein, M. (1956), The Unconscious Meaning of the Marriage Bond. In: *Neurotic Interaction in Marriage,* ed. V. Eisenstein. New York: Basic Books, pp. 65-80.

SUGGESTED READING

Benedek, T. (1959), Parenthood as a Developmental Phase: A Contribution to the Libido Theory. *Journal of the American Psychoanalytic Association,* 7:389-417.
Beres, D. (1953), The Person and the Group: Object Relationships. In: *Psychoanalysis and Social Work,* ed. M. Heiman. New York: International Universities Press, pp. 53-75.
Bergmann, M. (1971), Psychoanalytic Observations on the Capacity to Love. In: *Separation-Individuation—Essays in Honor of Margaret S. Mahler,* ed. J. B. McDevitt & C. F. Settlage. New York: International Universities Press, pp. 15-40.
Deutsch, H. (1945), *The Psychology of Women.* 2 vols. New York: Grune & Stratton.
Evans, W. (1953), Two Kinds of Romantic Love. *Psychoanalytic Quarterly,* 22:75-85
Lidz, T. (1968), *The Person.* New York: Basic Books.
Sternschein, I., reporter (1973), Panel on "The Experience of Separation Individuation in Infancy and its Reverberations through the Course of Life: Maturity, Senescence, and Sociological Implications. *Journal of the American Psychoanalytic Association,* 21: 633-645.

CHAPTER FOURTEEN
Symptom Formation

JULIAN L. STAMM, M.D.

Emotional illness has plagued man since the dawn of his existence, and yet, in terms of the vast epoch of time spanning his history on earth, it has only been in the past century, especially during the last 60 to 70 years, that psychology has made valid claims to a truly scientific explanation of mental illness.

This brings us to the present-day psychodynamic point of view which has already been carefully explored and developed in the early chapters of this book, namely, that every aspect of human behavior is multidetermined and can only be understood in terms of the emotional, ideational, and neurophysiological aspects of the individual's internal milieu, which is the result of his previous growth and development interacting with the current external environment. Consequently, we no longer think in terms of heredity vs. environment, development vs. maturation, or normal vs. abnormal; instead, we attempt to understand all behavior as a composite and outgrowth of hereditary, maturational, developmental, and environmental factors constantly interacting with each other and constantly evolving new homeostatic equilibria. So it is with symptoms and symptom formation, which are, after all, a part of behavior.

For our purposes, the term symptom is to be understood primarily from a psychological frame of reference, although the same term is employed in a medical sense to include a much broader group of disturbances and physical findings. In medicine, a finding usually refers to an objective factor elicited by the doctor on physical or laboratory examination such as a rapid pulse or cardiac murmur or rales in the chest heard on auscultation, whereas the symptom is usually the subjective complaint of the patient—cough, headache, weakness, or shortness of breath.

Symptom Formation in Relation to Topographic and Structural Theory

Freud early came upon the important discovery that wish-fulfilling fantasies in infancy and early childhood represented a source of gratification together with conflict and therefore were subject to repression but continued to operate as unconscious dynamic forces seeking to gain re-entry into consciousness. Owing, however, to defenses (censorship) interposed between the unconscious and preconscious, these forbidden fantasies could gain entry to consciousness only by becoming disguised. This constitutes the explanation of symptom formation in accordance with the topographic theory.

Freud then postulated that the symptom, when it appeared in consciousness, represented not only an infantile wish in disguised form, but was a compromise formation between the repressed instinctual derivative—id impulse—and the repressing forces—ego defenses. The concept of a struggle or conflict between ego and id was termed an intersystemic conflict and represented the outgrowth of his later structural theory as distinct from the earlier topographical viewpoint.

Our current understanding is that when intrapsychic conflict is resolved through a return of the repressed in disguised form, this constitutes a symptom. Past traumatic situations—actual or fantasied—developmental defects and arrests, and increases in instinctual pressure are among the important factors that genetically contribute to symptom formation.

When finally organized, a newly formed symptom is experienced as something foreign, or recognized as strange or bizarre and is especially frightening in its acute states. This aspect of the symptom is termed ego-alien or ego-dystonic. Strictly speaking, it would be more accurate to use the terms "self-alien" or "self-dystonic."

As we have seen, Freud, almost from the very beginning of his work, viewed the symptom as an end product of conflicting tendencies within the psychic apparatus. He concluded that the subject was avoiding the overt recognition of the forbidden instinctual wish, since to do so would be painful to him because it would stir up anxiety, guilt, or other painful affects. With the advent of the structural theory, signal anxiety was regarded as the primary factor motivating repression and all the other defense mechanisms of the ego.[1] Generally speaking, anxiety may be defined as the psychological and physiological manifestations representing a reaction to a conflict and danger from within, i.e., from an intrapsychic source.

The source of anxiety experienced changes as the person progresses through the various developmental changes from infancy to adulthood. The earliest anxiety experienced by the infant is anxiety about the loss of the object; this is followed by anxiety about loss of love, then by castration anxiety, and finally by superego anxiety. Unacceptable thoughts of either a libidinal or aggressive nature, such as incestuous or death wishes regarding parents or siblings stir up anxiety, self-reproaches or other painful emotions, lead to repression or the use of other defense mechanisms, and eventually to the formation of symptoms.

Finally, the symptom itself always provides both a primary and secondary gain. The primary gain consists in the relief experienced by warding off anxiety or guilt feelings, as well as in a disguised, partial gratification of the underlying instinctual impulse. The secondary gain is represented by the advantages obtained from the environment as a result of the symptom. For example, a person may get special

[1] Freud earlier believed that anxiety resulted from dammed-up libido. That is, as a result of repression of the forbidden libidinal impulse, the energy connected with the repressed impulse was converted into anxiety which was experienced consciously. The toxic state resulting from dammed-up libido was exemplified in the so-called *aktual* neuroses supposedly induced by unsatisfactory sexual practices.

help, care and attention from his family and friends because of his psychological disability.

For many people with weakened egos the symptom is preferable to the experiencing of anxiety or guilt. The symptom thus enables them to avoid feelings of anxiety or other painful emotions. It also enables them to hold on to their relationships with ambivalently loved parents, siblings, etc.

Fixation Points

Furthermore, during every individual's maturation and development, both psychosexually and in the differentiation of ego functions, various libidinal fixation points are laid down in the psychic apparatus. These in turn are based on phase-specific experiences of a traumatic nature; overindulgences or deprivations at certain crucial life periods may lead to developmental arrests in important ego functions—object relationships, control over affects, motility, reality testing, etc. These fixation points and developmental arrests in turn provide the nuclei for later conflict formation in the growing child and adult.

In the process of growth and development each person acquires certain fixation points. There are some with very marked oral tendencies and others in whom anal or phallic fixations are evident. Still others may display arrested development with respect to the various personality functions, as exemplified by the preservation of markedly ambivalent or sadistic types of pregenital object relations, defective development of the superego or of other aspects of the personality. These developmental arrests and fixation points not only leave lasting imprints on the evolution of character structure, but also have an important bearing on the kinds of symptoms produced when regression occurs.

With each step in growth and development the child must struggle with the activities and problems that are specific for that given phase. Side by side with his psychosexual development, we witness the growing differentiation and strengthening of the ego, so that gradually he is able to postpone gratification and establish reality testing in place of fantasied wish-fulfillment. If, as a result of undue environmental stress or excessive pressure of instinctual drives, intolerable inner conflicts occur, he regresses to an earlier libidinal or ego state, i.e., to one which has already been left behind in the course of developmental progression and which offers him a state less threatening than the one he is now enduring. If, as a result of environmental stress or excessive pressure of instinctual drives, earlier infantile conflicts are reactivated, he must either fall back on earlier defensive patterns or utilize newer defenses in order to deal with the intolerable inner conflict. When viewed along developmental lines, therefore, it follows that each person will employ a hierarchy of defenses in response to conflicts stemming from different developmental levels.

A 45-year-old man had, as a child, been doted on excessively by his voluptuous mother. Every morning she allowed him to come into her bed and caressed him. As a result, he grew up with strongly fixated passive oedipal fantasies in which he was seduced by an older, voluptuous woman, a thinly disguised mother substitute. After he married, he unconsciously equated his wife with his mother. This was amply corroborated by dreams in which he often confused the two. During the engagement period he was quite potent with his wife-to-be, but almost immediately after the marriage he developed a physical revulsion for her, based on a reaction formation against his oedipal wishes. As a further protection, he regressed and developed counting compulsions and obsessive ideas related to cleanliness and orderliness. He also began to bicker violently with his wife, abusing, criticizing, and ridiculing her.

In brief, he had regressed to an earlier anal-sadistic state in order to ward off his oedipal conflict. This, in turn, reactivated conflicts of sibling rivalry with a younger sister, conflicts centering around aggression and impulse control of this earlier period. His compulsive, anal-sadistic behavior represented a symptom formation based on the libidinal regression to the earlier anal phase, as well as the activation of earlier defenses, such as reaction formation against those anal-sadistic conflicts. The result was the appearance of the obsessive-compulsive reaction. After a regression to an earlier level of development—in the present example, from the oedipal to the anal-sadistic—the return of the earlier fantasies aroused conflict between ego, id, and superego. The symptoms represent the return of the repressed in disguised form. The neurosis serves the function of warding off the tensions occurring at a higher developmental level and is set in motion by a regression to earlier fixation points, with the reactivation of the predominating fantasies of that period and their accompanying defenses. The resulting symptoms fulfill the purpose of expressing the forbidden wish, albeit in disguised form, and serve to limit the degree of anxiety experienced by the ego.

It should be emphasized that there is no certainty that a particular type of childhood neurosis will be either a prototype or model for a later adult neurosis. Even though the dominant drive components may remain the same, the choice between two opposing pathological entities depends on the interaction of these drive derivatives with corresponding ego functions and defenses at different developmental levels. Hence, it follows that a child who has had a phobic neurosis at age six may, as an adult, develop an obsessive-compulsive condition just as readily as another phobic neurosis or some other symptoms.

Various external events, such as the loss of a loved person or a disappointment in career, may lead to a transitory weakening of the ego and a tendency to retreat to earlier fixation points, to experience the reactivation of earlier intrapsychic conflicts, and to develop symptoms as a compromise formation.

In addition to external precipitating events, there are various periods when physiological factors—puberty, menopause, senility, or physical illness—may lead to a weakening of the ego defenses and loss of self-esteem; intrapsychic conflicts may then be exacerbated and lead to symptom formation. There might, for example, be a depressive reaction to an acute heart attack, or a psychosis that follows a major surgical intervention, or an anxiety or depressive state in response to waning potency in the climacteric.

Although the tendency to classify symptoms as neurotic or psychotic is still widespread, much greater clarity will be achieved if they are understood developmentally according to the structural theory. Every symptom should be understood as the result of the need to avoid anxiety arising from unconscious conflicts, be they libidinal or aggressive. Specific defenses are erected against these conflicts, and the symptom is the disguised compromise. Furthermore, the choice of symptoms and defenses employed will depend on the degree of ego, superego, and libidinal regression encountered. This is based, not only on current precipitating stress, but also on the subject's past history and the nature of his fixations, object relations, and environment.

It is impossible to make a clear-cut diagnosis of psychosis or neurosis on the basis of a single symptom. When viewed along developmental lines, it is possible for someone to develop different symptoms on different developmental levels, a hierarchical series, so to speak, according to the particular level of psychic conflict, anxiety, and defense in operation. To obtain a true diagnostic picture, there must therefore be a thorough knowledge of the entire personality functioning, the interpersonal relations, and the adaptive capacities.

We have not yet developed a fully satisfactory classification of psychological symptoms. We believe, however, that at this stage of our knowledge it is preferable to discard the classification of symptoms as psychotic or neurotic and instead to use the categories of functional, organic, and psychophysiological (psychosomatic). Whether a symptom is part of a psychosis or neurosis depends on the total picture.

By definition, a *functional* symptom is of a psychological nature without any lasting observable structural or functional impairment of the brain. A *psychological* symptom caused by organic factors, conversely, shows observable damage of the central nervous system due to injury, toxicity, infection, aging, etc. This damage may be either reversible or permanent. Important ego functions, such as memory, control of motility, thought, speech, and reality testing, may become impaired as a result of organic damage. This may lead to marked regression and helplessness.

Anxiety and depression are symptoms forming part of almost any emotional disorder. As unpleasurable and painful affective states, they also mobilize the defense mechanisms of the ego and contribute to the formation of functional psychogenic symptoms. Anxiety and depression are, of course, reversible functional states in the sense that they are not based on structural changes within the central nervous system, even though they also leave physiological manifestations of the most varied kinds. To mention just a few examples: in anxiety there may be a speeding up of the pulse, breathing, bowel evacuation, etc., and in depression loss of appetite, fatigue, constipation, and the like. Depression, like anxiety, is a primary affect. It is based on a particular subjective state or mood experienced by the ego in response to a host of factors—object loss, narcissistic injury, etc. Depression normally is part of a mourning reaction to the loss of a beloved person. Pathologically, it may be based on unconscious factors and reflect ambivalence and the subject's narcissistic orientation.

Functional Symptoms

Some of the most important *functional* symptoms other than anxiety and depression are phobias, obsessions and compulsions, conversions, dissociations, illusions, hallucinations, and delusions. We will describe each of these briefly; they receive more detailed examination in subsequent chapters.

In *phobias,* the subject experiences a fear of specific external objects or situations that he is compelled to avoid. This fear represents a displacement of some danger generated by intrapsychic conflict to some part of the external environment.

An *obsession* is the tendency to be unpleasantly preoccupied repeatedly with some thought or wish. It may represent a forbidden impulse, prohibition against it, or a combination of the two. It expresses both the unconscious wish and defenses against it. The most prominent defenses in the obsessions are isolation, undoing, and reaction formation.

A *compulsion* is the need to repeat over and over again a particular act or ritual. The act may symbolize an unconscious impulse or the prohibition of it, such as a superego injunction against a forbidden libidinal or aggressive wish. It always expresses an unconscious conflict in disguised form and, like all neurotic symptoms, is ego-dystonic. The major defenses employed are identical with those seen in the obsession.

Conversion is a symptom that serves as a defense against a conflict over forbidden, unconscious ideas and emotions and is expressed in bodily form. The site chosen involves either the voluntary skeletal musculature or any of the special senses—sight, hearing, taste, olfaction, or touch; it may lead to varying degrees of anesthesia. The symptom is functional, can always be translated into unconscious psychological derivatives, and expresses both a return of the repressed in disguise as well as the defense against it. The choice of organ is considerably influenced by identifications and somatic compliance.

Dissociation represents an alteration of consciousness in which varying parts of the personality are split off or repressed from the main stream of consciousness. The cause is invariably an unconscious conflict, which is thereby repressed and defended against. Outstanding examples of dissociation are various forms of amnesia, fugue states, hypnagogic or twilight states, and the rarely occurring instances of multiple personality.

Depersonalization is a form of dissociation wherein bodily and mental changes are experienced, leading to feelings of estrangement from oneself. There is an alteration of the ego with a split into a part which feels estranged and one which carries on in the observer's role. Frequently there is also a corresponding state of *derealization* in which the external world appears changed and unfamiliar.

An *illusion* is a distorted perception based on a false interpretation of external stimuli. It may occasionally occur in a healthy person as a result of overpowering wishes, severe fatigue, or marked sensory deprivation.

A *hallucination* is a false sensory perception based on projections of internal stimuli or fantasies that are experienced as though they come from without. Hallucinations invariably result from loss of reality testing. They may involve any of the special organs and, hence, may be auditory, visual, tactile, olfactory, or gustatory. Apart from psychotic hallucinations, there are transient conditions resulting from toxic substances or excessive fatigue as well as hypnagogic imagery prior to falling asleep. There may also be hallucinations caused by permanent brain damage, as seen in various organic states.

A *delusion* is a manifestation of a disorder of thinking based on defective reality testing and a projection of the individual's internal conflicts. It is a false belief adhered to in spite of evidence to the contrary—evidence accepted by the individual's peers. Denial and projection are important defense mechanisms underlying the formation of delusions.

Organic mental symptoms are based on underlying structural damage in the central nervous system which causes varying degrees of impairment in memory (remote and recent), judgment, recall, and in the capacity to think clearly. In addition, there are sensory disturbances leading to distortion of perception, such as occur in patients suffering from alcoholism, cerebral arteriosclerosis, senility, or general paresis.

Organic States

In all organic states, illusions, hallucinations, and delusions may occur as a result of brain damage that impairs reality testing and the capacity to think clearly. In organic conditions, however, in contrast to functional disorders that display similar symptoms, there will invariably be physical signs and laboratory findings corroborating underlying brain damage.

A prize fighter, punch-drunk after innumerable bouts during which he suffered from repeated minute hemorrhages throughout his brain, finally suffered complete loss of memory, even for current events, and was no longer able to recall his own past. His amnesia was based entirely on organic damage to the brain. In contrast, another patient suddenly became amnesic when he was told he would be one of the first soldiers to undertake a hazardous mission. His amnesia was entirely emotional in origin.

Psychosomatic Symptoms

The various psychophysiological symptoms result from a combination of organic and physiological changes in the respective organ systems, either organically induced or enhanced by emotional factors. These psychophysiological symptoms, however, do not express intrapsychic conflicts through unconscious symbolic language. There are many groups of gastrointestinal, genitourinary and cardiorespiratory symptoms—nausea, vomiting, diarrhea, increased frequency of urination, palpitations, dyspnea and precordial pain, to mention only a few—that represent equivalents of anxiety. Peptic ulcer and essential hypertension are further examples of psychophysiological symptoms, as are bronchial asthma, ulcerative colitis, vasomotor rhinitis, and various types of neurodermatitis.

While it should be quite apparent that one cannot predict with any degree of accuracy when a symptom will develop, or the specific nature of the symptom per se, especially because of the operation of the law of multidetermination, it is also true that if one understands thoroughly the nature of the given person's psyche, his previous life history, his current conflicts, and his predominant defenses and character traits, one can readily appreciate the particular symptom as an outgrowth of that structure rather than an event foreign to it.

In conclusion, the following points ought to be summarized:

First, a symptom—whether neurotic or psychotic—always expresses an intrapsychic conflict in disguised form and is always multi-determined. Its primary purpose is to avoid the anxiety that would be experienced if the intrapsychic conflict were admitted into consciousness undisguised.

Second, the precipitating event, either an external trauma or some internal factor—weakening of the ego, increased pressure from the id—reawakens conflicts of earlier phases of development.

Third, a regression ensues to the earlier fixation point, eliciting childhood fantasies and the corresponding defenses against them.

Fourth, the resultant symptom is always a compromise formation between the forbidden instinctual wish of early childhood that has been regressively revised and the defenses against it.

REFERENCES

Arlow, J. & Brenner, C. (1964), *Psychoanalytic Concepts and the Structural Theory.* New York: International Universities Press.

Brenner, C. (1955), *An Elementary Textbook of Psychoanalysis.* New York: International Universities Press, revised edition, 1973.

Fenichel, O. (1945), *The Psychoanalytic Theory of Neurosis.* New York: W. W. Norton.

Freud, S. (1926), Inhibitions, Symptoms and Anxiety. *Standard Edition,* 20:77-175. London: Hogarth Press, 1959.

CHAPTER FIFTEEN
Anxiety Neuroses and Phobias

JULIAN L. STAMM, M.D.

We have seen that symptom formation is in part activated by signal anxiety arising from intrapsychic conflicts. We shall now examine two specific symptom pictures: anxiety neuroses and phobias.

Anxiety and Fear

It is important to distinguish between anxiety and fear. Both are affective states with identical somatic manifestations, the potential for which is present at birth. But whereas anxiety is the reaction to inner dangers such as the threatened emergence of forbidden libidinal or aggressive wishes, fear is the reaction to a real external danger. Anxiety may also be adaptive as, for example, when signal anxiety activates the defense mechanisms of the ego (see Chapter Three).

Although anxiety and other unpleasurable affects are seldom absent in psychoneuroses, in anxiety neurosis, as the term implies, the anxiety and its physiological manifestations constitute the predominant element in the clinical picture. Anxiety is felt as a distressing affect which may be experienced as a feeling of worry, vague anticipation of danger, dread, or, in its severest form, panic. It has various physiological manifestations, usually resulting in increased activity of bodily functions that are controlled by the vegetative or autonomic nervous system. This may lead to any one or a combination of symptoms, such as palpitations, rapid breathing, increased blood pressure, nausea, vomiting and diarrhea, sweating, increased urgency and frequency of urination, muscular tenseness, and trembling. Some of these symptoms may in turn cause additional anxiety when the subject misinterprets them as indicating the presence of serious organic disease such as heart trouble or cancer.

Anxiety neurosis occurs when anxiety stemming from intrapsychic conflict cannot be successfully mastered by the ego through its defense mechanisms. It can be distinguished from other forms of psychoneuroses, psychoses, and personality disorders, although anxiety is present as one of the symptoms in most psychiatric disturbances.

Freud postulated two types of anxiety. The first is the automatic variety in which the organism, confronted with a dangerous situation coming from within or without, is unable to master it, and experiences a feeling of helplessness. Conditions producing this reaction are called traumatic. The second type is called *signal anxiety*. This is the ego's reaction to an anticipated danger which threatens to evoke the memory of a traumatic situation. Signal anxiety thus makes it possible to avoid the repetition of the intense anxiety experienced in the earlier traumatic situation by mobilizing the defense mechanisms of the ego. An adult, for example, may experience signal anxiety in the face of a separation from a loved person. The anxiety is not caused by any current danger of being helpless, but rather by the danger of a breakthrough of the memory of an experience of helplessness in the face of a separation in childhood. The ego may defend itself from the danger of re-experiencing the anxiety caused by the original danger situation by any of a variety of defenses, such as intellectualization, detachment, denial or projection. In an anxiety neurosis, the defensive measures of the ego have failed, and the subjective and objective manifestations of anxiety appear.

Anxiety Neurosis

The diagnosis of anxiety neurosis should be reserved for those syndromes in which the primary complaint is a pervasive anxiety that is not limited by specific defenses or neurotic symptoms. Anxiety is frequently seen at the onset of an acute psychoneurosis or psychosis before the ego's defenses have succeeded in binding the anxiety into more specific forms of psychopathology. The anxiety syndrome may develop gradually or it may be of acute onset, precipitated by some shocking external event. It may be self-limited in duration, evolve into another form of psychopathology, or become chronic.

Several factors are involved in causing anxiety neurosis. First, constitutional factors may be of some significance. Some people seem to have a predisposition for the development of anxiety; almost from birth they respond with anxiety to stimuli which others take in their stride. They are often unable to cope with the stresses and strains of everyday life without developing excessive anxiety.

In the course of development, traumatic fixations may produce an inability to deal with the anxiety that is normally expected to occur later in life, that is to say, with phase-specific anxiety, thereby increasing the possibility that anxiety neurosis will develop. This may manifest itself in a "free floating" anxiety, which differs from the circumscribed or bound anxiety to be found in phobic, conversion, and obsessive-compulsive neuroses.

Cultural and family influences are also important factors in determining readiness to express or even to be aware of anxiety. For example, in certain families a premium is placed on control of the expression of affects. To reveal anxiety would hence be regarded as a sign of weakness and would have to be guarded against at all costs. Here, one can see how important are the early identifications with parents or parental surrogates.

Many people whose constitutional endowment and defenses are quite adequate may nevertheless develop acute anxiety reactions in response to exceptional environmental stress, to, for example, severe physical illness, marked fatigue, or severe loss of self-esteem. In short, any environmental situation that causes a sufficient degree of stress may disrupt the ego's defensive system and may encourage regression to an earlier ego and libidinal state and precipitate anxiety.

It may be useful to present some actual examples of people who have developed an anxiety neurosis.

One such was a 22-year-old enlisted man who saw several of his buddies blown up by a mortar shell. He went into a panic, began to run aimlessly and to scream for help. When seen a few days later, he was wide-eyed, perspiring profusely, and complained of fatigue, insomnia, and headaches. He exhibited a marked, coarse tremor involving forearms, hands, and legs. There was also a severe startled reaction to the slightest sound. This acute anxiety state, precipitated by fear of death and marked feelings of helplessness, persisted for several weeks and eventually responded to reassurance, drug treatment, and rest.

An unmarried woman, age 22, came for psychotherapy because of a variety of symptoms of anxiety which permeated all aspects of her life and seriously interfered with her everyday functioning. This young woman had grown up in a highly sheltered milieu with a brother four years her junior who had been born blind. She had always suffered from feelings of self-consciousness and social anxiety, but had managed to graduate from an excellent college. Her acute anxiety syndrome developed after leaving college, when she was exposed to several new pressures. She was faced with the need to break away from her parents and the tensions involved in pursuing a career. In addition, her anxiety was especially stirred up by thoughts of heterosexual relationships, marriage, and childbearing.

When first seen, she suffered from many severe anxieties without any specific symptoms. For example, she found it difficult to converse over the phone. On a date, she felt inadequate and afraid she would be unable to interest the young man, becoming tongue-tied and suffering from pangs of anxiety and profuse sweating. At home she felt anxious if she sat on a couch near her father, or if her mother talked to her or attempted to kiss her. She also had vague fears that close relatives might have accidents or might become ill and die.

A nonpsychotic young man, age 26, entered therapy because of anxiety affecting him in many different ways. He was anxious about sexual intercourse with his wife, fearing that he could not satisfy her. He was also anxious at the thought that she might desert him, as his father had deserted his mother early in his childhood. He complained of headache, dizziness, and palpitations. Every time he had a mild cold he was terrified lest it develop into some deadly illness. He was of excellent intellectual endowment, displayed good capacity for introspection, and suffered no loss of reality testing.

Anxiety neurosis can be differentiated from conversion, phobic- and obsessive-compulsive neuroses (to be discussed later on) because these present specific symptoms in addition to varying degrees of anxiety. In the early stages of a schizophrenic breakdown, we often observe severe anxiety, bordering on panic. At the same time, feelings of estrangement and beginning signs of schizophrenic disorganization, such as loss of reality testing and disturbance in the thinking process, are present and help us to differentiate this condition from the less serious condition of anxiety neurosis. Some toxic states and acute infectious states may be accompanied by considerable anxiety. Usually, however, there is little likelihood of confusing such conditions with anxiety neurosis. Malaria or typhus fever, or the delirium tremens of alcoholism are examples of such states. Also, organic and psychophysiological disturbances such as hyperthyroidism, irregular heart rhythm, and even a chronic infectious disease such as tuberculosis may be accompanied by rapid pulse, excessive perspiration, and subjective feelings of anxiety. Of course, the underlying condition must be clarified to avoid mistaking these conditions for anxiety neurosis. Finally, the symptoms of anxiety neurosis may be produced chemically by the ingestion of a variety of drugs, especially amphetamines, a widely used and abused group of stimulants.

Phobias

The word phobia is derived from the Greek *phobos,* meaning fear. As is true of any psychological symptom-complex, it is always the end result of conflicts occurring with the personality. It is always multidetermined and can be understood when all the specific significant factors in the life history of that person are brought into consciousness. These will include the precipitating circumstances, which, in turn, revive earlier childhood memories, fantasies and conflicts, and the concomitant defenses called into play by the ego.

Equally important are the previous existence of early childhood traumata and early fixations. The phobia, therefore, is merely the symptomatic outgrowth of all these powerful forces that have remained in the unconscious; and it represents the ultimate compromise, the precarious psychological balance that emerged at a given point in the growth and development of the particular subject.

In the writings of the descriptive psychiatrists of the nineteenth and early twentieth centuries, the phenomenology of these conditions was elaborated in a descriptive way, but this did not shed any light on their etiology or psychodynamics. By and large, such reactions were regarded as constitutional or attributed to a form of degeneration of the nervous system. The prognosis was believed to be unfavorable. The American psychologist G. Stanley Hall suggested that phobic fears represented phylogenetic traces of ancestral experience. Toward the close of the nineteenth century, Janet began to apply a dynamic approach to phobias, linking them with the hysterias and calling them anxiety hysterias. But it was not until Freud made his extraordinary study of Little Hans that phobias could be understood as symptom-complexes specifically and dynamically determined in the context of the life history of each patient.

A phobic neurosis is a symptom-complex of functional origin which confines anxieties to certain specific external situations or objects. A great variety of phobic reactions have been described. Included among them are the following: agoraphobia (fear of open spaces); claustrophobia (fear of confined spaces); acrophobia (fear of heights); eating phobias in reference to specific foods; phobias pertaining to sexual activity or contact; phobias pertaining to dirt or to germs; phobias in relation to knives, scissors, or various other inanimate objects; erythrophobia (fear of blushing in public); phobias related to traveling in certain vehicles, such as airplanes, subways or buses; and phobias pertaining to the sight or smell of such things as blood, vomit, or feces.

The phobia may be of sudden onset or arise gradually. It may begin early in childhood, or it may develop abruptly in adulthood. It may remain relatively fixed and permanent or be subject to fluctuations in intensity. It may be limited to one situation or object, but it frequently spreads and becomes more complex. It may be confined to relatively unimportant areas of the subject's life or be so global that it is entirely incapacitating. We do not observe a phobic character structure as such, but we do encounter inhibited and restricted personalities who might be considered to have a latent phobic potential.

The classification of phobias on a purely phenomenological basis, however, is of little value because it does not help to explain their etiology or their dynamic function. In a phobia, the anxiety connected with repressed impulses, affects or ideas is displaced onto external situations or objects. The phobic patient usually recognizes the irrationality of his anxiety, but is entirely unaware of the unconscious intrapsychic conflicts which have generated the anxiety that we see projected and displaced. Displacement is the primary psychic mechanism in the formation of phobic symptoms. Repression, projection, and regression are, however, also involved to a greater or lesser extent. Prior to the development of specific phobias, which are manifested only after more complete structuralization of the psychic apparatus, children may display a type of anxiety called archaic. This kind of anxiety is not based on any actual experiences. It is almost universally observed among children and is believed to be due to innate predisposition. It appears to express the immature ego's disorientation when exposed to stimuli that cannot be assimilated and dealt with. Unlike a true phobia, it is not based on conflict, repression, or displacement. Examples include the anxiety response to sudden loud noises, to the dark, and to being left alone.

The following clinical example of an agoraphobia shows the mechanisms of displacement, projection, repression, and regression.

A 35-year-old woman in the throes of a depression following the loss of her beloved father awakened one day feeling terrified of leaving the house by herself. From then on, she refused to travel anywhere without being accompanied by her husband. The patient had for many years thought her husband undemonstrative and unaffectionate. By contrast, her father had doted on her and bestowed all kinds of attention on her from the time she was a little girl. After his death, the precipitating factor in her neurosis, she longed to recapture the attention she had received from him. Unable to feel adequately compensated by her aloof husband, she began to recall old memories of former suitors. What remained repressed were her wishes to have an extramarital affair. Since she was an exceedingly conscientous and faithful wife, even the thought of infidelity was repugnant to her.

Consequently, her fear of traveling outdoors was first of all a defense against her own fantasy of having a lover. The content of this fantasy was further distorted by means of projection—revealed in dreams of being accosted and raped. Then, to disguise her emotional conflict even more, the entire complex of ideas was displaced onto a fear of streets and a fear of traveling alone. By means of her phobia she was able to remain a faithful housewife, assuage her strict superego, remain unconscious of sexual fantasies and their connections with her father, and at the same time force her inattentive husband to accompany her wherever she went, thus giving her more of the attention she craved.

We see here the precipitating event—the death of her beloved father; the recollection of her childhood relation with him and her adolescent experiences with various suitors; and the threatened revival of repressed incestuous impulses.

The dwelling on her childhood relation with father and her adolescent dating experiences provided some compensation for the frustration she experienced at the hands of her cold and undemonstrative husband and enabled her to complete the work of mourning. The readiness to return in fantasy to these earlier pleasurable experiences was based upon an early fixation on her father.

The threatened return of her unconscious incestuous fantasies aroused intrapsychic conflict, which caused considerable anxiety against which she had to defend herself. The agonizing thought that remained repressed was: "I would like to leave my husband for another young man who will give me the same kind of love that I wanted from father." This thought, although repressed, was opposed by her superego and created anxiety which was then circumscribed by means of projection and displacement to the phobic situation.

Her inner impulse to seduce her father was projected onto the outside world in the form of a fear of being attacked and raped. She further concealed the real nature of her dread by displacing this fear to a fear of traveling alone in the street, the place where such an attack or seduction might occur. All these ideational complexes remained unconscious, and, prior to the onset of treatment, the patient was aware only of her fear of going alone into the street, i.e., her phobic symptom.

Originally, Freud saw the phobic reaction as a defense against libidinal impulses centering around the oedipal conflict. The core of her phobia, then, was based on her positive oedipal wishes for her father and the ensuing anxiety resulting from her fear of being punished for these incestuous wishes.

As a consequence of her phobia, she was able to retain both mother and father as love objects. Her need for punishment was also fulfilled by limitation of her freedom to travel, which was necessary in order to avoid encountering the phobic object, the forbidden suitor.

The primary gain, as in all phobias, was the confinement of her anxiety to the phobic situation which could then be avoided. The secondary gain was the extra attention and concern that she obtained from her husband and others as a result of her symptoms.

Helene Deutsch put more stress on the defense against aggressive wishes in the phobic neurosis. Bornstein has shown that preoedipal sources of anxiety, such as fear of the loss of love, or separation anxiety are powerful factors that influence and enter into the origin and subsequent development of a given phobia.

In addition to the emphasis on the influence of libidinal and aggressive derivatives in the formation of phobias, attention more recently has been directed to the importance of ego and superego deficiencies in the evolution of the phobic reaction. This point of view, in addition to taking into account the earlier stress on drive vicissitudes, also gives consideration to the ego and superego developmental sequences (Wangh, 1959).

To summarize, in phobias, as in other neuroses, we observe symptoms that defend against the anxiety resulting from intrapsychic conflicts around libidinal and aggressive impulses. By means of displacement as the primary psychic mechanism, the phobic patient is able to limit his anxiety to the specific phobic situation, which then can be avoided.

Although a phobia is classified as one of the psychoneuroses, phobic symptoms frequently occur in conjunction with other major diagnostic categories, such as schizophrenic psychosis, obsessive-compulsive neurosis, psychophysiological disorders, and depressions. It is valid to reserve the diagnosis of phobic neurosis for those in whom the predominant symptomatology is phobic in nature, whose major mechanism of defense is displacement, and in whom there is no evidence of the severe ego defects and ego regression seen in schizophrenia.

In the psychoneuroses, the treatment of choice is psychoanalysis or psychoanalytic psychotherapy which aims at bringing about a resolution of conflicts that have led to the formation of the neurosis. The severity of the anxiety and of the other symptoms may be diminished by the use of drugs and by supportive treatment. Casework, using supportive techniques, can be of great help in many instances of psychoneuroses, including phobias.

The prognosis depends on many factors, including the duration of the symptoms and the patient's capacity for insight, reality testing, and object relationships.

REFERENCES

Bornstein, B. (1949), The Analysis of a Phobic Child: Some Problems of Theory and Technique in Child Analysis. *The Psychoanalytic Study of the Child,* 3/4:181-226. New York: International Universities Press.

Deutsch, H. (1928), Agoraphobia. In: *Neuroses and Character Types.* New York: International Universities Press, 1965, pp. 97-116.

Freud, S. (1909), Analysis of a Phobia in a Five-Year-Old Boy. *Standard Edition,* 10:3-147. London: Hogarth Press, 1955.

Wangh, M. (1959), Structural Determinants of Phobia. *Journal of the American Psychoanalytic Association,* 7:675-695.

CHAPTER SIXTEEN

Hysterical Neurosis

JULIAN L. STAMM, M.D.

We now turn to another form of psychoneurosis, the hysterical neurosis. This disorder is subdivided into two main groupings: the conversion and the dissociative types. Of all the various psychological disturbances, the conversion type of hysteria is historically one of the best known to medical science. Hysteria, a term originally introduced by the ancient Greeks, described illnesses found among women and attributed to the "wandering" of the womb—in Greek, *hysteros*—from its original site to other parts of the body. In the Middle Ages in Europe many persons afflicted with hysteria and other mental illnesses were considered to have sold their souls to the devil. They were thrown into dungeons and often tortured and burned at the stake as heretics, witches, or warlocks.

Beginning with the Renaissance, the belief in demonology gradually subsided, to be replaced by an approach to mental illness corresponding to the evolving scientific climate of the age. In the nineteenth century most psychological disturbances, including hysteria, were assumed to be hereditary. Treatment at that time consisted primarily of rest cures, mineral baths, and medication that at best had a suggestive effect. In the last quarter of the century, hypnosis and suggestion, as well as weak electric currents became the prevalent forms of therapy for hysteria and other functional disorders. The investigation and psychological treatment of hysteria were spearheaded by the eminent French psychiatrists Charcot, Janet, and Bernheim.

Freud studied psychopathology, especially hysteria, in Charcot's clinic in Paris in 1885-86. While he also accepted the importance of the hereditary predisposition in the origin of hysteria, he came to place an even greater emphasis than Charcot on the psychological and functional aspects. Collaborating with the Viennese internist J. Breuer, Freud (1893-1895) arrived at the realization that hysterical phenomena were functional disturbances based on psychological traumas. He discovered, furthermore, that there was usually a precipitating traumatic event, the memory of which had been repressed. At first he believed that a cure could be accomplished simply by uncovering the memory and re-experiencing the affect of the traumatic event. This early method of treatment was termed abreaction or catharsis. Although Freud originally employed hypnosis as a treatment technique, he found that many individuals could not be hypnotized effectively, and that even those who could did not necessarily benefit from hypnosis, since the mental content brought back to consciousness under hypnosis was not always recalled and assimilated after the patient had been restored to his usual state of consciousness.

And so, in the 1890's, Freud replaced the use of hypnosis with the method of "free association." He encouraged his patients to say freely whatever came to their minds. Based on the material he obtained through hypnosis and with the help of this new method, he arrived at the conclusion that hysterical patients had suffered sexual abuse at the hands of their parents or older siblings, usually before the age of eight. This assumption, based on the reports of patients, could not be verified, and seemed implausible. Freud finally concluded that a great many stories of early sexual seduction were fantasies that had arisen in the course of early psychosexual development, had become repressed, and eventually contributed to the hysterical neurosis.

It is important to stress that in the conversion type of hysterical neurosis the symptoms are functional, i.e., not based on structural organic change. Of course, a competent neurological examination must be performed to make sure that an organic impairment of the nervous system is not mistaken for conversion hysteria. Multiple sclerosis, for example, may be incorrectly diagnosed as conversion hysteria, especially in its initial stages, if a neurological examination is omitted. In multiple sclerosis, as in any organic disease involving the nervous system, the symptoms correspond to the distribution of the nerves supplying the various muscles, areas of the skin, and mucous membranes. In hysteria, the symptoms do not follow the actual distribution of the nerves, but rather the sick person's assumptions and fantasies which are expressed in "body language" without regard to organic anatomical factors. The functional disturbance in hysteria may be severe, but because it does not involve any organic impairment of the nervous system it is reversible with proper treatment.

Conversion hysteria is frequently manifested by a variety of symptoms involving the motor function, the sensory qualities, and even the visceral organs. Conversion hysteria may, however, be monosymptomatic and manifest itself by only one symptom, for instance, the paralysis of one limb, lack of sensation in the hand, hysterical blindness, or vomiting.

The motor disturbances of hysteria may manifest themselves in hypo- or hyperfunction. The instances of hypofunction, i.e., decreased function, include partial or complete paralysis of muscles and muscle groups that can be moved voluntarily. This may result in the inability to stand, walk, write, or perform any other tasks involving the voluntary musculature of the body. If we speak of decreased function, it may actually be a masked hyperfunction—or increased function—of certain muscles which, through excessive nervous stimulation, are kept in a state of spastic immobility that either interferes with or prevents skilled performance, as, for example, writer's cramp which makes writing clumsy, slow, or even entirely impossible. In hyperfunction, epileptiform attacks may occur and be associated with changed states of consciousness. Isolated spasms and tics may also be based on conversion of anxiety aroused by primitive prephallic impulses. In epileptiform seizures, as well as in tics, an organic causation has to be exluded by a thorough neurological investigation before a diagnosis of hysteria can be made.

A brief example of a hysterical affliction interfering with motor performance will illustrate the general description.

A soldier in the Second World War saw his close friend killed by a shell only a few feet from him. The following morning he was picked up on the field and had to be transported on a stretcher because he was unable to walk. Physical examination was entirely negative, reflexes were active and equal. He could execute all voluntary movements while lying down. This was a case of astasia-abasia, i.e., an inability to stand and to walk, a conversion reaction precipitated by an overwhelming emotional trauma. The emotional conflict was then expressed in body terms by conversion, culminating in an inhibition of motor activities.

In the sensory sphere, all the senses may be symptomatically affected in the hysterical neurosis. Hysterical blindness, deafness and deaf-mutism, the latter a combination of a sensory and motor disturbance, have been known for a long time and often have yielded to various kinds of miracle cures which are based on strong belief and suggestion. The most common forms of hysterical symptoms in the sensory sphere are anesthesia (lack of sensitivity) or hyperesthesia (abormal and increased sensitivity) of the skin and mucous membranes. In glove or stocking anesthesia the patient complains of loss of sensation corresponding to a glove or stocking distribution on the limb; this rules out organic pathology, for it does not correspond to the anatomical distribution of the peripheral nerves. Sexual frigidity, so often encountered in women, is also considered a form of conversion hysteria.

In hyperesthesia we observe pain or increased sensitivity to touch that cannot be explained by organic factors, does not conform to any specific anatomical or neuromuscular innervation, and, hence, is of functional origin.

Loss of response to pain and even complete anesthesia may also form part of a dissociated state in which the subject becomes oblivious to pain. Rituals and trance states among primitive tribes at times involve hypnotic phenomena in which the subject is able to endure piercing wounds by sharp instruments or exposure to flames without experiencing pain. Other symptoms quite frequently seen are impairment of swallowing and gag reflexes (globus hystericus) in which the patient complains of a lump in his throat and an inability to swallow.

Painful sensations in any part of the body, often mimicking organic illness other than a neurological disorder, are frequent symptoms of conversion hysteria. Hysterical hypochondriasis in which the patient complains of various types of body ailments, such as pain in the chest, shortness of breath, believing he has an organic heart or lung disease, etc., must also be differentiated from schizophrenic hypochondriasis. In the latter, however, the somatic delusions are more bizarre than in hysteria, and there are other accompanying manifestations of severe ego-regression, especially loss of reality-testing, that are not part of a conversion-reaction.

The affect of many hysterical patients is one of indifference and unconcern—originally called *la belle indifference* by the French psychiatrists who were the first to describe it. The unconcern and even serenity of some hysterics is often in stark contrast to their severe disability. Quite at variance with the affective tone of hysterical neurotics, the hysterical personality disorders show emotional liability and excitability.

Psychodynamics of Conversion

In conversion reactions, the various physical symptoms represent a distorted expression of repressed, unconscious strivings or memories of fantasies and/or traumatic events through "body language." If the repressed material were permitted to gain access to consciousness, anxiety would be generated. The ego, therefore, sets up defenses against the forbidden instinctual wishes and the memory of the trauma, initially by means of repression and, if repression fails, by the mechanism of conversion. The final symptom then represents a compromise between the unconscious wish and the defense against it, as well as unconscious punishment for it.

By conversion, the symptom is expressed in physical language, and the body part is said to be instinctualized, i.e., it expresses unconscious sexual or aggressive fantasies. This may be manifested as a disturbance of motor function, sensation, or certain visceral functions. As was stated, in all instances of true conversion there is no organic defect, and the physical symptom, after being translated into the underlying ideational and emotional factors in treatment will ultimately be abandoned when the individual is aware of his unconscious conflicts and can work them through on a psychological level.

As in all forms of psychopathology, there may be one or more psychological traumas that precipitate the neurosis. These episodes, however, are only triggers and set in motion the process of regression.

In hysterical neurosis, the basic conflict is at the oedipal level. Forbidden oedipal wishes threaten to emerge into consciousness and are expressed in a more or less distorted form through the hysterical symptoms. It is important to bear in mind that there may be strong oral and anal fixations in hysteria. These fixations then lend an oral and anal coloring to the oedipal-genital fantasies. Sometimes the genital fantasies will seize on pregenital routes as a means of discharge, as in the case of hysterical vomiting.

Sometimes hysterical symptoms, usually of a transitory nature, may be based on the process of identification.

A man developed severe abdominal pain when his wife went into labor. He had strong unconscious pregnancy fantasies which were expressed in the painful conversion symptom. Another man, who had never suffered from asthma previously, developed severe wheezing two weeks after he witnessed the death of his son. The boy had sustained a fatal chest injury as a result of an auto accident while his father was driving. In part, the wheezing represented a hysterical identification with his dead son, who had literally gasped for breath as he lay dying from chest hemorrhages, and, in part, it expressed his guilt for contributing to the fatal accident.

Hysterical Dissociative Reactions

In the second major type of hysterical neurosis, the dissociative type, there is an altered state of consciousness, a change in the sense of identity, or both. Hysterical epileptiform seizures, now only rarely encountered, are accompanied by a clouding or loss of consciousness. Hysterical seizures may take the form of isolated spasms or of convulsions involving the whole body, simulating *grand mal* epilepsy. The seizures represent distorted pantomimic expressions of underlying sexual or aggressive fantasies, and may be accompanied by screaming, crying, or hysterical laughter. Somnambulism, amnesia, fugue states, and multiple personality are also considered dissociative hysterical conditions. Whether the grouping of these varied conditions as dissociative-type hysteria is justified on etiological grounds, i.e., on the basis of similar origin, is not certain. The most frequently encountered disturbance, somnambulism or sleepwalking, may include the performance of complex actions in an altered state of consciousness. Sleepwalking may not be remembered at all upon awakening, or may be recalled only in the way that a dream is remembered. As with dreams, behavior during sleepwalking may reflect conflicts, fears, and wishes.

A middle-aged man reports that he has had frequent episodes of somnambulism since early childhood. He invariably finds himself walking toward his mother's bedroom. After marriage, in addition to the episodes of somnambulism, he frequently embraces his wife, calling her endearingly by his mother's and sister's names, and then awakens in a state of acute anxiety.

In this case, during the spells of sleepwalking, oedipal strivings were clearly expressed. In hysterical attacks and in somnambulism, other unconscious wishes may be represented in a more or less distorted form, for example, wishes and fantasies having to do with pregnancy, childbirth, sexual intercourse, and the like.

Amnesia is the result of repression. Dissociative hysterical amnesia is massive and may blot out important, sometimes traumatic, periods of a person's life. There are instances where people forget their entire past and assume a new identity. This type of amnesia is a precondition for fugue states and multiple personality. In contrast to organic types of amnesia, a recovery of the forgotten memories in dissociative amnesia can either occur spontaneously, or else be achieved by hypnosis or by the administration of drugs (barbiturates).

Someone in fugue states may appear normal to the casual observer, but has actually assumed an identity different from his real one. This new, spurious sense of identity is based on unconscious fantasies. The rare instances of double or alternating personality may be considered to be prolonged and, as it were, more stable fugue states. An example of a shift in identity in a hysterical fugue state will serve to illustrate this condition:

During the Second World War a young soldier entered a battalion aid station dressed in an Italian uniform. He could speak only Italian and was taken prisoner by the American troops. Examination soon revealed that he suffered from total amnesia and had adopted another personality in which he presented himself as an Italian soldier. He could not recall his name, address, the names of family members, or whether he was married or single. Under chemical hypnosis his exclusive use of the Italian language gradually disappeared and was replaced by English with a foreign accent, and then finally by fluent English. He turned out to be American-born, a resident of the midwest and a married man with two children. The last time he had spoken Italian was with his grandmother as a little boy. The amnesia was precipitated by a series of shell explosions nearby. He showed a massive amnesia for the past, an altered state of consciousness, a change in his identity. His fugue state subsided under hypnotic therapy.

Hysteria Superimposed on Organic Conditions

As was stated earlier, hysteria must be distinguished from organic neurological illness. At times, it is difficult to differentiate hysteria from organic illness, if malingering is involved to support insurance claims following an injury or to escape from some onerous, unacceptable task. There are many instances of painful hysterical sensations being superimposed on an organic condition. Pain in the location of an operative site may continue long after surgery is completed and the operative site healed. Pain in the chest following recovery from a heart attack may persist without any organic cause and represent a conversion of the severe anxiety following a life-endangering illness.

The treatment of choice in hysteria is any form of uncovering therapy which will give the patient insight into his unconscious fantasies and memories, thereby translating his somatic symptoms into their underlying psychological equivalents. The various types of therapy may include psychoanalysis, psychoanalytically oriented psychotherapy, or hypnosis.

REFERENCES

Breuer, J., & Freud, S. (1893-1895), Studies on Hysteria. *Standard Edition.* 2. London: Hogarth Press, 1955.

Freud, S. (1905), Fragment of an Analysis of a Case of Hysteria. *Standard Edition.* 7:3-122. London: Hogarth Press, 1953.

——— (1908), Hysterical Phantasies and Their Relation to Bisexuality. *Standard Edition.* 9:157-166. London: Hogarth Press, 1959.

SUGGESTED READING

Abse, D. W. (1959), Hysteria. In: *American Handbook of Psychiatry,* ed. S. Arieti. New York: Basic Books, pp. 272-292.

Deutsch, F., ed. (1959) *On the Mysterious Leap from the Mind to the Body.* New York: International Universities Press.

Deutsch, H. (1965), *Neuroses and Character Types.* New York: International Universities Press, pp. 29-73.

Engel, G. L., & Schmale, A. H., Jr. (1967), Psychoanalytic Theory of Somatic Disorder: Conversion, Specificity, and the Disease Onset Situation. *Journal of the American Psychoanalytic Association,* 5:344-365.

Fenichel, O. (1945), *The Psychoanalytic Theory of Neurosis.* New York: W. W. Norton, pp. 216-235.

Schur, M. (1955), Comments on the Metapsychology of Somatization. *The Psychoanalytic Study of the Child,* 10:119-164. New York: International Universities Press.

Rangell, L. (1959), The Nature of Conversion. *Journal of the American Psychoanalytic Association*, 7:632-662.

CHAPTER SEVENTEEN

Obsessive-Compulsive Neurosis

IRVING STERNSCHEIN, M.D.

One who suffers from an obsessive-compulsive neurosis is compelled repeatedly to think or to avoid thinking certain thoughts, or to do or to avoid doing certain acts, in order to ward off feelings of anxiety or guilt. Obsessional thoughts may be formed from any kind of idea. They may be "wishes, temptations, impulses, reflections, doubts, commands or prohibitions" (Freud, 1909), and they may seem to be without motive or meaning. Some are such simple thoughts as a word, a name, an odor, a seemingly nonsensical phrase, or a bothersome mental image. Others are more complex: a musical motif, a mathematical problem, a philosophical notion, a religious system, or a conscious fantasy. They frequently concern disagreeable or disgusting things, immodest or blasphemous thoughts, or morbid fears of some threatening misfortune. The great attention given to these seemingly inappropriate, nonsensical, or indifferent ideas suggests that they are distortions of another mental product for which the emphasis would be more understandable. Psychoanalysis has shown that the force behind these repetitive thoughts comes from a warded-off, associatively linked idea of which the subject is unaware.

An unmarried young accountant had the conviction that his penis was underdeveloped and doubted that he could father a child. He had forfeited several chances for marriage because of these persistent notions. He submitted to examination by an eminent medical authority in the field of fertility, but this did not help him to overcome his doubt. It was only after considerable psychoanalytic treatment that he succeeded in uncovering the latent obsession that if he married, his mother would die.

A recently married, devout young woman became obsessed with the thought, "The Virgin Mary is a whore." Because of her shame and because of a fear that she might sometime speak her thought aloud, she began to withdraw from social contacts. Her early history included frequent exposure to the sounds of parental intercourse and her mother's evident pleasure from it. The thought that was being warded off was "mother is a whore."

The obsessive neurotic is disturbed by the peculiarity and strangeness of his abnormal thoughts. Even if he expresses some measure of belief in his ideas, he struggles to eliminate them, usually by bringing about some change in himself. In contrast, the psychotic with a delusional idea that may be even more bizarre or inappropriate accepts his false belief as the truth and thereby attempts to transform reality into conformity with his views.

Obsessive thoughts about murderous or incestuous acts are not uncommon. It is possible for these thoughts to enter consciousness because they are not accompanied by the appropriate emotion. The feeling has become separated (isolated) from the thought. Consequently, there is no pressure for discharge through action.

A good mother who loved her infant son sought psychiatric help because she was tormented by frightening thoughts of injuring or killing him. She had tried desperately to force these thoughts out of her mind by a variety of diversions and by drinking excessively, but these efforts were unsuccessful.

An unmarried middle-aged man developed the obsessive fear that he would punch the pregnant wife of his friend in the stomach and kill her child. When he was a child, a much wanted sister was born into a family of three boys and became a focus of his jealousy. He was repeatedly cautioned to treat her gently and frequently forbidden to play with her because he was too rough.

Compulsions are essentially obsessions in which there is an insistent urge to act. They are made up of a combination of instinctual and anti-instinctual forces and are often experienced as if they were commands or prohibitions coming from within. The symptom may stress either the instinctual drive or the superego's inhibiting position.

A female patient who had unconscious death wishes for her four younger brothers would awaken regularly to watch their breathing in order to reassure herself that they were alive and that she loved them. Her checking soon became insufficient to allay her fear of their death, and she began to awaken them. But in doing this, she simultaneously allowed some of her hostility to break through by becoming the disturber of their sleep.

This example clearly illustrates the typical two-phase structure of many compulsive symptoms. Either love or hate may be expressed in the first phase and then be undone by the second. The true significance of his actions escapes the compulsive. He is unaware of the ambivalence conflict in which love and hate are of approximately equal strength. Unconscious guilt feelings about either the love of a forbidden object or the hate expressed by the ritual makes necessary the undoing that takes place in the second phase. Complications arise when other people are required as witnesses of positive feelings. When the patient awakened her brothers, she told them she wanted to see if they were "all right" (i.e., alive). They were being forced to learn of her concern for their well-being (i.e., love). A compulsion such as this is usually a defense against an unconscious murderous impulse.

Phobic situations that are avoided may become obsessive preoccupations or may be replaced by compulsive acts to further insure avoidance of that which is feared. Thus, a fear of germs (mysophobia) may be overshadowed by a constant consuming preoccupation with cleanliness. Such compulsive cleansing operations as hand and body washing compulsions or strict household cleaning rituals may follow. These practices and others like them may even expand into compulsive systems. Intrafamilial disharmony between husbands and wives, mothers and their children, or between siblings is often caused by opposing or different compulsive systems.

When obsessive thoughts and compulsive actions occur and recur, one is readily aware of their driven quality. They may range from mild ego-syntonic eccentricities to exceedingly neurotic disturbances bordering on schizophrenia proper. The characteristic symptoms often have a tendency to spread and become relentlessly chronic, causing a neurosis in which the suffering is intense and the internal equilibrium and external adaptation badly crippled. In the most advanced cases, the preoccupation with obsessional ideas and compulsive behavior can lead to a complete paralysis of action and will. Failure to submit to the inner commands or prohibitions of this disease evokes tormenting states of tension, anxiety, or guilt feelings. Obsessive and compulsive symptoms are triggered by small quantities of anxiety (signal anxiety) in an effort to forestall the appearance of the more massive anxiety (traumatic anxiety) that would occur if the pathogenic unconscious fantasy or urge were permitted to erupt into consciousness. Guilt feelings are the principle underlying motive for the defense.

Psychodynamic Considerations

As a childhood neurosis, this psychopathological reaction generally does not appear before the age of five, when the required intellectual powers (ego functions) and moral and ethical standards (superego functions) have been sufficiently developed. Pregenital fixations and the pressure of heightened instinctual forces at puberty and during adolescence are the other basic factors that contribute to the succumbing of otherwise predisposed individuals. Because constitution and heredity affect drive and ego development, they also play a varying role. An environment in which parents or parent surrogates with obsessive traits cause or allow anal seductions, or interfere with anal development by excessive, early, and strict bowel training, is conducive to the appearance of this disorder. Any of life's crises or stresses that can precipitate other mental disorders may also initiate the chain of psychic events that leads to formation of an obsessive-compulsive reaction. Failure or success, loss or danger of loss of a loved one—either by departure, illness, or death—an overwhelming sexual experience, marriage or impending marriage, the birth of a child, or an unexpected catastrophic event may be followed by the appearance of obsessions or compulsions, or both.

Because neurotic symptoms are the result of intrapsychic conflict, it is evident that for such conflict to develop there must be a sufficient differentiation of the psychic structures id, ego, and superego. Such a degree of differentiation occurs by the time of the phallic-oedipal phase of psychosexual development. As in other neuroses, the unconscious Oedipus complex, that is, the phallic and incestuous strivings for the parent of the opposite sex and the death wishes against the parent of the same sex, with the resultant guilt feelings and anxiety, is of central importance.

Typically, for the obsessional neurotic, a situation in life which comes to represent an oedipal victory may cause enough stress on a tenuously resolved Oedipus complex to upset the prevailing emotional equilibrium. The psychological defenses that previously sufficed are no longer adequate to the test of keeping incestuous desires and death wishes from coming into consciousness. Sometimes before and sometimes after these forbidden wishes reach consciousness, the ego's "alarm" system, aroused by unconscious guilt feelings, evokes a signal of anxiety. This initiates a regressive process that enables the ego to utilize more primitive and, up to now, sparingly used mechanisms of defense and modes of adaptation. These psychological devices, which originated and were predominant in the anal phase of psychosexual development, are once again called into service by the ego to supplement or replace the presently ineffective methods of defense. The ego regression also results in a return to magical thinking, to a tendency to primary-process thinking, to a loosening of reality testing, and to a weakened capacity of the ego to synthesize opposing mental currents. Moreover, there is also an instinctual or drive regression, so that a shift takes place from the dangerous oedipal wishes to the developmentally more primitive and less dangerous interest in the excretory processes, in the anus, and in the fecal product, and to derivative phenomena that are associatively linked to them. As a result, obsessional and compulsive symptoms that become clinically manifest are concerned with destruction, cruelty, dirtiness, domination, parsimony, order, lateness, and their antitheses.

PHENOMENA RELATED TO INSTINCTUAL REGRESSION

Frequently, contradictory behavior occurs in which opposites such as disorder and order or dirtiness and cleanliness coexist. Obsessives can have scatological—excretory—practices of which they are ashamed, so that they are either kept secret or rationalized as natural or necessary. The act of defecation itself may become affected. The fecal mass may become small, hard, and fragmented as a result of retention, or unformed from a need to frequently and hurriedly expel rectal contents that are unconsciously regarded as dangerous. Thinking and speech undergo changes because they become unconsciously representative of anal processes and because of the ego regression leading to magical thinking.

With the obsessive-compulsive neurosis, the total behavior is changed to a greater or lesser degree by the marked anal regression. The distortions of character and the symptomatic elaborations which have as their chief aim the relief of anxiety may be successful in reestablishing the psychic equilibrium for a time, but the cost to total adjustment is usually considerable. The internal contradiction of the coexistence of love and hate—ambivalence—which typifies the anal stage of psychosexual development reappears when the ego's capacity for fusion of these opposing affects decreases. This is a major reason for the impairment of the capacity for sound object relations and the consequent distortions of interpersonal relationships. The compulsive's ambivalence also can make him turn against his previously established protective rules and systems so that he may sometimes oppose his superego as well as his instinctual drives.

The concurrence of masculine and feminine strivings in the same person—bisexuality—another aspect of the anal period, is also an important factor in symptom formation. For example, the fact that the anus (and rectum) is a hollow organ which can receive as well as expel is utilized by most compulsives for the expression of receptive fantasies. The unconscious wish is to have something inserted or retained in the body as a woman does. The symbolic castration implicit in this feminine identification is not what is sought; rather, surrendering the masculine position has the aim of relieving anxiety by disavowing the guilt-provoking oedipal desires. On the other hand, the same male compulsive may simultaneously build up his body through ritualized gymnastics, thereby expressing the unconscious fantasy that his body is a giant phallus whose power he is enhancing. The conflict of passivity versus activity is likewise a frequent component of the obsessive-compulsive neurosis.

Genital sexuality is also altered so that it is viewed in anal terms as a dirty act, or as a financial matter in prostitution fantasies. The semen may be withheld—ejaculatio retardata—or expelled prematurely—ejaculatio praecox—to avoid soiling the partner, or the vagina may be confused with the rectum (cloacal theory). In addition, anal-sadistic fantasies may become linked with sexual intercourse, unconsciously equating it with a fight in which one partner is physically destroyed or castrated.

One compulsive woman would acknowledge her desire for sexual intercourse and then retire to the bathroom for extended periods to "prepare" herself by going through an elaborate body and vaginal cleansing ritual while her eager and aroused husband waited for 30 minutes to an hour. In this way she asserted her dominance and control over him. While waiting, her husband's annoyance built up to the point where he was often unable to achieve or sustain an erection when his wife emerged. After having been symbolically castrated by being kept waiting, her passive husband became impotent as a defense against his retaliatory sadistic urges. In so doing, he denied his wife his penis, thus underscoring her penislessness (castration). This contest had many parallels in their everyday life.

Phenomena Related to Ego Regression

As mentioned before, ego functions regress along with the instinctual drives, so that thinking becomes interlaced with archaic elements. A failure to distinguish sufficiently words or thoughts from deeds causes the former to evoke superego censure that is appropriate for the latter. Words are dealt with as if they can kill or revive, can perform magic or bring back the past. This omnipotence of thought has its source in the characteristic fantasies of omnipotence originating in the anal and even in the more primitive oral periods.

Doubting, another common symptom, arises from the weakening of reality testing produced by perceptual distortion and by the use of denial mechanisms. The doubting is basically a displacement of the obsessive's underlying doubt about his ability to love and about his sexual identity. Hence, ambivalence and bisexuality are the essential psychic determinants of this symptom as well. In daily life, doubt is displaced onto minor issues and decisions so that feelings of uncertainty abound. The underlying ambivalence and bisexuality that is expressed through the characteristic defensive measures and the typical symptoms contribute to the two-phase structure of the symptoms and to their tendency to progression or spreading. The ambivalence and bisexuality conflicts also markedly affect the intellectual sphere and can produce preoccupations with issues and questions for which no one has absolute certainty, e.g., the length and meaning of life, life after death, etc. When ruminations about life and death or other such matters persist and expand, with much time and energy given over to them, we have a condition of obsessive brooding. If sexual significance has been unconsciously attached to the brooding, an otherwise painful experience becomes a source of masochistic gratification.

The obsessive is notorious for his tendency to procrastinate. He exaggerates preparatory acts because he is afraid of the "real thing." If his procrastination becomes intolerable, he may act without thought or devise a compulsive scheme to break the impasse. This may then be followed by doubts or falsification of facts, generally of small or unimportant details. The tendency to falsification may be in striking contrast to the conscientiousness and exactness of the obsessive-compulsive person.

The intellect of the compulsive neurotic, though often highly developed, is nevertheless concerned with magic and superstition. The superstitutions are not the unsophisticated ones of ghosts and goblins, but rather have to do with such things as premonitions, prophetic dreams or pseudoscientific fads, errors of memory, and visual illusions. Minor scientific observations or facts are used for substantiation. Just as material things can be used as talismans, so can thoughts become "good luck" charms.

A patient who made a point of carrying at least a sliver of wood for use in an eating ritual and as a protection against his own death, occasionally found himself without it. If there was no wood object that he could touch as a substitute, thinking about wood could mitigate his anxiety.

The absolution and redemption that compulsive ceremonials afford offer a protection similar to that offered in religious rituals. Freud (1907), therefore, spoke of the compulsion neurosis as a "private religion." The conscious ego usually knows what is true and what is false, but an unconscious part of the ego attempts to alter or repudiate reality by the formation of ceremonials. This requires some reversion to early infantile omnipotence with its accompanying narcissistic overevaluation. The compulsive is thus one notch closer to psychosis than the hysteric.

The prominently used defense mechanisms of undoing, reaction formation, isolation of thought and affect, intellectualization, and regression supersede repression in importance. When repression occurs, it is mostly secondary and often accounts for the vagueness and "burned-out" or dream-like quality of long-standing obsessions and compulsions. The defense of doing-undoing is directed against real or imaginary acts of soiling and against aggressive wishes or acts. Compulsive and ritualized washing, a common symptom, is meant to do away with sins or dirt and is related to conflicts over masturbation. The touching compulsion *delire de toucher,* which is often carried out in a numbered sequence, is likewise the reflection of a superego attitude that is opposed to the instinctual intention. Such compulsions may be replaced by compulsive counting, which has the same dynamic significance. "Odd" numbers, whether in an action or by counting, usually reflect the aggressive instinctual wish, and "even" numbers the love demanded by the superego. The compulsive act of touching may also be displaced to other sensory modalities, for example, "touching with the eyes," or it may be otherwise disguised.

One angry compulsive man often avoided looking at hated male passenger-rivals in subway trains. Instead he looked to the right or left where he usually lined up their symbolic substitute in the form of the supporting tunnel beams.

Sighting in this way served as a simultaneous doing and undoing. He was taking aim as if with a gun but also was protecting his rivals by unifying them into one solid indestructible symbolic mass onto which he directed his hostility.

Reaction formation, which is directed primarily against unconscious hostility and sadism, accounts for such ego-syntonic traits as excessive gentleness, kindness, orderliness, or frugality. These traits are frequently found in compulsive characters as well as compulsive neurotics. Because they are a source of pride and heightened self-evaluation they are not readily accessible to change and add greatly to the difficulties in the treatment of obsessive-compulsive neuroses.

Isolation of affect, one of the most pervasive mechanisms of defense, refers to the disconnecting of thoughts from the emotions with which they are linked. This may be done by inserting spatial or temporal intervals between the ideational and emotional realms to keep them separate. Thus, expressing of feelings may be postponed until some time has elapsed.

An extreme but by no means unusual example is that of a patient who went through an intense emotional crisis and then revealed only weeks later, after the crisis had subsided, that he had learned of the mortal illness of a dear friend at the time his panic anxiety began. The chronological relationship and the fact that the woman was dying of cancer, as had his mother, had not occurred to him. Even after these connections were pointed out to him, he responded with a "so what?" defense. He felt the necessity of clinging to the original isolation out of fear of his own ambivalence and because of the magical notion that his hostility could have brought about her death, as he had felt it had brought about his mother's death.

Unlike the hysteric who has amnesia for the pathogenic traumas of childhood, the obsessive feels that he has always known the traumatic events of the past. He fails, however, to recognize their true significance. When he is first informed of their importance, he is likely to negate it for a time. The obsessive's traumatic childhood memories often have an interrelationship. As with two dreams occurring in the same night, the relationship may be that of cause and effect. The obsessive-compulsive also may discuss the most exciting events with complete calm. At another point in the same discussion an incomprehensible and disproportionate emotion may appear without there being any awareness of the shift of the affect.

An obsessional woman could fully experience emotions about having had an illegal abortion for an out-of-wedlock pregnancy because she didn't think of either the pregnancy or the abortion as "serious." In fact, this was a defensive attitude she adopted generally. She had suffered the trauma of a sordid separation and subsequent divorce of her parents when she was four years of age. In comparison with that, nothing was serious.

In addition, the obsessive may convert total feelings into localized feelings, or specific feelings into generalized ones. Important life activities may be disconnected from the rest of life by seemingly innocent rituals before and after the important activity.

The isolation of tender from sensual components of sexuality is a frequent occurrence among compulsive men and women. Sexual enjoyment in such instances can be experienced with a partner for whom there is no tender feeling. Some men put one type of woman on a pedestal and avoid them sexually, while they find "degraded" women intensely exciting. Such people "cannot desire where they love and cannot love where they desire."

Genetically, the mechanism of isolation is related to the ancient—and childhood—taboo against touching. This taboo is directed against the unconscious instinctual urges to commit incest and to kill; consequently, it is also directed against the urge to masturbate, which is so regularly accompanied by oedipal fantasies and their manifold derivatives. Another antecedent of isolation, which has its roots in the anal phase of libidinal development, is the admonition to keep dirty and clean things apart. The normal prototype of isolation is "logical thinking" which consists of the elimination of emotionally tinged wishful elements in the interest of objectivity and not for defensive reasons.

Phenomena Related to Superego Regressions

As mentioned earlier, the obsessive-compulsive submits to and obeys superego dictates, but he also rebels against them. The utter absurdity of many of the pseudoproblems that are the subjects of obsessive thoughts indicates a malicious and mocking attitude toward the superego. Moreover, morality often becomes a pseudomorality; the superego of the obsessive is a corruptible superego. Concomitant with the instinctual and ego regression, there is partial superego regression, so that its archaic, sadistic precursors become reactivated. Moral masochism, or the need for punishment, is the complement of the sadism of the regressed superego. Thus, the compulsive accepts and seeks punishment and opportunities for expiation, sacrifice, and even torture to a remarkable degree. The need for punishment is a reflection of the more basic need for absolution. Consequently, external assurances are sought to prove reliability and worth. One of the more frequent reasons for suicide in the obsessive is his need to be rid of the unbearable tension evoked by unconscious feelings of guilt. The obsessive-compulsive differs from many guilt-ridden and more dangerously suicidal depressives, however, because of the numerous pathways available to him for partial or distorted expressions of aggression against objects. This diminishes the need for large amounts of aggression to be turned against the self. Of course, when the obsessive-compulsive neurotic decompensates sufficiently for a depression to develop, the suicidal possibilities are the same as in depressive conditions of equal severity.

Anal Character Traits

Those with anal-sadistic predispositions do not always go on to develop an obsessive or compulsive neurosis. They may exhibit only the anal character traits without the obsessive or compulsive symptoms of the fully developed neurosis. To the well-known triad of orderliness, parsimony, and obstinacy of the anal character may be added the traits of conscientiousness, punctuality, meticulousness, propriety, and scrupulous honesty and fairness. All of these traits are related in one way or another to bowel training, the child's first developmental experience in which he learns to postpone or renounce a direct instinctual pleasure for the sake of the environment. This is the time when the adult first must depend on the child. For the young child, feces, as a concept, usually becomes connected with the idea of gifts.

Later on in childhood, the concept of feces becomes linked with the idea of money. Feces and money ultimately become deindividualized possessions which are simultaneously valued and regarded with contempt. Childhood attitudes connected with toilet training persist in self-satisfaction or discontent with the self, in collecting manias or in miserliness, in mannerisms of speech and thinking, in desires for power, in fears of starting something or of changing the status quo, and in deciding everything for oneself or in needing others to do everything for one. Such character patterns are, in part, reaction formations, but may also serve as sublimations. In either case they are ego-syntonic. An overly sympathetic attitude toward the bereaved and a great awareness of death and length of life is also not uncommon. Many anal characters regularly study obituary columns, and some feel obliged to attend numerous funeral services, even those for remote acquaintances or for relatives of friends.

At times, the individual with an anal character or with compulsive traits shows a general muscular rigidity with muscular spasms or its opposite, a flabby hypotonus. Either type of physical "armoring" causes an unreadiness for action. The vegetative nervous system may also be involved, so that many obsessive-compulsives suffer from constipation with rigid regularity of bowel movements while others may have frequent loose stools with rectal urgency.

Differential Diagnosis

The obsessive-compulsive neurosis characterized by anal-sadistic regression sometimes may be difficult to differentiate from schizophrenia, particularly from its latent, incipient, or ambulatory forms. Obsessive thinking and compulsive actions may be a last line of defense preceding the development of a catatonic or paranoid type of schizophrenia, or they may supplant the psychotic symptoms when a remission occurs. In such cases, there are anal fixation points and a history of anal regression in childhood. In rare instances, when an obsessive fear of touching due to fear of contamination is extreme, the muscular rigidity may result in a state of immobility, making for possible confusion with a catatonic state of withdrawal.

The fully developed schizophrenic, however, shows more marked disturbances of ego (and superego) functions than the obsessive compulsive. His defects in reality testing are severe enough to make it possible for delusions and hallucinations to occur. The schizophrenic's thinking also becomes more childlike, grossly illogical and full of symbolism. His intellect suffers as a result of a significant loss of the capacity for abstraction and because of memory abnormalities and serious perceptual distortions. The relationship to objects in schizophrenia is severely hampered by poor control of the drives which leads to impulsivity, and by the deeper narcissistic regression which can result in various degrees of withdrawal.

Although it is ordinarily not difficult to distinguish an obsessive-compulsive reaction from an anxiety or repressive reaction, anxiety and depression may become prominent features of this illness, especially when a progressing obsessive-compulsive neurosis decompensates. Phobic symptoms, as mentioned earlier, sometimes become obsessive preoccupations. When genitality is relinquished in hysteria, or sometimes after the menopause, regression to a compulsion neurosis may follow.

The presence of reaction formation and intellectualization in compulsives helps to distinguish their acts from the behavior of addicts, psychopaths, and many delinquents whose actions are compelled by the impact of the instinctual drives themselves. Similarly, the repetitive actions of very young children and of mental defectives can be differentiated from compulsives because these defenses are not involved.

Treatment

The treatment of choice for this tenacious neurosis is classical psychoanalysis. Even the analyst, however, may have to content himself with less than optimal results. Accordingly, psychoanalytic psychotherapies at times achieve only modest results or no results at all. When psychotherapy, including casework treatment, has a beneficial effect, this usually occurs through modifying or eliminating stressful reality situations or by reinforcing the obsessive-compulsive defensive structure or by offering psychological support that enables the obsessive patient to break out of a specific impasse in which his ego is caught in a state of ambivalent paralysis. Even these accomplishments, temporary or meager as they may be, are welcomed by the harassed patient. The difficulties involved with any of the expressive-analytic therapies arise from the patient's inability to speak freely and his ever-present tendency to "split hairs." Magical thinking renders the best, intellectually comprehended interpretations ineffective, because intellectual understanding is placed in the service of resistance to emotional grasp. Sometimes the neurotic pleasures accruing from sexualized thought and speech will adversely affect communication with the therapist. The compliant compulsive who overvalues his reaction formations invariably regards the therapist as a seducer. In the psychoanalysis of an obsessive-compulsive, greater therapeutic penetration is required than in hysterical reactions, and sometimes serious psychosomatic complications occur when the obsessive-compulsive is unable to deal with the strong emotions that are released. Such an eventuality may force an interruption or termination of treatment.

Of the available types of treatment, psychopharmacological and somatic therapies have a lesser role to play. It has been claimed that prefrontal lobotomy in the most severe and resistant patients can reduce anxiety and tension, but the possibility of some permanent brain damage with irreversible intellectual impairment is a significant deterrent. Electrocerebral convulsive therapy—shock treatment—may conceivably be of some help to those deteriorating obsessives who develop a severe depressive reaction. If such treatment is used, it is directed against the depressive symptom. Obsessive thinking may be blocked for a time by the electrically induced confusion, but it returns as soon as the confusion clears. These somatic treatments are rarely used by careful and knowledgeable psychiatrists, but drug therapy may be helpful at times of panic or when suicidal wishes must be vigorously and promptly combatted. When suicide is a definite possibility, or when the symptoms markedly disrupt a household, or in those rare cases where complete immobility occurs, hospitalization for protection or for preparation for psychotherapy or psychoanalysis may have to be employed.

REFERENCES

Abraham, K. (1921), Contributions to the Theory of the Anal Character. In: *Selected Papers.* New York: Basic Books, 1953, pp. 370-392.

Bychowski, G. (1966), Obsessive-Compulsive Facade in Schizophrenia. *International Journal of Psycho-Analysis,* 47:189-202.

Deutsch, H. (1945), *Psychoanalysis of the Neuroses.* New York: W. O. Norton.

Fenichel, O. (1945), *The Psychoanalytic Theory of Neurosis.* New York: W.W. Norton.

Ferenzci, S. (1914), The Ontogenesis of Interest in Money. In: *Sex in Psychoanalysis.* New York: Robert Brunner, 1950, pp. 319-331.

——— (1916/1917), The Compulsion to Symmetrical Touching. In: *Further Contributions to the Theory and Technique of Psychoanalysis.* New York: Basic Books, 1952, pp. 242-243.

——— (1923), Washing Compulsion and Masturbation. In: *Further Contributions to the Theory and Technique of Psychoanalysis.* New York: Basic Books, pp. 311-312.

Freedman, D. A. (1971), The Genesis of Obsessional Phenomena. *Psychoanalytic Review,* 58:367-384.

Freud, A. (1966), Obsessional Neurosis: A Summary of Psychoanalytic Views. *The Writings of Anna Freud,* Vol. 5. New York: International Universities Press, 1969, pp. 242-264.

Freud, S. (1907), Obsessive Acts and Religious Practices. *Standard Edition,* 9:116-127. London: Hogarth Press, 1959.

——— (1908), Character and Anal Eroticism. *Standard Edition,* 9:168-175. London: Hogarth Press, 1959.

——— (1909), Notes upon a Case of Obsessional Neurosis. *Standard Edition,* 10:153-249. London: Hogarth Press, 1955.

——— (1913), The Predisposition to Obsessional Neurosis. *Standard Edition,* 12:313-326. London: Hogarth Press, 1958.

——— (1917), On the Transformation of Instincts as Exemplified in Anal Erotism. *Standard Edition,* 17:127-133. London: Hogarth Press, 1955.

Gero, G. & Rubinfine, D.L. (1955), On Obsessive Thoughts. *Journal of the American Psychoanalytic Association,* 3:222-243.

Jones, E. (1913a), Anal-erotic Character Traits. In: *Papers on Psychoanalysis.* Boston: Beacon Press, 1961, pp. 680-704.

——— (1913b), Hate and Anal Erotism in Obsessional Neurosis. In: *Papers on Psychoanalysis.* Boston: Beacon Press, 1961, pp. 553-561.

Menninger, W. (1943), Characterological and Symptomatic Expressions Related to the Anal Phase of Psychosexual Development. *Psychoanalytic Quarterly,* 12:161-193.

Nacht, S. (1966), The Interrelationship of Phobia and Obsessional Neurosis. *International Journal of Psycho-Analysis,* 47: 136-138.

Nemiah, J. C. (1967), The Obsessive-Compulsive Reaction. In: *A Comprehensive Textbook of Psychiatry,* ed. A. M. Freedman & H. I. Kaplan. Baltimore: Williams & Wilkins, pp. 912-928.

Ramzy, I. (1966), Factors and Features of Early Compulsive Formation. *International Journal of Psycho-Analysis,* 47:169-176.

Sandler, J. & Hazari, A. (1960), The "Obsessional": On The Psychological Classification of Obsessional Traits and Symptoms. *British Journal of Medical Psychology,* 3:113-122.

——— & Joffe, W. G. (1965), Notes on Obsessional Manifestations in Children. *The Psychoanalytic Study of the Child,* 20:425-438. New York: International Universities Press.

Weissman, P. (1959), Characteristic Superego Identifications of Obsessional Neuroses. *Psychoanalytic Quarterly,* 28:21-28.

CHAPTER EIGHTEEN

Personality Disorders—I

MERL M. JACKEL, M.D.

The term "personality disorders" includes a large heterogeneous group of emotional and developmental disturbances, usually ego-syntonic, which manifest themselves primarily in the person's characteristic modes of response and behavior.

Our knowledge of personality disorders is based largely on the work of psychoanalysts. Prior to Freud, psychiatrists worked largely with psychotics and usually in institutions. Freud began his work by treating hysterics who presented physical symptoms such as paralyses and anesthesias. The focus was on making the unconscious conscious, and interest centered on the drives. His description in 1908 of the anal character constituted a milestone in that it was the first attempt to connect normal developmental processes with character traits. However, a classification based solely on the drives proved inadequate. In working with patients, he and his colleagues became aware of resistances to getting well. These came largely from the ego and were manifestations of each patient's personality structure. The introduction of the structural hypothesis (id, ego, superego) brought some order into the field and supplied a framework for the investigation of personality structure. Anna Freud's *The Ego and the Mechanisms of Defense,* (1936), established the close relationship between defense mechanisms and personality structure. Confirmation of these findings in adults and further contributions came from child therapists and researchers studying the earliest years of life. Gradually it became clear that in addition to the psychoneuroses there could be disorders of the personality, called character disorders by psychoanalysts. It became evident that patients could react *unconsciously* with repetitive patterned responses that pushed them into characteristic difficulties. These patterned responses had a marked bearing on choice of career, choice of mate, marital adjustment, and many other aspects of social conduct.

Nomenclature

Because much of our understanding of personality disorders originated in psychoanalytic studies, a number of terms derived from that discipline pervades the literature. The most common is character disorder, which is often used interchangeably with personality disorder. Insofar as personality encompasses a wider area and is the term that has been officially accepted, it will be favored here, except where clear reference is being made to psychoanalytic findings. Other terms derived from psychoanalysis are character neurosis, neurotic character, behavior disorders and acter-outer. The first two blur the lines between character disorders and psychoneuroses and should be dropped. The behavior disorders apply to children and adolescents and should be so restricted. Acter-outer is a term essentially misused by some who seem to regard it as the only descriptive term for one small group of personality disorders.

It should be noted that the term personality in psychiatry has only a distant connection to the ordinary use of the word, connoting glamour or charisma. It is a scientific term and may be defined as the total combination of relatively permanent tendencies to act, think, or feel in specific ways. It is unique for each individual. It may be thought of as a composite of many personality traits. These traits form a highly heterogeneous group, the classification of which must vary with the frame of reference.

It is important to make a distinction between a *descriptive* frame of reference and a *dynamic* one. Descriptive psychiatry tells *how* someone behaves. Dynamic psychiatry tells *why* he behaves as he does. Similar behavior may result from various dynamic constellations, and, conversely, a particular dynamic constellation may lead to a variety of behavioral manifestations. An adolescent may steal because, under stress, his ego is not able to distinguish between what is his and what belongs to someone else, or because his ego has not yet developed the ability to postpone gratification of instinctual drives, or because an unconscious sense of guilt pushes him to seek punishment by being caught. Conversely, a sense of guilt may lead to oversolicitude for an ambivalently loved person, or to antisocial behavior, or to philanthropic acts, or to failures in life.

In the early days of psychiatry, when dynamic explanations were not available, classification was based entirely on description. With the introduction of psychodynamics, descriptive psychiatry was gradually derogated. This is unfortunate. It is frequently forgotten that one must know in exact detail how an individual reacts before one can hypothesize why he reacts that way. Furthermore, descriptive aspects may be intertwined with sociological problems. Children who are behavior problems in school or adults whose illness is manifested by antisocial behavior or who are addicts, have similar social problems as a group, regardless of varying dynamics. It is not a question of dynamic psychiatry *versus* descriptive psychiatry, but of dynamic psychiatry *and* descriptive psychiatry. This, however, makes integrated classification an unattainable goal. The official classification compromises by using that frame of reference which is most useful in a particular instance and accepts some unavoidable inconsistencies.

Personality traits should be distinguished from symptoms. Symptoms are usually felt as painful or in other ways undesirable by the one who has them. He wants to get rid of them and may seek help in doing so. Personality traits are felt as very much part of the self. The idea of change is felt as undesirable or impossible. In this sense, a personality trait is described as ego-syntonic, as opposed to a symptom which is ego-dystonic.

Mrs. B., a 30-year-old married woman, came for help because of the obsessive thought that she would kill her seven-year-old daughter. These thoughts had become more frequent in the past few months, terrifying the patient and making her feel guilty. She could not understand having such thoughts, for she felt, if anything, overly fond of her daughter. In the course of taking her history, it was learned that she placed great emphasis on cleanliness. The little girl was always immaculately dressed. The mother bathed her twice a day and even woke her to give her a bath. Mrs. B. kept her house very clean and prided herself on this. The kitchen floor was washed twice a day, and her husband routinely took off his shoes when he came into the house after work. Both her husband and daughter, at least consciously, accepted this situation, and even took some degree of pride in Mrs. B's reputation for cleanliness.

Here, the personality trait of cleanliness, although exaggerated, and, one would suspect, unconsciously a great source of irritation to those around her, is accepted by the woman as part of herself, that is, it is ego-syntonic. Her obsessive thought about killing her daughter, however, is painful to her, and is seen as an alien instrusion, that is, it is ego-dystonic. She wished to be rid of the symptom, she did not want to change the personality trait.

Personality traits also differ from symptoms in their history. Symptoms usually have their origin at a particular time. Character traits, on the other hand, are perceived as having existed throughout the person's adult years, often as far back as he can remember. Frequently, a patient with a neurotic symptom can date its onset, for instance, to the death of a loved one, a failure in business, or the birth of a child. Although investigation may reveal that the reported onset may not actually have been the first time the symptom occurred, this does not invalidate the observation that there is a specific time of onset for the symptom.

The distinction between a personality trait and a symptom may be of great practical importance in treatment. For example, consider the client who consistently comes late for interviews. What is said or done about this practice is very much determined by whether it is a personality trait or a symptomatic reaction to the treatment. If lateness has been a problem for the client most of his life, and if he is late for all appointments, whether they are anticipated with pleasure or not, one can assume that lateness is a personality trait. As such, it is ego-syntonic, has a complicated set of dynamics, is apt to be multidetermined, and serves some necessary psychic function. Incorrectly perceiving this lateness as a symptom rather than as a personality trait and interpreting to the client quickly that he is late because he is afraid of what he will uncover or because he is angry at the caseworker can mean only criticism and disapproval to the client, even though such an interpretation may contain elements of truth. Often it may lead to arguments, so that the few minutes remaining for helping the client to deal with his problems are used up fruitlessly. The client is then likely to leave the session feeling frustrated and resentful and will often miss the next appointment or discontinue treatment entirely. The caseworker must accept the fact that, for such a client, lateness is a part of his personality structure and that attempts to "attack it" or to modify it by direct interpretation will be of no avail.

To illustrate:

A 27-year-old man came for help because of a moderate chronic depression. He was seen once a week and was invariably late for the hour. Because he was late for appointments everywhere, his friends made allowances for it. In high school he was frequently called into the principal's office because of his habitual tardiness. He had difficulty awakening and had an arrangement which included three alarm clocks and a friend to call him each morning. For a month in the treatment nothing was said about his lateness; instead, if possible, the hour was slightly prolonged. Attempts were made at each interview to help the client with some current problem. The aim was to have the client leave each interview with the feeling that it had been worthwhile for him to come. After some months, the client was asked what he thought about his lateness for interviews. At first, he found the question incomprehensible. He subsequently explained that since he was at least a half hour late for all other appointments and was only 10 to 15 minutes late for the interviews, he felt that he was doing very well in the treatment, was being completely cooperative, and had gained in self-respect because of it.

Personality traits, as a rule, involve broader and more complex reactions than do psychoneurotic symptoms. Furthermore, personality traits have a quality of constancy not evident in the psychoneurotic symptom. That this quality is commonly recognized is indicated by the well-known expression, "he is acting in character." This is true as well for pathological personality structure—for example, the girl who repeatedly falls in love with the wrong man or the man who marries two or three times, each time, by some peculiar coincidence, a woman who turns out to be frigid.

To summarize, personality traits differ from psychoneurotic symptoms in that they are habitual modes of acting, thinking, and feeling and therefore relatively constant, in that they are ego-syntonic, and in that they are broader and more complex reactions than symptoms.

It is very difficult to define what constitutes a normal personality trait, although it is possible to set up some criteria to distinguish between a normal and an abnormal personality trait. It should not be forgotten that what is a normal personality trait in one historical and social setting may be abnormal and maladaptive in another. Characteristic of the "abnormal" personality trait is an inflexibility and rigidity that makes the trait a poor adaptive tool in relating to the environment and often a source of suffering for the subject. The abnormality may be evident in the lack of specificity of the stimuli that elicit the characteristic response or in the quality of the response itself.

This may be illustrated by the case of a woman who reacted to almost all situations as though she were being humiliated. If she were accosted by a man, she felt humiliated; if she was not, she imagined she was unattractive—and felt humiliated. In her office work, if she was told to do something, she thought the other person was showing his authority—and felt humiliated. If she was not told what to do, she was being ignored, was not valued, and this, she felt, was humiliating. If she was unable to do a particular task, she felt humiliated by her inadequacy; if she could do it and it was part of her job, she felt humiliated that she had to perform such undemanding tasks.

Some people are incapable of responding to a particular situation with the appropriate affect, but instead respond with different or even opposite affect, as is illustrated in the following case:

A woman never recognized in herself feelings of jealousy. In situations where one might expect such a reaction, she experienced consciously a feeling of pity. She could agree intellectually that feelings of jealousy might in certain circumstances be warranted, but unconsciously she could not accept having such feelings. She had to defend herself against experiencing feelings of jealousy, but she was not aware of this defensive process, because defense mechanisms work unconsciously. She was therefore unable to react with appropriate jealousy even in situations that realistically warranted it.

Here is an example of a fixed response to a specific situation:

A 26-year-old attractive unmarried woman, in treatment for two years, described the following incident. She was thinking of changing jobs and responded to an advertisement placed by a moderate-sized business firm. As she came into the office, she saw a young man to whom she felt emotionally and physically attracted. In the course of waiting to be interviewed by the personnel manager, she was told that the young man was the owner and boss of the firm. Her feelings about him changed immediately. Instead of finding him attractive, she found herself disliking and criticizing him, her "characteristic" response to bosses.

As indicated in the definition given at the beginning of the chapter, those suffering from personality disorders maintain their equilibrium not by intrapsychic changes, but rather by their behavior and by their use of the environment. Usually they come for treatment, if at all, when the environment has changed or, for one reason or another, no longer adjusts itself to their character needs. This makes them anxious or depressed. They seek "cure," however, by a change in the environment or in the significant people in their life. This is common in marital situations. These patients usually come hoping that in some way the therapist will either change their spouse or show them how to make their spouse change. They rarely complain about their own personality traits, except those which they believe make them unable to deal with their spouse. Similarly, the mother with personality problems will come for help saying: "My son is a brat; he disobeys and is always provoking me. What can I do to make *him* behave?"

The following case, paraphrased from F. Alexander (1930), will illustrate this.

The history obtained and later remembered by the patient was that he had refused to give up his nursing bottle and had persisted in drinking his milk from it up to at least the age of five. This elicited a great deal of teasing from his siblings, although not from his mother. As a compensation for this attack on his pride, he prematurely developed the ability to ride his bicycle on the street alone, a feat which brought him respect and admiration. When the patient became an adult, he expected his wife to guess his every need and to satisfy his desires without his asking (the bottle); in business, however, he was capable, daring, and successful (the bicycle). This psychic equilibrium, established in childhood, was satisfactorily maintained until a new boss was appointed who dominated and used the patient. Psychologically, this removed the patient's defense (bicycle). At this juncture, and without making any connection, the patient became involved with the wife of a superior, succeeding in establishing her as his mistress. This, then, was the new defense, the re-establishment of masculinity (the bicycle). At home, he continued as before with the childlike demands with which his wife complied (the bottle).

Here we see that the defense constituted an action affecting the patient's environment. No internal psychological changes were made. When the new boss was introduced, the patient conceivably could have reacted in one of four ways: (1) He could have developed a psychoneurosis, perhaps a street phobia that would have kept him at home. He would thus have avoided being exposed to the new boss. (2) He might have developed a psychotic reaction, paranoid delusions for example, about the new boss. (3) He could have developed a psychosomatic disorder, such as colitis or a stomach ulcer, the symptoms of which would have allowed him to avoid his boss on days of particular stress. (4) He could have solved the conflict by a complicated piece of behavior in which he used people to re-establish a defense. This last was, in fact, what the patient did, and is characteristic of a personality disorder.

It should be emphasized that the various ego functions are not usually affected all to the same degree. Even in the most severe personality disorders, some ego functions may be preserved or even highly developed. In evaluating the total personality, it is as important to recognize these as it is to consider the pathological ones. Furthermore, most adult personality traits are the result of many vicissitudes in the interaction between drive and defense. An exhibitionistic impulse, well developed at age four, may be inhibited by the birth of a sibling at age five, return in the form of truancy and provocative behavior in school during latency, turn to religiosity under the impact of sexuality in adolescence, and end up as a masochistic form of exhibitionism in adulthood.

The diagnoses of psychoneurosis and personality disorder are not mutually exclusive. On the contrary, a full diagnosis of any psychoneurosis should include the personality structure, e.g., phobic neurosis in an obsessive-compulsive personality, or conversion hysteria in a borderline personality. This is dynamically sound. All adults have developed definite personality structure which helps them cope with their daily life. Under stress, the first reaction may be an intensification of some character traits. If this is insufficient to defend against the stress, a psychoneurosis or even a psychosis may develop.

A study of the *causes* of personality disorders involves all that we have learned about psychic development. We regard personality disorders as resulting from distortions, inhibitions, or exaggerations of developmental processes qualitatively not different from those of normal character development. The difference is quantitative. All of us have had developmental tasks to accomplish and conflicts to resolve.

Innate potentialities are determined by heredity and constitution. There is every reason to assume that just as there are variations in the physical make-up of human beings, so are there variations in the drive endowment and in potential for ego and superego development. Longitudinal studies confirm that differences are apparent immediately after birth. Infants vary in their response to loud noises as early as the second day of life. Some children are more irritable, others are more passive. There is variation in the type of "cue" by which infants signal their distress. The importance of the mother's ability to adjust to the child's temperament and to recognize the cues has already been described. One way in which heredity affects future personality structure is in regard to intellectual endowment. Apart from the effect of his abilities on general development, an intellectually precocious child elicits responses from his environment which differ from those of a more limited child. This may also be seen in children with specific talents who, with a minimum of effort, can elicit love and approval from their environment. The unusually beautiful child, as well as the excessively tall or small child, evoke special responses from those around them. The characteristics producing these responses are largely determined by heredity. The child also comes into a world that includes a specific family history and environment. Even siblings who have died before he was born may be woven into his personal mythology and dynamics, thus affecting his personality structure.

To "blame" the parents for all psychological disturbances in the child and adult is to misuse present psychodynamic concepts. We have come to recognize that many things happen that are beyond the parent's control. The effect, for instance, of even a minor congenital deformity, or of an illness early in life, can be devastating.

There should at this point be no need to stress the importance of psychosexual development, identifications, and defense mechanisms in the development of personality structure. It would seem, however, that it is necessary to re-emphasize the importance of the Oedipus complex and its resolution, inasmuch as there has been some tendency to devalue it as a result of the surge of interest in the earliest years. In fact, much of the importance of disturbances of the earliest years lies in the very fact that the child reaches the oedipal stage inadequately prepared to deal with these new conflicts.

Even in the normal mature adult, oral, anal, and phallic drives are not extinct, but exist side by side with the genital organization. Normally, however, they are in the service of the ego and are controlled by it. Similarly, the child ideally enters the oedipal phase with oral and anal drives attenuated and with phallic drives at a peak. Where, for instance, anal conflicts remain unresolved, sado-masochistic impulses are strongly incorporated into the oedipal conflict, which then cannot be satisfactorily resolved, and the personality structure retains excessive amounts of anal character traits or is prone to regress to them.

It is also a misconception to believe that personality development ends with the resolution of the Oedipal conflicts. The importance of identification in adolescence has been stressed. Furthermore, environmental and accidental factors may be of extreme importance. One could mention sexual seduction in early adolescence, physical illness, such as a kidney or bladder disease, death of a parent or sibling, greatly delayed or accelerated physical development; all may markedly affect the subsequent personality development. It is in adolescence that moral values are consolidated in the individual, the result of a blending of early superego standards and more recently acquired attitudes and ideals. As we have seen, growth and development continues into the mature years with marriage, children, and choice of occupation. These affect the self-image and subsequent personality development.

Recent studies have resulted in new criteria for the observation and study of personality disorders. We now consider such factors as frustration and anxiety tolerance, object constancy, reality constancy, ego autonomy, superego autonomy, neutralization, self and object differentiation. As was noted previously, these are usually unequally developed in any given case. This results in such seemingly contradictory pictures as severely disturbed people being highly successful in their work, or overtly stable persons breaking down because of apparently minor environmental changes. It is not sufficient to speak in general terms of a "weak" or "strong" ego. One must add specific information about the areas of function in which the ego is weak or strong. These relatively new concepts have expanded our understanding of personality development and in the future may contribute to an improved classification of these disorders.

Treatment Aspects

In discussions of treatment, one frequently finds the division "supportive" versus "uncovering" or "modifying" techniques, often without making clear what is being supported and what uncovered. Unless this is clearly formulated, treatment can only be haphazard. In structural terms, it is the ego that is being supported. What is uncovered are defenses and the underlying conflicts. Patients with personality disorders come to treatment at a time when the environment for some reason no longer "cooperates" with their pathological emotional needs, or when a faulty pattern of behavior again fails. The girl who repeatedly gets involved with the wrong man may come when a break-up of a relationship is threatened or has actually taken place. A mother will come when the school authorities have insisted she must do something about her child. In the first case, treatment may tide the patient over until she establishes a relationship with another man, or it may prevent the threatened break. In the second case, treatment may help the mother to deal more effectively with the school authorities or with her child. These methods are largely supportive, but not entirely so. No treatment can be entirely supportive or entirely uncovering. Sometimes an uncovering technique is in itself supportive. Treatment aimed at resolving the girl's repetitive need for becoming involved with the wrong man, however, would necessarily use a largely uncovering technique. An assessment of the ego is necessary to assure that it is strong enough not to be overwhelmed by the conflicts stirred up by this kind of treatment. The enthusiasm for psychoanalysis and for a full uncovering technique often has as its basis a neurotic need for perfection. In reality, analysis is not always possible or desirable. A supportive treatment which restores the individual to his previous level of functioning, even if it was neurotic, is frequently most desirable. The choice may not be between illness and health, but rather between one illness and a more severe one. Defenses are always there for a good reason, and to attempt to "break" them in pursuit of unrealistic treatment goals is extremely dangerous. A bad marriage may be a defense against schizophrenia or homosexuality. One must guard against accepting without question the patient's complaints about his environment. The woman who complains that her husband is cold and unfeeling and that she therefore cannot be expected to respond sexually has not demonstrated that she could live with a warm, giving man who expected her to respond in a similar manner. It should be remembered that the solutions a person has spontaneously worked out, no matter how disturbed they seem to the observer, often meet personality needs that should not be disturbed lightly.

Any attempt to treat a personality disorder by techniques aimed at basic change in personality is a difficult procedure and requires sound motivation on the part of the patient. Treatment is particularly arduous because personality traits are ego-syntonic. If the patient is not discomforted by them, does not reject them even on an intellectual basis, treatment will fail. Patients often stop treatment when a transient improvement occurs. The more the environment "cooperates" with neurotic needs, the more difficult will be the treatment. This is particularly important, for instance, in adolescent delinquents, where almost invariably one or the other of the parents unconsciously or consciously contributes to the delinquency.

REFERENCES

Alexander, F. (1930), The Neurotic Character, *International Journal of Psycho-Analysis,* 11:292-311.

American Psychiatric Association (1968), *Diagnostic and Statistical Manual of Mental Disorders,* 2d ed. Washington, D.C: American Psychiatric Association.

Fenichel, O. (1945), *The Psychoanalytic Theory of Neurosis.* New York: W. W. Norton, 1945, pp. 465-570.

Hartmann, H. (1939), *Ego Psychology and the Problem of Adaptation.* New York: International Universities Press, 1958.

——— (1964), *Essays on Ego Psychology.* New York: International Universities Press.

Freud, A. (1936), *The Ego and the Mechanisms of Defense. The Writings of Anna Freud,* Vol. 6. New York: International Universities Press, 1966.

Freud, S. (1908), Character and Anal Eroticism. *Standard Edition,* 9:167-175. London: Hogarth Press, 1959.

SUGGESTED READING

Freud, A., Nagera. H. & Freud, W. E. (1965), Metapsychological Assessment of the Adult Personality. *The Psychoanalytic Study of the Child,* 20:9-42. New York: International Universities Press.

Lampl-De Grott (1963), Symptom Formation and Character Formation. *International Journal of Psycho-Analysis,* 44:1-11.

Michaels, J. J. (1959), Character Structure and Character Disorders. In: *American Handbook of Psychiatry,* Vol. I., ed. S. Arieti. New York: Basic Books, pp. 353-377.

Nunberg, H. (1955), Character and Neurosis. In: *Principles of Psychoanalysis.* New York: International Universities Press, pp. 303-320.

CHAPTER NINETEEN
Personality Disorders—II
MERL M. JACKEL, M.D.

There are certain dangers in applying labels to normal or deviant personalities. Without such labels, however, communication concerning this important aspect of psychopathology would be very difficult, if not impossible. It must be kept in mind that "typical" or "pure" instances of personality disorders as defined in any manual or textbook are not found in real life. Yet, in various individuals we find clusters of behavioral traits, normal or abnormal, that provide an adequate basis for classification as to personality type. We will now proceed to examine the various personality disorders.

Hysterical Personality

The hysterical personality is characterized by histrionic, excitable, attention-seeking behavior and emotional lability. If these traits are sufficiently intense, they can dominate the personality and make it pathological. Hysterical characters coincide more closely with the popular concept of hysteria than does the conversion type of hysterical neurosis. One would expect from the terminology that conversion symptoms would occur predominately in hysterical characters, and, conversely, that hysterical personalities would be particularly liable to develop conversion symptoms. Neither assumption is correct, and this has led to some confusion. Individual hysterical traits may occur in all types of emotional illness, including schizophrenia, and their presence should not alone determine the diagnosis or mislead one into overlooking the more serious disease. In the "normal" personality as well, there is a scattering of such traits, which may actually make the person more interesting and enhance his popular appeal.

Hysterical personality is said to be more common in women than in men. If so, this is culturally determined, inasmuch as histrionic traits are more acceptable to society in the female. The male defends himself against these traits, because, for him, they represent effeminacy. The male often expresses his hysterical tendencies by some variety of Don Juanism or by other forms of exaggerated "masculine" behavior. When we take this into consideration, we find the hysterical personality by no means rare in men.

The hysterical woman has a flair for the dramatic and seems always to be play-acting. She is "on stage" most of the time, demanding to be the center of everyone's attention. If frustrated in this, she becomes angry, sullen, and at times self-depreciatory. She often distorts the truth and seeks to shock, to impress, and to win attention. Those who take her words at face value are often confused by her actions, which are at variance with her stated attitudes. The hysteric is constantly in a crisis situation. Exaggeration and hyperbole are the order of the day. She never feels merely slighted, she feels rudely insulted; she is never merely upset, she is "miserable," "wretched," her "stomach is in knots," and she "wants to die." Favorable happenings are equally overstated and dramatized. She is constantly ready to be excited, whether by good or bad news. Irrational emotional outbursts of love, hate, or self-depreciation are frequent. This lability of affect has a false quality, puzzling to the observer. The excessive emotional reactions may cover emotional shallowness and a lack of genuine concern for others. They may also be a distortion of feelings which may really exist, but which the hysteric makes unreal even to herself by her exaggeration.

Hysterics are commonly regarded as suggestible. Closer examination, however, reveals that they often succeed in getting others to suggest what they wish to hear. They may select from what is said those parts which fit into their fantasies, while remaining psychologically deaf to the rest. They readily form superficial identifications, elaborate these into fantasies, and tend to "try out" their roles. They are sexually provocative, but deny any awareness of this to the extent of appearing completely naive.

The hysterical woman is frequently coquettish in dress and behavior, yet is surprised and shocked when the man responds accordingly. She is terrified by real sexual feelings in herself and either avoids sex or engages in it compulsively—at times even promiscuously—but without a full sexual response. She may be demanding and markedly dependent. She may communicate helplessness or aggrieved innocence. She completely denies responsibility for her actions and their consequences. She begs for help and advice, but then ignores or rejects it. Some hysterics develop vague conversion symptoms and have a history of repeated examinations by doctors and, occasionally, of several surgical procedures. A childhood history of temper tantrums, bedwetting, and nailbiting is common. Hysterical women are often young in appearance and are regarded by their family, in whose presence they are prone to regress, as immature, inefficient, and dependent—but also as cute and loveable.

The "Don Juan" has many of the characteristics of his female counterpart. Just as she uses sexuality to reassure herself of her attractiveness and to be the center of attention, the Don Juan pursues women in order to be reassured of his masculinity. His aim is not to establish a love relationship with his partner, but to outwit and conquer her. In order to do so, he, too, exaggerates, lies, shows off, and play-acts. When success seems imminent, he may reject his partner and repeat the procedure with someone else. If he becomes involved in an affair, he usually becomes disenchanged and unfaithful.

The hysterical woman has an overwhelming need to be reassured that she is desirable and worthy of interest and affection. She cannot, however, seek this reassurance directly and openly because the sexual connotations she attaches in her fantasy to all relationships make it difficult for her to accept such feelings in reality. She manipulates people and situations in such a way as to maintain a shaky equilibrium between her wish to be courted and her fear of genital sexuality.

Many hysterical women had mothers, often masochistic or themselves hysterical, who were incapable of giving genuine love. Early in life, and again in adolescence, the girl turns to her father for emotional support, enhancement of self-esteem, and reassurance as to her femininity. But hidden sexual feelings, frequently mutual, arouse guilt and anxiety in both. The girl comes into competition, both desired and feared, with her mother. If these conflicts continue into adulthood, they lead to character distortions.

Mrs. G. was a 28-year-old housewife who came for treatment because of an unhappy marriage she wished to salvage. This was her second marriage. She was first married at 17 to a man a year older than herself. She thought she married her first husband to spite her parents, particularly her father, who disapproved of him. Soon after marriage, she "discovered" that her husband was infantile, avoided responsibility, and shirked work. The sexual relationship was unsatisfactory to both. Ostensibly to determine who was at fault, she started an affair with her boss, a much older man. She preferred sex with him, but still did not experience orgasm. Guilty and depressed, she sought psychotherapeutic help. During treatment, she felt frustrated and exasperated by the therapist's "coldness," and simultaneously felt abandoned by her husband, who was now turning to other women. In the presence of her husband, she took a moderate overdose of sleeping pills. Shortly after this suicidal gesture, she left her husband, but continued in treatment until she married again. Her second husband was a withdrawn, obsessive-compulsive lawyer, 12 years her senior. They had two children. She had many girl friends and at parties was gay, outgoing, and popular. At home, she was terrified of her husband's criticism and frequently lied to him. Sometimes she was submissive, but on other occasions she exploded with rage. She felt inadequate as a mother and as a wife. In the course of her second marriage, she again started an affair, this time with her dentist. She did not experience orgasm, but pretended that she did.

Mrs. G. was an only child. Her mother was a masochistic woman who imposed guilt feelings on her daughter and fostered overattachment. Her father drank and was overtly unfaithful. There was much marital strife, and when Mrs. G. was 15 her mother divorced her father and married a wealthy surgeon. In treatment, Mrs. G. recalled that her father had been quite affectionate to her in her early years, but she had always known that he would have preferred a boy. In latency she began to resent him, and from early adolescence on they quarreled incessantly. Mrs. G. also gave a history of temper tantrums in childhood, "nervousness," and many somatic complaints.

The usual problem in differential diagnosis is to ascertain whether or not the patient's hysterical traits hide more severe pathology, in particular, a borderline or schizophrenic state. Some hysterics, under stress, regress to an unreasonable, demanding attitude, which at times approaches psychotic behavior. In crucial situations, however, the hysteric is much more able to function than is the borderline or psychotic. The histrionics of the hysteric do not lead to the severe types of acting out of the borderline patient, whose behavior is less attention-seeking and determined instead by other inner needs. The self-image of the borderline is more distorted than is that of the hysteric. Such physiological disturbances, as prolonged delay in the onset of menstruation, marked obesity or extreme underweight, and severe allergies are more common in borderline disorders than they are in hysteria.

Conversion hysteria has traditionally been regarded as the classic case for psychoanalytic treatment. The same, however, may not apply to the hysterical personality disorder. This is partly because of the hysteric's provocativeness and tendency to "act out." Even more important is the disposition in some hysterics to regress, when frustrated, to an oral, demanding, dependent relationship which makes any treatment, including analysis, long and difficult. If hysterical patients are responsive to psychoanalysis, the results may be excellent. Where they are unable to tolerate the analytic treatment situation, supportive psychotherapy or family therapy can be helpful, especially in diminishing acting out and excessive demands.

Obsessive-Compulsive Personality

This psychiatric syndrome is probably the most common personality disorder in our culture. It has much in common with its counterpart, the obsessive-compulsive neurosis. Many of the symptoms evident in the neurosis are reflected in the traits of the personality disorder, where they are rationalized, isolated, and intellectualized so that they become ego-syntonic. The obsessive-compulsive character disorder includes a wide variety of character traits, most of which are based on conflicts between good and bad, cleanliness and dirtiness, right and wrong, conformity and rebellion. The compulsive person tends to be overly meticulous and conscientious, pedantic, worrisome, and frequently intolerant and stubborn. He may be diligent and industrious, but often gets so lost in details that his total accomplishment is minimal.

Ambivalence is especially marked in the obsessive-compulsive personality. Opposing feelings and attitudes to other people exist simultaneously in everyone, but as a rule, either positive or negative feelings and attitudes prevail. In the obsessive-compulsive, affectionate and hateful feelings may exist in continuing opposition to each other. This leads to an indecision that, at times, may involve all kinds of minutiae of every day life. Because of this ambivalence, the obsessive-compulsive lacks spontaneity and frequently has severe emotional inhibitions. He may not be aware of feelings, or he may be aware of them but unable to show or act on them. He has difficulty falling in love or in properly evaluating his attachments. Sexual feelings and tender feelings are often separated, and one or the other repressed. Sometimes, tender feelings are reserved for one person and sexual feelings for another. Strangely, some people find it easier to admit to sadistic feelings than to talk about feelings of tenderness, which they regard as "corny" and even shameful. This attitude, however, is frequently a rationalization with which the obsessive person covers up his inability to feel love. He may become attached to a woman, get married, and even have children, maintaining throughout that he feels no love for his wife and denying inwardly that he is really married. Having difficulty with his own feelings, he is unable to empathize with those of others. Although sensitive to being hurt, he has difficulty in understanding that others, too, can be hurt, and he is often unwittingly cruel.

The obsessive-compulsive personality suffers from an archaically severe superego, which utilizes the principle of "an eye for an eye, a tooth for a tooth." In fact, he goes even further and believes that if he even thinks of hurting someone he will be hurt in exactly the same way. Because of this, thinking becomes dangerous and much psychic energy is utilized in attempts to repress or isolate unacceptable thoughts. This leads to constriction in thinking and lack of imagination. To reinforce repression, the defense mechanisms of reaction formation, reversal, projection, and denial are used.

The following examples illustrate some aspects of the obsessive-compulsive personality:

Mr. T., a student at a school of music, was given a week in which to write an original musical composition. He chose to do it on parchment and meticulously drew lines in India ink. Hours were spent in lettering the title, using old English script. Each note was carefully and perfectly drawn. As a result, he was five weeks late turning in the assignment, and failed to receive credit for it. He rationalized his behavior as an attempt to please the instructor and to produce a perfect job.

Still another example is that of a patient in his mid-thirties who came for treatment because of depression, poor functioning on his job as a research assistant, and worry that he might be fired. His rationalization for his poor performance was that he was too sick to work. In treatment he became aware that he was angry at his employers because he felt that they did not recognize the value of his work or admire his capabilities. Actually, his performance had always been spotty. As his poor functioning on the job continued, he accused himself of being stubborn, but also realized that by working poorly he was trying to punish his employers. This went on for several months. He then became aware that, whenever he was praised, he reacted by functioning even more poorly. He came to realize that he was afraid his employers would then expect more of him and that he would be unable to satisfy them and be fired. He defended himself against this fear of being thrust into a helpless position by being inefficient on his job, which, paradoxically, gave him the feeling of being in control rather than helpless.

This patient was the oldest of three siblings, a sister having been born when he was four and a brother when he was six. When he was seven, his mother developed tuberculosis. She was hospitalized for six months, and he saw her only occasionally. In treatment he became aware that he had always felt guilty, believing that he was in some way responsible for his mother's illness, and that she had left because he had in some way disappointed her. He further became aware that at the birth of his sister he felt that his mother had been dissatisfied with him and had therefore given birth to another child, a girl at that.

The compulsive person is often self-depreciating, suffers from a sense of inferiority, and is shy and diffident, largely because of his pervasive feelings of guilt which derive from his ambivalence. He is constantly warding off self-accusations. He projects these accusations onto people in the environment who must then be placated. He views life entirely from the standpoint of whether he is a good or a bad person. To be good is to be lovable, to be bad is to be rejected. He feels that only if he is perfect will he be loved, and he is constantly in search of that love. As a result, he sets up impossibly high standards for himself. When he fails to meet these standards, he is apt to become depressed. The obsessive-compulsive person overvalues intelligence. Although he is frequently of superior intelligence, he is dissatisfied because he feels only perfection merits admiration. Very often one discovers in analysis that the self-depreciatory person unconsciously fantasies himself as superior to everyone, and a very special person. He despises people he regards as inferior and is jealous and envious of those he regards as superior. As a result, he withdraws from social relationships, is lonely, feels uninvolved and unhappy. Because of his harsh superego, he is prone to worry more or less constantly and tends to be pessimistic and moralistic. Frequently, he lacks a sense of humor. His jokes, if he has any, are usually sadistic in nature and defensive in purpose. He tends to be indecisive, but resents advice, which he regards as an attempt to control or dominate him. The fear of being controlled often gets him into difficulties with authority. He imposes his demand for perfection on authority, and is enraged when he is let down. Sometimes, conflict with authority is displaced and disguised by participation in truly worthy causes. Here too, however, his rigid conformity to the standards of the group makes for an inflexibility that interferes with his adaptation to the group as well as with success in his conscious goals.

The obsessive-compulsive personality can deal objectively with neither time nor money. Time is handled as a commodity which can be bartered; used spitefully to humiliate or as a vehicle of self-punishment. Compulsive people are usually punctual or early, although they may sometimes be compulsively late. This behavior is usually a defense against submission, and they will be late even for events they enjoy. This is one cause of procrastination, a common characteristic of compulsive personalities. The compulsive person is often penny-wise and pound-foolish. Very often he is a hoarder, but because he regards this as "bad," he may be inconsistently wasteful as well. He may develop elaborate ways of hiding his way of handling money from himself. As a result, he presents a pseudonaive attitude to it. He will have no idea what his income is, will never ask how much an item costs, and will pretend to be totally indifferent to money. He will engage in complicated bookkeeping so that he never knows whether he is making or losing money. Sometimes he keeps his money in five or six different banks, each account having a special meaning. He uses the federal tax system to further complicate and confuse the situation.

The obsessive-compulsive person fears failure because failure means that he is totally worthless and despicable. He also fears success because this gratifies hostile impulses for which he will be punished. He therefore avoids putting himself into situations that would provide a clear-cut test of his abilities. What constitutes a "meaningful" test is specific for each individual. Some obsessive persons are brilliant in all avocations, but are unable to put their energies into their vocation. Sometimes they will manage to succeed, but appear surprised at, and naive about their success.

It bears repeating that compulsive traits are present in everybody and that this is a desirable state of affairs. Without such traits, little would be accomplished and few relationships maintained. Too often, the term "compulsive" is used glibly as a derogatory epithet. Compulsiveness becomes pathological only when it is so rigid and inflexible that it interferes with a satisfactory self-image and efficient functioning.

Genetically, the obsessive-compulsive person is either fixated in, or has regressed to, the anal-sadistic phase of development. The regression is from the phallic phase, and is usually a consequence of inadequate resolution of the Oedipus complex. The regressive process may take place in varying degrees in the id, ego, or superego. The ego may regress in one area, e.g., magical expectations, and yet be overdeveloped in other areas, e.g., intellectual development. Such variations make for the uniqueness of the personality structure.

Because obsessive-compulsive character traits are present in everyone from the normal to the most severely psychotic, the diagnosis of obsessive-compulsive personality is based on the severity of the disturbance, its rigidity, and the degree to which the individual is incapacitated by it. It must be differentiated from more severe illnesses such as borderline conditions and schizophrenia, which may be excluded when symptoms characteristic of these diseases are absent.

Obsessive-compulsive personality types usually come for help when their defensive mechanisms are proving inadequate, that is, when they are anxious or depressed. This acute phase can often be treated by any of the forms of psychotherapy. Change in their basic ambivalent attitudes about themselves and about persons important to them, however, requires psychoanalysis. Their ambivalence may then focus on the therapy, so that it is often prolonged and difficult.

Paranoid Personality

This disorder is characterized by a persistent tendency to blame others and ascribe hostility or evil motives to them, evidenced by hypersensitivity, marked suspiciousness, a tendency to be querulous, litigious, and to fight excessively over minor issues, and by implied or expressed feelings of excessive self-importance. Paranoid people frequently become involved in causes or in political activity, and paranoid traits may influence the choice of occupation. The need to defend against a hostile world, or to be involved in conflict, is an externalization of internal aggressive impulses and conflict. Paranoid types become extremely adept at sensing unconscious aggression in others, and there is often, therefore, some kernel of truth in their accusations.

It is unfortunate that the term "paranoid" has become part of our daily language, where it is essentially a form of name-calling. It should be carefully noted that paranoid mechanisms (projection) are present in normal people, can be quite mild in the neurotic, and are not incompatible with excellent functioning in many areas. The difference between the normal, the paranoid personality, and the paranoid state is essentially one of degree, of conviction, and of rigidity. To hurriedly label someone of his thinking as "paranoid" is in itself often a "paranoid" mechanism.

The paranoid mechanism is essentially a defensive one, defending against either an underlying feeling of guilt or an underlying masochistic trend, both originating from within. The former is often seen in accusations of infidelity. The marital partner who has transgressed, either in reality or in wishful thinking, accuses the other of infidelity. The mechanism is obvious—if the partner has been unfaithful, he or she is not in a position to be critical of or angry at the accuser.

A patient who had intense conflicts over masturbation periodically became highly critical of the therapist, accusing him of reading a magazine, etc. while the patient was talking. He criticized the therapist's interpretations of the preceding day, saying that he talked too much and that he gave unnecessary advice. It soon became apparent that these criticisms invariably followed instances when the patient had given in to his masturbatory impulses.

The mechanism is clear; if the therapist was inadequate, if he was a transgressor, then he was in no position to judge or criticize the patient.

There is an element of masochistic suffering in all paranoid mechanisms. The paranoid person implies that he is unattractive, hateful, unworthy, etc. Paranoid thinking, however, may reflect masochistic wishes even more specifically. A woman who has an underlying wish to be overcome, to be helpless, to be attacked by a man, may defend herself against awareness of this wish or its consummation by accusing the man of being tyrannical or sadistic to her.

Freud's earlier writings on paranoia (the Schreber case, 1911) approached the problem largely from the standpoint of the instinctual drives, which were his main concern at the time. Paranoia was seen as a defense against homosexuality. In the paranoid person, the unconscious homosexual thought "I love you, a man like myself" is not acceptable, and is denied by its opposite "I hate you." Because of fear and guilt, this aggressive attitude is then projected and becomes, "You hate me." While in agreement with the second part of this formulation, many psychiatrists take issue with the idea of an invariably homosexual basis for paranoid mechanisms.

It should be noted, however, that the homosexual basis has its genetic aspects in childhood. Niederland (1959) has shown that even in the Schreber case the delusions had a core of reality in Schreber's early relation with his father. The paranoid man is unconsciously repeating with some person in the present the attraction his father had for him as a child. This feeling is denied and replaced by hostile wishes, which are then projected.

The paranoid personality is difficult to treat. Because many paranoid people deny illness, it is difficult to get them to seek help. In the treatment situation, one must guard against becoming involved in their projections, which must be constantly interpreted.

The Antisocial Personality

The diagnostic category of antisocial personality (psychopath) has been, and continues to be, one of the most confused entities in the classification system. The succession of terms which have been used to designate this disorder reflect the changing attitudes of society and of the medical profession to mental illness. In the late nineteenth century, constitutional psychopathic inferiority, as the condition was then called, was considered to be essentially an organic disorder characterized by "moral idiocy," a defect in moral development, as opposed to "mental idiocy," a defect in intellectual development. Psychopathic individuals were considered to be depraved, lacking in normal human feelings, and incapable of conducting themselves with decency and propriety. Included were all types of criminals, army deserters, swindlers, pathological liars, sexual deviates, and even persons who were simply unable to cope with the demands of everyday life.

Antisocial personalities, according to our present definition, are immature, intolerant of frustration, are basically egocentric and unsocialized, irresponsible, impulsive, and do not benefit from experience or punishment. They tend to rationalize their behavior or to blame others for it. There is a defect in the superego, and there appears to be an absence of guilt feelings. Closer examination, however, frequently reveals that the superego is not totally defective, but rather presents lacunae in specific areas.

The typical psychopath (antisocial personality) is a person of ingratiating manner and often of superior intelligence. At first meeting, he appears warm, friendly, and likeable. Because of this, he is often initially successful in whatever he attempts to do. This success, however, is temporary,and eventually there come failures and disappointments. At such times, the psychoapth may voice feelings of deep remorse, sincere regrets, and intentions of change. Given another chance, however, the same pattern is repeated. He is eventually fired from his job, antagonizes his friends, loses his wife, and alienates his family. Attempts by psychiatrists, social agencies, and others to help him are ineffectual in the long run. Antisocial types with a severe personality disorder may commit aggressive acts, forge checks, steal, swindle, and be highly disturbed sexually. Verbally, they may express quite normal feelings, but they make no connection between this expression and their actions. Many are "con artists" with an uncanny ability to know how to gain the favor of their victim. They can be entirely callous, show poor judgment, and evidence no sense of loyalty or responsibility.

As one would expect, psychopaths are notoriously poor candidates for any psychological treatment, and there are, therefore, few studies in depth. Much has been learned, however, from the simultaneous study of delinquent children and their parents (Johnson, 1949). The surprising finding is that the behavior of these children is almost invariably one that is unconsciously wished for or needed by the parent. (The family scapegoat is in a similar predicament.) The child recognizes the parental need and unconsciously gratifies it. A parent who listens with obvious enjoyment and a half-smile to an account of his child's misdemeanors, and then punishes him, confuses the child and encourages him to further delinquency. Similarly, a parent who constantly warns against or accuses the child of stealing, lying, or promiscuity, at a time when the child has not even thought of committing such acts, is communicating to him an unconscious wish that he do so. Normal ego and superego development under such conditions is impossible.

The split between the verbalized and nonverbalized attitudes evident in the parent may, by identification, be incorporated into the character structure of the child. Underlying both the sociopathy and the identification is a deep hostility to and resentment against the parent who has failed to give emotional support, is ambiguous, seductive, and often punitive. A distrust of authority, often of colossal proportions, may result.

The problem of differentiating diagnostically between the antisocial personality and other conditions is quite a difficult one. The antisocial personality must first be distinguished from the "normal," inasmuch as what is displayed is a facade of normality. The early recognition of the psychopathic personality as such will save those who must work with him much frustration. Suspicion should be aroused by discrepancies in the history and by frequent moves or changes in jobs, no matter how plausibly explained. A knowledge of the locale or industry described is helpful. The psychopath may answer questions "truthfully," but secretly interprets the question either so narrowly or so broadly as to deceive. The examiner must be alert to such evasions. He should be particularly suspicious if he finds that he himself is suddenly talking about his favorite project or pet idea; or if he is finding exonerating reasons for obvious delinquency or callous behavior.

The irrational thinking of the schizophrenic differentiates him from the psychopath who acts irrationally but usually does not think irrationally. The psychopath can be distinguished from the criminal (dyssocial personality) because the criminal has more logic and purpose to his actions, whereas the psychopath seems to act on whims and without clear desire for gain (Cleckley, 1959). The criminal is more consistent in avoiding consequences; the psychopath may be ingenious, but sooner or later "loses interest" in protecting himself. The criminal is capable of loyalty to the members of his group; the psychopath is incapable of loyalty to anything or anyone. The dyssocial behavior of the criminal is acquired by identification with his family and social group. Even though his behavior is in conflict with the rules of behavior of the larger society, he is still conforming to his social group. In contrast to the dyssocial, criminal personality, the psychopath who commits criminal acts is very much at odds with the standards of his family and at times with his social group.

Single and isolated antisocial acts are not in themselves indicative of an antisocial personality. Nor would deviant behavior that is observed in a significant number of persons belonging to any social class or group be considered conclusive evidence of an antisocial personality disorder. The total functioning of the personality must be evaluated, and only when the antisocial behavior is a major element in the psychological make-up are we justified in making the diagnosis of antisocial personality or psychopath.

Although we have used the term psychopath synonomously with antisocial personality, it should be noted that the two terms are not always used interchangeably. Frequently, the terms "psychopath" and "psychopathic" are used in a less specific way than the term "antisocial personality." In such instances, they are used as descriptive terms, connoting a variety of behavioral manifestations that are at variance with the accepted cultural milieu. These may include such varied conditions as promiscuity and criminality. These terms are often added to a primary diagnosis, e.g., borderline personality with psychopathy. As has already been emphasized, the therapeutic problem may be greatly affected by whether psychopathy is also present in any given personality disorder.

Treatment, thus far, of psychopaths has been largely unsuccessful and unrewarding. Forthright confrontation in a nonpunitive atmosphere is indicated. Reassurance and relief of guilt, however, are undesirable. If possible, the patient should be helped to avoid situations that will further his guilt feelings by demonstrating better ways by which to attain his aims. He must see in the therapist his ego ideal, an omniscient, omnipotent protector who will use his power to keep the patient from harming himself. Few therapists at present have the skill or stamina for such a task.

Masochistic Character

This diagnostic category is not listed in the official psychiatric nomenclature, but is instead usually included in the passive-aggressive personality category. Some forms of the masochistic character have traits in common with the paranoid personality and may be so classified. Considering the masochistic or sadomasochistic character as a separate diagnostic category, however, has considerable merit, insofar as it is a formulation that contains both descriptive and dynamic aspects. The masochistic character is of special interest because it appears to contradict the pleasure-unpleasure principle which has been recognized to be fundamentally important in our personality functioning.

The term masochistic character should not be used to describe any and all emotional conditions that entail suffering. All neurotic and psychotic conditions have suffering as a by-product. In fact, the ability to tolerate the suffering that is an unavoidable aspect of normal living is an essential part of healthy ego development. The term masochistic character should be restricted to those instances in which suffering is sought as a necessary condition for a stable inner emotional equilibrium. It is incorrect to say that masochistic people "like to suffer." Conscious pleasure in suffering is true only in sexual masochism, a perversion that is not our subject matter in this chapter. In psychic masochists, the "pleasure" in suffering is unconscious and often minimal.

Clinically, sadomaschism is seen most frequently in the form of "sadomasochistic marriages." It should be noted, however, that the partners in these marriages are bound, not only by unconscious gratification through their sadomasochistic relationship, but also by significant defensive aspects of that relationship. At varying levels of consciousness, separation may be feared for any number of reasons. It may threaten a sense of identity which has been maintained through close dependence and symbiotic ties, or it may lead to severe regression, even to a schizophrenic reaction. Separation may provoke homosexual fantasies or behavior or excessive masturbation, which can cause feelings of guilt and worthlessness, or it may arouse anxiety related to previously warded-off impulses toward promiscuity or prostitution. Clearly, urging separation, no matter how bad the marriage, is dangerous unless these pathological needs have been understood and dealt with.

The problem of treatment in sadomasochistic marriages is complicated because the pathology is usually ego-syntonic and unconscious. Each partner maintains the illusion that the marriage would be all right if only the other person changed. They are unaware of their own inability to love, and find justification for their own behavior in the behavior of the partner. The criticism of the spouse is often valid, but this does not mean that if the spouse were different either would be happy. The following example illustrates this point.

The client, a woman, came for treatment because her husband was an alcoholic who frequently brought home drinking companions he picked up on the street, causing her anxiety and shame. When the husband was seen by the therapist, he acknowledged that his alcoholism was a problem, but complained that his wife was a nagging, perpetually dissatisfied woman who made him feel like a guilty and helpless child. He felt she had no respect for him as a man. He agreed to treatment, joined Alcoholics Anonymous, and stopped drinking. Shortly after, his wife began to feel restless, anxious, and irritable. She could no longer blame this anxiety on his drinking. She wanted to nag her husband, but found no valid cause. As her distress became worse, she began subtly to push him into resuming his drinking. In joint therapy, both were made aware of this. He was able, with support, to resist her temptation and pressure. Her own neurotic needs were exposed, and she then wanted help with her anxiety and her unexplained depression.

It is important to note that masochism is invariably bound up with sadism. This may be seen in the subtle or not so subtle ways through which the masochist punishes the sadist. In addition, by identifying with the aggressor, the masochist gratifies his own sadism. Stated differently, masochism is sadism turned on the self. The masochist who, by his complaints, is saying or implying, "See how I suffer for love of you" is also saying, "See how you allow me to suffer without coming to my rescue." In this way, he imposes guilt on the "aggressor." Frequently, this arouses resentment and bewildered anger in the "aggressor," who then becomes more sadistic, setting up a vicious circle. In fact, the masochist may create a sadomasochistic situation by exactly this technique. Guilt favors turning of the aggression on the self. The masochist feels guilty for many things but basically for unresolved oedipal wishes. This is central to many sadomasochistic marriages.

As an example, a 34-year-old accountant came for treatment because of an unsatisfactory marriage. He claimed that his wife was personally unclean, did not take care of the house properly, constantly criticized him, and was basically unfeminine in her attitudes. She, on the other hand, criticized him for being cold, unresponsive, and sexually uninterested in her. The last, he said, was true, but he believed that she destroyed any sexual desire in him by her domineering, "castrating," behavior. Quarrels and fights alternated with withdrawal and acts of spite on both sides. Repeatedly they discussed separation, since both were miserable, had few friends, and received no conscious gratification from the marriage. Both turned their affection on their only child, a girl four years of age. Questioning brought out the fact that during courtship their sexual life had been active and pleasant. As the date for marriage approached, however, the husband began to have anxiety which interfered with the sexual act. Following marriage, sexual intercourse became less and less frequent. For a brief time he turned to prostitutes, but this made him feel guilty, so he resorted to masturbation.

Here, the regression from a mature heterosexual relationship to a sadomasochistic one is clear. In normal child development, the boy gives up his sexual desire for the mother under the threat of punishment by the father and because he also loves his father. The masochist does not really give up his sexual wishes, but regresses to the anal phase in which conflicts between submission and domination, dirty and clean, giving and withholding are central. Masochism thus becomes both punishment for, and gratification of, incestuous sexual wishes. A masochist loves by suffering, just as the masochistic pervert can achieve orgasm only under conditions of suffering and pain.

A variety of the masochistic character is the "moral masochist." Here, the masochism is not as directly involved with people as it is with the person's own superego. "Moral masochists" are those who must suffer in order to satisfy a constantly critical superego. They unconsciously seek out humiliation and failure because success is not allowed them. They attribute their difficulties to fate, bad luck, or their own high standards.

Genetically, masochism can be understood in terms of the child's relations with his parents. Those parents whose relations with their own parents and siblings were markedly ambivalent may, usually without being aware of it, behave sadistically to their own children. The child soon learns that his provocations allow the parent to gain satisfaction by discharging sadistic impulses. In this way, the child pleases the parent through his provocative behavior and the subsequent punishment for it. He incorporates the parent's sadistic attitudes into his own superego. The masochistic pattern can then be duplicated intrapsychically between the child's ego and his superego. In later life, the moral masochist unconsciously treats himself as his parents treated him, by imposing feelings of humiliation upon himself, by failure and suffering. The source of his suffering is attributed to fate, or if projection is used, to authority figures in a more or less paranoid way.

As-If Personality

Helene Deutsch (1942) described a specific type of personality disorder which she labeled "as-if characters." This is an interesting group, not yet officially recognized as a diagnostic category. The initial impression these people give is one of complete normality. Their object relations "are usually intense and bear all the earmarks of friendship, love sympathy, and understanding." They are socially active and apparently successful. But soon even the untrained observer begins to sense something is lacking, and asks what is wrong. Actually, these people are devoid of real warmth, their expressions of emotion are not genuine and exclude all inner experience (Deutsch, 1942). They are emotionally empty and only *behave* "as if" they had the appropriate feelings. They are quite unaware of this. Although such extreme cases are rare, milder forms are not. In the mildest form, usually neurotic, there is a conscious feeling of "not being with it," a feeling of being an observer rather than a participant in life situations. In severer instances, the subject may feel depersonalized: it is not he who is experiencing or doing, it is a stranger—he feels himself an observer to his experiences and actions. The external situation likewise may appear unreal. This state of mind is related to problems of identity. Feelings of identity require a sense of individuation and a sense of continuity within oneself, as well as continuity with one's culture. It implies a past and a future. It is necessary to feel that one is the same person who experienced certain feelings and relationships in childhood and that, although one may have changed, one is still the same person, and will be the same person in the future. Repression or denial of large parts of the self, or of one's past self, gives rise to feelings of emptiness and deprivation. This problem is basic for some disturbances in adolescents. Driven by feelings of emptiness, some young people frenetically seek emotional stimulation, identification with groups, new sets of ideals, new forms of excitement (drugs, sex) to fill in the sense of emptiness which pervades their life.

In addition to the personality types so far described are several others which are largely self-explanatory and will be dealt with more briefly.

The *cyclothymic* or *affective* personality is manifested by alternating periods of elation and depression. During the elated period, the person may be full of energy, optimism, and enthusiasm. He may be able to work very efficiently, get along with very little rest, and be extremely outgoing in his relations with other people. These elated periods may alternate with periods of depression, during which the person appears to be tired, without energy, pessimistic, and worried. His capacity to work may become greatly diminished. No sufficient external cause is usually found to account for these changes in mood. We also find those in whom the mood may be constantly one of depression or elation, without any alternation between the two states. The description of the cyclothymic personality clearly shows that it can be understood as a mild form of a cyclothymic psychosis. It is a kind of borderline condition, with reality testing and logical thought left relatively intact.

A similar situation exists with regard to the *schizoid* personality. Here, too, we find certain traits that in a severe form, together with an impairment of reality testing, and marked regression, constitute a schizophrenic psychosis. The schizoid person is characterized by autistic thinking, shyness, seclusiveness, and excessive sensitivity to slights. He usually avoids close relationships and frequently shows a detached and seemingly unfeeling attitude toward disturbing experiences. He is unable to express either affectionate or hostile feelings. The schizoid person may choose occupations where there is little involvement and contact with people, and is sometimes an eccentric.

The *asthenic* personality cannot be readily differentiated from an affective disturbance, such as a chronically depressed personality. The depression, however, is not in the foreground of this condition, which is, instead, marked by low energy, a tendency to become easily fatigued, the lack of capacity for enjoyment, and excessive sensitivity to stress. It is difficult to distinguish between the asthenic personality and the neurasthenic neurosis. It may very well be that the somatic manifestations of both the neurasthenic neurosis and the asthenic personality are the equivalents or masked manifestations of a chronically depressed state.

The category, *inadequate* personality, although not identical with the asthenic personality, overlaps it. Primarily, the inadequate person is characterized by ineffectuality in his response to ordinary social, emotional, and intellectual demands. This leads to ineptitude, instability, and inadaptability. It is obvious that this diagnostic category depends very much on the social criteria by which a person is judged. It is one of the prime examples of a socioevaluative approach to the classification of personalities.

The diagnosis *explosive* personality or *epileptoid* personality disorder is not too frequently used in everyday psychiatric practice in the United States. Those with this type of personality are inclined to have gross outbursts of rage, verbal or physical. They seem to be unable to control outbursts, which they may regret later on. If a person with an explosive personality has amnesia for his outbursts of rage, the diagnosis of hysteria may be indicated, and if there is evidence of epilepsy, then the diagnosis of psychosis with epilepsy should be considered. The category of explosive personality overlaps with the so-called passive-aggressive personality, aggressive type. The diagnosis passive-aggressive personality is only used in the United States and has become, to some extent, a wastebasket diagnosis for those personality disorders that do not fit into any other category and are characterized by aggressiveness, passivity, or both. Aggressiveness and passivity may coexist and the so-called passive-aggressive person may be aggressive in certain situations and passive in others. Frequently, aggression is expressed in a passive way, by obstruction, procrastination, and stubbornness.

A scientifically valid classification of personality types and disorders will be possible only when personality development is more clearly understood and the interaction between nature and nurture—constitution and environment—can be specifically formulated. Until then, we must remain satisfied with the rather imperfect nomenclature at our disposal to communicate our evaluation of the various personality disorders.

REFERENCES

Cleckley, H. M. (1959), Psychopathic States. In: *American Handbook of Psychiatry*, ed. S. Arieti, New York: Basic Books, pp. 567-589.

Deutsch, H. (1942), Some Forms of Emotional Disturbance and Their Relation to Schizophrenia. In: *Neuroses and Character Types*. New York: International Universities Press, 1965, pp. 262-286.

Easser, B. R. & Lesser, S. R. (1965), Hysterical personality. *Psychoanalytic Quarterly*, 34:390-405.

Freud, S. (1908), Character and Anal Eroticism. *Standard Edition*, 9:167-176. London: Hogarth Press, 1959.

——— (1911), Psychoanalytic Notes on an Autobiographical Account of a Case of Paranoia. *Standard Edition*, 12:3-82. London: Hogarth Press, 1958.

Johnson, A. M. (1949), Sanctions for Superego Lacunae of Adolescents. In: *Searchlights on Delinquency*, ed. K. R. Eissler. New York: International Universities Press, pp. 225-245.

Moore, B. E. & Fine, B. D., eds. (1967), *A Glossary of Psychoanalytic Terms and Concepts*. New York: American Psychoanalytic Association.

Niederland, W. G. (1959), The "Miracled-Up" World of Schreber's Childhood. *The Psychoanalytic Study of the Child*, 14:383-415. New York: International Universities Press.

SUGGESTED READING

Blinder, M. G. (1966), The Hysterical Personality, *Psychiatry*, 29:227-235.

Chodoff, P. & Lyons, H. (1958), Hysteria; The Hysterical Personality and Hysterical Conversion. *American Journal of Psychiatry*, 114:734-740.

Nydes, J. (1963), The Paranoid-Masochistic Character. *Psychoanalytic Review*, 50:215-251.

CHAPTER TWENTY

Sexual Disorders and Variations

GEORGE H. WIEDEMAN, M.D.

The development of human sexuality, like other lines of development, proceeds in a sequence that follows the epigenetic principle (Erikson, 1959, p. 52). As we said in Chapter One, various erogenic zones have their time of ascendancy or dominance, the earlier ones being succeeded by the later ones without, however, altogether losing their erogenic significance. "Dominance" is the key word here, in that nothing is fully erased. The dominance of the oral zone gives way to the dominance of the anal zone, which, in turn, yields its dominance to the phallic zone. The latter becomes the center of sexual sensation in the oedipal period. After a time of relative quiescence of the sexual drives during latency, sexuality is reorganized under genital domination. Although the vast majority of people reach genital primacy and heterosexuality, many developmental disturbances may deflect psychosexual progression. These disturbances, as we have pointed out in the chapters on development, have their source in the nature of the child's object relations during the early developmental stages. Fixation to early phases of psychosexual development and interpersonal relations, persistence of excessive erogeneity of the oral and anal zones (and of the skin), and the presence of primitive psychic mechanisms—inability to withstand delay in gratification—are characteristic of those with sexual deviations.

The deviations or variations from the epigenetic sequence can be viewed in terms of deviations from the aim of genital union with an adult partner: fetishism, sadomasochism, voyeurism/exhibitionism, pedophilia, and transvestism; or they can be viewed in terms of the choice of an object: homosexuality. Sexual dysfunctions of heterosexuals—impotence and frigidity—have been described in Chapter Thirteen.

Deviations of the aim and of object choice cannot always be neatly separated. Sadomasochism, for example, can be combined with either hetero- or homosexual object choice. Or, again, fetishism can be a solitary form of sexual gratification leading to masturbation, but the fetish may also serve as a preliminary means of arousal that culminates in a sexual act with a partner. When a sexual disturbance or maldevelopment is thoroughly investigated and repressed material is uncovered, then the roots of the disturbance, dating from the earliest phases of childhood to adolescence, can be understood. The variations from the ordinary heterosexual pattern originate postnatally and are due to experiential environmental factors and not so far as is known to biologic-genetic ones. What causes sexual variations cannot be ascertained by questionnaires or a few interviews because most of the essential experiences that have determined the deviation have succumbed to repression or isolation. Inasmuch as the sexual variation offers the possibility of sexual gratification, the person afflicted with it considers it as part of himself—it is ego-syntonic and seemingly not subject to change without endangering any sexual satisfaction and even the sense of identity. This is the chief reason why most people with sexual deviations do not seek treatment even if it is available.

The majority of people look upon deviations from the socially recognized norm with disapproval, disgust, and/or ridicule. It is true that some forms of disturbed sexuality represent a danger to others—pedophilia and rape, for instance—but in the vast majority of cases, sexual deviations practiced in solitude or covertly with consenting adults constitute no danger whatsoever to society. Their persecution is a remnant of medieval attitudes when any deviation from the permitted sexual act was considered a sin akin to heresy. The "sinfulness" of sexual variations was succeeded by the conviction that it was a sign of hereditary biological "degeneracy." This point of view has become untenable due primarily to research initiated by Freud (1905) and since then extended by psychoanalysts and psychiatrists. The tenacity of derogatory popular attitudes can be explained by people's reluctance to tolerate deviations in general and, especially, sexual variations, roots of which go back to the early psychosexual stages traversed by everybody in the course of development and eventually repressed. Sexual deviations represent the persistence and dominance of some aspects of childhood sexuality in adult sexual life.

Sadism, masochism

Sadism and masochism are probably second in incidence only to homosexuality. They occur among both heterosexuals and homosexuals. The masochist experiences sexual arousal and pleasure up to the point of orgasm if pain is inflicted on him. The masochist—male or female—has his own set of fantasies which he strives to enact with a partner. These fantasies may include bondage (being tied up), verbal abuse, humiliation, domination, and actual beating and flogging. Most masochists do not experience pleasure when the pain oversteps the degree of intensity that they desire and does not correspond to the enactment of their fantasies. In masochistic personality disorders, the original sexual masochistic wish has undergone desexualization: these people unconsciously desire actual suffering and achieve it in nonsexual circumstances. It is often quite transparent that the sexual masochist re-enacts in his fantasies and sexual activities childhood scenes of submitting and being punished by the powerful parent, usually the father—which by no means implies that the masochist has actually been cruelly punished by his parents. Usually, the psychodynamics and history disclose difficulties during the oedipal period; a great deal of guilt over incestuous desires is generated and activates a defensive regression to the anal-sadistic phase. The unconscious desire to be anally penetrated by the father is replaced by masochistic submission and beatings. The man who submits masochistically to a woman unconsciously imagines a woman equipped with a phallus—in terms of early childhood fantasies; he can thereby submerge any homosexual anal wishes that would be too threatening to him.

The sadist is one who inflicts humiliation and pain on the partner in order to achieve sexual arousal and orgasm. It appears that sadism is a more serious disturbance than masochism. It involves a greater disturbance of the ego functions and, paradoxically enough, may be coupled with masochistic character traits. Some sadists achieve gratification through rape; they are impotent unless they use violence or threats of violence. Yet, not all rapes are committed by sadists. Many are performed by immature teenagers, sometimes acting in groups and raping the same victim in rapid succession. They feel compelled to prove their "masculinity" to themselves and to other members of their gang. This sexual behavior does not necessarily carry over into adulthood, especially among those who are the followers of a gang leader. Other sexual aggressors use force when they are drunk, especially if they are, when sober, under the sway of sexual inhibitions. There are egocentric delinquents with a defective superego who do not care to make the effort to woo the woman they desire, but use force instead; forcible rape, to them, is not necessarily a precondition for being potent and sexually gratified as it is to the sadistic assaultive type of rapists. To them, the age and appearance of their victim may be a matter of indifference.

We frequently speak of sadomasochism because a mixture of sadistic and masochistic sexual features can exist in the same individual. Psychodynamically, the sadist identifies with his masochistic partner and the masochist with the sadist. This identification is mostly unconscious.

Fetishism, voyeurism, exhibitionism, pedophilia

Fetishism, voyeurism, and exhibitionism are limited almost exclusively to males. The fetishist is sexually attracted and aroused by an object rather than by a person. This object may be a woman's shoe, a female undergarment, a piece of fur, or one of any number of things. Sometimes the fetish is used to achieve sexual arousal in order to be able to perform the sexual act with a partner, sometimes the use of the fetish is sufficient to produce sexual arousal, with masturbation to full orgasm. Unconsciously, the fetish represents the fantasied female phallus. The fetishist, as a small boy, could not, because of castration fear, conceive of anybody without a penis and therefore, as an adult, created a substitute penis in the form of a fetish. He has suffered a split within the ego. He realizes, on one hand, that women do not possess a penis, but, unconsciously, he is compelled to recreate this female phallus in order to reassure himself against his castration fear and to be able to achieve sexual gratification. The split in the ego represents the persistence of a primitive mental mechanism.

The voyeur is intent on watching a couple engage in sexual activity or a woman undress. He usually does it stealthily, becomes sexually aroused, and masturbates. The exhibitionist is the counterpart of the voyeur, He shows his, usually erect, penis to a woman or girl. It is essential for him to provoke surprise and fright in the woman. Neither the voyeur nor the exhibitionist is likely to attack a woman, as is a rapist. Rather than desiring to overpower the woman physically, the exhibitionist has to keep his sexual activity at a distance from her. Both the voyeur and the exhibitionist experienced a disturbance during the oedipal phase of development. Despite being adult, the exhibitionist shows off his penis as might a little boy of three or four. The voyeur is constantly engaged in gratifying the sexual curiosity and excitement he experienced as a child, namely: what goes on between adults, especially between the parents in the bedroom.

The pedophile, or child molester, is fixated on certain sexual experiences in childhood and is usually afraid to engage in sexual relations with adults. The pedophile usually molests a relative or some child known to him. When the pedophile is apprehended, it is especially important to protect the child from undue alarm by not stressing the dangerous aspects. The alarm and the disgust expressed by the adults would compound the actual effect of the sexual seduction and make it even more traumatic than it actually was.

Transvestism, transsexualism

The transvestite is one who has a very strong desire to wear garments of the opposite sex and may experience sexual arousal by doing so. He is usually heterosexually oriented and may be married and have children. In some instances, the wife goes along with his "habit," in other instances it may disrupt the marriage, once the wife discovers it.

The wearing of feminine clothing and make-up by homosexuals has a different significance. It may be done to attract other homosexual men, and the use of exaggerated female mannerisms and movements usually contains an element of mockery toward women.

In transsexualism, a rare condition, represented in males at least 10 times more frequently than in females, the man, from early childhood, considers himself a member of the opposite sex. If possible, he will undergo surgery to have his genitals removed and replaced by an artificial vagina; he will also take hormones to achieve a feminine appearance. There have been numerous reports of surgical sex transformations; the subjects conduct themselves as women and even marry. The few attempts to create an artificial phallus in transsexual women have been fiascoes.

Homosexuality

Homosexuals have the normal complement of sex chromosomes: XX in the female and XY in the male. Homosexuality is a psychosexual phenomenon caused by a variety of factors that take place during development, not by genotype.

As with the other sexual deviations, the homosexual's gender identity, which is established by the age of three, may be conflicted and uncertain. In other words, the toddler was not treated unequivocally as a boy or girl and did not acquire the full conviction of being either male or female. Male homosexuals, like other small boys, develop a strong attachment to their mothers. Their mothers usually reinforce the attachment by being overly seductive, and some are both seductive and hostile at the same time. The fathers may be either absent, detached and ineffectual, or hostile. In any case, these children do not achieve a successful resolution of the Oedipus complex. They identify with their mother rather than their father and take themselves narcissistically as their sexual objects. The fixation on the mother creates a very strong incest taboo, which is extended from the mother to all women. They also have intense castration fears, which generate a feeling of disgust and horror of female genitalia and make it impossible for them, later on, to approach any woman sexually. Instead, they look for a man whom they may love as their own mothers loved them. Paradoxically enough, many homosexual men run away from women and transfer the sexual excitation to men in order to remain faithful to their mothers. Sometimes a strong attachment to the mother and early jealousy of older brothers may undergo a transformation, and the rival of an early period becomes the homosexual object later on. The retention of the erotic significance of the anal zone is likewise of great importance as a determinant of homosexuality. The homosexual who has anal intercourse identifies with the woman—the anus becomes his vagina. These determinants, of course, are all unconscious. Primitive unconscious oral impulses also play a considerable role, and the partner's penis frequently is important as a means of incorporating the partner's masculinity in order to reinforce his own.

Female homosexuality has received much less attention and has been less subject to social sanctions than has male homosexuality. In the female, as in the male, cumulative disturbances during various stages of development, especially during the oedipal phase contribute to homosexual object-choice. The inability to resolve the oedipal relation to the father causes a regression to the early attachment to the mother. An identification with the father or brother likewise plays an important part in the genesis of lesbianism.

Freud (1914) described four possible types of homosexual object-choice: the man may choose (1) what he himself is, (2) what he himself was, (3) what he would like to be, or (4) someone with whom he at one time identified.

Kinsey et al. (1948) proposed a scale for classifying homosexual behavior from zero to six: (0) is exclusively heterosexual; (1) has incidental homosexual experiences; (2) has more than incidental homosexual experience, but is still predominantly heterosexually inclined; (3) has sexual activity that is evenly balanced in terms of hetero- vs. homosexual object choice; (4) is predominantly homosexual, but retains substantial heterosexual interests; (5) has only incidental heterosexual interests and activity, and, finally, (6) is exclusively homosexual. The Kinsey scale would roughly correspond to Freud's (1905) broader clinical classification as follows: groups one and two would be considered "contingent"; groups three and four, "amphigenic," and groups five and six, "absolute inverts." Statistics concerning the incidence of homosexual behavior depend on how many of the groups on the Kinsey scale are included in the statistical sample. If all males who ever had a homosexual experience or wish are included, the incidence of homosexuality would amount to one-third, inasmuch as occasional homosexual contacts are not infrequent among adolescent boys. If only groups five and six are included, then the percentage of homosexual men would come close to two per cent of the population.

In 1974, the American Psychiatric Association abolished the term "homosexuality" as one of its diagnostic categories and replaced it by "Sexual Orientation Disturbance," to apply only to those homosexual men and women who are distressed by their homosexual orientation. It is not a mental illness, but a developmental deviation. The psychiatric diagnostic manual contains several other diagnoses—for instance, the psychosomatic conditions such as peptic ulcer, hives, bronchial asthma, etc., which are hardly considered "mental" illnesses. The exclusion from the official psychiatric nomenclature was urgently advocated by the homophile groups, for they considered it demeaning to be classified as one of the psychiatric categories. Whether the deletion as a diagnosis will contribute to a change of public attitudes and help eliminate discriminatory legislation against homosexuals remains to be seen. The overwhelming majority of the helping professionals—psychiatrists, psychologists, etc.— have always advocated the removal of any stigma and discrimination against people with sexual variations that do not harm others.

If we are confronted with people having various sexual disorders and deviations, we must keep in mind that nobody should be pressured to undergo treatment against his will. Therapy of any kind is ineffective under duress. Sexual deviates who are in a state of conflict should be given the opportunity to have psychiatric or analytic therapy. Behavioral modification techniques have been used to modify sexual deviations, although their efficacy remains to be proven. If the sexual deviation serves as a defense against an underlying serious mental disorder, it should be left alone. Of course, casework and other forms of treatment should be made available to those suffering from social maladaptation, neurotic, or characterological disturbances, whether or not they also have a sexual deviation.

REFERENCES

American Medical Association (1972), *Human Sexuality*. Chicago: A.M.A. Committee on Human Sexuality.

Erikson, E.H. (1959), *Identity and the Life Cycle* [*Psychological Issues*, Monogr. 1] New York: International Universities Press.

Freud, S. (1905), Three Essays on the Theory of Sexuality. *Standard Edition*, 7: 239. London: Hogarth Press, 1953.

——— (1914), On Narcissism: an Introduction. *Standard Edition*, 14: 69-102. London: Hogarth Press, 1953.

Kinsey, A., Pomeroy, W. & Martin, C. (1948), *Sexual Behavior in the Human Male*. Philadelphia: W. B. Saunders.

——— ——— ——— (1953), *Sexual Behavior in the Human Female*. Philadelphia: W. B. Saunders.

SUGGESTED READING

Benedek, T. (1959), Sexual Functions in Women and their Disturbance. In: *American Handbook of Psychiatry*, Vol. 1, 2nd edition, ed. S. Arieti. New York: Basic Books, 1974, pp. 569-591.

Karlen, A. (1971), *Sexuality and Homosexuality*. New York: W. W. Norton.

Lief, H. (1974), Sexual Functions in Men and their Disturbance. In: *American Handbook of Psychiatry*, Vol. 1, 2nd edition, ed. S. Arieti. New York: Basic Books, 1974, pp. 545-568.

Masters, W. H. & Johnson, V. E. (1966), *Human Sexual Response*. Boston: Little, Brown.

Socarides, C. (1966), Homosexuality. In: *American Handbook of Psychiatry*, Vol. 3, ed. S. Arieti. New York: Basic Books.

Stoller, R. (1968), *Sex and Gender*. New York: Science House.

Vincent, C. E., ed. (1968), *Human Sexuality in Medical Practice*. Springfield, Ill.: Charles C Thomas.

CHAPTER TWENTY-ONE

Alcoholism

DONALD L. GERARD, M.D.

Alcoholic beverages have been used for thousands of years, and for all this time drunkenness has been a familiar phenomenon. Most adults drink alcoholic beverages today; but why so many drink to such an extent that their health is jeopardized and their social relations impaired is far from a simple question—and it is an important question. Although we lack clear and simple criteria for identifying them, an enormous number of people—competent authorities estimate more than four million adults in the United States alone—suffer from alcoholism. Not only do they themselves suffer, but they and their drinking problems adversely affect the lives and welfare of others. Alcoholism is the most serious—in terms of prevalence, morbidity and mortality—drug-abuse problem in contemporary society.

Many fields of knowledge have made salient contributions to the understanding of this problem; biochemistry, neurophysiology, sociology, biostatistics, internal medicine, experimental and clinical psychiatry, and psychoanalysis have helped elucidate its etiology, clinical course, and prognosis. Unfortunately, none of these fields, nor any conjunction of them, has as yet provided a powerful enough grasp on the phenomena of alcoholism to significantly enhance our ability to modify the life course of the many who suffer with it.

This chapter should provide an introductory framework of basic information and current perspectives, useful for clinicians, or prospective clinicians, who will have to take care of patients with this problem.

On Alcohol

Alcohol is a food, a substance that, under certain conditions, can be directly harmful to health, and a potent drug affecting the nervous system.

Alcohol as a Food

Although alcoholic beverages have played an important role in the dietary practices of countless societies and cultures since antiquity (McCarthy, 1959), they are *inadequate* foodstuffs. They are rich in potential for providing quickly available energy, but are totally deficient in the vitamins, minerals, and proteins necessary to sustain normal growth, or to assure the proper functioning of biochemical systems in the body. It is known that people who obtain much of their daily caloric supply from alcoholic beverages acquire vitamin deficiencies which may result in acute or chronic disease of the nervous system, heart, skin, or other organs. (Such illnesses as alcoholic neuritis, Wernicke's encephalopathy, Korsakoff's syndrome, beri-beri, and pellagra, do occur secondary to alcoholism, though other sources of dietary deficiency may also generate these syndromes.) In addition to these relatively specific syndromes, chronic vitamin and protein deficiencies (along with some of the vicissitudes of chronic abuse of alcohol) make those who use alcohol as a major source of calories more susceptible to, and less capable of recovery from a variety of infectious diseases, especially tuberculosis and pneumonia. In fact, the age-specific death rate among alcoholics is three to four times higher than that of the general population (Schmidt & deLint, 1969).

Alcohol as a Toxic Substance

The local irritant action of alcohol on mucous membranes may cause acute or chronic inflammation of the lining of the stomach. This often results in disturbances of appetite with insidious nutritional consequences. In some cases, pain, vomiting, and hemorrhage may occur. (Alcoholics also suffer from peptic ulcer to a far greater degree than does the general population, or at least from severe complications of peptic ulcer through a variety of direct and indirect effects.) The major pathological effects of alcohol occur after the alcohol has been absorbed into the blood stream. Recent medical research indicates that absorbed alcohol causes damage to liver cells (leading via fatty liver, through cirrhosis, to serious medical and surgical conditions) interferes with the formation of red blood cells (anemia), and impedes the circulation of blood—via "sludging" of blood cells—in the small arteries that deliver oxygen to the brain, heart muscle, and kidneys (causing cell damage in these organs owing to insufficient oxygenation). It is important to note that these effects may occur under conditions of optimal nutrition, and the effects are cumulative with chronic use of alcohol. These toxic effects, together with nutritional deficiencies, contribute to the high morbidity and mortality of those who use alcoholic beverages frequently and in large quantities.

Alcohol as a Drug

Alcohol affects the central nervous system. As with all drugs affecting brain function, the behavioral consequences of imbibing alcohol are a result of the interplay of three factors: the neurophysiologic disturbance directly related to the drug, the psychological state of the subject prior to and during intoxication, and the social context of the drug use. From a purely neurophysiologic standpoint, alcohol interferes with the transmission of electrochemical impulses among the cells of the brain; like the anesthetics, it is a *depressant* of neural activity. However, the different functional areas of the brain are not all affected at the same time. At minimal blood-alcohol levels, those areas of the brain which regulate and integrate the higher mental functions—the synthetic ego functions of judgment, restraint, delay of gratification, frustration-tolerance—are the first to be impaired. At the same time, the diminution of vigilance and attentiveness to outer reality may be experienced as a gratifying relaxation. For those whose psychological control systems are intact and effective, minimal intoxication does not lead to marked behavioral alterations of a maladaptive nature. The converse is also generally true: those whose control systems are impaired, either because of major psychiatric illness or neurologic impairment, may manifest serious disturbances of behavior in response to small quantities of alcohol.

As the blood alcohol level rises subsequent to continued drinking, neuromuscular coordination begins to be impaired. Even prior to the moment when performance is grossly impaired, the drinker's judgment about fighting—or flirting—may go awry, which is why people do things when drunk that they would not do when sober. However, as drinking continues and the blood level continues to rise, the drinker becomes incapacitated—i.e., "drunk." Not only is his judgment impaired, his coordination is disrupted; he staggers, lurches, falls. His irritability is increased. His state of consciousness becomes labile, shifting back and forth from drowsiness to intense wakefulness. Finally, he may enter a drugged sleep from which he cannot be readily aroused. At very high blood alcohol levels—when, for example, large quantities of alcohol (perhaps a fifth of whiskey in half an hour) are quickly consumed the drinker may become anesthetized, comatose, and may even die as a result of depression of the respiratory centers.

It is not possible to drink alcoholic beverages without affecting the brain. Although there probably are only minor individual variations in brain physiology in response to small levels of blood alcohol, there are remarkable individual variations in the associated behavior. How the drinker feels and acts as he becomes progressively intoxicated, and how he interprets the experience, depend on his sociocultural background and his immediate circumstances, including his state of health and his basic personality. Interestingly, the behavior and the physiology of the drinker are also affected by the total past experience with alcohol. People with drinking problems of long duration may exhibit less behavioral malfunction than control subjects with the same blood alcohol level. Following the same amount of ingested alcoholic beverage, the blood alcohol level may be even lower for them than for normals. This explains why there is no predictable, uniform, or simple pattern of behavior in the initial phases of alcohol consumption.

Almost all human drinking behavior occurs under the influence of social expectations about the nature of alcohol and about the behavior drinking ought to elicit. Without trying to summarize the fascinating literature on this subject (see especially Bales [1946], Pittman & Gordon [1958], and Snyder [1958], it is worthwhile noting that, broadly speaking, Orthodox Jews drink with the expectation that they will not become drunk, whereas foreign born Irish-Americans do expect to become drunk. At middle-class cocktail parties the usual expectation is that drinking will enhance conviviality without enhancing intimacy. In some primitive groups (Horton, 1945), the purpose of taking alcoholic beverages is to become as drunk or as crazy as possible as quickly as possible. Whatever the expectations may have been at the initiation of a drinking bout, if the drinker becomes "drunk"—or acutely intoxicated, to use the medical euphemism—his behavior becomes less individualized and more toxically or organically stereotyped. He becomes less able to cope with his inner conflicts, to live up to his aspirations, or even to achieve his desires of the moment, and he enters into an altered relation with his physical and personal environment that may be quite hazardous. The nature and extent to which the relation with the physical and personal environment is altered, however, and the associated degree of hazard, is determined both by characteristics of the drinker and by the nature of his environment. In any instance, either or both sets of factors may enter into play. A man may be mugged and beaten while intoxicated because he has unconscious masochistic or suicidal impulses or because he lives in a neighborhood where preying on drunks is part of the delinquency subculture. In general, the more protective, tolerant, and supportive the environment, the less likely that intoxication will lead to dangerous consequences. In environments where violence, exploitation, apathy, or disinterest are the preponderant attitudes, the hazards of intoxication are greater. Therefore, for the urban poor, the hazards of intoxication are magnified.

Pathological Drinking Patterns

Acute alcoholic intoxication, with its associated medical and social morbid consequences (head injuries, fights, automobile accidents, etc.) is an organic brain syndrome, a psychiatric disorder, frequently but not regularly or necessarily leading to hospitalization, protective isolation in special centers for alcoholics, or being jailed. It may be that social custom rather than psychologic disorder is the basis for episodes of acute intoxication. No single episode of acute intoxication with alcoholic beverages warrants psychiatric concern. The important issue is the role that alcoholic beverages play in the drinker's life situation and adaptation.

Acute intoxication is a self-limiting disorder lasting for hours, not for days. Sooner or later, money runs out, friends or authorities intervene, or sleep interrupts the event. Whether or not the drinking is malignant or symptomatic of psychiatric illness may be more clearly recognized by what the subject is and does when he is sober than by what he did when he was drunk.

Frequent drinking without episodes of acute intoxication is customary in many national groups. The beverage alcohol is usually of low alcoholic content, beer or wine, for example, often diluted with water. The conscious motive for drinking, aside from the gustatory enjoyment, is to aid digestion and to improve appetite. Such drinking is almost always done in a social context. In some societies, beverage alcohol can be a major foodstuff for the poor (Jellinek, 1960); wine can be a less expensive or as inexpensive a source of calories as bread or other grain products. Hence, the motivations for drinking wine and eating are inseparable, and the widespread cirrhosis of the liver which occurs in these contexts is a consequence of alcohol usage without "psychiatric" alcoholism. As a dietary pattern, the consumption of beverage alcohol contrasts sharply with the kind of regular drinking without acute intoxication that is consciously motivated by an attempt to relieve feelings of sadness, loneliness, tension, inadequacy, or pain. This drinking is more often solitary and surreptitious than it is "social." Such behavior is rationalized by the belief, which is widespread, that relief from emotional distress can be obtained by drinking. This belief is not supported by scientific study or by careful clinical observation. Mendelson (1964) has shown that alcohol actually intensifies rather than alleviates depression and anxiety. There are real effects of alcoholic beverages on emotional states, but they are mediated by complex symbolic, unconscious, and neurophysiologic processes.

The point to be emphasized here is the paradoxical one that dramatic public instances of acute intoxication may not warrant psychiatric concern, whereas regular drinking even without acute intoxication may be indicative of serious psychiatric illness; regular drinking without intoxication, whether surreptitious or public (the so-called heavy social drinker) may well be an attempt to cope with persistent disturbances of mood, thought, and personal relationships. Very often those who exhibit this latter kind of pathological drinking pattern reject the idea of treatment. They are satisfied that alcohol provides them with sufficient relief at little cost to themselves. Nevertheless, such a background of alcohol use without acute intoxication, intended to diminish conscious distress, is often noted in the history of those who are later on regarded as suffering from alcoholism.

Chronic intoxication is a drinking pattern characterized by recurrent episodes of acute intoxication, interrupted only by sleep, to the exclusion of other activities or responsibilities. The chronically intoxicated eats less and less, does not go home, and does not go to work. Though the drinking may have begun in the company of others, it becomes an increasingly solitary activity. Under these conditions, alcohol is rarely absent from blood or brain. During sleep, the blood alcohol level gradually diminishes, for the drinker is no longer drinking, and previously ingested alcohol is metabolized. On awakening, he is never as drunk as when he fell asleep; however, on awakening, or soon thereafter, he again begins to drink until judgment, coordination, and consciousness are once more seriously disrupted. The intervening periods of sleep become progressively less restful, less recuperative, and the general state of feeling on awakening worsens. In the vernacular, he becomes more and more "hung-over." Indeed, the hangover, with headache, depression, tremulousness, irritability, etc., is often the stimulus or the rationalization for more drinking.

Even among people who go through episodes of chronic intoxication or "binges," as they are called in the argot of alcoholics, there are individual variations. Some remain sober and abstinent for a large part of the year, but on a regular anniversary basis, perhaps around Christmas or New Year, deliberately start out on a binge, which usually continues until they land in a hospital. The commoner pattern is to go from one binge to another, with brief periods of abstinence usually enforced by such changes in circumstances as being jailed or hospitalized or being controlled by the family. Most striking is that usually this type of drinker does not wish to go on a binge. Each time he has the opportunity to drink, however, he is apparently unable to use judgment based on the recollection of prior experience with drinking and to control the amount he drinks. He may intend to have a few drinks for sociability's sake, but he recurrently ends up in a state of chronic intoxication.

Sequelae of Intoxication

Both acute and chronic intoxication with alcohol may be and often are accompanied or followed by disturbances in sleep such as insomnia, restlessness, or early awakening; disturbances in memory such as "blackouts" and amnesia; and loss or diminution of appetite. The hangover, a state of general malaise, with headaches, digestive system comlaints, and, often, anxiety or depression, is the most common sequela. The precise mechanism for the formation of these symptoms is not understood. Probably both disturbed physiology and psychodynamic factors play a role. In any event, nobody really knows how to "cure a hangover." Like the common cold, it is a self-limiting disorder. For those with drinking problems, the usual remedy is to take a drink on awakening. As we have said, this often turns out to be the first step to resuming a binge.

The most serious and occasionally even fatal complication of chronic intoxication with alcohol is *delirium tremens.* Isbell et al. (1955) have shown that this syndrome can be precipitated by the withdrawal of alcohol from chronically intoxicated human subjects in the experimental psychiatric laboratory. The usual course of this acute psychiatric illness follows after the patient has been having a prolonged episode of chronic intoxication. When he is abruptly placed in an environment—in jail or a hospital—where he can no longer obtain alcohol, the drinker begins to experience marked restlessness, anxiousness, and insomnia, which progresses into a state of disorientation for time, place, and person. He further experiences *hallucinatory perceptions,* usually of small biting animals or insects, and *tremulousness* (hence the term delirium tremens), accompanied by *dehydration* and fever. Exposed to the stimulation of restraint or merely to questioning, the drinker may become violent, not because he is aggressive, but in an attempt to ward off what he regards as an attack. Delirium tremens usually last from three to six days. On recovery, the patient is in a highly weakened state, usually vaguely aware that he has been through a life-threatening, medical psychiatric crisis, and that this came about in consequence of his chronic intoxication.

Another phenomenon, less common but not infrequent, that may follow acute withdrawal of alcohol from human volunteers and clinical (post-binge) subjects is the "rum-fit" (Victor, 1968). This is a seizure state indistinguishable in appearance from an attack of idiopathic grand mal epilepsy. It almost always consists of a single episode of sudden loss of consciousness with diffuse convulsive movements and loss of sphincter control, and it occurs from six to 48 hours after the last drink. In approximately one out of three cases, the patients who have a "rum-fit" go into delirium tremens.

On Alcoholism

We have so far discussed acute intoxication, drinking for symptom relief, binges, and the sequelae of intoxication. We have made a distinction between instances of malfunctioning or pathology involving the use of alcohol and *alcoholism.* Although this term is difficult to define, it does not suffer from lack of definitions. An examination of three definitions of alcoholism will disclose some of the difficulties involved in trying to conceptualize this phenomenon.

According to the World Health Organization (1952), alcoholics, persons who suffer from alcoholism, are "those excessive drinkers whose dependency on alcohol has attained such a degree that [they show] a noticeable mental disturbance or interference with bodily or mental health, their interpersonal relationships, and their smooth social and economic functioning, or the prodromal signs of such developments." This formulation of the diagnostic criteria of alcoholism is unsatisfactory. The terms "dependency," "noticeable," "smooth," "prodromal signs," "such a degree," etc., are vague and undefined, and further criteria are required to help distinguish the "normal" drinker from one who "obviously" has serious difficulties in his life in which the use of alcohol seems to be a major significant element.

Mark Keller (1960) who, as editor of the *Quarterly Journal of Studies on Alcohol,* for many years has been concerned with clarifying terminology in this area, has defined alcoholism as a "psychogenic dependence on or a physiological addition to ethanol, manifested by the inability of the alcoholic consistently to control either the start of drinking or its termination once started" (p. 127). This operational definition has prospective or predictive aspects. But the phrase "consistently to control" is ambiguous. What frequency of drinking indicates loss of control? Must the rate of intake equal or exceed the rate of metabolism of alcohol? And for how long?

Based on his thoughtful review of the psychoanalytic literature, Fenichel (1945) defined alcoholism as a *psychological addiction.* The addict, whether to alcohol, morphine, or other substances, is one who doesn't use drugs as a protection against painful mental states, but rather as a means toward the unconscious satisfaction of inner needs. For such people, the effect of alcohol "has a subtle, imperative significance." The alcoholism grew out of a predisposition to attain certain effects which satisfy deep and primitive desires related to archaic, oral longings. The emphasis in this psychoanalytic definition is on the genetics or psychodynamics of alcoholism, but the disorder itself is not defined, nor are diagnostic criteria suggested to identify and discriminate those persons who use alcohol as a protection against painful mental states from those who use alcohol for the satisfaction of archaic oral longings.

All three definitions, though incomplete, are instructive. The first emphasizes the aspect of social or medical morbidity associated with the "disorder." The second emphasizes an undoubtedly important clinical phenomenon as the hallmark of an illness, and the third gives a partial theoretic perspective on its etiology. Supplementing these, we would suggest a definition of alcoholism based on clinical practice in psychiatry. We would remind the reader that in psychiatry there are few "diseases," many classifications, and a rich, descriptive vocabulary. If, as often happens in psychiatry, we use the term "alcoholism" to convey part of our differential evaluation of a particular patient, then the term acquires reasonable precision and consistency. The use of this term should imply that the clinician believes, based on study of the patient's difficulties in living, that the use of alcohol has become integrated with the disorder in the patient's life; the clinical comprehension and attempts at management of the patient's intrapsychic and/or interpersonal maladaptation would be grossly handicapped if one did not pay considerable attention to the patient's current use of alcoholic beverages. Thus, the term "alcoholism" operationally *refers to the clinician's judgment* about the importance of alcoholic beverages in the patient's disturbed behavior and inadequate adaptation, *and not to a disease* he has acquired or developed.

Although the term alcoholism is still widely used, there is a growing trend toward the use of two more elastic concepts, neither of which implies a specific disease. The first is "problem drinker," meaning someone with a drinking problem; the second is "drug abuse of the alcohol-barbiturate type," a behavioral-pharmacologic concept proposed by Eddy et al. (1966).

With this definitional framework in the background, we now turn to the question of what characterizes people who become alcoholic.

How this question is answered is often determined by the experience the responder has had with patients having drinking problems. At one time, the simple notion was widely held that alcoholism was a syndrome primarily associated with being a social derelict. The studies of Straus and Bacon (1951) and more recently those of Gerard et al. (1969) have amply documented that this notion is erroneous. Although the rate of alcoholism among those who are down and out—the drifters, hoboes, men on skid row—is vastly higher than in the remainder of the population, it is estimated that 97 per cent of the alcoholics in this country are *not* on skid row. In fact, the rate and prevalence of alcoholism off skid row is probably underestimated because many people who would be regarded as alcoholics never come to the attention of professionals interested in studying or documenting the true prevalence of the problem. Then, too, there are physicians who wish to protect their patients from the stigma they fear may be attached to the diagnosis of alcoholism. The patient may be truly described as having pneumonia, but the additional truth that the pneumonia was acquired in the course of a binge may be omitted from the hospital record.

It is generally accepted that alcoholism is preponderantly a *disease of men,* who are four to six times more likely than women to manifest this disorder. Men of Irish, Scandinavian, or Slavic origin are far more often observed to be suffering from alcoholism than white men of other ethnic origins, though ethnic differences tend to become smaller with increasing Americanization. For example, first-generation, foreign-born Jewish men are almost never observed to be alcoholics, while their American-born children and grandchildren are increasingly prone to manifest this syndrome. More recent studies, however, have indicated that blacks (or nonwhites, as reported in the Federal government publication of vital statistics) have the highest rates of alcoholism-related medical disorders, although nonwhite patients have generally not been referred to or treated in special alcoholism programs, in proportion to the incidence and prevalence with which they manifest alcoholism.

The psychiatrist views patients with alcoholism from two perspectives: first, according to the patient's psychological traits, and, second, according to the process—the interaction of the patients forces, motives, and needs with his life circumstances that eventuates in the integration of alcohol with his maladaptive personality traits.

Psychological Traits

Alcoholics do not exhibit psychological problems that make them intrinsically different from other psychiatric patients, though certain traits may be noted more readily among alcoholics than in the general population or in comparison groups of other psychiatric patients. Apart from their drinking problems, alcoholics may be diagnosed as manifesting neuroses, character or personality disorders, or any of the major functional psychoses. Similarly, the conflicts noted among alcoholics may be related to issues of dependence, autonomy, aggression, sexual assertion, or control. The predominant *defenses* may be those of repression, avoidance, projection, isolation, or denial and rationalization. The prominent *character style* may be passive-dependent, obsessional, psychopathic, or paranoid. It is true that certain kinds of conflicts, certain character styles, and certain defenses are more commonly noted among those patients studied in alcoholism clinics, but a point to be emphasized is that alcoholism cannot be forced into the mold of a single psychodiagnostic, psychodynamic, or etiologic conceptual framework. In the face of these facts, there have been several attempts to formulate a classification or typology of alcoholism in accordance with the life setting in which drinking becomes integrated with the person's difficulties in adaptation. Knight (1937), for example, has formulated a psychiatric typology of alcoholism in which he differentiates three types. The first is the *reactive* alcoholic, those usually of middle age who, subsequent to a significant trauma or loss, turn to drink. The second type is the *symptomatic* alcoholic. This is usually one whose drinking is clearly integrated with a prolonged and overt psychiatric illness, for example, paranoid schizophrenia. The third type is the *essential* alcoholic. This is usually somebody not so young who, as a young adult or adolescent, began almost with his first experience with alcohol to drink excessively and to acquire serious troubles in his personal relations and sexual functions as a result of drinking.

Although there is no personality or character type or constellation of psychopathology specifically associated with alcoholism, all alcoholics do have serious difficulties in living, some of which are clearly consequences of their drinking problem, but most of which existed independently of their drinking problems and very often continued when their drinking was interrupted, with or without benefit of formal treatment (Gerard et al., 1962). That serious difficulties preceded the drinking problem and in some way played a causative role in the problem is difficult to demonstrate in all instances, for many patients are not able or willing to provide data that would allow an objective exploration of the interplay between the life history and the development of the drinking problem. The study of alcoholic patients' present illness, life style, and adaptation, however, usually indicates that they are having difficulties in the areas of *personal relationships, sexuality,* and *dependency*.

Disturbed Personal Relationships

One of the stereotypes about alcoholics is that they have a facility for easy conversation and are even gregarious. However, examination of the actual nature of the relationships such patients have with other people reveals impairment in their capacity for emotional closeness or psychological intimacy. And though indeed some patients present a facade of gregariousness, most alcoholics are very aware that they are isolated, without friends or social acquaintances. Accompanying the disturbances in their overt social relations may be feelings of grandiosity and superiority, coexisting with or masking shyness and feelings of worthlessness. In general the disturbances in personal relations are most blatant in patients who have been hospitalized for psychiatric disorders concurrent with their alcoholism, or as a sequela of alcohol use (usually delirium tremens). In those patients seen for their drinking problems in psychiatric outpatient clinics or in private practice, but who have never been hospitalized, these trends are more frequently subtle, disguised, or partial.

Disturbances of Sexuality

The sexual organization and life of patients with drinking problems is characterized by disturbances in sexual function and in sexual identity. Their sexual histories are often characterized by a fear, avoidance, or disinterest in sexuality that began in adolescence and continued into adult life. Some patients claim that drinking results in a lessening of their sexual inhibitions. Although a compensatory facade of masculinity may be an important aspect of the alcoholic's style, this is usually expressed more with men than with women. The man may play the tough, virile role when out with the boys, but he cannot carry this off with his wife or girl friends, though he may adopt the facade when drinking. Such symptoms as impotence, premature ejaculation, or inability to have orgasm are quite common among alcoholics. For some, the impairment of sexual functioning is a consequence of alcoholic excess. For others, difficulties in sexual functioning are at times a major factor in causing their alcoholism. Disappointed with their inability to function in the sexual area, they turn increasingly to situations in which awareness of sexual or other inadequacies is minimized. And yet there are men who marry, have children, or claim to enjoy or to have enjoyed a satisfactory sexual life with their wives or other women, who nevertheless drink intermittently or become progressively more involved with drinking.

Although with most alcoholic patients the disturbances in sexuality are clearly evident, there is a substantial minority in whom disturbances in sexuality are not manifested in major inhibitions or malfunction of sexuality, but can only be discerned in the *quality* of their relations with women, for example, in such secret attitudes toward their sexual partners as disappointment, disgust, or revenge, or in the need for fetishes to sustain interest. Alcoholics, generally, operate at a pregenital level of sexual aim and object; their difficulties may be partial or they may be global; they may be transparent and readily verbalized, or they may be masked by complex defensive structures. The difficulties in sexual organization and functioning, just as the disturbances in personal relationships, are more evident in those patients with gross psychiatric disorder than in those who have been able to make apparently adequate or, in certain ways, successful social adaptation.

Dependency

People with drinking problems usually have poorly integrated, pathologic dependency wishes. Frustration of these wishes can intensify distress, and resultant behavior can take many forms, but some alcoholics are disturbed by the gratification of dependency. As a general rule, these wishes are defended against: if they are conscious, they are regarded as shameful immaturities; if they are unconscious, they are most commonly defended against by projection or by denial, often as part of a posture of stubborn independence.

The loss of institutional support (retirement or discharge from the army, for example) is often the precipitating event in the transformation of socially condoned, intermittent heavy drinking into alcoholism. Conversely, the threat of loss of institutional support can be a major force in initiating and sustaining abstinence. Pfeffer (1956) reported that the threat of losing job, employee benefits, and retirement pensions in an industry noted for its benevolent concern for employees' health and welfare could regularly get an alcoholic into usually successful treatment, whereas an already dismissed employee could hardly ever be motivated to enter or stay in treatment.

Many alcoholics take recurrent flights into custody where they can in large measure be dependently immersed in an institutional routine against which they consciously protest. Because they function well and thrive there, they are discharged to the community as "well" or "recovered." They thereupon quickly return to alcoholism, unemployment, and misbehavior, and again have to be institutionalized. Successful treatment of alcoholics often requires that the patient establish dependence on the therapist, group, or treating institution. Gerard et al. (1969) have encountered striking instances of patients who were salvaged from life-threatening alcoholism by falling into situations where their dependency wishes were satisfied.

Mr. X suffered from progressive asthmatic disease, which did not, however, prevent him from having frequent episodes of acute intoxication and binges. Eventually, Mr. X was declared to be totally disabled because of his asthma and placed on a comfortable pension. At this point, freed from economic responsibility, he voluntarily stopped drinking, and at the time of the last follow-up study, a year later, was still abstinent.

For that minority of patients with drinking problems who are predominantly distressed by the gratification of dependency wishes, treatment is an especially difficult problem. There are ambitious, competitive, pseudo independent men with drinking problems who cannot bear to acknowledge their wishes for tenderness, support, or concern from their wives or relatives. They also cannot bear to become involved with a psychotherapist, because they see the treatment situation itself as a form of dependency, the very condition they must at all costs avoid.

The Process

Although psychological difficulty in the three areas of personal relationships, sexuality, and dependency are regularly observed among alcoholics, it may be well to remember that these are not inclusive of all the psychological problems that individual alcoholics may manifest; that in any patient, problems in one of these areas may be more prominent than difficulties in the other areas, and finally, that these areas often are functionally interrelated. How do these psychological problems relate to the drinking problem? Because structure and function interpenetrate, we have not succeeded in discussing traits without at times giving illustrations of their dynamic, that is their motivating or driving, relevance. Similarly, as we turn our emphasis to the dynamic or process perspective, we shall not be able to totally dissociate the dynamic from certain structural or trait considerations.

To begin with, we note that both normal and pathological drinking start with a common conscious wish based on a conviction about the value and efficacy of alcoholic beverages. The wish is in some way to feel better; the conviction is that drinking can help one to feel better. In effect, drinking is regarded as a means to an end, both for the normal drinker and for the alcoholic. But the alcoholic, as perceived retrospectively through clinical studies, has had fewer ways, apart from drinking, to make himself feel better; he has developed fewer alternative resources—intrapsychically or in his social situation—for achieving gratification and recognition than has the "normal drinker." Furthermore, in consequence of his personality problems, he lives with, and is seeking to equilibrate, higher levels of distress than the nonalcoholic. The sources of his distress are manifold. In some patients it may derive from the anxiety related to intrapsychic conflict and failure of defense. In other cases it may be due to the pain of humiliation or self-disappointment, related to the fact that external realities are beyond the capacity to endure: chronic unemployment, discrimination, or illness, for example. It may also stem from internalized demands related to absurd or exaggerated ego ideals. Finally, it may spring from depression or guilt related to aggression against an ambivalently loved object.

The more the drinker's aim of "feeling better" is linked to unconscious goals originating in infantile oral yearnings, the less likely that ordinary achievements will be felt as satisfying. Getting a raise is a paltry substitute for getting mother's love. For the normal drinker, a cocktail celebrates the raise. For the alcoholic, or potential alcoholic, the function of drinking may be to diminish the paradoxic disappointment he experienced: instead of being pleased by the raise, he feels untouched, or perhaps even depressed because it does not in the least gratify the unconscious yearnings.

As we said earlier, experimental data indicate that people become more rather than less distressed as a result of intoxication. The restlessness and aggressiveness of drunks in a bar is not the outcome of feeling better, but rather the expression of counteraggression against a world increasingly perceived, as they descend into an acute toxic state, as dangerous, hostile, and beyond their control. Indeed, in the psychotherapeutic treatment of those suffering from alcoholism, it is often valuable to explore with the patient what actually happens to him as he becomes drunk. He is frequently surprised to learn of the discrepancy between his illusions about the nature of his intoxication, and his own reconstruction of what he actually experienced.

Inasmuch as "really" feeling better is not an observable consequence of progressive intoxication, clearly one must look elsewhere to understand the forces that lead a particular drinker to go beyond one or a few drinks. What is unquestionably true is that increasing the blood alcohol level alters the quality of consciousness; this altered state of consciousness is utilized by alcoholics to facilitate the gratification of some of their important psychic needs. For them, intoxication facilitates defensive processes, predominantly that of denial; it facilitates the acceptance of forbidden aggressive and sexual impulses, though often with only temporary success. Furthermore, the altered state of consciousness, in conjunction with the physiologic effects and the symbolic significance of alcohol intake, ceases to be a means of *attaining* gratification, but becomes, instead, the equivalent of the state of gratification itself. It may, for example, represent the satiated state of the infant after nursing.

The defense of denial

A brief description of a case will clarify how intoxication may facilitate denial.

Mr. B was a 19-year-old boy who had just dropped out of college, barely anticipating his being dismissed because he was failing all his courses. He was drinking daily, with episodes of acute intoxication, and was suffering from abdominal pains (due to peptic ulcer), blackouts, depression, and fears of being attacked by hoodlums. He was acquiring speeding tickets and parking tickets almost daily—paid for by his wealthy, indulgent parents, who were afraid to impose any limits on his behavior because of their fear that he would either commit suicide or leave home if thwarted. Prior to dropping out, Mr. B felt he was not accepted by his fellow students because of his unkempt appearance. He also felt that they were all angry with him and would beat him up if they were aware of his feelings of superiority to them. He had begun to drink socially in his senior year in high school; but after moving away from home into the college dormitory his drinking became a daily occurrence. After a week at college, his class attendance became sporadic and he did no homework at all. His days were filled with tension, despair, and fear of other students, whom he perceived as dangerous.

From the standpoint of the process of his becoming an alcoholic, it became more and more clear to the patient and to the therapist over the course of several years of treatment how the phenomenology of his drinking behavior related to the complexities of his interpersonal development. His dependence on his seductive mother, his rivalry and submission to his successful, dominating father, his resentment and rage against the brother who was born when he was 13 months old, were major genetic and experiential factors in the development of his character disorder. These issues were brought to a head by the adaptational demands of his becoming a college student, which required that he leave his mother and his wealthy home, where he had been able to bask in the reflection of his father's wealth, prestige, and power. It also intensified his jealousy of his brother, who remained at home with the parents.

Mr. B did not present himself at the beginning of treatment with these psychodynamics clearly formulated, or with available data from which they could be readily inferred. He spoke only of his troubles, his pain, and his wish for relief. In reviewing his current drinking behavior, it was possible to slowly piece together some understanding of what intoxication meant to him. Through drinking, he could avoid the locale that intensified his distress; he could only drink and get liquor off campus, away from associations with the young men he regarded unconsciously as rivals or as powerful figures to whom he must submit. Intrapsychically, he could get away from awareness of his tension and inner conflict. In fact, he bluntly denied the existence of these painful inner states. Though he felt his life was terrible, he almost angrily insisted that it had nothing to do with his own thoughts or feelings or prior life experiences. He had countless rationalizations for each episode of intoxication.

How did the intoxication facilitate denial? First the organic confusion experienced during intoxication *blurred the registration of experience,* and this in turn interfered with its recall. The waking life of a sober adult is dominated by conscious, secondary-process thinking in which experiences, thoughts, and feelings are organized into ordered sequences; conscious fantasies or daydreams take place, but are well differentiated from "reality." When an important segment of one's daily experience is poorly registered, however, its recall is apt to be distorted. Mr. B's drinking episodes were actually anxiety-ridden, meagerly gratifying encounters, but he reconstructed them as exciting, interesting experiences and glorious conquests that enhanced his self-esteem.

Secondly, as intoxication progresses, in proportion to the heightening blood alcohol level, more and more attention is required in order to cope with the increasing disturbance of perception, cognition, and the functioning of the autonomic nervous system. Put simply, when you get drunk, instead of attending to feelings or thoughts, your attention is drawn more and more to what is happening to you physiologically as you get drunker. Denial is thus further facilitated by this overlay of attention-absorbing stimuli.

Thirdly, as intoxication progresses to where the person is rendered stuporous or unconscious, even minimal self-observation is no longer possible. Both the internal distress and the distress superimposed by the lack of control disappear into what may be regarded as either death, paradise, or peace.

Denial is not only facilitated by intoxication, it is a defense very commonly observed, as Hartocollis (1968) has pointed out, among alcoholics both prior to and subsequent to their drinking. It was in the context of an inability to master a variety of real and fantasied losses and frustrations that Mr. B became an alcoholic—his previous use of denial as a defense against his tensions and conflicts no longer worked. For him, one major appeal of the intoxication experience was that denial would again be effective.

The superego deceived

The defense of displacement of responsibility is enhanced by drinking, partly because of the sociocultural meaning of alcoholic beverages for the drinker and partly because of the intoxication per se. Instead of being accountable to oneself and to others for sexual or aggressive behavior, expectations of conduct are modified through displacement of responsibility to the putative effects of the alcohol. The so-called "release of social inhibitions" associated with drinking is a normal variant of this defense. Relaxation of inhibitions at a drinking party does not as a rule occur because of the physiological effect of alcohol, but rather because of shared expectations about the effects of alcohol. This is attested to by the commonplace observation that merely sipping a drink or holding a drink in one's hand may often suffice to initiate either conviviality or aggression. Parenthetically, becoming intoxicated does not necessarily lead to such behavior.

Aggressive and disruptive behavior may erupt at any point in the course of drinking, from the first sip up to when the impairment of coordination is such that effective violence is impossible. In general, this is perceived or interpreted by the aggressive drinker in such terms as, "I didn't do it, the alcohol made me do it. I was drunk, and I'm sorry; I really didn't mean it. I wasn't responsible."

The displacement of responsibility to the alcohol serves to defend against the anxiety or guilt related to overt aggressive or sexual behavior. Indeed, some patients drink until they are stuporous in order to placate their conscience for aggressive or sexual behavior or fantasies occurring prior to intoxication; they relate their, to them, unacceptable behavior to the time when they were drunk, a retrospective falsification facilitated, as noted earlier, by the altered state of consciousness.

Intrinsic satisfactions

The actual experience of prolonged and disruptive intoxication with alcohol is observably distressful, yet many alcoholics return to this state over and over again, and many even recall it, though dimly and vaguely, as having been an attractive and pleasant experience. This is strikingly different from intoxication with heroin or other opiates, where apparent comfort and dimunition of overt anxiety or other mood disturbances are regularly noted by addicts and by those who observe them. Consciously, most alcoholics do not regard getting deeply drunk as intrinsically desirable. On the contrary, the wish is to drink "only enough," which, of course, they sometimes do. Consistent with the facilitation of denial by intoxication, and with the importance of denial in their psychic economy, most alcoholics are hesitant or negative about carefully examining the intoxication experience per se, except to disparage it. Nonetheless, it would be inconsistent with all psychological theory to believe that these patients regularly endanger their lives and well-being for no gain to themselves other than the facilitation of defenses. Indeed, psychoanalytic study of patients with serious drinking problems confirms the expectation that there are considerable psychic pleasures in the intoxication experience. However useful it may be to encourage and develop the patient's interest in recalling the intoxication experience in its psychological detail, this approach gives limited insight into the psychodynamic significance of his drinking. It is only when the patient is able to participate in the detailed exploration, through free-association, of his dreams, fantasies, and preoccupations, that one learns (1) that the episodes of intoxication are psychologically constructed out of *individualized* recurrent behaviors and themes (2) that are linked to persistent *specific* infantile wishes (3) that *this* person is striving to gratify. Such clinical study, has supported the generalization that those with a serious drinking problem have the gratifying unconscious fantasy that they gain access to vast supplies of nourishment, stimulation, and power through the intoxication experience.

The following formulation is based on psychoanalytic work with alcoholics:

In early childhood, being close to the mother, being fed, and being loved communicates (and perhaps instills) that the child is worthwhile and important; these intimacies are the substrate for feelings of personal worth and importance which help sustain the growing child and the grown adult when subject to subsequent strains and disappointments. By regaining access to and possession of the mother, the diminished self-esteem, which plays such an important role in the psychopathology of alcoholics, is enhanced. Under intoxication, the maternal object is unconsciously, symbolically, possessed. But because the maternal object is taboo and the legal proprietor, so to speak, has been displaced, the satisfaction is accompanied by guilt and anxiety. These painful affects are balanced by the distress of the intoxication experience. Suffering expiates guilt related to incestuous strivings, and the lesser punishment of the actual psychophysiological distress, the humiliation, and the progressive bodily illness associated with excessive drinking are accepted in preference to the worse punishment of abandonment, castration, or death for the expropriation of power. That so many alcoholics are unconcerned about or oblivious to the clear-cut relation between drinking and the disruption of their lives may be accounted for by the balancing role that distress plays in their psychological systems.

Treatment

There are no simple formulas for the treatment of alcoholics or alcoholism. As we have indicated, every patient for whom this diagnosis seems warranted manifests varying degrees and kinds of psychosocial pathology and physical consequences of his drinking. Taking care of him often entails the diagnostic and therapeutic skills of a variety of professionals and the important influence of nonprofessionals, both within and outside of his family. However there are some generalizations which can be offered about the treatment of alcoholics, based on research and our own clinical experience.

Each patient has very powerful motivations for continuing to use alcohol. The salient countervailing motivations are those interjected by the social environment, or by the recognition that organic illness associated with drinking (or illness etiologically independent, but exacerbated by drinking) threatens his life or imposes unacceptable disabilities. The therapist is more likely to help the patient to modify his drinking behavior by never allowing him to lose sight of the threat that continuation of his drinking proffers to his life and social adaptation.

Because alcohol contributes so much to the patient's intrapsychic adaptation, something must be supplied by the therapist to make up for the loss, or the prospect of the loss, of this valued substance. As a general rule, the compensation is provided by the supportive, controlling (in the benign sense) interest—without too much closeness—of the therapist, accompanied by whatever services the therapist can provide, such as medication, help with welfare, social rehabilitation. Insofar as the possibility of organic complications of alcoholism is always present, regular medical examination of the patient should be arranged. This has three functions. First, there may be treatable gastrointestinal or nervous-system illness requiring special care. Second, it serves as an effective reminder to the patient that his drinking is potentially at, if not present a threat to his life. Third, the physician's examination provides a concrete instance of reasonable concern for the patient's well-being.

Generally, alcoholics do not possess the kind of personal resources that facilitate involvement in a psychological investigation of their motives, relationships, and behavior. In order to participate and benefit from exploratory psychotherapy, the patient must possess a reasonable capacity or potential for introspection and for the delay of gratification, as well as an interest in strengthening internal sources of support and control. In addition, it is necessary that the environment be capable of tolerating and protecting the patient until changes in his cognitive and emotional framework lead to modification in his life style. It is a mistake—an exercise in futility for the therapist—to try to induce the typical alcoholic patient to explore his motives and feelings and the subtleties of his human relationships—it may well lead to failure, humiliating to the patient. Conversely, it is not useful to manage *all* patients with a drinking problem in a supportive-controlling framework. The problem is to weigh the degree of intrapsychic conflict and neurotic suffering against the extent of fixed characterologic or ego defects, and then to assume a therapeutic posture based on this appraisal. The social work admonition to work with a client "where he is" is especially important with alcoholics. The examination of the immediate reality problems and the consciously experienced distress, and an attempt to participate or influence the state of affairs at this level are more likely than any other approach to create a bridgehead into a treatment relationship, as well as to gain an operationally based diagnosis of how flexible, resourceful, and intelligent the patient really is.

The circumstances offering the best prognosis for the treatment of alcoholics are those involving a socially stable patient population whose continuing alcoholism confronts them with the prospect of loss of important sources of security. But, except for this special situation, the treatment of alcoholism is very frustrating. Most patients do not remain with the therapist or the responsible agency for more than a few consecutive interviews. Forces outside the confines of formal treatment often are far more influential than the therapist in continuing the patient's alcoholism, or, conversely, initiating and sustaining abstinence or controlled drinking. It is better to expect little cooperation, consistency, or responsiveness from these patients. In sum, it is difficult to enter into a treatment relationship with an alcoholic, and it is easy to drive him away by one's own impatience or disappointment.

For that prominent, though numerically minor segment of the alcoholic population who are homeless and unemployed, no outpatient service to which the patient or client makes visits is predictably helpful. Specialized programs offering medical and social rehabilitation and welfare services in a residential or a freely available lounge are necessary.

Outside the fabric of professional services, the organization of Alcoholics Anonymous (1957) has for almost 40 years played an important role in caring for those with drinking problems. For those patients who are able to accept its quasi-religious philosophy and can participate in its mutual-help programs, AA can provide anything from support in becoming abstinent to an opportunity to devote one's life to the organization. AA consists of a group of heterogenous chapters, each with its own type of membership and with its own method of influencing the drinking behavior of its members, ranging from an emphasis on public confessional and testimonials of success, at one extreme, to "encounter" or "analytic" group therapy at the other. What they have in common are the beliefs that only one alcoholic can help another to change; that once a person becomes an alcoholic he is always an alcoholic; that in order to be helped one must acknowledge the existence and the need for a force of power greater than oneself. Many clinics and hospitals dealing with alcoholics maintain a liaison with the local AA chapter and routinely offer their patients an opportunity to meet AA members or to supplement or replace health care by professionals. There have been no objective or critical evaluations of the work of AA. We have dealt with many alcoholics who went to AA but could not make successful use of its help. Conversely, we know patients who were unable to benefit from any other form of therapy.

Group therapy is regarded as an important treatment modality for alcoholic patients, not only for the practical reason that larger numbers of patients can be treated, but also because of certain advantages: the intensity of the relationship to the therapist is lessened; the patient is offered support from other group members who suffer with similar difficulties; and the patient may play a far greater variety of roles in the group—listener, supporter, leader, critic, rebel, protagonist, chorus—than he can in the one-to-one relation of individual psychotherapy. Because the demand and the stress on the individual patient are lessened in the group, the defensive distancing of the patient from the treatment situation is frequently diminished.

Alcoholic patients seen in group therapy maintained contact longer and were seen more often at the clinics where they were treated than patients who were not seen in groups. A crucial predictor of the outcome of treatment was the number of visits the patient made to the clinic. Although there is no clear evidence that group therapy per se is associated with a better outcome than is individual therapy, the fact that group therapy could better hold the patient in a supportive therapeutic context attests to its special usefulness in the treatment of alcoholism.

REFERENCES

Alcoholics Anonymous (1957), *Alcoholics Anonymous Comes of Age: A Brief History of A.A.* New York: Alcoholics Anonymous Publishing.

Bales, R. F. (1946), Cultural Differences in Rates of Alcoholism. *Quarterly Journal of Studies on Alcohol,* 6:482-498.

Eddy, N. B., Halbach, H., Isbell, H. & Seavers, M. H. (1966), Drug Dependence: Its Significance and Characteristics. *Psychopharmacology Bulletin,* 3:#3, 1-8.

Fenichel, O. (1945), *The Psychoanalytic Theory of Neurosis.* New York: Norton.

Gerard, D. L., Saenger, G. & Wile, R. (1962), The Abstinent Alcoholic. *Archives of General Psychiatry,* 6:83-95.

——— ——— ——— (1969), *Outpatient Treatment of Alcoholism.* (Brookside Monography No. 4). Canada: University of Toronto Press.

Hartocollis, P. (1968), Denial of Illness in Alcoholism. *Bulletin of the Menninger Clinic,* 32:47-53.

Horton, D. (1945), The Functions of Alcohol in Primitive Societies. In: *Alcohol, Science and Society* [*Quarterly Journal of Studies on Alcohol,* Monogr] New Haven, pp. 153-173.

Isbell, H., Frazer, H. F., Winkler, A. et al. (1955), An Experimental Study of the Etiology of "Rum Fits" and Delirium Tremens. *Quarterly Journal of Studies on Alcohol,* 16:1-33.

Jellinek, E. M. (1960), *The Disease Concept of Alcoholism.* New Haven: Hillhouse Press.

Keller, M. (1960), Definition of Alcoholism. *Quarterly Journal of Studies on Alcohol,* 21:125-134.

Knight, R. P. (1937), The Dynamics and Treatment of Chronic Alcohol Addiction. *Bulletin of the Menninger Clinic,* 1:233-250.

McCarthy, R. G., ed. (1959), Drinking Practices, Ancient and Modern. In: *Drinking and Intoxication.* Glencoe: The Free Press, pp. 39-175.

Mendelson, J. H. (1964), Experimentally Induced Chronic Intoxication and Withdrawal in Alcoholics. *Quarterly Journal of Studies on Alcohol,* supplement #2. Part 3, pp. 40-52.

Pfeffer, A. Z. (1956), A Treatment Program for the Alcoholic in Industry. *Journal of the American Medical Association,* 161:827-836.

Pittman, D. J., & Gordon, C. W. (1958), *Revolving Door; a Study of the Chronic Police Case Inebriate.* Glencoe: The Free Press.

Schmidt, W., & deLint, J. (1969), Mortality Experience of Male and Female Alcoholic Patients. *Quarterly Journal of Studies on Alcohol,* 30:112-119.

Snyder, C. R. (1958), *Alcohol and the Jews, A Cultural Study of Drinking and Sobriety.* Glencoe: The Free Press.

Straus, R., & Bacon, S. D. (1951), Alcoholism and Social Stability; a Study of Occupational Integration in 2023 Male Clinic Patients. *Quarterly Journal of Studies on Alcohol,* 12:231-246.

Victor, M. (1968), The Pathophysiology of Alcoholic Epilepsy. In: *The Addictive States,* Vol. 46, Research Publications Association for Research in Nervous and Mental Disease. Baltimore: Williams & Wilkins, pp. 431-454.

World Health Organization (1952), Second Report of the Alcoholism Subcommittee, Expert Committee on Mental Health. *WHO Technical Report Series,* 48.

CHAPTER TWENTY-TWO
Drug Addiction

JULIUS RUBIN, M.D.

In his long, precarious, and often hungry existence, man has sampled nearly everything that has ever grown, flown, crawled, run or swum. Many of these substances have nourished him, some have purged him, and others have provided him with various kinds of physical and emotional surprises. In early times, the priests or shamans, who also served as doctors and surgeons, assumed control over the use of all those substances—whether animal, vegetable, or mineral—which had strong somatic or psychological effects and over the millenia, an extensive pharmacopoeia was accumulated, carefully guarded, and handed down by the priestly class. Among these were pain relievers used in medical and surgical treatment, and consciousness-modifiers used in religious ceremonies.

Holy men and prophets have always sought states of ecstasy in which they felt closer to their gods. They learned that these states could be induced by certain substances. The priestesses of the famous oracle at Delphi are said to have delivered their prophecies after becoming intoxicated by inhaling gaseous vapors rising from a cleft in the earth. Even today, the sacred mushroom of Mexico is called "God's flesh," and rites of the Native American Church employ sacred peyote buttons. One might say, paraphrasing Marx: "Opium is the religion of the people."

Opium and cannabis, the latter known variously as marijuana, hashish, bhang, ganja, kif, etc., have been used throughout the Middle East, Africa, and India for thousands of years. The word "assassin" is derived from "hashish": the Assassins were a fanatical Moslem sect who specialized in political murder they allegedly committed under the influence of hashish. More recently, synthetic substances have been employed, as well as those derived from plants and fungi.

The Drugs

Drugs are usually divided into physiologically addictive "hard" drugs, and habit-forming but physiologically nonaddictive "soft" drugs. Actually, both "hard" and "soft" drugs are habit-forming. The classification of addictive as opposed to habit-forming drugs has contributed to a great deal of confusion, because the terms addiction and habituation have often been used interchangeably. It has been proposed that both terms be replaced by "drug dependence." It should be specified whether the dependence is physical as well as psychological, as is the case in addition to "hard" drugs, or whether the dependence is only psychological, as would be true in the use of many habit-forming "soft" drugs and substances. With the physiologically addictive drugs, there is an overpowering and compelling desire for the drug, with withdrawal or abstinence symptoms if its use is discontinued. Another characteristic feature of physical dependence is the development of *tolerance* to the drug. The addict must continually increase the dosage to achieve the same effect. People who use the physiologically nonaddictive drugs sometimes have a very strong desire for the drug in order to achieve a sense of well-being or relief from tension, but evidence no physiological withdrawal symptoms. The initial irritability and tension accompanying the renunciation of smoking cigarettes shows the power of habituation to one of the most widely accepted "drugs"—nicotine.

The addictive and habit-forming drugs can be classified into the following groups: opiates, hypnotics, stimulants, cannabis (marijuana and hashish), hallucinogens and miscellaneous other drugs. Alcohol, discussed in a separate chapter, may be considered a seventh category. Although the chemically active ingredient of marijuana is also a hallucinogen, its widespread use in dosages that do not include hallucinations justifies a classification separate from the hallucinogens proper.

The Opiates

Opium is derived from the juice of the unripe pods of the opium poppy. This juice coagulates into a gummy solid which may be eaten, drunk diluted with water or alcohol, or put into a pipe and smoked. The smoking of opium and marijuana began only after the discovery of America and tobacco. Addiction to opium in this country increased greatly during the building of the transcontinental railroad when many Chinese laborers brought their opium pipes along. A number of Chinese words that had to do with the preparation and smoking of opium came into common usage. Our slang word "yen" is derived from the Chinese—to have a yen originally meant to have a desire for opium. The isolation of morphine, the most active ingredient, comprising 10 per cent of raw opium, led many opium addicts to transfer their addiction from the pipe to the needle.

Morphine, one of the most potent pain relievers, is given by injection. Without it, many of the surgical advances of the twentieth century would have been impractical because of the unbearable pain during and after surgery. Because it has proved to be so addictive, a number of synthetic substitutes have been tried as substitutes. The best of these has been demerol, but it is also addictive; another is talwin which is said to be nonaddictive.

Heroin, a derivative of morphine, is a white powder, readily soluble in hot water, which has three times the euphoriant effect of morphine and is easy to manufacture and transport. It is also called H, horse, duji, schmeck (or smack), junk, stuff, skag, etc. It is possible to become addicted to heroin by absorption through the mucuous membranes of the nasal passages—"snorting"—or through subcutaneous injections—"skin-popping"; most heroin addicts, however, inject the drug directly into a vein—"mainlining." For this purpose only a simple apparatus—"works"—is needed. Water for dissolving the heroin powder can be heated in a spoon— "cooker"; an eye dropper with an intravenous needle—"spike"; and a belt for use as a tourniquet complete the equipment.

The veteran addict soon becomes adept at getting a needle not only into the large veins in the crook of the elbow, but also into the small veins on the back of the hand and at the ankles and feet. This procedure becomes necessary because the frequent injections—three to six or seven a day—irritate and cause closure of the veins. When veins are plugged up, they form strings instead of tubes and can be seen through the skin as bluish-brownish streaks called "tracks."

Heroin is sold in cellophane packets called "bags." Any white powder, especially milk sugar and quinine, can be used to adulterate heroin, so that the addict can never be sure of the potency or purity of the drug he buys. Because the body gradually develops an increased tolerance for heroin or the other opium derivatives, the addict soon needs more and more heroin to achieve the highly euphoric feeling he calls the "rush" and to avoid the withdrawal or initial abstinence symptoms. These withdrawal symptoms consist of shivering, discharge from the nose resembling a cold, nausea, diarrhea, muscular twitching, insomnia, and an almost intolerable craving for the drug.

The drug addict gives up all his former interests, and everything in life becomes subordinated to the need to procure heroin. No matter what the underlying personality structure, all severely addicted persons behave alike in the intensity of their pursuit of their pacifier. All efforts are directed toward establishing the necessary "connection" and securing the money to buy the necessary supply. Most male addicts sooner or later resort to stealing, and the women to prostitution, in order to provide the large sums of money needed for their addiction.

Codeine provides a much smaller analgesic and euphoriant effect than do morphine and heroin; correspondingly, addiction to it is less severe. It inhibits coughing and is frequently a component in cough medicines.

Hypnotics

A hypnotic is any pill or liquid used to induce sleep. The *barbiturates*—"goofballs, pills"—are derivatives of barbituric acid and are effective hypnotics used widely for legitimate medicinal purposes. Because the various barbiturates are packaged in capsules of different colors, the addict refers to them as "yellow jackets," "red devils," "green hornets," etc. Barbiturates make the user sleepy and provide him with a euphoria different from that caused by opiates. They lead to a carefree drowsiness in which the user feels as if he were floating on a cloud. He is likely to stagger around and bump into walls or furniture; and is endangered in traffic. Large doses of barbituates may be lethal, and they are frequently used for suicide.

Other sleeping medications have a similar effect; some of the antihistamines are also sleep-inducing. If there is any medication that will have some effect on the mood or state of consciousness, people intent on using drugs are likely to find it and try it. Heavy addiction to hypnotics and the abrupt cessation of their use leads to withdrawal symptoms, manifested by anxiety, trembling, and convulsions. Sedatives and hypnotics are called "downs" or "pills," and their users "pillheads." Minor tranquilizers such as meprobamate, popularly known as Miltown and Librium, widely used to counteract anxiety, have been taken in large dosages by some predisposed individuals. A sudden withdrawal may lead to restlessness and even convulsive seizures similar to those resulting from a sudden withdrawal of barbiturates.

Stimulants

Amphetamine is the generic name for a family of drugs of which the best known are benzedrine or "bennies," dexedrine—"dexies," and methedrine—"speed." These drugs, popularly called "ups," are frequently used by students cramming before examinations, long-haul truck drivers, and others who need to stay alert and awake. Amphetamines temporarily increase the sense of well-being and optimism and improve the capacity to work. Because of their widespread use in diet regimens, they have become the basis of small-scale partial addiction for millions of ordinary people. In large doses they cause overstimulation, euphoria, sleeplessness, palpitations, elevated blood pressure, diarrhea, and trembling. Large amounts of amphetamines interfere with sound judgment and can lead to psychotic reactions, with symptoms of paranoia and megalomania. Someone who is "brought down" from the overactive, euphoric, and sleepless state caused by amphetamines will feel completely exhausted and heavily depressed: he has "crashed" and requires careful medical and psychological treatment. It is not uncommon for barbiturate users to use amphetamines as well. A person who has taken barbiturates to fall asleep may find it necessary to take amphetamines in the morning to overcome the sluggishness caused by an excessive dose of barbiturates.

Cocaine, which at one time enjoyed a wide cult and had its own set of appellations—"happy dust," "snow," etc., fell into disuse with the advent of heroin. Medically, cocaine and its derivatives are used as local anesthetics; taken internally, cocaine produces a stimulant and euphoriant effect, abolishes feelings of fatigue and creates illusions of power and creativity. Prolonged use may lead to hallucinations, paranoid delusions, and recklessly aggressive behavior. Many addicts like the peculiar effect provided by taking a depressant and stimulant at the same time, i.e., heroin and cocaine—"speedball"—or barbiturate and amphetamine.

Marijuana and Hashish

Marijuana, popularly called "tea," "grass," or "pot," is made up of the leaves of the hemp plant, *cannabis sativa,* and is generally dried and smoked like tobacco. It has a mildly euphoriant effect, and may produce a feeling of outgoingness and cheerfulness, particularly if consumed in the company of others. Marijuana, even in small quantities, while enhancing subjective reaction to sounds and colors, does not improve performance, but, on the contrary, impairs it; alteration of perception and memory hinders performance that requires skill and mental concentration. Scientific research into the immediate and long-term effects of marijuana resulted in the isolation of the drug's active ingredient, tetrahydrocannabinol, or THC. The short-term effects are extremely variable, depending on the state of mind of the user, on the social situation, and on the amount of THC absorbed. Marijuana, highly popular among teenagers, college students, and young adults, is used to enhance social situations in much the same way as alcohol by older people. For many, the use of marijuana may be on a temporary, experimental basis or it may continue in a limited, moderate manner. Others, however, especially those with serious intrapsychic conflicts, may come to rely more and more on its use as an escape from work and involvement in social problems. For a predisposed minority, marijuana will become the stepping stone to the use of drugs with a more powerful impact.

Hashish, or "hash" contains much more THC than marijuana and therefore has a much stronger hallucinogenic effect. It is a resin secreted by the cannabis plant and is molded into bricks from which shavings are sliced off and smoked. If used habitually and heavily, it becomes a "hard" drug. Reports from India and North Africa state that psychosis, brain damage, and serious habituation can develop. In this country, hashish is used more cautiously and is often mixed with marijuana to "spice it up."

The more potent drugs such as hashish, the strong hallucinogens, and opiates, while temporarily providing escape from serious conflicts and satisfying deep primitive needs, also seriously threaten the organization of the personality. One cannot constantly revert to severely regressive gratifications without serious damage to the personality organization and its psychophysiological balance.

The Hallucinogens

Hallucinogenic drugs are also known as psychedelic and psychotomimetic drugs. The most frequently used of these is d-LSD-25—lysergic acid diethylamide—"acid." It was discovered in 1943, but its use did not become a social problem until approximately 20 years later. Since its discovery, it has been extensively studied in medical and physiological laboratories as a possible therapeutic agent in the treatment of many types of mental illness, particularly the psychoses and alcoholism. Its possible treatment benefits are overshadowed by the unforseeable. LSD exerts a very powerful impact upon the central nervous system so that all sensations are felt to be enormously more intense, especially the perception of colors. Also released are all sorts of memories and phantasmagorias of hallucinatory vividness. An alleged "expansion" of consciousness that has been compared to that of religious revelation is reported by users of LSD. The hallucinations induced by LSD and other hallucinogenic drugs may be visual or auditory and rarely include the other sensory qualities. Distortion of the body image and feelings, especially depersonalization and a loss of the sense of reality, are common.

A colorless, odorless, tasteless liquid, LSD is easy to ingest, either in a capsule or absorbed in a cube of sugar or on a piece of paper; it is easy to transport and relatively simple to synthesize. With its power to disorganize the personality system, LSD poses a serious threat to someone whose integration is weak in the first place. Many cases have been reported where the ingestion of LSD has led to severe psychotic outbreaks, with bizarre behavior and even suicide. LSD is dangerous taken habitually because at any point a "trip" may activate a latent psychosis. The hallucinogenic effects of LSD may be repeatedly experienced even months after the last ingestion of the drug—"flash backs." Users of the drug place considerable emphasis on having an experienced person present and a setting conducive to a feeling of security, inasmuch as acute depressive and paranoid reactions are fairly common after taking it. The adverse publicity on LSD has led to a decline in its use.

Mescaline is the active ingredient of the mescal cactus or peyote. The use of the drug by the Indians of the Native American Church in some of the Southwestern states has the sanction of the government, because the peyote is given only by a priest in certain specific rites. The effects of mescaline, while similar to those of LSD, are milder and potentially less destructive to the personality structure.

Psilocybin, the active ingredient of a Mexican mushroom, also produces mind-altering effects and hallucinations. It has been claimed that it enhances so-called extrasensory perception, and some users can allegedly locate missing persons or objects under its influence.

Other natural agents that supposedly engender hallucinatory or mood-altering effects are constantly being tried out by those attempting to cope with their conflicts and give meaning to their lives. Many substances temporarily acquire the reputation of being "mind-expanding," and a fad leading to their mass use may rapidly develop and just as rapidly pass. Synthetic compounds with chemical acronyms such as DMT and STP have already been created and other are undoubtedly on the way.

Other Drugs with Habituating Properties

Any agent, whether synthetic or natural, that has the property of alleviating pain, reducing anxiety, acting as a stimulant, or in any way causing a change of mood or a state of "high" is potentially habit forming. It was accidently discovered that a solvent in the glue used to assemble plastic model airplanes, a common toy for boys, produced a "high" when inhaled. Anything that dissolves fatty substances is likely to have some effect on nervous tissue, which contains many fatty compounds; many commercial spot-removers and other solvents can be used to get "high." Medicaments are pressed into use for whatever effects they may offer, including whole families of tranquilizing and sedative agents, no matter how slight their potency may be.

The Addict

Having surveyed the drugs, let us now take a look at the addict. Drug addicts run the gamut of character types, and addiction is found in every social class, intellectual level, and vocational group. Practically all addicts, however, develop similar traits based on a common, deeply ingrained need for nirvana, for a return to the breast, for a degree of mothering available only to infants. When a substance is encountered which satisfies this lurking and insatiable demand, it is seized upon and then becomes the mainspring of the addict's life. The choice of the drug by the potential addict is influenced by his personality in ways that are as yet not fully understood. Addiction depends as well on such socioeconomic factors as the availability of the drug, the pull exerted by peer groups, on a feeling of not belonging or of alienation from the society at large, and on the current sources of political and social mismanagement and misery.

The addict's personality contains a strong oral-aggressive element—"give me"—which shows itself in his utter disregard for others and in his demand for medication. In hospital wards where addicts are detoxified, the staff are subject to continual bombardment by the unreasonable demands of the patients: they want medicine, pills for everything, a magic chemical solution for all discomforts. During the normative crisis of adolescence, drugs—aside from their physiological danger—hamper the consolidation of the personality; the acquisition of a sense of identity may become impossible under conditions of drug use and abuse.

Treatment

Treatment of Opiate Addiction

Individual therapy, including psychoanalysis, has not, as a rule, been effective in curing opiate addiction. Efforts at treatment in hospitals or prisons, where detoxification and abstinence from the addicting drugs were the only techniques employed, have been proven of little lasting effect—most addicts on returning to their drug-using communities sooner or later revert to their drug habits. Group therapy in the community after short-term detoxification has also proved a failure. It is true that in all these modes of treatment some alleged "cures" have taken place, but they have been extremely rare and are attributable more to the determination of the addict to stop his habituation than to the efficacy of the treatment.

The only substantial "cures" have been accomplished by two methods: pharmaceutical and the "therapeutic community."

Pharmaceutical

One method here is that of substitution. Methadone, a synthetic opiate, if administered in sufficient quantities in the absence of heroin, apparently fills up "receptor sites" in the nerve cells, and if heroin is taken subsequently it finds no entree and is ineffective or blockaded. Methadone, however, is itself addictive, but much less pernicious than heroin, thus permitting the addict to work and maintain significant personal relationships.

The other pharmaceutical method is by means of "antagonists." These are compounds whose affinity for the receptors is greater than that of the opiates, so that when taken in the presence of the latter they evict them from the receptors and take their place. Antagonists are therefore life-saving in treating coma caused by overdosage of opiates and also provide blockade in the proper dosage. Nalline, Cyclazocine, and Naloxone are the more widely used antagonists.

The search for better substitutes and antagonists is of course continually going on.

Other blocking, replacing, or antagonizing drugs are currently being tested and still others will surely be synthesized in the future. The chemical mode may prove to be the method of choice in the treatment of large masses of addicts: it requires a relatively short period of time in a hospital for detoxification and replacement (this may even be accomplished on an outpatient basis), while further group, vocational, and other therapy can be carried on in the community. The need many addicts have for comfort and security is so great that they will require protection with the help of drugs rather than the type of treatment which is described immediately below.

The Therapeutic Community

Perhaps the best results have been achieved by the method originated and developed at "Synanon" in California and its independent derivative, "Daytop Village" in New York. This encompasses a residential program of at least a year and a half, a schedule of hard work, stringent adherence to rules and regular group therapy in a community setting. All residents regard each other as "brother" and "sister"; the staff, except for medical consultants, consists of former addicts. The building and grounds housing the community provide a focus for the process of rehabilitation. Like pioneers, the residents repair, paint, garden, cook, and clean, maintaining both the property and themselves. To root out and replace the tenacious grasp of the drug which, like a virus, has altered the personality of the host, a powerful counterforce is necessary. This is provided by the close "family" relationship, purposeful activity, and rigid discipline. The addict's rationalizations to justify his need for the drug are pounded out of him in the sometimes brutal group sessions, but the wounds are immediately soothed by the community brotherhood and by the feeling of accomplishment as the house and property improve and as the addict's status in this new family is enhanced by his taking on more responsibility. The method is not new: it has been utilized by monastic groups and is recognizable in the sometimes brutal training program of elite military troops and other select groups.

The overindulged orality of the drug user is replaced by masochistic gratifications; the neophytes are punished for their past indulgences, and they derive satisfaction from their suffering: they have trespassed and need to atone for it. Synanon and Daytop both, as a matter of policy, used to detoxify the addict without any palliative drugs—"cold turkey." The addict went through his withdrawal on a couch in a common room where the other residents could talk to him, give him a massage, hot drinks, and sympathy. All those who have gone through "cold turkey" withdrawal in these agencies have said that it was much less harrowing than on other occasions, in jail or even in a room with a friend. Furthermore, they felt they accomplished it themselves and also felt a sense of satisfaction for having atoned for their past sins. It is likely that addicts detoxified under a more "humane" program using palliating medication acquire less resistance to drug use and are more liable to relapse. At the group therapy sessions, or "encounters," the older residents who have "kicked the habit" unmercifully expose the rationalizations and evasions of the newcomers. They may derive a sadistic sort of satisfaction from this; they are having revenge for their own past suffering. Sadomasochism is an integral component of all such programs; it must be recognized and kept in check in order to prevent excesses.

In most therapeutic communities, for the first six months the resident may not leave the premises; during the next six months he may perform outside assignments, such as speaking to various groups or picking up supplies, but is always accompanied by an older, more reliable resident; during the third six months he may work outside the residence and live in. After this, he may leave the house if the board of directors, all of them exaddicts, judge him sufficiently improved. Daytop and Synanon each have a number of branches throughout the country; their method is being applied with inmates of jails and other disturbed and alienated people.

An agency called Phoenix House has been operating in New York City since 1967. Here, groups of addicts, instead of living in isolation, are residing in therapeutic communities in heavy drug-using neighborhoods, under the auspices of the New York City Addiction Services Agency. A number of other similar projects under the aegis of various agencies are underway.

Clearly, the use of one drug to substitute for another does not constitute a cure; it blocks the acceptance of the other drug, but does not alter the underlying need. Therefore, some people on opiate-substitution programs may continue to use marijuana, alcohol, or other drugs; others have been able to give up the maintenance drugs, while some who have attempted this have failed and gone back to maintenance. Even among the ones who have conquered the drug habit through Synanon-type programs, there is a need for further help. Many if not most of its graduates work in the field of the treatment of drug addiction and, helping to combat addiction in others, reinforce the resistance to their own addictive trends.

Treatment of Addiction to Hypnotics

Whereas many opiate addicts have "kicked the habit" at home or in jail without dire results, this procedure is dangerous for those dependent on barbiturates because sudden withdrawal of the drug frequently produces convulsions and even death. Hospitalization is therefore advisable for barbiturate detoxification, which is accomplished by careful gradual withdrawal, following which a rehabilitation similar to the one described for opiate dependency is recommended to attempt to cure the addiction.

Chloral hydrate, paraldehyde, doriden, and many proprietary drugs are also addicting and dangerous. A drug that induces sleep usually has anticonvulsant effects as well, and an abrupt discontinuation of the drug after addiction to large dosages may then cause a convulsion on the rebound. Hospitalization, as in barbiturate detoxification, is therefore advisable.

Treatment of Marijuana Habituation

The increase in the use of marijuana is hardly a treatment problem. The casual smoker of marijuana does not consider himself a subject for psychiatric treatment any more than does the social drinker. Like the social drinker, he may occasionally smoke one or two "joints" by himself if he feels depressed or anxious, but usually confines his usage to social situations. The neurotic or otherwise severely disturbed marijuana user, of course, is in need of treatment for the underlying disorder, especially if there is any danger of progression to other, more hazardous drugs.

Treatment of Habituation to Hallucinogens

Many marijuana users try LSD, psilocybin, or mescaline once or twice; most never use it more than that, for they do not desire the violent cataclysm that these drugs, especially LSD, are capable of causing, and they fear the dangers involved in their use. Those whose dissatisfaction with their lot in life is great enough, however, find in the exotic LSD "trips" sufficient satisfaction to overcome their fears. There are some, in fact, who crave these garish metamorphoses of mood and perception and who may become habituated to them, just as there are people who learn to enjoy the thrills connected with other dangerous activities.

Some call the LSD experience "religious" and "transcendental" and say that in it they attain peace, deep insight, and a "cosmic consciousness." Such trance states have been and can be achieved not only through drugs, but also by fasting, flagellation, meditation, and other means. Psychologically speaking, what may take place is a fusion of the unconscious and the conscious, whereby the immensely rich buried resources of old wishes and images enter awareness. Perhaps the most important of these wishes is the primeval one of fusion with the mother, translated into unity with the universe.

Treatment for habituation to the hallucinogens is generally a by-product of treatment for the subject's underlying problems. The nature of the treatment will, of course, depend on the therapist's assessment of the personality strengths and weaknesses as well as on the specific problems arising from drug use.

Narcotics and the Law

In the United States, during the early part of the nineteenth century, opiates were the basic component in many freely sold medications, including soothing syrups for children and elixirs for "female complaints," and considerable addiction developed. By the time of the Civil War, the hypodermic needle had been invented, and, with a huge toll of wounded soldiers who had received morphine by injection, morphine addiction became so common as to be called the "soldier's disease." Addiction was hence regarded as an unfortunate illness, and understanding and sympathy were extended to its victims. But with the introduction of opium smoking by the Chinese, the public attitude changed. The white working man saw the Chinese, who were willing to work for very little money, as a threat to his livelihood. With the flourishing of the myth of the "yellow peril," the unfortunate addict became the sinister "dope fiend."

The regulation of addictive and habit-forming drugs in the United States goes back to the first Food and Drug Act of 1906. To implement the control of addictive drugs, the Harrison Narcotic Act was enacted by the federal government in 1914. It provided, through licensing, for control of import, manufacture, and distribution of "narcotics," including the opiates, cocaine, and marijuana. It stated that physicians could prescribe or dispense opiates only to bona fide patients, not to addicts, and established clinics under federal jurisdiction which furnished free opiates to addicts, somewhat like the system operating in Great Britain. The addicts, many of them delinquents, congregated in the vicinity of the clinics, as did black-market vendors. Some registered at more than one clinic, and other abuses were common. As a consequence, organized American medicine in 1921 condemned the ambulatory treatment of addicts, whether carried out privately or in clinics. The Treasury Department eventually closed down the clinics. During the nineteen thirties, federal treatment centers working on a voluntary, inpatient basis were opened at Lexington, Kentucky and Fort Worth, Texas and are still in operation.

Legislative control measures contributed to a great drop in the incidence of drug addiction. After World War II, however, it began to rise again, concurrently with the massive Negro and Puerto Rican migration to the large urban centers and the gigantic increase in the population of the big city slums. In 1957, the American Medical Association stated that because of the sociopathic character of most addicts, it would be improper to give them drugs gratis, but it also deplored the hysteria concerning drugs and held that the penalties were too severe. The AMA recommended criminal penalties for the sale of narcotics, but suggested civil commitment to a hospital for detoxification and long-term aftercare for the addict.

REFERENCES

Freedman, A. & Kaplan, H. I., eds. (1967), *A Comprehensive Textbook of Psychiatry*. Baltimore: Williams & Wilkins, Chapters 27, 41.

Lingeman, R. R. (1969), *Drugs from A to Z: A Dictionary*. New York: McGraw-Hill.

Yablonsky, L. (1967), *Synanon: The Tunnel Back*. Baltimore: Penguin Books.

SUGGESTED READING

Burroughs, Wm. S. (1959), *Naked Lunch*. New York: Grove.

Kaplan, E.H. & Wieder, H. (1974), *Drugs Don't Take People, People Take Drugs*. Secaucus, N.J.: Lyle Stuart.

Solomon, D. ed. (1964), *LSD: The Consciousness-Expanding Drug*. New York: Putnam.

——— ed. (1968), *The Marihuana Papers*. New York: Signet.

Wakefield, D. ed (1963), *The Addict*. New York: Fawcett.

CHAPTER TWENTY-THREE
Psychosomatic Disorders

IRVING STERNSCHEIN, M.D.

Psychosomatic disorders comprise a vaguely delimited borderland between the predominantly psychological and the predominantly physical diseases. Some clinicians have objected to the term psychosomatic because they think it implies a dichotomy between the psyche and the soma that does not exist. (The same criticism could be made of the terms psychobiologic or psychophysiologic.) These linquistic symbols can serve only as a semantic convenience, indicating that the mind plays more or less of a role in the abnormal physiology of some physical symptoms and diseases, and vice versa (somatopsychic). Hippocrates and other early thinkers who lived before the advent of modern medicine recognized mind-body interrelationships in the causation of disease. By the eighteenth century, Lord Chesterfield, the English statesman and writer, perceptively stated: "I find, by experience, that the mind and the body are more than married, for they are most intimately united; and when one suffers, the other sympathizes." Louis Pasteur, who discovered the bacterial etiology of many diseases, may have inadvertently contributed to the trend of looking for a single causative agent for disease ,a trend which prevailed until World War II. He was aware that disease could result from a variety of diverse external and internal causes. He felt, however, that emotions could not be subjected to scientific scrutiny, and so he excluded them from his list of pathogenic agents.

In the nineteen-thirties and early forties some leading psychoanalysts had begun to study and record their findings in a group of illnesses wherein psychic mechanisms and organic pathology were clearly operating together. During World War II, masses of data from a vast number of observations by military physicians were psychodynamically interpreted by their psychiatric colleagues, stimulating a renewed interest in the multifactor etiology of disease, and more particularly in the role of emotions in pathogenesis. Of course, thoughtful and wise physicians had always taken the psyche into account in their treatment of their patients, but they had to rely heavily on their personal gifts of observation and intuition. The great clinician, Sir William Osler, once said: "What happens to a patient with tuberculosis depends more on what he has in his head than what he has in his chest." During the period when psychoanalysts were expanding their clinical "research" and describing their developmental concepts and psychological theories, the Russian physiologist and experimental psychologist, Pavlov, whose life span (1849-1936) is almost identical with that of Freud (1856-1939), discovered conditioned-reflex phenomena and developed a mechanistic theory of human behavior. His experimental work demonstrated conclusively a fundamental link between bodily and behavioral events. Although Freud acknowledged the physiochemical substratum underlying the mental phenomena in the neuroses and psychoses, his direct references to the effect of the emotions or the mind on the pathological physiology of the body are curiously meager.

Psychological Considerations

Now that multicausality has been re-emphasized in the study of the human organism in health and disease, more attention is being paid to the interaction of the organism and its internal and external environment. The state of the organism and its central nervous system in particular, the input of excitatory stimuli, and the modulating and regulating mechanisms of the psyche and the soma all play a significant role in the adaptive behavior of bodily structures. In a general way, the psychosomatic concept comprises the systematized study and understanding of biological processes that are fused and amalgamated with emotional processes. The use of this broader point of view provides a better understanding of such phenomena as the yogi's skill at controlling his heart rate or the hypnotist's ability to suggest the appearance of a blister by a mere touch with an object that does not actually burn, and, more importantly, of the complexities of psychosomatic disease. The genesis and nature, however, of the disrupted physiology are as yet incompletely understood. A number of psychoanalytic explanations and theories have been advanced, but they, too, leave important questions unanswered. Dunbar's personality profiles and Alexander and French's proposal of unresolved core conflicts have not clarified why an individual becomes afflicted with one and not another of these illnesses. Neither do we have an answer to the question of why a psychophysiologic reaction occurs and not a neurosis or a psychosis.

It has been found that the bodily malfunction in psychosomatic illness often has a relation to early psychogenetic or physiological traumas around the time of birth or soon after. At this time the body's organ systems are grossly immature, and physiological mechanisms and neural processes are incompletely developed and unstable. They are unusually vulnerable to the damaging events of life, some of which can leave psychological and physiological imprints which become preconditions for disease in later years. When the ego is faced with new dangers in later years, it makes use of "selected" bodily structures and bodily functions for defensive purposes. Parts of the body, which have been "preprogrammed" by heredity and "weakened" by disease, trauma, or faulty development at an earlier period, will be affected so that their functioning is altered or modified in a maladaptive way that we then refer to as a psychosomatic illness. This explanation forms the core of Schur's psychoanalytic concept of somatization. He suggests that the malfunction in psychosomatic disease is dependent upon the liberation of quantities of unneutralized aggression resulting from a defensive regression of some ego functions and of pregenital instinctual drives.

Physiological Considerations

Studies have demonstrated that there are physiological developmental sequences for brain centers, such as the amygdala, the limbic system of the temporal cortex, etc. and their afferent and efferent pathways that regulate organ functioning. These mature alongside the psychological development sequences, and the physiological and psychological sequences are thought to influence each other's development. Reiser (1966), in an attempt to integrate all the factors involved in psychosomatic illness, has elaborated an ingenious plan. He postulates that the potential for the appearance of psychosomatic symptoms is probably always present. A preference or predilection for malfunction of particular cellular circuits in the brain, based on genetic constitution and growth experiences, is what accounts for the appearance of a particular psychosomatic syndrome. Reiser also thinks that, under stress, vulnerable neural centers and circuits that may or may not have been operative before are capable of being activated and producing symptoms.

Basic Clinical Concepts

The psychological state of the individual changes once the disease has begun. The secondary psychological reactions (epiphenomena) appear after the onset of the disease and are often difficult to distinguish from the preconditioning factors. Similarly, the fantasies and affects relating to the predisposing conditions and the precipitating circumstances need to be differentiated from fantasies and emotions which are secondarily produced. To obtain this kind of knowledge of the psyche, specialized techniques of observation or treatment based on psychoanalytic psychology or the utilization of psychoanalytic therapy itself are required.

Certain emotional processes are constantly operative, and every bodily function is available for the expression of some emotional need. The control and synthesis of emotional states is one of the principle maturational tasks and an essential function of the ego. The body musculature, for example, may serve to relieve anxiety by purposeful or nonpurposeful action. With bouts of hyperventilation, the main purpose may not be to provide more oxygen, but to relieve anxiety by rapid, rhythmic contractions of the muscles of the chest wall and abdomen. Also, where internal inhibitions against muscular movement exist, attacks of meaningless movements—mannerisms or tics, for example, can occur in an effort to relieve tension or anxiety More complex and purposeful activities, such as those involved in many hobbies, are aimed, at least in part, at ridding the individual of anxiety. Emotional states are complicated and have visible and invisible physiological correlates: blushing often accompanies shame; nausea may be present with disgust; pallor, elevated blood pressure, and increased heart rate are concomitants of anxiety. The physiological correlates may also appear without a subjective awareness of the emotion. Thus, some of the physical symptoms of a psychosomatic disease are affect equivalents which serve to ward off unwelcome emotions and their associated mental content. The following case example will serve to illustrate some aspects of psychosomatic illness.

A patient developed a repetitious noisy throat-clearing symptom as a substitute for unconscious murderous rage. This symptom did not, however, afford an adequate means for the expression of his anger, just as his character traits of passivity and compliance had not always sufficed to deal with his unconscious aggression. As a result, he had developed an elaborate system of fantasies of the Walter Mitty type in which he performed heroic deeds, frequently involving the destruction of malevolent forces—perhaps to save his town and attract the attention of his lady love, while winning the acclaim of his fellow citizens. For a time in this man's life there was a relative psychic equilibrium. He had married and had fathered three sons. The carping behavior of his unloving wife seemed to be counterbalanced by the admiration of his young children and by some business successes. The youngest of his sons, who had suffered from eczema as an infant, developed a severe bronchial asthma, which was a constant source of worry. He unconsciously resented the attention paid to his son by his wife, so that his relationship with her became more strained. Consciously, he blamed her for the illness. The patient was now approaching 40 years of age, the age of his father at the time of his death. From the age of six, when his father had died from an industrial accident, he had idealized him in order to deal with his deeper ambivalent feelings. During a routine physical examination, his blood pressure was found to be elevated. He had had recurrent headaches in the past, but no evidence of hypertension, although there was a familial history of this disease. His mother and a maternal aunt had suffered from the effects of hypertension for many years. There was unconscious hostility toward his mother for her ineptitude and persistent ridicule of him. He had concealed his anger by compliance and solicitude. The prolonged inhibition of aggression seemed finally to have triggered a neuroendocrine change affecting the vegetative nervous system so that hypertension developed as an additional means of warding off the mental content and the physical equivalent of an affect, i.e., the unconscious murderous rage.

Every infant has certain basic biological needs. One of these, feeding, involves a dependence on the mother or her surrogate. Gratification or frustration during the nursing and feeding processes are inevitable, so that these processes become more or less emotionalized; that is, patterns of emotional response become laid down in relation to eating and the suppliers of food. Frustration of the pleasures of feeding may eventually mobilize aggressive activity in the form of biting and thumbsucking in some children. If the latter persists, or if the former is replaced by grinding of the teeth, malformation of the jaw and malocclusion of the teeth can occur. In that event, the psychosomatic "deformity" that occurs is not directly psychogenic, but is instead the result of an unconsciously determined pattern of behavior, that is psychogenic.

Transient and harmless organic disease in early childhood, if it recurs frequently or requires repeated involvement with the child's body, may influence the child's relationship to his body. In addition, any bodily disorder that occurs while developmental processes are in a state of flux can bring about a continuing associational link, which throughout life becomes part of a pattern of psychosomatic behavior that may persist as a possible response to stress. In psychosomatic disorders, the illness itself represents a needed solution of a conflict (primary gain). The illness often resists treatment because the sufferer may prefer to remain sick and be cared for as an invalid with a minimum of responsibility and an abundance of attention (secondary gain). In the psychosomatic patient, the underlying emotional conflict is almost always completely divorced from the somatic symptoms, so that he is totally unaware of his wish to remain ill or the reasons for it. The shift of interest from the outside world to the body that occurs may also be difficult to reverse and thus constitutes an added treatment problem.

Psychophysiologic Disorders

Excretory functions constitute another biological need involving the child in an emotional interaction with the parents. The eliminative act becomes a medium for gaining approval or disapproval. The child soon senses a potential for power because of his parents' need for his cooperation. The very time and place for the child's bowel movement can become part of a contest for control, during which behavior patterns of defiance and submission may be formed which profoundly influence the future personality and health of the child, as the following case history illustrates:

A five-and-a-half-year-old boy who had been admitted to the hospital for the third time because of serious bloody diarrhea and weight loss due to ulcerative colitis had a recurrence or exacerbation of diarrhea for one or two days after each of his mother's departures following a hospital visit. Data obtained from a detailed longitudinal history, direct observation, and play therapy with the boy revealed an abnormal degree of separation anxiety for his age. He reacted to separation with vengeful destructive fantasies for which his diarrhea served as an outlet. He fantasied, too, that his mother could be brought back in a magical way by his diarrhea. The history revealed that he had been vigorously toilet-trained at nine months of age by his grandmother when his mother went back to work following the death of the boy's father. The frequency of his stools were a barometer of his unconscious hostility, usually triggered by some form of separation or loss. The transfer of a favorite nurse or a brief holiday of his psychiatrist could also initiate a bout of bloody diarrhea. A vital part of the total treatment plan involved casework with the mother to help her understand the vulnerability of the child to separations that were either too abrupt, unexpected, or too prolonged, and his unintentional bodily response to her leaving.

The gastrointestinal tract is the organ system most frequently involved in psychosomatic disease In addition to ulcerative colitis, peptic ulcer is an excellent example of the interaction of somatic and psychosocial factors to produce bodily symptoms. Research has shown that gastric secretions increase with great joy, intense anger, or chronic fear. The hyperacidity that occurs, however, does not produce ulcers. Studies have proven that a genetically-determined physiological factor is necessary but insufficient to produce an ulcer. Other factors, such as stress caused by emotional conflict, are also necessary. In spite of the mysteries and uncertainties that surround the psychosomatic diseases of the gastrointestinal system and those of other systems, some degree of improvement with unilateral—organic or psychological—treatment programs has occurred. There is a growing recognition, however, that the multilateral "team" approach is most likely to be successful. Family members often require guidance or counseling, too, as part of the total treatment plan.

The usefulness of interprofessional collaboration can be seen in the case of an obese adolescent who was beginning, through psychotherapy, to understand the meaning of her "binges" of overeating. But she continued to have difficulty in controlling them because her mother insisted on overstocking the family larder with delectable and irresistible foodstuffs. The mother was intensely competitive with her daughter, whom she considered a rival. She turned this into a seductive overindulgence, a mechanism that had to be exposed by casework therapy before she could modify her buying and supplying habits. With the reduction in the temptations offered and with the understanding of the psychosomatic symptom, the obesity could now be corrected.

Respiration often dramatically reflects emotions. This is very clear when its rate and depth increase with anxiety; but it is also involved when amusement evokes laughter or when sadness causes crying. In children and adults, "spontaneous" attacks of hyperventilation can cause fainting or blackouts. Even when the subject knows that the overbreathing is of psychological origin, it cannot be deliberately halted. Psychological stress has also been observed to lower the resistance of the upper respiratory tract to the common cold. Separation, disappointment, or loss has been correlated with the appearance of recurrent colds in a group of psychoanalytic patients. In many but not all bronchial asthmatics, psychological events play a role as precipitating or predisposing conditions. The asthmatic attack has been thought to be the equivalent of a suppressed cry for help from the mother. Even if the passive longing for the mother is met, or the asthmatic can be induced to cry, his labored breathing and wheezing will not subside. Such observations raise questions about the reasons for remissions, maintenance, or exacerbation of psychophysiological reactions. Partial answers in individual situations are sometimes discernible, but an over-all theory is not yet available.

There is usually a striking interaction between emotional and metabolic processes in such endocrine disorders as hyperthyroidism. Very often the cluster of symptoms that constitute the "nervousness" of the anxiety neurosis is difficult to distinguish from the hypermotility, emotional excitability, tremulousness, hyperalertness, markedly increased tempo of living, irritability, apprehensiveness, and the sensation of "the motor racing" that can be observed in Graves' disease or hyperthyroidism. In some intensively studied patients (Lidz) an overattachment of the patients to their children—found to be related to an overdependent, clinging relationship to their own mothers—was a characteristic precondition for the illness. The loss of a key person, such as a child, through maturation or marriage, or of the mother or a mother figure through separation or death, has been implicated as a precipitating cause of the overactivity of the thyroid gland in a large number of cases. It may be impossible in many of such multiply-caused diseases to say which of the findings are secondary to the illness itself and which predate it and play a causal role. Thus, an extreme fear of dying that occurs in hyperthyroid patients has been said to have a specific etiologic significance, but this fear could just as plausibly be a response to the feeling of helplessness in relation to the body processes consequent to the disease.

Psychosomatic dysfunction involving the genitourinary system is nearly as common as it is in the gastrointestinal system. With this system, the close anatomical relationship between the sexual and excretory organs is often of considerable importance. The conditions of impotence in the male and frigidity in the female are primarily related to emotional factors. They are almost always caused by anxiety, guilt, shame, or anger. The psychological value and meaning of the sexual act affect the desire for intercourse, the nature of the orgasm, and the enjoyment that is experienced. Persistent difficulties with, or failure of, erection or ejaculation are only rarely the result of spinal cord or other organic disease. Inhibitions related to conscious and unconscious prohibitions are the usual reason for malfunction and for the various degrees of aversion to sexual union, such as lack of pleasure, inability to achieve orgasm, pain with intercourse (dyspareunia), spasm of the muscles of the pelvic floor (vaginismus), or complete absence of lubricating secretions which can occur in the frigid woman. Similar inhibitions are responsible for erectile impotence, penile anaesthesia, and premature or retarded ejaculation in the male. Any of these may occur occasionally in sexually "normal" people with particular partners, or at times of stress and with inexperience. When these disturbances are the result of severe sexual traumas in early life, they are not likely to respond to the simpler therapeutic procedures, such as re-education or reassurance (Masters and Johnson, 1966) but will require some form of insight psychotherapy. The most effective method in these instances is psychoanalysis.

Menstrual difficulties (amenorrhea and dysmenorrhea), infertility, habitual abortion, menopausal reactions, enuresis, and encopresis are most often psychosomatic in nature. The complete list of psychophysiological conditions is extensive and also includes some diseases of the skin, like the neurodermatoses, pruritus, eczema, urticaria and others; some diseases of the musculoskeletal system like rheumatoid arthritis and some cases of low back pain; and an assortment of other conditions, from tic syndromes to diabetes mellitus and stuttering.

Every illness, regardless of its etiology, has some damaging effect on the body, disturbing the psyche so that there is a greater or lesser disruption of the personality. Each person reacts differently to sickness, but usually in a way characteristic for him. Most people react with some anxiety; others with impatience; many with denial of the existence of an illness or denial of its implications; some welcome the chance to be dependent, others abhor the dependence and become anxious about it; occasionally, unwarranted optimism is the response, but more often one comes across a feeling of helplessness or a loss of hope. These responses reflect character traits, actual or latent. Illness can serve as a punishment, as a source of relief from guilt feelings, or as a way to place blame on others in whom the patient may wish to evoke guilt for self-serving reasons. On the other hand, illness may become an avenue for aggression against others: a mother may unknowingly wish her child to remain ill so that she can be overprotective and thus conceal her unconscious hostility.

Principles of Treatment

When planning the psychosocial aspects of a comprehensive treatment program for the psychosomatic patient, the caseworker, the psychiatrically oriented physician, and the psychiatrist must be alert to the social implications of the disorder. They will want to assess the effect of the emotional behavior and bodily symptoms at the hospital, in the home, at work, or in school. They must know what kind of supportive services, including financial aid, are required and available. They will also want to think of means for relieving the patient's daily burdens during periods of incapacity, the nature of the transference relationship they can expect, and how they can effect and maintain an optimal therapeutic atmosphere. Obtaining the necessary psychological data may be initially difficult, because the patient is usually unaware of his use of his symptoms as a solution for emotional conflicts. In time, essential points relating to the old conflict, to the recent conflict, and to the temporal factors can be elucidated. It is important to determine who is the most significant person in the environment. It is necessary to know about the patient's life motivations, his reaction to the people with whom he has been living, and his relationships to members of his family in his early life. During treatment, clues as to why and when his symptoms developed may eventually be brought out. Their influence on his personality make-up should be ascertained. Knowing how organic disturbances were used in the past and determining the role of the diseased organ in the psychosomatic pattern are important. With improvement or disappearance of the physical symptoms, a shift in the psychic economy occurs and is often accompanied by the appearance of a neurotic symptom. If and when this happens, the patient may become even more interested in participating in some form of insight psychotherapy in the hope of finding a better solution for his pathogenic conflicts.

REFERENCES

Alexander, F., & French, T. M., (1948), *Studies in Psychosomatic Medicine*. New York: Ronald Press.

Cannon, W. (1929), *Bodily Changes in Pain, Hunger, Fear, and Rage*. New York: Appleton Century-Crofts.

Dunbar, H. F. (1943), *Psychosomatic Diagnosis*. New York: Paul B. Hoeber.

Deutsch, F., ed. (1953), *The Psychosomatic Concept in Psychoanalysis*. New York: International Universities Press.

Engel, G. L. (1967), The Concept of Psychosomatic Disorder. *Journal of Psychosomatic Research*, 11: 3-10.

Groen, J. J. & Welnor, A. (1966), The Biological Losses of Psychosomatic Medicine. *Israel Annals of Psychiatry*, 4: 36-147.

Gosliner, B. J., reporter, (1960), Panel on Psychosomatic Disorders in Children and Adolescents. *Journal of the American Psychoanalytic Association*, 8: 152-158.

Jackel, M. (1968), Common Cold and Depression. *Journal of the Hillside Hospital*, 17: 165-177.

Lerner, J. & Noy, P. (1968), Somatic Complaints in Psychiatric Disorders: Social and Cultural Factors. *International Journal Of Social Psychiatry*, 14: 145-150.

Lidz, T. (1949), Emotional Factors in the Etiology of Hyperthyrodism. *Psychosomatic Medicine*, 11:2-8.

Mason, J., et al. (1963), Limbic System Influence on the Pituitary-Adrenal Control System. Abstract in: *Psychosomatic Medicine*, 22:322.

Masters, W. H. & Johnson, V. E. (1966), *Human Sexual Response*. Boston: Little, Brown.

Nemiah, J. C. (1961), The Concept of Psychosomatic Medicine. In: *Foundations of Psychopathology*. New York: Oxford University Press, Chapter 18.

Noyes, A. & Kolb, L. (1968), *Modern Clinical Psychiatry*. Philadelphia: W. B. Saunders.

Reiser, M. (1966), Toward an Integrated Psychoanalytic and Physiologic Theory of Psychosomatic Disorders. In: *Psychoanalysis—A General Psychology*, eds. R. M. Loewenstein, L. M. Newman, M. Schur, & A. J. Solnit. New York: International Universities Press, pp. 570-582.

Ruddick, B. (1963), Colds and Respiratory Introjection. *International Journal of Psycho-Analysis*, 44:178-190.

Schur, M. (1953), Comments on the Metapsychology of Somatization. *The Psychoanalytic Study of the Child*, 10:119-164. New York: International Universities Press.

Stunckard, A. (1969), Hunger and Satiety. *American Journal of Psychiatry*, 118:212-217.

von Bertalanffy, L. (1964), The Mind-Body Problem—A New View. *Psychosomatic Medicine*, 26:29-45.

Winnicott, D. W. (1966), Psychosomatic Illness in its Positive and Negative Aspects. *International Journal of Psycho-Analysis*, 47:510-516.

Wittkower, E. D. et al. (1969), A Global Survey of Psychosomatic Medicine. *International Journal of Psychiatry*, 7:499-524.

CHAPTER TWENTY-FOUR

Depressions

MERL M. JACKEL, M.D.

In common usage, the term "depression" is used to describe a variety of affective states, including sadness, grief, dejection, apathy, loss of self-esteem, or even general unhappiness. These terms are not synonymous, and psychiatry attempts to distinguish between them and to determine specific dynamics for each. Because our present knowledge is limited, however, and because human beings invariably present complex pictures, this is not always possible. Psychiatry also attempts to distinguish among "depression" as a mood, as a symptom, and as a diagnostic category. To describe a mood as depressed is to imply that the person feels sad and that his behavior and verbalizations are in keeping with such an affect. Because most people, at one time or another, suffer from such an affective experience, it may be regarded as a normal reaction to life's vicissitudes. Depression as a *symptom,* however is by definition pathological. Furthermore, depression is so regularly accompanied by a variety of other symptoms, that its use in psychiatry has come to refer to a complex of symptoms, rather than to an affect alone. These include symptoms commonly regarded as somatic, such as insomnia, loss of appetite, chronic fatigue, constipation, generalized vague pains, and other hypochondriacal complaints. Psychological symptoms which may be included are obsessive worrying, overeating, impulsive acts, and even some addictions. Not infrequently, the depressed person is unaware of feeling depressed until his attention is called to it, and in some cases the affect of depression may in fact be absent. In such cases one may say that the symptoms replace the affect, although more correctly, they are defenses against it. Because of the somatic aspects of depression and the natural tendency of people to attribute discomfort to physical causes, people who are in actuality suffering from depression constitute a large percentage of patients who seek help from medical doctors. They are also the willing victims of the many nostrums advocated in the various media. "Tired blood" is more often a depression than any form of anemia. Depression is the most common symptom which brings the patient to the psychiatrist. It is also the most frequent motivation for people seeking help from social workers, marriage counselors, clergymen, and others. The senescent seeking help with a housing problem is often unknowingly trying to alleviate an inner depression by an external change. The spouse who has for years endured an unsatisfactory marriage may finally be motivated to seek help only when some precipitating event has resulted in a depression. Even the antisocial characters referred to psychiatrists and casework agencies by the courts may in the final analysis be depressed people who have been covering over their depressions by antisocial acts.

Descriptive Aspects

The symptoms of depression may vary widely in intensity. The subject may feel mildly "blue" or may be so depressed that he feels hopeless, apathetic, and even stuporous. Typical pictures of normal depression (sadness, mourning, grief), moderate (neurotic) depression, and severe (psychotic) depression, follow.

Normal depression includes normal mourning and normal depressive reactions in other situations. Normal mourning occurs in relatively normal character structures, and, theoretically, in such cases the depressive reaction is proportionate to the importance of the object loss. Actually, because none of us is entirely free of neurotic traits or ambivalence, mourning is rarely free of neurotic components. It should be recognized that mourning serves a useful psychic function. The first response to the death of a loved one is denial. Continuation of this denial is evidenced by lapses in memory in which the lost object is thought of as being alive. Gradually these lapses occur less and less frequently. Libido is withdrawn from the object itself, a small quantity remaining attached to the memory, while the rest is freed to attach itself to a new object. During the mourning period, minor guilt reactions in relation to the lost object are re-evaluated and resolved. For these reasons, it is important that the mourning reactions, despite their attendant suffering, be allowed to take place. Otherwise, libido remains attached to an object that does not exist, guilts remain unresolved, and the realistic possibility of new and satisfying object relations is blocked. Reassurances of well-meaning relatives and friends that deny the essential significance and reality of death are not constructive.

Mourning may be pathological in quality, quantity, and duration. The major portion of the mourning process should have been accomplished by the end of a year. Denial of loss may reach psychotic proportions, as in the case of a mother who had lost a child, yet, for twelve years continued to keep the child's room and toys intact and spoke as though the child would imminently return.

It should also be recognized that sadness or depression resulting from a failure in performance or a deprivation, and which is proportionate to the cause, is also normal and serves a purpose. The pain of failure or deprivation must be experienced in order to effect changes and adaptation to reality. To put the matter in a negative form, it may be said that the inability to develop a depression where one would be expected is pathological.

The *moderately depressed* person is sad, unhappy, pessimistic about life in general and about his own future in particular. He feels inadequate for tasks he was quite capable of performing prior to his illness. He belittles his capabilities and tends to withdraw from challenges he would ordinarily accept. He must drag himself to work. He becomes somewhat careless about cleanliness and in his dress. He exaggerates ordinary cares and worries, so that he is unable to obtain pleasure from anything or from anyone. Periods of feeling guilty or remorseful alternate with periods of feeling irritable and resentful. His thoughts dwell obsessively on the particular event he feels precipitated the depression, for example, a failure in business or a broken love affair. There is a diminution in sexual drive, which adds to his worries. The tendency to withdraw may lead to an excessive desire for sleep. In other cases, insomnia is a prominent symptom, particularly early awakening in the morning. Despite increased rest, and no matter how little work he has done, he is constantly tired. Frequently he has vague pains, headaches and upset stomach, and he worries about physical illness. He questions the worth of all he is doing and sometimes of life itself.

In *severe* depression all these symptoms are greatly exaggerated. Sadness becomes painful dejection or utter despondency. There is a complete loss of interest in the world, including loved ones. Work is impossible. The patient is self-reviling, and expresses feelings of utter worthlessness. Minor indiscretions of the past are exaggerated with most intense feelings of remorse. Sometimes he may have strong feelings of having committed some unknown but unforgiveable act. All attention to dress or appearance is gone. There may be delusions of extreme poverty, of being dirty, of being infested by vermin. The delusions are frequently somatic and of a bizarre quality. A patient, for example, said, "Oh doctor, my stomach's gone, I had no intestines, and now my liver is rotting away."

The picture of dejection may be further evidenced by a characteristic posture in which the head is bowed, the body arched, and the knees flexed. All motor functions are slowed down, as are thinking and speech. Insomnia becomes severe and intractable. Aversion to food may be so severe as to require forced feeding in order to sustain life. There is a decrease in bodily secretions, resulting in dry mouth and dry skin. Menstruation may be irregular or absent. In both sexes, the loss of sexual drive is characteristic. Suicidal preoccupation is common.

No one symptom is sufficient to establish a diagnosis. In the milder forms of depression, there may be some diagnostic confusion between a normal reaction and a pathological one constituting a symptom. Factors to be considered in making an evaluation are the precipitating circumstances, the intensity of the depression, its duration, and the relationship among these three factors. In general, the more disproportionate the reaction in intensity and duration to its precipitating causes, the more pathological it is. It would not, for instance, be normal for a man to go into a severe depression over a minor business loss, or for a housewife to be depressed for weeks over breaking an ordinary dish. To be depressed at the death of a loved one is a normal grief reaction. If, however, there is no lessening of the intensity of depression after a year or more, one would begin to question its normality. To be depressed when a love affair ends is normal. To be suicidal because of it would be abnormal.

Etiology

Insofar as heredity is a factor determining character development, it is also a factor in the predisposition to developing depression. Both the strength of the drives and the potential for the development of various ego functions are determined by heredity. Culture, too, may play a role, in that it supports or alleviates conflicts that might lead to depression. Heredity and cultural factors appear to play a specific role in the development of manic-depressive reactions. Nevertheless, depression is never without psychogenic determinants, and, in all depressions, one must regard developmental factors as etiologic.

Psychodynamics

The dynamics of depression may be studied in terms of the interrelations of the id, ego, and superego. Abraham (1911) was the first analyst to study and write about depression. His cases were patients suffering from manic-depressive psychosis, and his observations dealt chiefly with the nature of their drives (id) and their guilt reactions (superego). He pointed out that these people invariably had a highly ambivalent attitude toward their love objects. Abraham's observations remain a cornerstone in our understanding of depression. Because of hostility to the love object, there is a feeling of guilt, which is unconscious and is often displaced onto minor—even picayune—incidents. This accounts for the bizarreness of some of the complaints and the intensity of the self-reproach. Abraham traced ideas of impoverishment, so common in depressives, to the unconscious awareness of an incapacity to love. Freud, in his classic paper, "Mourning and Melancholia," published in 1917 before he had developed the structural theory of personality, contrasted mourning ("normal" depression) with melancholia (manic-depressive reaction). He added to Abraham's observations, pointing out that in mourning there is no lowering of self-regard as there is in a pathological depression. He postulated that in melancholia, as in mourning, there is also a loss of a love object, but that this was not necessarily by death and therefore not always perceived by the melancholic. What happens is a change in the relationship between the depressed person and his love object. Freud noted that the self-accusations of the severely depressed person, which seemed so completely inappropriate and even delusional in quality, could be understood and were valid if applied to the "lost" object. For instance, a man who had always been a dutiful son to his father might, in his depression, accuse himself of having been stingy, spiteful, and jealous of his father, whom he portrays as only good and kind. Impartial friends would be well aware that these unpleasant traits were actually characteristic of the father rather than the son. From our more recent knowledge of defense mechanisms, we would say that the son has identified himself with his father and now directs onto himself the critical feelings previously felt, unconsciously, for his father.

An essential aspect of depression, therefore, is a disturbance in object relations, and, in order to understand depression, we must understand the nature of the depressive's prior relation to his object (the term depressive, here, referring to people who are prone to develop depression). When we examine the history of such a person, we usually find that there have been few important object relations in his life. Furthermore, these relations have been largely on an oral level. Characteristically, he is one who is hypersensitive to frustration and who experiences even minor disappointments as oral deprivation. He feels himself at the mercy of people to whom he tries to attach himself in a dependent way, hoping to force them to give. His desires are usually insatiable and have an all or nothing quality. Because he cannot love, he can never convince himself that he can be loved. Such people are often unable to be alone, requiring the physical presence of the object in order to maintain a feeling of relatedness. The depressive cannot tolerate the idea that the same person can give both satisfaction and disappointment. The object must be regarded as either entirely good or entirely bad. The object is not loved as a real object, but is clung to in an attempt to feel loved and so to help bolster the ego in its effort to maintain a state of equilibrium in relation to instinctual drives and the superego. The depressive needs to feel loved in order to feel lovable and to counteract his hostility. Loss of love precipitates a depression. The loss is felt as a blow to the ego; hostility is released and, in the weakened state of the ego, is turned against the self, resulting in a depression. The loss may be actual, as when a spouse walks out on a marriage, or it may be only imagined, as in cases of pathological jealousy. The depression may be the result of neither a real nor imagined loss of object, but rather of the loss of ability to love or feel loving. Anything, therefore, which changes the relationship between the person and the ambivalently loved object so as to either increase hostility or decrease love may precipitate a depression. The depressive cannot cease loving or being loved without feeling hostile, guilty, and in danger. From this description, it becomes clear that the predisposing factors for future depression are present in the character structure of the depressive. In an earlier chapter (Six), Spitz's observation on "anaclitic depression" in hospitalized infants is described.

The superego of the depressive is characteristically severe, and, in the throes of depression, it may regressively become archaic and tyrannical (Cameron, 1963). The talion law reigns supreme—an eye for an eye, a tooth for a tooth, "I wished you dead, I deserve to die." Some authorities consider guilt reactions rather than object loss central in the development of "true" depression. Actually, these factors are interrelated, and we are dealing with relative quantities of one or the other.

The ego ideal, another aspect of the superego, is characteristically high in depressives. A common precipitating cause of depression is a failure to meet this ego ideal. This is particularly true of compulsive characters. A teacher who, for example, in spite of an unsatisfactory marriage, maintained her narcissistic equilibrium by her excellent work in a nursery school, became depressed when she was unable to deal with the parents of the children, thus failing to meet her own ego ideal.

Depressive Illnesses

As we stated previously, the term depression is applied to specific complexes or groups of symptoms, as well as to a particular mood or affective state. These groups of symptoms (syndromes) are, in turn, the basis for the delineation of certain specific diagnostic categories. Unfortunately, the human psyche is complex, and these clinical entities are not always as clearly defined or readily recognizable as one might wish. Difficulties also arise because several terms are used for the same clinical entity. In the subsequent sections, the official classification of the American Psychiatric Association is followed by synonymous terminology added in parenthesis.

In describing any one of the depressive illnesses, it is customary to include where possible a description of the premorbid personality structure, the presence or absence of precipitating traumata, the mode of onset, the symptomatology, and the course of the illness.

Depressive Neurosis (Reactive Depression, Neurotic Depression)

This is a psychoneurotic disorder in which depression is the outstanding symptom. As stated previously, depression may occur in any or all other psychiatric conditions, and therefore, the presence of depression is not in itself conclusive evidence of a depressive neurosis. In general, the more serious condition determines the diagnosis: when depression occurs in a schizophrenic, the primary diagnosis would be schizophrenia; in other situations, the more prominent symptom or group of symptoms determines the diagnosis.

The characteristic picture of a neurotic depression has already been described. Neurotic depressions differ from psychotic depressions in the following ways:

There is usually a precipitating event which is known to the individual or is readily apparent to the observer. For example, a man denies that his depression has anything to do with separation from his wife because he has been separated for three years and he has only had the depression in the past year. At another point in the interview, however, he mentions that he has been divorced for a year. Obviously, until the actual divorce he had managed in some way to deny the separation. The connection in this instance is made by the observer and not by the client.

A depressive reaction which appears paradoxical may be observed occasionally when someone achieves or fulfills some long-sought-after goal. A student, for example, who has sacrificed much and worked long and hard for his Ph.D. degree becomes depressed after passing his examinations instead of feeling jubilant. A woman, who has been in love with a man for some time, becomes engaged to him. Instead of great happiness, she becomes more and more depressed and doubtful about the approaching marriage. To both the observer and the sufferer these reactions are inexplicable. A clue is provided in the following example:

A man who has been vice-president of his company for many years, upon the death of the president, succeeds to the presidency. He reacts by becoming depressed. This is at first explained as a mourning reaction, but it is too intense and lasts too long. As he continues to function poorly, all become concerned. He has no explanation.

Analysis usually shows that *unconsciously* he feels his *unconscious* wish that the president should die has been fulfilled. In primary-process thinking, he has killed him. This revives his earlier oedipal guilt. Similarly, for the Ph.D. student, success meant killing his father. The woman who became engaged unconsciously felt her success as oedipal, getting her male ideal, originally her father, for herself and displacing (killing) her mother. The resultant guilt led to depression. Freud labeled these types of reaction "success neuroses."

Neurotic depressive symptoms are apt to be less severe, less disruptive to work and to love life than are psychotic depressions. Neurotic depression frequently manifests itself in such masked form as somatic symptoms or psychic equivalents; delusions are absent, and self-accusations are more in line with reality.

Mrs. M. suffered from a severe neurotic depression. She was referred for consultation by the minister of her church. She came from a lower middle-class Italian family and a broken home, her father having "walked out" when she was seven years old. Shortly after he left, a brother was born. She had two older sisters and one older brother. She had been married 12 years, with two daughters, 11 and eight years of age, and had her fortieth birthday two weeks before she sought help.

Mrs. M. impresses the examiner as a very unhappy woman who is desperately looking for someone to listen to her, to sympathize with her, and in some magical way to make things better. Her present problem is a marital one. Her husband owns and manages a small music school and is completely involved in it. He does not, however, earn enough to support the family. She tries to help him by keeping the school's books, but he does not want her to be involved in his business activities. He insults and berates her. He is a poor bill-collector, and in desperation she calls on his father to make collections for him. She tries in every way possible to please him, but he is never satisfied and will criticize her for doing the very things he has asked her to do. She recalls having been left at home, as an adolescent, to do the work while her mother took her siblings into town. Although she worked very hard, her mother invariably pointed to what was not done and never gave her recognition for what had been accomplished. This situation is being repeated in her present life with her husband. She does not think he is malicious, but rather that he is basically insensitive. He has always been like this. Periodically, when she fails to please him, she feels aggrieved, hopeless, and depressed. She is usually behind in her housework, but at such periods lets everything go, so that her husband becomes furious with her. Mrs. M.'s mother lives in an apartment in the same building and does the cooking for the entire family. Mrs. M. does not think this is right, but rationalizes that her mother is lonely.

Several times during the interview, Mrs. M. was on the verge of tears. She revealed that she often feels that living is not worthwhile. If it were not for the children, she is quite sure she would not be here. She is not sure but what one can will oneself to die. She thinks that her age may have something to do with her feelings at present. She has always hoped that something would happen to change her life. Now she finds she is getting old and there is no likelihood of change. She feels she has accomplished nothing worthwhile in her life.

Mrs. M. dates the onset of the acute marital difficulty to the time of the birth of their second child. At that time Mr. M. stopped approaching her sexually. She waited a year before she decided to raise the question with him. His response was that she had a problem, that he was completely satisfied with their life, and that she should see a psychiatrist. She recognizes that her need is not a sexual one, but rather that of being wanted and needed. She has never experienced orgasm. She punishes her children severely and is afraid she will seriously hurt them. She has a fear of "going crazy." She readily accepts the suggestion she may be displacing anger from her husband onto the children. She mentions casually that she says a prayer for their safe return each morning when they leave for school.

The dynamic interaction in this couple is between a passive-aggressive woman married to a nonaggressive man. The relationship is sadomasochistic. Mrs. M. attempts to get the security of love and approval by trying to be "good" as she conceives it. Due to Mrs. M.'s inconsistencies and her own ambivalence, this fails. This augments her hostility, with a consequent threat of loss because of it. Her age undoubtedly is contributing to her present depression. It is not likely that she would commit suicide, but it is not at all impossible that she may unconsciously arrange to get herself killed accidentally.

The treatment of choice for depressive reactions is either psychoanalysis or a psychoanalytic form of psychotherapy. These patients may improve quickly on a transference basis, but cure in the sense of preventing recurrences requires a thorough analysis of their ambivalence, oral fixations, and immature object relationships.

Manic-Depressive Reaction (Melancholia)

This condition is a psychotic reaction which is marked fundamentally by severe mood swings and a tendency to remission and recurrence. The resultant disturbance in thought and behavior is in consonance with the affect.

In this condition, heredity and cultural factors seem to play a significant role. Studies of identical twins show that if one twin has developed manic-depressive psychosis, in more than half the cases the other twin will also develop the disease. Manic-depressive psychosis is three times as common in the highest social class as it is in the general population. It is twice as common in women as in men. According to statistics, the incidence of manic-depressive psychosis in the United States has decreased sharply in recent years. This is probably the result of more careful diagnostic study: many cases that would previously have been diagnosed as manic-depressive reaction are now seen to involve a thought disorder which cannot be explained by the change in mood. Such cases are now classified as schizophrenic reactions, and these have therefore had a relative increase in incidence.

Theoretically, the disease is characterized by alternating phases of elation and depression. Clinically, however, there is no constant sequence, and recurrent depression may be the only manifestation of the disease. Manic-depressive patients have a premorbid history of wider-than-normal mood swings. In the depressed type, one is apt to get a history of a tendency episodes of mild depression. In the manic type, there may be a history of having been generally ebullient, outgoing, optiministic, and hyperactive. The first diagnosed attack of manic-depressive psychosis usually occurs in early maturity, each attack lasting an average of six months.

In the depressive phase, the depression is severe, with correspondingly sagging posture and sad appearance. All activity is retarded, including thinking and verbalization. Disturbance in psychophysiological function is marked. Delusional ideas of guilt and suicidal preoccupations are common. Somatic delusions, frequently of a bizarre nature, often occur.

In the manic phase, elation and good humor are striking and infectious. The patient is in constant motion, singing, shouting, assuming dramatic attitudes. He seems imbued with boundless energy. His rate of thinking and talking is so increased that it has been termed "flight of ideas." His attention span is limited by this constant influx of ideas and by his hyperactivity. Grandiose delusions are common. Activity is so accelerated that there is danger of death through exhaustion.

One may wonder why such a condition is included among the depressions. Empirically, it is known that the two conditions (mania and depression) frequently occur in the same person. There is much psychoanalytic evidence to indicate that the manic behavior is a denial and avoidance of depression. Another possible explanation is that, having expiated his sins through suffering in depression, the manic-depressive now feels that he is permitted to enjoy optimism and elations, or, conversely, having dared to be elated and grandiose, he must now punish himself by becoming depressed.

Psychotic, as opposed to neurotic, depression, will be suspected when one or more of the following malignant symptoms is present: severe hypochondriacal preoccupation, delusions, often somatic, agitation, severe irrational guilt feelings, intractable insomnia, severe psychomotor retardation, or suicidal rumination.

Manic-depressive psychosis is differentiated from schizophrenia principally because all of the symptoms in manic-depressive psychosis are in keeping with the affect. For example, in depression, the thoughts expressed are pessimistic and the activity retarded. In schizophrenia, however, there is a disharmony between feelings, thoughts, and actions. Furthermore, manic-depressive psychosis does not usually show the thought disorder characteristic of schizophrenia. Nevertheless, since depression may occur in schizophrenics, the differentiation in practice may be difficult, as is illustrated in the following case:

Mrs. E.M., 51-year-old dentist employed in a city clinic, has had five attacks of depression in the past 10 years. On three occasions she was given electric shock treatment. Her condition has worsened in the past six weeks. The depressions last from three to six months, depending upon the treatment. She says that she is depressed, but looks impassive and denies that she is slowed down. On the other hand, she is silent through most of the interview, speaks very slowly, has difficulty in thinking, and says she would "like to lie down flat and do nothing all day." She complains incessantly to her husband about her condition and has difficulty sleeping. She is concerned that she is letting people down, particularly her son, her husband, and her employer. She worries what will happen to her and although she cannot feel that she will get over this attack, she also worries that if she does, there will only be recurrences. She worries about a recent loss of memory, and "disorientation," which on examination proved rather to be distraction and preoccupation. Tests of her ability to conceptualize show marked deterioration. At home she forces herself to attempt minor household duties, but is completely inefficient. On such occasions she will talk to herself, exhorting and reprimanding herself. About a year before her latest attack, her husband had a stroke and has worked only irregularly since. He is a periodic drinker and on one occasion took an overdose of sleeping pills. Their married life has been marked by great strife and frequent threats of separation. Her son, now in his twenties, has been unable to keep a job and shows little desire to do so. He and his father quarrel incessantly.

With antidepressants and psychotherapy, the patient improved over the next couple of months. She was taken off drugs and continued to do well for another two months. One day she came in and stated that something seemed to be happening to her and she was not as well as she had been. No cause was apparent. Within two weeks she was again in a deep depression. Placed on antidepressant drugs again, she quickly improved and in a month returned to work.

This case again shows the difficulty of placing depressive illnesses into clear-cut diagnostic entities. This woman certainly had much cause for depression. The depth of the depression and its recurrence would, however, favor the diagnosis of manic-depressive psychosis. The defect in concept formation might suggest a schizophrenia, but she does not show the disharmony between affect, ideation, and behavior that might be expected in such an illness. Her age is in keeping with an involutional psychotic reaction, but the history of five similar attacks makes such a diagnosis unlikely.

In the acute phases of a manic-depressive psychosis, hospitalization is frequently mandatory. Shock treatment (ECT), drug treatment, or both, are used. In the less acute phases and in the periods of remission, psychotherapy is indicated and psychoanalysis occasionally possible. In working with severely depressed persons, it should be kept in mind that it is exhausting for them to maintain a relationship and to have to think or concentrate. It is necessary for the therapist to lessen this load for them as much as possible. Shorter interviews may be necessary and no emotional demands should be made of them. In cases of severe guilt, routine manual tasks, even though unpleasant, may be insisted on. Because depression is largely a disturbance in object relationships, the therapist must offer himself as an object in order to form a bridge to other object relationships. Frequent contact may be necessary either in person or by telephone in order to accomplish this.

Involutional Psychotic Reaction (Involutional Melancholia)

This category covers psychotic depressions occurring for the first time during the involutional period—the years between the end of maturity and the beginning of senescence. Involution is more clearly defined in women, where the end of maturity is marked by the cessation of the menses. No such clear delineation is possible in the male, but a psychologically similar phenomenon has been described, beginning in the early fifties. Originally, this group of psychotic reactions was separately classified because it was believed that endocrinological factors were responsible. There is no scientific evidence for this, and it is now accepted that the symptomology can be explained on the basis of psychological changes that usually take place at this period of life. The disease is twice as common in women as in men. The prepsychotic personality is usually that of a superego-dominated character structure. These patients have been tense, compulsive, scrupulously honest, and self-denying all their adult life. The illness tends to run a prolonged course.

The basic dynamics are those of all depressions. Specific factors are the changes in the way of life inherent in this age period. For the woman, the reproductive phase is ended, and the children are grown and out of the house. A feeling of uselessness is common. For the man, success is either attained or no longer seems possible. For both, the awareness that many dreams will never be fulfilled is brought home. The future looks bleak, and the possibility of death becomes more real.

Perhaps the most severe depression one ever sees is the involutional type. Along with the profound depression, there is marked anxiety, restlessness, agitation, and intractable insomnia. Delusions of sin, disease, guilt, and imminent punishment are characteristic. Of all psychiatric illness, this one has the highest incidence of suicide.

While one might conservatively question the use of shock treatment in other illnesses, it is the treatment of choice here. Occasionally, if the patient can be kept under 24-hour surveillance, one may temporize and test the benefits of antidepressant drugs.

Psychotic Depressive Reaction (Psychotic Depression)

This diagnosis is used in cases where the depression is psychotic in degree and yet there is no history suggestive of manic-depressive reaction, involutional reaction, or schizophrenic reaction. Environmental precipitating factors are usually present, as in depressive reaction. The difference lies in the intensity of the symptoms. This diagnosis is also used occasionally in state hospitals for those cases of depression of a psychotic degree which for some extraneous reason cannot be fully studied, if, for example, the patient does not remain in the hospital long enough, or is mute, and there is no one to supply the necessary information.

Suicide

Regardless of diagnostic category, the most serious danger in any depression is the possibility of suicide. Suicide has ranked among the first 10 causes of death in adults for the past half-century, and among white males between the ages of 15 and 45, it ranks fifth. In 1960 (the most recent available statistics) about 20,000 people committed suicide. When one considers that these statistics do not include the numerous cases which occur but are not recognized, or if recognized are not reported, and the many psychologically determined fatal accidents, the enormity of the problem is clear.

Suicide is the clearest example of turning against the self. Freud originally wrote on the dynamics of suicide in "Mourning and Melancholia" (1917). Since that time, psychoanalytic studies have emphasized that, no matter how inexplicable a suicide may seem, unconscious motivations are always present. Psychoanalysis has also shown that the method the individual chooses to commit suicide is unconsciously determined.

Although depression is a frequent concomitant, if not cause of suicide, it is not invariably present. People may commit suicide in rage or in a state of beatific elation. Karl Menninger (1939) has pointed out that each suicidal act contains three elements in varied proportions. There is a wish to kill, a wish to be killed, and a wish to die. The wish to kill may arise from rage at an ambivalently loved object, rage which is then turned against the self. This may be phrased, "I identify myself with my parents and kill the parent within myself." Recent psychoanalytic studies have stressed, in addition, the identification with the superego of the ambivalently loved object. This may be described as, "I identify myself with standards (fantasied or real) of my parent and kill the bad self in me."

The wish or need to be killed is usually derived from a sense of guilt for fantasied aggression, in accordance with the talion law, "I wish to kill someone, therefore I deserve to be killed." In some cases, the act of being killed is clearly sexualized and represents an extreme form of physical submission. Because of the aggressive or libidinal determinants, the act of suicide itself is often attended with a feeling of guilt. This may play a role in unconsciously determined accidents where the responsibility for the suicide is avoided. In someone who has lost a parent through suicide, the wish to be killed may represent an attempt at identification with that parent.

The wish to die may contain within it the fantasy of being reborn. At other times, it may represent the wish to join a loved one who is dead. More commonly, the wish to die is a wish to obtain relief from intolerable fantasies and intrapsychic conflicts, to escape intolerable life situations. Unconscious fantasies of martyrdom are frequent in suicide.

The act of suicide may have many more determinants. It may be a coercive act to impress others with one's goodness, suffering, or desperation. It may represent a denial of the feeling of helplessness. "I may be helpless in all other situations, but this one thing I can control and do." It may be a defiance of authority. It may represent such opposites as assertion of identity or destruction of identity. It may be an exhibitionistic act, as in public suicides. The suicidal person may conceive of death as a return to perfect love, union, a condition of loving and being loved.

These various motivations also determine the method of suicide. Menninger points out that although one would expect someone who had made up his mind to commit suicide to do so in the easiest, most convenient, and least painful way, the opposite is often true. Fantastic, horrifying, excruciatingly painful methods are sometimes chosen. Very often the method chosen is symbolic. Death by burning may symbolically gratify a wish to be emotionally warm and loved. Drowning may be a return to mother.

It is extremely difficult to predict whether or not someone will commit suicide. Two common misconceptions should be cleared up. The first is that people who threaten suicide rarely commit the act. This is definitely untrue. The second is that, by making suicidal wishes explicit and conscious, the danger of a suicidal attempt is increased. Quite the contrary, only if the suicidal wish is made conscious can the ego be on guard against it. A forthright approach is often necessary in order to determine the danger.

The danger of suicide is greater under the following circumstances: where a parent or other meaningful person has committed suicide; where there has been an acute personality change with unconscious self-destructive behavior now evident; where there has been a previous suicidal attempt; where a person has decided on a time, place, or method for the proposed suicide; where the threat of suicide follows the death of a loved one within a year; where an elderly person has had a great deal of surgery; where the individual's object relationships have narrowed or are narrowing to the point where no one is left; where the depressed or enraged individual has always shown poor ego control or where there is indication that such controls are rapidly being lost. Statistically, the older the person, the greater the danger. Unusual preparation for a trip, or the making out of a will, may also be a warning sign.

Where suicidal danger is suspected, one should not be loath to recommend psychiatric consultation, nor should one be dissuaded by the reluctance of the depressed person or his relatives. In this connection, it should be remembered that the danger of suicide in severely depressed people is greatest when they are apparently starting to improve. This is probably due to the fact that at the depths of the depression the individual is unable to mobilize himself sufficiently to commit the act. Relatives are often insistent on taking depressed patients out of institutions at the first sign of improvement. Too often, the results are disastrous.

This description should make it clear that the suicidal person's "cry for help" (Farberow and Schneiderman, 1961) is not as silent as some would believe. Signs are there for those who are willing to see and hear. When even a suspicion is present, professional help must be sought immediately. There is no substitute.

A number of cities have established agencies especially to deal with suicidal crises. Los Angeles has a "Suicide Prevention Center," New York a "Save-A-Life League," Boston a "Rescue Incorporated."

REFERENCES

Abraham, K. (1911), Notes on the Psycho-Analytical Investigation and Treatment of Manic-Depressive Insanity and Allied Conditions. In: *Selected Papers on Psycho-Analysis.* New York: Basic Books, 1953.

Cameron, N. (1963), *Personality Development and Psychopathology.* Boston: Houghton Mifflin, Chapter 12.

Engel, G. L. (1962), *Psychological Development in Health and Disease.* Philadelphia: W. B. Saunders.

Farberow, N. L. & Schneiderman, E. S. (1961), *The Cry for Help.* New York: McGraw-Hill.

Freud, S. (1917), Mourning and Melancholia. *Standard Edition,* 14:237-258. London: Hogarth Press, 1957.

Hill, D. (1968), Depression: Disease Reaction or Posture? *American Journal of Psychiatry,* 125: 445-457.

Menninger, K. (1939), *Man Against Himself.* New York: Harcourt, Brace & World.

Schneiderman, E. S., Farberow, N. L. & Leonard, C. V. (1961), *Some Facts About Suicide.* Washington, D. C.: U. S. Health Service Publication.

CHAPTER TWENTY-FIVE

Schizophrenia

LEONARD A. WEINROTH, M.D.

Schizophrenia, sometimes referred to as the group of schizophrenias, is a frequently encountered mental disorder which produces a disturbance of the total personality organization. Thinking, feeling, and overt behavior regress to a primitive level and appear irrational, inappropriate, and bizarre. In some cases, the overt manifestations of the disease may be quite subtle and difficult to detect. Close study, nevertheless, will reveal a personality structure in which the ego is weak or vulnerable, especially in the areas of reality testing, control over instinctual drives and superego demands, and appropriateness of affect; as a consequence, adaptation to the environment and interpersonal relations, as well as the individual's sense of identity and self-esteem are adversely affected.

Nearly one-quarter of all patients admitted to psychiatric hospitals are diagnosed as schizophrenics, and more than half of the psychiatric hospital beds are occupied by people suffering from schizophrenia. The incidence of schizophrenia, i.e., the number of new cases occurring in a given period of time, usually one year, is between 50 and 250 per thousand of population in the western industralized countries.

The maximum incidence of schizophrenia is between the ages of 25 and 34. The distribution between the two sexes is approximately equal. It has been stated that .3 per cent—and probably more—newborn babies are likely to become ill with schizophrenia, regardless of their social and historical environment but accurate statistics in relation to schizophrenia are very difficult to compile for a variety of reasons. In many instances, the schizophrenic never comes to the attention of the psychiatrist. He may live in his community, where he may be considered "odd" but never be hospitalized or diagnosed. Furthermore, because many schizophrenics recover, if not completely, at least partially, without hospitalization, and do not progress to a state of mental deterioration, they may not be included in any statistical compilation. There is also a general lack of agreement among psychiatrists on what constitutes schizophrenia or other disorders similar to it. In the United States, the term schizophrenia is applied to a broader group of conditions than in most other countries. There are many conditions which are actually on a borderline between schizophrenic disorders on the one side and severe neuroses or character disorders on the other. (These borderline conditions are frequently encountered by the helping professions and are therefore taken up in a separate chapter.) All these variables contribute to the general uncertainty of the statistics on schizophrenia.

The diagnostic term "schizophrenia" was coined in 1911 by the Swiss psychiatrist Eugen Bleuler (1950) on the basis of his observations of common fundamental symptoms that appeared in the different types of the disease. "Schizophrenia" is derived from two Greek words meaning "split" and "mind" and was intended to indicate that essential psychic functions are split and fragmented and that the integration and unity of the personality is lost. Different forms of "madness" corresponding to schizophrenia have been described and studied since the beginning of recorded history. In 1856, the French psychiatrist Morel introduced the term "dementia praecox" ("demence precoce") to identify psychoses which began early in life and led to mental deterioration. By 1870, the catatonic and hebephrenic forms of mental illness had been described as separate entities. The German psychiatrist Kraepelin, working at the end of the nineteenth century, extended the term dementia praecox to include the catatonic, hebephrenic, and paranoid types of what we now call schizophrenia. "Dementia praecox" is a term that describes mental deterioration beginning early in life. Kraepelin assumed that the condition was a disorder of metabolism. Until recently, the terms "dementia praecox" and "schizophrenia" have been used interchangeably. Dementia praecox, however, is no longer in general use or listed in the present official nomenclature, inasmuch as schizophrenia includes a broader range of syndromes than were originally covered by the older term.

In the United States in the twentieth century, psychiatric attitudes to schizophrenia were fashioned by the psychodynamic approach elaborated by Freud and his followers, by Adolph Meyer, who considered schizophrenia to be largely a reaction to the experiences of the subject's life, and by Harry Stack Sullivan, who stressed the role of social experience and communication in the etiology of the disease.

Bleuler divided the manifestations of schizophrenia into the fundamental—or primary—and the accessory—or secondary—symptoms. The primary and basic manifestations are thought disorder, disturbances of affects and ambivalence. In the schizophrenic thought-disorder, primary-process thinking becomes prevalent. The logical associations between various thoughts are disrupted. Ideas which do not belong to one another may be condensed into one thought. The ability to form concepts and to generalize is impaired; thinking becomes "syncretistic." Essential content is omitted, the unessential is pushed into the foreground, and sometimes a chain of thought is completely blocked. Frequently, associations are based on similarity of sound and not on any valid logical connection. The goal-directedness of thinking is very much determined by the subject's inner life, his daydreams, fantasies, and impulses. Bleuler called this kind of thinking, which is detached from reality "dereistic," and he termed the state in which the individual primarily focuses on his own fantasies and thought processes, without regard for external reality, "autism."

The affective life of the schizophrenic shows a disruption comparable to the disruption of thinking. The affect does not correspond to the content of the thought that is being communicated. The schizophrenic may, for instance, talk about tragic events and serious thoughts with a silly grin or laughter. Conversely, he may cry when there is no reason for sadness in the thought that he presents. The expression of feeling thus appears inappropriate to the observer. Many schizophrenic patients show a geneal flatness of affect, that is, in a reduction in the intensity and modulation of the emotional response. In some instances, these responses are excessive, in others, shallow and indifferent.

A further manifestation of schizophrenia is ambivalence. The same thought content may be accompanied simultaneously by both pleasant and painful feelings; this is affective ambivalence. The person may also show ambivalence of will; he may want and at the same time not want to perform a given act.

The accessory or secondary symptoms are usually very much in evidence in schizophrenia and are displayed by the patient in more obvious ways than are the primary ones. They are sometimes considered to be attempts at restitution of mental functioning and reestablishment of object relationships on a delusional level. The secondary symptoms most frequently encountered in schizophrenia are delusions and hallucinations. These determine much of the schizophrenic's behavior. Illusions, i.e., mistaken perceptions of external reality, are also of frequent occurrence in schizophrenia. Most schizophrenic hallucinations are of an auditory type. The patient perceives his own thoughts as if they were being communicated from outside through his sensory apparatus. He may hear threatening and accusatory voices expressing his own feelings of worthlessness. The voices may also be soothing and consoling, visionary and prophetic. Hallucinations of visual imagery, of touch, smell, and taste, likewise occur, but are more frequently encountered in the organic psychoses. In his delusions, the schizophrenic feels influenced by malevolent or sometimes by divine agents. Occasionally, he develops delusions on which he may base schemes to save the world, or make claims of spectacular inventions or discoveries.

Psychomotor symptoms appear in all forms of schizophrenia. They are the most conspicuous manifestations in the catatonic type of the disease.

Types of Schizophrenia

The group of schizophrenias is subdivided into four main types: the simple, hebephrenic, catatonic, and paranoid types. A fifth form is designated the schizo-affective type. There exist, in addition, other subtypes of schizophrenia, as well as such related conditions as the borderline and paranoid states, and paranoia. The four classical types of schizophrenia often show the same symptoms throughout the course of the disease. There may also be instances in which the initial diagnosis is catatonic type (or any type), but, during the second or third hospitalization, the combination of symptoms is more indicative of the hebephrenic or paranoid type, i.e., there is a transition from one type of the illness to another.

The *simple type of schizophrenia* is manifested by gradual decrease in attachments to people and interest in the outside world. Interpersonal relations become impoverished, there is a lowering of mental efficiency and a sinking to a lower level of functioning. The dramatic accessory symptoms of other types of schizophrenia are usually missing. In the beginning stages of this condition, the patient may be diagnosed as an inadequate personality.

In the *hebephrenic type of schizophrenia,* there is a marked inappropriateness and shallowness of affect. The patient behaves in a silly way, grimaces and giggles, and exhibits mannerisms. His mental life is fragmented, and even his delusions and hallucinations are poorly organized and transitory. Frequently, there are delusional hypochondriacal complaints. This form has a very marked tendency to result in deterioration.

The *catatonic type of schizophrenia* can be divided into excited and withdrawn or stuporous subtypes. In the excited catatonic state, the patient, aside from sudden outbursts of aggressive behavior, may become exhausted, lose body fluids without replacing them, and even develop fever because of the constant overactivity, lack of sleep, and refusal to eat or drink. The withdrawn type of catatonia shows a great deal of negativism; frequently the withdrawn catatonic is mute and stuporous for prolonged periods of time. He may refuse to take any food, to move his bowels, or to urinate. Stuporous states may suddenly be followed by excitement, and vice versa. Waxy flexibility of the musculature and catalepsy—prolonged maintenance of sometimes very artificial postures—occur in catatonic types of schizophrenia. An organic neurological factor may contribute to these somewhat rarely encountered symptoms. The onset of catatonia may be quite sudden and acute, but the prognosis is not necessarily unfavorable, especially in the acute cases, if proper treatment is undertaken in time. Other psychomotor symptoms observed in catatonia, and in other types of schizophrenia as well, include echolalia (repeating what others say) and echopraxia (copying what others do). This may be considered the opposite of negativism. Odd and stilted movements and speech, as well as stereotyped movements and mannerisms are also observed in different types of schizophrenia, frequently in the form of bizarre gestures and grimacing.

The *paranoid type of schizophrenia* often begins later in life than the other three forms. Aside from the primary symptoms of schizophrenia, this form is characterized by delusions and hallucinations of a persecutory or grandiose nature. Sometimes both megalomania and delusions of persecution are expressed by the same patient. Delusions may take on the coloring of religion or science fiction. The general attitude of the patients is often aggressive and hostile, quite in line with their delusions of being the victims of persecution. Prior to the outbreak of the psychosis, the patient may show some of the features of the paranoid personality: he is cold, distrustful, and hostile. The total personality of the paranoid type schizophrenic is less disorganized than is that of the other three types. This is probably because the paranoid schizophrenic defends himself against the inner conflicts that tear him apart by projecting them onto others. As the sickness progresses, the organized but pseudo logical system of delusions becomes more and more disjointed.

The *schizo-affective type of schizophrenia* includes those basically schizophrenic patients who also show marked elation or depression. For diagnostic purposes, this group may be subdivided into excited and depressed subtypes. At times, the manic-depressive psychotic may show a considerable amount of disorganization of thought and, sometimes, paranoid ideation, but in the manic-depressive the affective symptoms are very much in the foreground, and a periodic change from elation to a relatively neutral state and to depression, i.e., the periodicity of the illness, differentiates it from the schizo-affective type of schizophrenia. The depressed schizo-affective sometimes commits suicide in a conspicious and dramatic way, in line with his delusional system.

In addition to the types of schizophrenia just described, there is a diagnostic category called *acute schizophrenic episode*. It is characterized by a very acute onset of symptoms, "with confusion, perplexities, ideas of reference, emotional turmoil, dreamlike dissociation, and excitement, depression, or fear" (American Psychiatric Association, 1968). In some instances, patients may recover from the acute episode; within weeks in others, the features of catatonic, hebephrenic, or paranoid schizophrenia eventually become discernible.

The official nomenclature also contains the diagnostic group of *schizophrenia, latent type*. This category is only of statistical interest, for the adjective "latent" refers to something that cannot be observed. It includes the borderline and pseudoneurotic types of schizophrenia described elsewhere in this book.

In order to provide a diagnostic pigeonhole for schizophrenia with mixed symptoms, a category called *schizophrenia, chronic undifferentiated type* has been created.

Aside from the paranoid type of schizophrenia, other *paranoid psychotic states* exist, in which the predominant symptoms are based on delusions of a persecutory or megalomanic nature. It is sometimes difficult to differentiate the paranoid states and the paranoid personality on the one side from the paranoid schizophrenia on the other. Which category an individual case falls into is largely a matter of degree. There is no severe fragmentation of the personality observed in paranoid states, but there may be hallucinations, and disturbances in mood and behavior which are based on paranoid delusions. On the other hand, these latter symptoms are absent in the paranoid personality, which is described in Chapter Nineteen.

Another syndrome, called *paranoia,* rarely comes to the attention of the helping professions. Paranoiacs are those who develop a frequently elaborate and consistent paranoid system that proceeds logically from a delusional premise and is frequently based on certain facts or observations that fall in line with the subject's preoccupation. Paranoiacs frequently pursue their arguments logically and forcefully and may become convinced that they must right wrongs or follow causes with complete disregard for the actual situation. At times, paranoics acquire followers who will participate and help them further their "cause," however unreal it may be. Some paranoiacs engage in litigation before the courts—occasionally the term "litigious paranoia" is used. The accusations may be completely unfounded and yet be presented with a forcefulness and logical coherence that leads to endless court proceedings and often to the impairment of the reputations of those whom they accuse. Some paranoiacs develop delusionally based jealousy and are absolutely convinced that their spouses have been unfaithful to them. They may proceed to violent and even murderous actions. The essential aspect of true paranoiac conditions consists of the encapsulation of the paranoid system within an otherwise intact evaluation of reality, and with the preservation of the formal logical structure of thought and language. The paranoiac is absolutely convinced that he is right and that anyone who opposes his views is wrong. He therefore never seeks psychiatric or other professional help, and if he is forced to undergo a mental examination or is hospitalized, the hospital personnel become his enemies, i.e., part of his delusional system. In certain historical circumstances, persons who might be considered paranoiacs because of their relentless and fanatical dedication to some cause may become leaders or martyrs. As with all psychological disorders, we observe in the paranoid conditions a gradual transition from the normal to the grossly pathological. The vigilance and the occasional suspicion of the average person certainly cannot be considered "paranoid." A consistent coldness and suspiciousness and hostility characterizes a paranoid personality. If such suspicion becomes systematized and more or less pervades the person's life, we are dealing with a paranoid state or with paranoia. Eventually, if there is a thought disorder and other manifestations of schizophrenia, we are confronted with a paranoid type of schizophrenia.

Differential Diagnosis

The differentiation of psychoses, including schizophrenia, from neuroses has been very clearly formulated by Arlow and Brenner (1964). In psychoses one finds a greater degree of instinctual regression or infantilism, a greater prominence of manifestations of the aggressive instinctual drive and of conflicts over such manifestations and more severe and more widespread abnormalities in various ego and superego functions. These last are generally motivated by a need to prevent the emergence of anxiety in a situation of inner conflict, i.e., they serve a defensive function primarily. The type of anxiety which is defended against in schizophrenic illness is much more intense than that in neurosis and is based on the sense of an impending disintegration of the personality and the loss of identity. In schizophrenia, depersonalization is very frequently observed, especially in the initial stages of the illness. The subject feels as if he were another person observing himself from the outside. There may also be a feeling of estrangement from one's own body. Depersonalization, however, may also occur in its milder forms in some neurotic conditions. Loosely related to depersonalization is the feeling of derealization, in which external reality is perceived as different, strange, and usually frightening. The use of hallucinogenic drugs frequently induces depersonalization and derealization, much as does schizophrenia.

Underlying Dynamics

We now consider the manifestations of schizophrenia in terms of our personality theory, with its subdivisions of id, ego, and superego. The above reference to regression refers to changes which occur in the id. This regression brings out more primitive manifestations of the instinctual drives and interferes with their control. The primitive fashion in which the instinctual drives manifest themselves disturbs the autonomous functioning of the ego and sublimation. Yet, quite remarkably, we frequently observe that many skills acquired earlier in life remain outside of the pathological process. For instance, an otherwise severely regressed schizophrenic may preserve his knowledge of a foreign language, some of his mechanical skills, and even be able to perform such a relatively complex mental activity as mathematics. In other words, in most instances of schizophrenia, the regression is not global, but partial. Islands of autonomous functioning still remain intact.

In schizophrenia, the severe and extensive abnormalities in ego functions are the most significant features of the disease. *Consciousness* is usually not grossly disturbed, with the exception of some clouding in stuporous catatonic states. Autism may result in impairment of attention. This sometimes leads to a lessened awareness of the surroundings. *Sense perception,* as a rule, is not impaired, but frequently is distorted because of the general fragmentation of the mental life. Perception may regress to a global, diffuse level. Synesthesias occur: an auditory stimulus may be accompanied by visual perceptual effects, and vice versa. Illusions and hallucinations, of course, can be said to affect perception, in the sense that in illusions the perception of the object does not correspond to the external stimulus, and in hallucinations inner thoughts and fantasies are perceived as if they were coming from the outside. *Control of motility* is very conspicuously disturbed from the point of view of the observer. Aside from the psychomotor symptoms already mentioned, other changes in muscular control, including stiltedness, grimacing, and stereotyped movements, appear in the various forms of schizophrenia. There is no specific disturbance of the *memory function,* but the general fragmentation of the mental organization may affect the recall of the past, which can be incorrect, jumbled, and influenced by hallucinations and delusions that are considered to be events which have actually taken place. The schizophrenic also has distortion in recall because of *déja vu*—already seen—and *déja entendu*—already heard—phenomena which, by the way, are not in themselves an indication of schizophrenia, since they occasionally occur in normal or neurotic persons. It is remarkable how some schizophrenics are able to recall years later what other people said and did in their presence while they seemed to be completely out of touch with their environment. In addition to the description already given, the thought processes are highly charged by the schizophrenic's individual idiosyncratic types of symbolism; his concepts of time and space may be markedly distorted.

Perception and expression of affects are two of the basic ego functions impaired by the schizophrenic illness. In advanced stages of the disease, the patient may seem to be completely devoid of any emotional responsiveness. If this condition is combined with mutism or severe impairment of language, the schizophrenic in this deteriorated state appears to be vegetating. The *language* in schizophrenia is just as fragmented and impaired as the thought processes. Speech becomes circumstantial and incoherent, and, at times, blocking and mutism interfere with any verbal communication. The patient often coins his own neologisms. The schizophrenic may perseverate, repeating the same sentence over and over again. Language and speech may also be characterized by disregard for the rules of grammar, and eventually the schizophrenic may express himself by speech in which sounds are combined in his own way and are completely unintelligible to others—speech referred to as "word salad." Whereas *reality testing* and the *sense of reality* are disturbed in any psychosis, this disturbance is especially noticeable in schizophrenia. It is obvious that when severe regression and interference with the basic ego functions has taken place, good judgment and correct evaluation of reality are all but impossible. The schizophrenic patient frequently has difficulty in sensing the boundaries between the self and the outside world. This, in turn, interferes with proper reality testing. Mental processes that go on within the individual are readily presumed to go on in the outside world.

Defense mechamisms, which have been described in Chapter Three, are used by the schizophrenic in an excessive and exclusive way that accentuates the secondary symptoms. Projection and denial are of special importance in schizophrenia. Many other defense mechanisms, including isolation, reaction formation, and somatization, are also employed in an excessive and one-sided way by schizophrenic patients.

The statement that one of the main aspects of the schizophrenic illness is the fragmentation of the psychic life can be formulated in other terms: the synthetic or organizing function is impaired in moderate cases and is nearly abolished in severe instances of the disease.

As we have seen, the basic structure of the superego is laid down during the oedipal period, but many other components of the conscience, including moral and ethical attitudes, are acquired later in the course of development and modified even in adult life. The regression of the mental organization to a primitive level especially affects the conscience functions of the superego. This does not mean that schizophrenics will necessarily engage in criminal or antisocial activities; but because of their poor judgment and the alteration of moral standards, schizophrenic patients in advanced stages may publicly masturbate or defacate, undress when it is inappropriate, or attack others without any obvious reason. This, of course, reflects the disorganization of the ego and the superego, as well as the prevalence of primitive unchecked instinctual impulses.

Etiology

The etiology of schizophrenia cannot be stated with any degree of exactitude. During the nineteenth century, all mental illnesses were considered to result from impaired structure and function of the brain. This point of view contributed to a host of important discoveries where anatomical changes in the brain could be correlated with psychological disturbances. At the present time, it is not even certain that the various subtypes of schizophrenia have a common origin. For instance, it is assumed that some catatonic conditions may be based on an organic disturbance of the midbrain, but this explanation would certainly apply to only a very few exceptional cases of even the catatonic type of schizophrenia. This leaves us with a general assumption of some organic predisposition, probably based on biological-genetic factors. Extensive studies of fraternal and identical twins have shown a 15 per cent concordance in fraternal and an 86 per cent concordance in identical twins for schizophrenia. Kallmann (1953) found that even in those identical twins who were reared separately, the concordance for schizophrenia was still 77.6 per cent. Some authorities are, however, critical of the theory of primary hereditary transmission of schizophrenia.

The role of adverse life experiences in the causation of schizophrenia is likewise by no means clear. Sometimes it appears that traumatic events, especially cumulative ones, precipitate the outbreak of the psychosis, but there is no direct correlation between the severity of the trauma and the development of a schizophrenic psychosis. It is well known that many, even under the most adverse life situations, do not succumb, while in other cases schizophrenia can be precipitated by relatively trivial events which at face value do not seem to be particularly pathogenic. This, of course, can be explained by assuming a lesser or greater predisposition.

Psychoanalysts have introduced the concept of a weak or a strong ego; strength is characterized by a lesser tendency to regress when confronted with traumatic situations or intrapsychic conflicts. The ego of schizophrenics is generally weak. This statement, however, is descriptive and not explanatory (Redlich and Freedman, 1966). Other environmental factors that presumably contribute to the causation of schizophrenia include disturbances during the early stages of development, as far back as the symbiotic stage.

Inconsistency, ambivalence, detached attitudes, serious neurotic and psychotic disturbances are some of the important characteristics of the parents which have been considered to contribute to schizophrenic illness in the offspring. With the help of the psychoanalytic understanding of the personality, the meaning of many manifestations of schizophrenia have been elucidated, but we should be careful not to confuse meaning with cause.

It has also been hypothesized that schizophrenia results from a faulty communication system in the family, with the child receiving contradictory messages. This results in "double-bind" situations in which the cues coming from the parents are ambiguous and frustrating. For example, the child may be asked in the friendliest way to approach the parent and then be treated harshly.

In the present state of our knowledge, we are not able to pinpoint the specific causes of schizophrenia. Both biological and environmental factors are undoubtedly involved, and, furthermore, we are probably not dealing with a single entity, but with a group of different illnesses with different causes.

Prognosis and Treatment

The course of schizophrenia and the paranoid states varies greatly, and it is very difficult to predict whether the end result will be recovery with hardly any defect, recovery with defect, or progressive deterioration. Before the advent of drug therapy, one quarter of schizophrenic patients ended up as deteriorated wrecks in the back wards of mental institutions. With drugs and enlightened methods of treatment, the number of deteriorated schizophrenics is much less. An attempt has been made to divide schizophrenia into two general groups, the reactive and the process types. The reactive type are those schizophrenics who had functioned adequately in their premorbid state. The sickness was precipitated by a traumatic event, and the onset was usually acute. In the process type of schizophrenia, the patient had never been able to function adequately, the onset of his sickness was gradual, and eventually he progressed to a deteriorated state. Family stability prior to the outbreak of the psychosis is considered a good prognostic sign.

Treatment methods consist of various organic therapies, including drugs and milieu therapy, and various forms of psychotherapy, i.e., individual, group, and family treatment. Efforts at rehabilitation and reintegration into society are of paramount importance. Hospitalization used to be the only treatment available in schizophrenia; now it serves to initiate a treatment program and to protect the patient from any danger to himself or to others which might be caused by his disturbed behavior. The hospitalization at times is also helpful in order to isolate the patient from the emotional tensions related to family, work, and the other demands of everyday life. A good hospital offers the patient a structured situation which has a calming effect and facilitates recovery. Some have established psychiatric sections which integrate hospitalization with an over-all care of psychiatric illness furnished by the community mental health center. Of course, hospitalization can only be therapeutic in those institutions which have adequate staff and other facilities for the treatment and rehabilitation of the patient. The hospital must offer the proper milieu for a recovery of the patient. In effect, it should represent a therapeutic community in which all types of activities are available.

As soon as possible, a patient must participate in such group activities as group therapy, patient government, and recreational and vocational programs.

Various organic therapies have been used in the treatment of schizophrenia and other psychotic disorders. In the nineteen thirties, shock treatment with metrazol, insulin coma, and eventually electroconvulsive treatment (ECT) were applied to schizophrenics. In the nineteen forties and fifties, schizophrenic patients who showed no improvement with the help of any treatment approach were subjected to lobotomy, i.e., the nerve fibers connecting the frontal lobes to other parts of the brain were surgically severed. Lobotomy has been generally abandoned because of the uncertainty of its therapeutic effects and the severity of its side effects. Since the early nineteen fifties, a great many psychotropic drugs have come into use. This has made it possible to shorten the hospital stay of many schizophrenic patients and to maintain them outside the hospital in states of at least partial remission. The psychotropic drugs belong essentially to two groups: the tranquilizers and the antidepressants. By counteracting the severe underlying anxiety and disturbance of affect, these drugs have made it possible to eliminate restraints, isolation cells, and even most closed wards in psychiatric institutions. Recently, however, the so-called "revolving door syndrome" has been observed. Patients are discharged after a short hospitalization, suffer a relapse, and must be readmitted. This may happen repeatedly. The treatment of schizophrenia is largely pragmatic because the etiology of the illness is unclear. Reliance on drug treatment alone is insufficient and unsatisfactory. When the patient is discharged from the hospital, arrangements must be made for his life in the community, without exposure to the stress which contributed to the outbreak of his illness. If a full return to family or community is impossible, day or night hospitalization may be indicated. The patient, for instance, goes to work, but spends the time after work in the hospital. In other instances, he participates in the daytime activities of the hospital community, i.e., in individual, group, and milieu therapy, but spends the night and weekends with his family. At times, something akin to a foster home must be found for the patient after his discharge from the hospital. Half-way houses are extremely helpful in rehabilitating schizophrenic patients, in that they facilitate the transition from hospital to life at home and in the community. Patients can attend school or go to work and return to an atmosphere more acceptable to them than that provided by their families. The relationships formed at half-way houses are easier to tolerate than the more involved and ambivalent ones at home. The readily available activities at the half-way house are helpful to prople who find it difficult to reach out. Such institutions give the patients an additional opportunity to strengthen their defenses and bolster their self-esteem. It goes without saying that vocational retraining, job placement, or a return to school are likewise important measures to be planned and put into effect with the schizophrenic patient. It is obvious that in order for the patient to get the most effective treatment, social workers, nurses, psychiatrists, psychologists, and paraprofessionals must all make their contribution.

There are two essential aspects that may determine success or failure in the treatment of schizophrenia, aside from the training and competence of those engaged in the helping professions. First, it is necessary to respect the dignity of the patient, whatever his manifest behavior. Second, it is necessary for all members of the therapeutic team to work together in a concerted way to help facilitate the recovery of the patient.

REFERENCES

American Psychiatric Association (1968), *Diagnostic and Statistical Manual,* 2nd edition. Washington, D.C.: American Psychiatric Association.

Arlow, J. & Brenner, C. (1964), *Psychoanalytic Concepts and the Structural Theory.* New York: International Universities Press.

Bellak, L., ed. (1958), *Schizophrenia: Review of the Syndrome.* New York: Logos Press.

——— & Loeb, L., eds. (1969), *The Schizophrenic Syndrome.* New York: Grune & Stratton.

Bleuler, E. (1950), *Dementia Praecox or the Group of Schizophrenias,* trans. by J. Zinkin. New York: International Universities Press.

Cancro, R., ed. (1971, 1972), *The Schizophrenic Syndrome,* Volumes 1 and 2. New York: Brunner/Mazel.

Heston, L. (1970), The Genetics of Schizophrenic and Schizoid Disease. *Science,* 167:249-256.

Jackson, D., ed. (1960), *The Etiology of Schizophrenia.* New York: Basic Books.

Kallmann, F. (1953), *Heredity and Health in Mental Disorders.* New York: W. W. Norton.

Klein, D. & Davis, J. (1969), *Diagnosis and Drug Treatment of Psychiatric Disorders.* Baltimore: Williams & Wilkins.

Lidz, T. (1963), *The Family and Human Adaptation.* New York: International Universities Press.

———— (1973), *The Origin and Treatment of Schizophrenic Disorders.* New York: Basic Books.

Redlich, F. & Freedman, D. (1966), *The Theory and Practice of Psychiatry.* New York: Basic Books.

CHAPTER TWENTY-SIX

Borderline Personality Disorders

MERL M. JACKEL, M.D.

Although not officially recognized, the diagnostic term "borderline" has attained *de facto* recognition through common usage. It encompasses an apparently increasing number of people who simultaneously present indications of psychosis, neurosis, and health. The psychopathology lies primarily in disturbances in object relations, disturbances in relation to the self, and maturational failures in the development of certain basic ego functions. In daily life the "borderlines" may appear normal, or peculiar, eccentric, and even bizarre. Particularly in well-structured situations, as, for instance, in work, they may function well—at times even brilliantly. In unstructured situations, however, or under mild stress, their behavior may appear puzzling, incomprehensible, and even psychotic. This paradoxical picture led to a number of inappropriate diagnostic terms in the earlier psychiatric literature—"incipient schizophrenia," "pseudoneurotic schizophrenia," "ambulatory schizophrenia," "pseudopsychopathic schizophrenia." Today, these cases are set apart from schizophrenia and are considered borderline states or borderline personality disorders. In addition, many cases of psychosomatic illness, perversions, and addictions have an underlying borderline personality disorder and may be so classified. It should be noted that borderline states are not transient conditions occurring in the course of a breakdown from neurosis to psychosis, but stable ones reflecting the basic organization of the personality. Even where the behavior is, in ordinary descriptive terms, unstable, this has been a characteristic trait of the borderline personality all his life—the instability is predictable. Under great stress (or under the influence of drugs), he may decompensate and become overtly psychotic, but this usually is a transient phenomenon and he soon returns to his usual borderline state. From the standpoint of psychopathology, however, one may say that the borderline conditions are intermediate to normal, neurotic, and psychotic and may "border" on any one of these states.

What significantly differentiates the borderline patient from the psychotic is his ability to test reality, an ego function which remains *relatively* well-preserved (Frosch, 1960, 1964). What makes the borderline ill is that, despite this ability, he has difficulty in dealing with reality adequately.

A woman with a borderline disorder, married to a psychotic man, knew that he was "crazy," that he became violent, and that he constituted a real physical danger to herself and their children. Nevertheless, she was quite unable to take steps to protect herself and them, even when specifically advised to do so.

No one symptom is pathognomonic of borderline conditions, although there are some combinations of symptoms (to be described) which alert one to the possibility. What characterizes the borderline is failure in development and maturation of important ego functions. Often, stable secondary-process functioning has not been attained and regression to primary process is frequent. Such basic ego functions as the capacity to tolerate reasonable frustration, to delay discharge of tension where it is necessary, and to tolerate anxiety or guilt, are impaired.

A dentist developed pain in his abdomen. He correctly suspected he had appendicitis and decided to call the doctor. However, he knew the doctor would hospitalize him and forbid him to eat. He could not tolerate the frustration, so he had dinner and then called the doctor.

This man knew the dangers and consequences of his actions, but he could not act in accordance with his knowledge. Not infrequently, borderline patients are unable to think of the consequences of their actions. They seem, then, to lack "common sense." They will take out a loan without having in any way considered how they will repay it. They are often unable to think of alternative solutions in a conflict situation. For them, there is only one possible way to respond. In narcissistic types of borderline pathology there is an acute intolerance to feelings of shame or humiliation.

Some borderline patients are unable to differentiate within themselves a feeling, an impulse, and a body sensation. They tend to confuse past and present, with a readiness to recreate past experiences.

A young man re-created on his job his early family constellation. His boss represented the father he loved ambivalently; an elderly woman played the role of his mother, whose sympathy he sought and to whom he voiced many complaints about the boss; he was rivalrous with a younger female employee for the approval of the older woman, as he had been with his sister in the past. Under these circumstances he kept the job for two years. Then his boss was transferred and the elderly woman retired. The young man became so anxious he had to leave his job.

The borderline ego fails in its integrative and repressive functions. Marked opposites remain unresolved and unintegrated. Impossibly high ideals may be retained in the presence of gross delinquency. Primitive regressions occur quite readily. Overt incestuous fantasies or dreams may be readily reported. Often there is a preoccupation with fantasies of extreme aggression and with chaotic perverse sexual fantasies that interfere with the performance of routine tasks. The capacity for enjoyment is often limited, and emotions seem to lack depth or are distorted. Their inability to separate an observing self from an experiencing self is of great importance and makes therapy more difficult.

All borderline patients suffer from more or less severe disturbances in their object relations. This may be, in part, a consequence of basic ego defects as described above, but also may occur because the borderline patient has failed to negotiate successfully the separation-individuation phase (see Chapters Four and Five) and subsequent developmental steps. At first, will be remembered, the infant does not recognize the angry or frustrating mother as being the same person as the warm, feeding and caring mother. Eventually he acknowledges that the "good" and "bad" mother is one and the same person, but, under stress, he again splits the object image into two, one all good and all giving, and the other all bad and dangerous. This "splitting" mechanism persists in the borderline personalities, and, according to Kernberg (1967), is central to their pathology. As opposed to this primitive defense, the *neurotic* favors repression as his major defense. In order to go beyond the use of the primitive splitting defense, the young child must develop the capacity for object constancy.

Some borderline patients are fixated in a symbiotic phase. Separation for them means one or both partners will die. To counteract this, they cling, but then fear fusion and loss of their sense of identity. They may act and feel as if they were an appendage to the other person, or vice versa. At later stages of development, they experience every separation as tantamount to rejection. Some borderline patients project their own aggression onto the object and then feel the need to protect themselves from the aggression they have ascribed to others. Because they cannot feel separate, they have to control the object in order not to be destroyed themselves. They may defensively devaluate others or themselves. Some develop a completely passive attitude to the object, barely distinguishing their own wishes and drives from those of the object. The object then replaces some of the functions part of their own ego, superego, or even id should carry out. These mechanisms and needs are much more primitive than object choices based on sexual maturity, and it is a mistake to think of them as homosexual or heterosexual.

These primitive mechanisms also involve the nascent attitudes to the self. The all-good mother is associated with the all-good self, and the same applies to the all-bad mother.

Kohut (1971) has described a particular group of patients, generally included in the borderline category, although not quite as sick as most borderline cases, whose problems center around a particular type of narcissistic disturbance. Kohut points out that narcissism has its own lines of development, and that it is an error to think of narcissism and object relations as related purely reciprocally, that is, the greater the narcissism the less the object cathexis and vice versa. He points out that there is a healthy form of narcissism that shows itself as normal self-esteem, based on real accomplishments realistically evaluated. Such narcissism does not detract from, but rather enhances the possibilities of good object relations. In early years, the child idealizes the parents, regarding them as omnipotent and omniscient. The child can then have trust in them and use their protection in developing his own autonomous ego functions. At first, the infant requires the mother's constant physical presence. Gradually he strays further and further from mother, returning to her side periodically for "refueling." This is also seen in some borderline patients who use the treatment session in the same way. The basic trust in the mother, and, later, father, allows the child to use them for his own ego ideal, as well as to develop his own autonomous ego functions. He tries to be like them and think of them as being in many ways like himself. If this idealization is abruptly terminated for whatever reasons, the weak ego of the child has no alternative but to fall back on his own unrealistic fantasies of omnipotence. As a result, he cannot build up realistic self-esteem and is constantly in search of the idealized parent of his childhood. In a treatment situation, the therapist becomes the idealized omnipotent person, and must at all costs be kept in that role by the patient. Any sign of "weakness" in the therapist stirs up intolerable tension.

The borderline personality is often unable to maintain a consistent concept of the self. A man elected to Phi Beta Kappa, for example, may feel strongly that he is a moron. This can assume almost delusional proportions. A highly successful businessman felt that he really was a preadolescent boy who was fooling his associates. He was in constant fear of being "exposed."

In some cases, the ego boundaries are fluid. These people need closeness so as to get narcissistic supplies, yet simultaneously fear closeness because they are afraid of losing their identity. They are extremely vulnerable to narcissistic injuries, are readily hurt, and withdraw into haughty coldness. This alienates friends, and the alienation causes them additional pain. Because of their narcissism, they are unable to empathize with others, and instead feel confused and attacked by them.

Etiology

The basic causes, if one can speak in such terms, of borderline personalities lie in severe traumata occurring in the early years of life that leave in their wake developmental ego defects or weaknesses. Loss of one parent through death or separation before the age of six is common. Some of these patients had psychotic parents, or parents with severe emotional disturbances who constantly failed them in furthering maturation, and were unsuitable objects for identification. Others have a history of a severe illness in the first few years of life. If early hospitalization has been necessary and prolonged, one can be almost certain that there will be some lasting aftereffects. Congenital defects, whether apparent—as in birth marks on the face—or hidden—as in chest deformities or in cases of undescended testicle, leave their mark in disturbances of body ego concept and the sense of self. Similarly, severe illness, physical or emotional, on the part of the parent during the person's early life will leave its effects. The death of siblings when the person is young, or severe chronic illnesses of siblings can also disturb personality development. A common finding in borderline personalities, and one which often serves as a chronic trauma, is sexual overstimulation. Many patients tell of parents or a parent who customarily walked around the house nude, or report repeated exposure to the primal scene, or actual seductions by siblings of the same or opposite sex, or parents who carried on sexual affairs within the home, often in the presence of the child.

Differential Diagnosis

It is often difficult to differentiate a borderline personality structure from a neurotic and even from normal personalities in a single interview, for their psychopathology may not be readily discernible. Several interviews may be necessary in order to appraise ego functioning. We are alert to peculiarities in expression, blocking of thoughts, obliviousness to obvious implications of what the individual is saying, arbitrary inferences, inappropriate affect, suspicion-laden behavior, all of which may be clues to more serious disorder. A lack of purposiveness in an interview, inability to convey the reasons for their coming or the inability to identify with the interviewer and judge what information is pertinent, provide further clues. Similarly, the lack of evidence of unusual stress which might account for an emotional breakdown, or a lack of expectable concern in the presence of reality predicaments in their life, point toward a diagnosis of borderline personality. Inappropriate outbreaks of affect of any kind are noted. The difficulty the examiner feels in empathizing with the person is a similar warning. One should not content oneself with a history of the present behavior only. Past history may reveal, for instance, severe adolescent upheaval, with criminality, fire setting, robbery, etc., in someone who in his present behavior appears to be highly moral. In women, a history of marked promiscuity, of several marriages, of many hospitalizations, of several abortions, is significant. In men, frequent changes in jobs or long periods of unemployment need careful investigation. In both men and women, the fact that long periods of life are unexplained, or vaguely or poorly remembered, is suggestive of borderline pathology.

Borderline conditions must be differentiated from neurotic illness, even though neurotic symptoms, such as phobias and obsessions, may be presented as the chief complaints. The presence of marked free-floating anxiety despite definite neurotic symptoms is suggestive of a condition more serious than a neurosis. The presence of *multiple* phobias, especially those which impose severe restrictions on the patient's life, or phobias related to the body, e.g., fear of being looked at, or obsessive-compulsive symptoms that are rationalized and close to being ego-syntonic, or one or more somewhat bizarre or peculiar symptoms, or severe hypochondriasis are all suggestive of a borderline state—as are polymorphous perverse sexual trends and bizarre forms of perversion. Severe psychophysiological disturbances, such as prolonged amenorrhea without cause, marked and rapid fluctuations in weight, "binges" of any type, suggest more than a neurotic disturbance. Infantile behavior of significant degree, e.g., thumb-sucking, bed-wetting, or a generally infantile attitude toward life in an adult should also be viewed as indication of marked regressive trends and possible borderline pathology. Severe sadomasochistic behavior, particularly if not regarded as ego-alien, also belongs here.

Treatment

In general, working with those who present borderline pathology is more difficult and frustrating than working with neurotics. This is particularly true if one has in mind effecting internal changes. Some borderlines, however, are more capable of instituting changes in external life circumstances than are neurotics. Important in enabling them to do this is providing them with a constant relationship with someone they can feel is basically on their side. With this support, they institute changes, which, in turn, improve their sense of well-being, leading to most gratifying results.

Some borderlines are difficult to work with because they resent feeling dependent. Their need to test the limits in their conflict of dependency versus independence demands flexibility on the part of the caseworker. According to the type of borderline being dealt with, one may have to help him see alternatives, help him see the reality of a situation, define his affect for him, or even show him the appropriate affect. At times we may be dealing with a typical neurotic conflict and at other times with borderline pathology, all in the same person. Borderlines tend to be easily hurt (narcissistic injury) and prone to conceal their hurt in unexpected ways. Particularly difficult are these borderlines who seek closeness but fear identification or fusion. They mislead the therapist because, at the time when they are most desirous of closeness, they are most frightened of fusion and therefore seek escape. This may appear as negative transference or lack of interest. The therapist is required to tread a very narrow line between threatening the borderline's sense of identity or imposing feelings of rejection.

REFERENCES

Frosch, J. (1960), The Psychotic Character. *Journal of the American Psychoanalytic Association,* 8:544-548.

——— (1964), The Psychotic Character: Clinical Psychiatric Considerations. *Psychiatric Quarterly,* 38:81-96.

——— (1970), Psychoanalytic Considerations of the Psychotic Character. *Journal of the American Psychoanalytic Association,* 18:24-50.

Jacobson, E. (1964), *The Self and the Object World.* New York: International Universities Press.

Kernberg, O. (1966), Structural Derivates of Object Relationships. *International Journal of Psycho-Analysis,* 47:236-254.

——— (1967), Borderline Personality Organization. *Journal of the American Psychoanalytic Association,* 15:641-685.

——— (1970), A Psychoanalytic Classification of Character Pathology. *Journal of the American Psychoanalytic Association,* 18:800-822.

——— (1971), Prognostic Considerations Regarding Borderline Personality Organization. *Journal of the American Psychoanalytic Association,* 19:595-635.

Knight, R. (1952), Borderline States. In: *Psychoanalytic Psychiatry and Psychology,* eds. R. Knight & C. Friedman. New York: International Universities Press, 1954, pp. 97-109.

Kohut, H. (1971), *The Analysis of the Self.* New York: International Universities Press.

Mahler, M. (1968), *On Human Symbiosis and the Vicissitudes of Individuation.* New York: International Universities Press.

Rangell, L., reporter (1955), Panel on "The Borderline Case." *Journal of the American Psychoanalytic Association,* 3:285-298.

CHAPTER TWENTY-SEVEN

Senescence

MERL M. JACKEL, M.D.

Senescence is best regarded as a developmental phase comparable to latency, adolescence, and maturity. Such a view favors an objective approach and prevents both the overidealization and the pessimism so common in discussions of aging. We have seen how each developmental phase imposes demands on the ego's adaptive, integrative, and synthetic abilities. This is equally true of senescence. Whereas adaptation in other developmental phases deals with expanding potentialities for ego development, the senescent must adapt himself to diminishing abilities and shrinking opportunities.

It is difficult to obtain a consensus on when "aging" begins. Aging cannot be defined out of context; an athlete may be on his way out at 30; a businessman or professional of the same age may be merely beginning. In a sense, aging begins at birth. There is great variation in time of onset and rate of progress of physical aging from one person to another. Furthermore, individual parts of the human body may age at differing rates. Premature balding, graying, deafness, or loss of teeth are familiar examples, and the heart, blood vessels, joints, and musculature may show similar variations. The causes of physical aging are by no means clear. Heredity is certainly an important factor, and recent work in that field will undoubtedly make important contributions to our understanding. Environmental and emotional factors are also important. There is some evidence that atomic radiation accelerates aging in animals. We are familiar with those who, after a severe emotional trauma, "age overnight." Studies are being done of concentration camp victims in whom the same phenomenon occurred.

Psychologically, too, there is great variation. Some people are inflexible in their thinking and attitudes at 40, while others are still flexible at 80. This is not well understood. The chronological age at which a person begins to "feel" old is also variable and not always directly related to physical aging. The death of a spouse, relative, or friend may stimulate such awareness. Curiously, the occurrence of an illness unrelated to aging may produce an awareness of aging, leading to a depression which is otherwise inexplicable. Lack of awareness of aging involves mechanisms of rejection and denial, which will be discussed later.

The problem of the senescent can be subsumed under three categories: physical, psychological, and socioeconomic. Within each of these, the problems are almost invariably those of loss: loss of physical abilities, loss of psychological abilities, loss of family, friends, job, and status. The degree and extent of these losses and the individual's adjustment to them constitute the developmental phase of senescence, the subject matter of this chapter.

Physical and Physiological Changes in Aging

Although there may be great variations in the process of physical aging, sooner or later and to a greater or lesser degree, there are typical changes. The five major sensory modalities are all affected. Vision is altered by the loss of lens elasticity, and consequently bifocals are commonplace among the aging. The fact that bifocals do not fully compensate means there is a constant source of discomfort to which old people must adapt (and of which they may not even be aware). In addition, peripheral vision deteriorates, so that crossing a street becomes more dangerous. The old are also slower in adapting to changes in light intensity, and generally require more intense light to read or work comfortably. These changes may stimulate feelings of insecurity and are a source of strain throughout the day.

In the auditory sphere, deterioration is progressive in variable degrees. It involves high and low pitches unequally. As a result, the senescent may hear one person better than another, or hear one part of what is being said and not another. This exposes him to accusations of "hearing only what he wants to hear," a charge that may be true in some cases but does not rule out organic impairment. Important is the fact that deafness, partial or complete, pushes the senescent toward isolation and also makes him feel isolated. Loss of perception of background noises, such as street noises, birds singing, or door shutting, increases this feeling. The world outside becomes, acoustically speaking, dead. Curiously, it has been shown that the senescent's hearing ability in noisy surroundings is better than that of his younger counterpart. Such a paradox points up the need for accurate evaluation in situations where, for instance, the choice of job is involved.

The old person has less sensitivity to pain than the younger. This may mislead the family in evaluating illness, and the physician in diagnosing it. The sense of equilibrium may become disturbed, particularly when the head is tilted upward, making standing on chairs or stepladders particularly dangerous. The senses of taste and smell also deteriorate. Other significant physical accompaniments are wrinkling of the skin (due to loss of skin elasticity). Deterioration of the skeletal muscles impairs speed, strength, and endurance. Physiologically, throughout the body generally and in all organs there is a decrease in homeostatic function, that is, in the ability to return quickly to a previous level of functioning, to "bounce back." The old, when exposed to cold, take longer to warm up, when fatigued, need longer rest, when short of breath, take longer to recover.

The psychological impact of these physical changes is extensive and varies with the specific meaning of the particular loss to each individual. For a woman whose self-esteem has always been centered on her appearance, the impact of facial wrinkling may be devastating, whereas loss of physical stamina might be unimportant. The opposite would be true of a man who has prided himself on his physical strength. When physical changes lead to a loss of income, this becomes an additional trauma; when they interfere with pleasure previously derived from eating, reading, music, sports, or any other hobby, the deprivation can be severe. Many of these physical changes, by making reality testing more difficult, lend support to psychopathology latently present in the mature years. A disturbed sense of taste can encourage suspicions of being poisoned. A young person who suspects people of talking about him or laughing at him can, by approaching and listening, convince himself that it is only a fantasy. The older person, with some deafness, has less opportunity to correct such distortions. Uncorrected, these fantasies increase anxiety and further isolation. Isolation, whatever its cause, in itself affects reality testing because environmental responses, the ordinary give and take of life, serve as checks on uncontrolled fantasy life.

Failing physical functions make the preservation of the familiar important to the old. He is less afraid of the dark if he knows where every door and hallway is, where each piece of furniture is, and where help can be obtained on short notice. It is also easier to prepare for an event if it has been established as a routine. Unfortunately, at the very time that the familiar is most important, socioeconomic factors frequently make change necessary.

In considering the physical aspects of aging, one must include chronic illnesses. Although technically speaking this is not part of normal aging, statistically it occurs so often that it has been called "secondary aging." Almost 80 per cent of those over 65 have some form of chronic physical disorder; for 35 per cent of these, the disorder is severe enough to cause some disability. Two per cent of the aged are reported to be bedfast and six per cent are confined to their room or living quarters. Common conditions are cataract and glaucoma; chronic bronchitis and emphysema; arthritis; arterial hypertension; arteriosclerosis affecting either the coronary, cerebral, or kidney arteries; and malignancies of various kinds. The impact of these chronic illnesses is obvious. When it takes all one's energies to handle the everyday processes of dressing, bathing, combing one's hair, and moving about the house, little energy is left for interest in the outside world. This further tends to isolate the senescent and to cut him off from his established place in the family and in society. Furthermore, as with most people who become ill, the senescent often asks himself, "Why did it happen to me?". There is resentment at fate and at the world. When his resentment is directed against ambivalently loved ones, it is compounded by feelings of guilt. He also reacts with increased concern about his family's feelings for him, because feelings are now being put to the test by his increased needs. When the aggression is turned on himself, he may give up, become uncooperative, and unconsciously self-destructive.

Intellectual Functioning

Probably no aspect of geriatric research has given rise to more controversy than the standard test of intellectual functioning and performance. This is owing to the inherent complexities of human functioning as well as the difficulty in evaluating the intelligence test when performed on senescents. Memory, for instance, may be affected by emotional factors, accuracy of perception, and degree of interest and attention. Most intelligence tests emphasize speed and the ability to solve difficult problems. This handicaps the senescent and gives a distorted picture of his potentialities. In the important decisions in life, accuracy and judgment are more important than speed. Most intelligence tests do not allow for life experience, which may be more important than basic capacity. Standard tests measure disparate abilities, which may hold up differently—a fact not represented in the final score. Birren (1963, 1965) has shown that those subtests in the Wechsler-Bellevue test that measure stored information accounted for most of the loss in senescence. It has been shown that with aging, "set" (readiness to learn) for an activity assumes importance. Continuation of one activity results in better performance of that activity than if it immediately follows a distinctly different one. The senescent needs to be protected from the fatigue involved in lengthy tests and yet must be allowed time to "warm up." Lower scores achieved by the senescent have been shown to be due largely to defects in short-term memory. Here, inadequate perception and susceptibility to distraction are involved. There is evidence to show that skills which are maintained suffer less deterioration than those which are not. We do not know what effect the long-term lack of learning experience has on learning ability in general. Comparison between the senescent and the young can be invalid because of differences in background, schooling, and training. Other factors to be considered in evaluating these tests are motivation, anxiety, and depression. Old people are often not motivated to take these tests—or worse, are angry, rebellious, and actively nonmotivated. Anxiety and depression, so common in the old, handicap performance. The implications of these facts for rehabilitation of the senescent and for employment is obvious.

Social and Economic Aspects

Loss is the key word in senescence. The old loses family and friends, economic independence, status, familiar surroundings. Perhaps the greatest strain imposed on the senescent is the loss by death or otherwise of people important to him. These may be parents, children, siblings, spouse, friends, or employers. The effect will vary with the role the missing person played in the life (fantasy as well as reality) of the senescent. The effect is a constriction in his world, with a need to find substitutes, a task that might well strain the adaptive abilities of a younger person. When someone dies who has been loved ambivalently, unconscious feelings of guilt develop and contribute to depression. Furthermore, deaths are reminders of aging and impending death. Most important is the fact that these losses deprive the senescent of the opportunity to satisfy the basic human needs to love and to be loved, to have someone to care for, and to be needed.

Statistically, less than half of the population over 65 are employed. The economic consequences of this are apparent. Yet the functions of employment in the psychic balance of the individual extend far beyond economic aspects. Work has an organizing and regulating influence on his daily life. It often determines where he lives and what friends he has. It regulates when he goes to sleep and when he gets up. It is a source of prestige affecting his self-image and his sense of identity. For some, it is a symbol of the ability to function and imparts a sense of growth and development. For the man, and sometimes for the woman, it may symbolize masculinity. By its demands, it assumes superego functions; in the pleasures it gives, it gratifies the id through sublimations. By identifying with his firm or his work, the senescent establishes a sense of continuation of life after death. Work may satisfy a neurotic need to suffer and be punished. It may also serve to occupy time and as a distraction from feelings of unhappiness. It structures the day for the family as well. Many homes are disturbed when the father (or husband) remains home and no longer goes off to work each day.

America is traditionally a land of the young, the aggressive, and the pioneer. Rapid technological advances render the skills and knowledge of the senescent obsolete. Our society provides no clear socially recognized and approved way of aging. Unlike other cultures, ours does not offer the senescent a picture of how to grow old gracefully, effectively, and with dignity. Neither does his family. The attitude of the family (and of others who work with the elderly) is largely determined by attitudes learned in childhood. This includes, for any one individual, the attitude of his parents to his grandparents, as well as his own attitude to his parents and grandparents. As a result, the family and society at large often have for the old many of the irrational expectations a child has for his elders.

Perhaps in no area is this more apparent than in that of sexuality. The senescent is expected by his family and society to have given up all sexual desires and practices. Actually, sexual desire remains active throughout life, even if only expressed in fantasy. Research has shown that where opportunity is regularly available, sexual activity is maintained, although with less frequency, through late senescence. Yet the elderly male who exhibits sexual feelings is regarded as a lecher, and such desires in the female are regarded as unspeakably disgusting and "sick." The senescent himself often shares these views and suffers considerably from anxiety and guilt because of his continuing desires. For those senescents who accept sexuality in themselves, the attitude of society remains a potent deterrent, imposing unnecessary hardships on them. The atmosphere is so charged that often the senescent is prevented from showing ordinary physical affection to loved ones—the desire to be needed and to have love and affection is misinterpreted as sexually motivated. When old people marry someone much younger than themselves, it is usually as much for the need for love and affection as for sex.

Society and family frequently expect of the senescent that he give up without regret or resentment such feelings as a desire for a function in life, the need to feel loved and wanted, the need for security the desire to be respected as an individual, the desire to belong to and be a contributing member of a group. He is expected to no longer need rewards, gratification, or pleasure. Grandchildren may express it as "he has lived his life, now it is my turn." The family is surprised and disgusted when the elderly parent shows such human qualities as envy, jealousy, anger, or hurt. They are confused by the reversal of roles in which they are the ones who have the power to make the decisions, and are asked to give love and approval. This is particularly true when they themselves still unconsciously retain the desire for approval and authority from their parents.

There are both realistic and unrealistic reasons why the family and those required to work with the old have difficulty. Empathy depends on the ability to identify with the other person at least temporarily. Fears of identification prevent empathetic responses. People who have strong fears of growing old, of dying, of being helpless, of being useless and unwanted, fear identification with a person who epitomizes these fears. Similarly, people who are struggling to repress and control regressive impulses in themselves resent and reject elderly people who show regressive tendencies, even though these may be unavoidable.

Although one may recognize the reasons for the senescent's being as he is, there are realistic factors that make it unpleasant and difficult to work with him. He may exhibit depression, irritability, stubbornness, and garrulousness. He is sometimes physically repulsive in terms of odor, posture, cleanliness, and other personal habits. Often because of this, a vicious cycle of rejection and increasingly severe symptoms is established.

In contrast to the rather dark picture of senscence just described is another side which should not be ignored. Many old people report that they are as happy or happier than they were in maturity. Occasional ones may obtain their greatest success and productivity in old age. The relief from the economic and social responsibilities of maturity is welcomed to many. They now have time for hobbies and "doing what I want to do." Travel and other gratifications not available before can now be enjoyed. Those who have attained success and status can now enjoy it. Grandchildren are a source of endless pleasure. Some neurotic conflicts are attenuated in senescence, but others may then be gratified. A man's conflict, over passivity, for instance, may be lessened when there is no longer a need to be aggressive. If heterosexual functioning has been a problem for either man or woman, senescence makes avoidance acceptable. If the woman has resented family obligations and has desired a career, she may now gratify her desire.

From the psychoanalytic standpoint, one can examine the effects of aging on the id, ego, and superego. There is some question of whether id drives per se are decreased in the aging process, but there can be no question that the opportunities for discharge are lessened. This is particularly true at the genital level and to some extent accounts for the frequent regression (a subject to be dealt with shortly). The ego, weakened by physical deterioration, finds it more difficult to repress ego-alien drives and develops more and more anxiety. Under the pressure, the superego may regress in such a way that part of its function is given over to society or to important people in the immediate environment. In part, there is an attenuation of the superego. It has been suggested that modification of the superego in lessened demands for cleanliness, for instance, is an essential aspect of adjustment in aging.

The ego of the senescent, weakened by internal and external losses, consciously or unconsciously develops anxiety or depression. These differ from neurotic responses in that the losses have been real. The senescent does not merely fear the loss of his object relationships—he has in many instances actually lost them. He not only fears bodily damage; he has actually sustained such damage. Death is not only a threat in fantasy, it is an imminent possibility. The ego attempts to defend itself against these affects, first, by denial. Where such a defense is used excessively, it may threaten physical safety. Having denied physical aging, the senescent may also deny illness connected with it. He then may neglect proper treatment and engage in activities that can actually endanger his life. Moreover, denial often leads to unrealistic self-expectations with consequent frustrations, disappointment, and sense of failure. It often increases discomfort, for instance, by preventing the use of a hearing aid, glasses, or cane where needed. Rejection of one's own aging leads to rejection of other senescents and thus prevents replacement of friends and relatives who have been lost. At best, the denial of a reality which is omnipresent requires a great deal of psychic energy. Whenever events break through the denial, attacks of anxiety or depression follow. The ego then attempts to deal with this threat by an intensification of earlier defense mechanisms. Those who have been suspicious now may become paranoid; those previously using compulsive defenses now may become even more compulsive; those who have been overly careful in handling money now may become penurious. This mechanism is part of the basis for the broad statement that the kind of adjustment someone will make in the aging process is dependent on the kind of person he was in adult life. Failure in sustained adjustment in adolescence and maturity, often accompanied by neurotic illness, chronic unhappiness, unfulfilled and unsublimated yearnings, makes maladjustment in senescence more likely. Those who have felt cheated in maturity will feel more so in senescence. Conversely, when maturity has been satisfactory and gratifications have been reasonably sufficient, old age will be accepted and even enjoyed. When the ego's defenses become either greatly exaggerated or fail, the response is no longer within the normal limits of aging and may be regarded as pathological. Under such circumstances the senescent may develop any of the neurotic or psychotic illnesses that occur in maturity.

The common idea that the senescent regresses is expressed in the term "second childhood." Closer examination, however, makes it questionable whether the phenomena described fit into a psychoanalytic definition of regression. One must distinguish regressive-like behavior that is adaptive from regression that is defensive. Given the physical, psychological, and socioeconomic problems of the senescent, the reversal of roles so often taking place between him and his offspring may represent adaptation to reality. The elderly man who has become forgetful is not regressing when he asks his daughter to remind him of an important appointment. It is debatable whether the senescent's preoccupation with food and with bowel functioning, also cited as regressive—by implication, from the genital level—can be called regressive when, for various reasons, genitality is not available. Furthermore, such preoccupation is encouraged by the digestive and eliminative symptoms that go with deteriorated physiological functioning. Certainly, the elderly woman who has married and has raised children and now, in her later years, is preoccupied with food is not manifesting the same dynamics as the young woman who fears both sex and marriage and turns to food for consolation. The relaxing of standards of personal cleanliness is not necessarily a regression to the anal level, but rather an acceptance of the slowing-down process which makes adherence to earlier standards impossible. Often, of course, behavior contains elements of true regression as well as adaptive aspects. Miserliness, for instance, can serve both functions. Dwelling in the past, although a temporal "regression," may represent an attempt to hold on to memories of a time when functioning was on a more mature level. It is unlikely that the senescent's memory is actually better for past events than for the present. The present may be bleak; the past, particularly in distorted, idealized form often proves more gratifying.

Regressive behavior may be recognized as true regression when it is emotionally determined and is not realistically appropriate. Then too, many families tend to infantilize their senescents. This may be a mistaken way of being "good" to them, but it often happens because, consciously or unconsciously, it is more convenient for the family. It may be easier to make the elderly comfortable though inactive at home than to take them places and help them maintain contacts with the outside world.

The acceptance of a reasonable dependency by the senescent represents good adaptation. Many senescents maintain an irrational obstinate clinging to independence, which often makes them suffer unnecessarily and which may actually endanger them. This is a familiar problem to those who work with them. Elderly people, destitute and ill, live alone in walk-up flats, even when relatives are available and willing to help. Berezin (1965), who has written about this, points out that independence and dependence can have many meanings for the elderly. Independence may represent strength, whereas dependence represents weakness and helplessness. To some, independence represents usefulness and being alive, as opposed to aging and nothingness. Independence may be a compensatory device to combat feelings of inferiority and inadequancy. These feelings may always have been present, though defended against. Now they are accentuated because the defenses are threatened by physical and psychological decline. Secondarily, independence may be used as an act of hostility to arouse feelings of guilt and anxiety in the family. Also, the senescent may gain comfort from the fact that the family is concerned and thinking about him. A fear of imposing, with consequent loss of love, is often a factor.

In summary, we can include the following as being within the "normal symptomatology" of aging: the senescent shows a progressive decrease in self-sufficiency, regressive behavior, periodic mild depression, moodiness, irritability, querulousness, sensitivity to hurt, and often a tendency to cry. He may tend to withdraw or be annoyingly garrulous. He shows a clinging dependence or defiant independence. Life-long character traits, prejudices, and biases are intensified. He can be spiteful, sulky, and cunning. His interest in all things new, in forming new friends, in adopting new ways, is attenuated. There is a tendency to dwell in the past and to reminisce. Physically, he tires readily, is subject to insomnia, has a poor appetite, is prone to hypochondriacal complaints, and suffers from various psychophysiological disturbances and diminished sensory functions.

Protection and Promotion of Mental Health in Senescence

An effective program for dealing with the problems of the senescent must involve every level of our social structure. It requires effort at the federal, state, and community levels, as well as the specialized knowledge of sociologists, social workers, physicians, psychiatrists, architects, economists, teachers, industrialists, and union representatives. Finally, it requires a change in the attitudes and understanding of the family and of the public at large.

One important area in which effort can be directed is in the maintenance of optimal physical condition for the senescent. Diet must be regulated, and dentures, glasses, and hearing aids must be provided when needed. Anemia, failing heart function, and arthritic changes must be detected early and treated. Many senescents accept their aches and pains as "natural" and do not seek help. Regular and thorough physical check-ups are necessary. A tremendous stride in this direction has been taken by the creation of Medicare. This too, however, may go awry if the attitudes of families and physicians remain negative. The senescent has the right to live out his life in the best physical condition possible for him. The idea that the senescent's years are numbered encourages a pessimistic and neglectful approach. If one believes that nothing can or will be done, the need for accurate diagnosis is regarded as superfluous, and this will deprive the senescent of his right to the maximum help in the maintenance of his health.

One of the great fears of the senescent is that of being useless and therefore unwanted. This problem cannot be met by increasing his opportunities for leisure-time activities. He must have the chance for a useful and gainful occupation. As a group, senescents form a pool of manpower with experience, judgment, and conscientiousness, which could be used with advantage to both them and society. It is certainly incongruous that senescents are considered eminently qualified to sit on the Supreme Court and considered unsuitable for lesser activities. If retirement age were made flexible, depending on the individual abilities and the requirements or dangers involved in any particular occupation, a great deal of distress could be avoided.

Experience has shown that in our society the elderly do not do well living with their offspring. Freedom and a sense of independence are fostered by living away from the family, but this must not go so far as to encourage isolation. It has been shown that families that have been freed of feelings of guilt for not wanting to have senescent parents live with them are able to be more accepting. Studies in England have shown that even where the senescent lives with his family, the family members are more accepting of him if they can be assured that for a month out of each year he will be happily established elsewhere. It would be desirable to have low-cost housing units for the elderly interspersed throughout the general population centers. Tentative steps are being taken in the construction of dwelling units that take into consideration the physical limitations of the aged, their tendency to be forgetful, their need for the familiar, their need for adequate lighting, and other general pecautions for their safety. Where senescents cannot live alone, they may still be cared for in private homes geared to reminding them of such things as when it is time to eat or to take a bath.

A great deal can be done for the family of the senescent, and this would be indirectly helpful to the senescent as well. Education and simple explanation of some of the facts outlined in this chapter can be reassuring. Emotional support of the family in making the decision to institutionalize a senescent member where it is realistically indicated can be invaluable. It is important to deal with the relatives' feelings of guilt and with their rationalizations for not seeking placement of the senescent. Frequently it will be necessary to refer the family to appropriate agencies specifically geared to helping with these problems. As the senescent population increases, more and more of such resources are becoming available.

It is important to recognize that the goals of psychotherapy must be modified for the senescent. The aim is to enable him to continue in his ability to function, or to restore him, if possible, to previous levels of functioning. Here one must distinguish between reversible processes and those which are irreversible, either because of physical damage, or because the pattern is deeply rooted in the personality structure. One does not try to "break down" old defenses or to establish new ones; rather one tries to help the patient to re-establish or function with old defenses. Education, simple explanation, and practical suggestions can be of great value. For instance, the senescent whose movements are slowed may feel that he is lazy, and he may feel guilty because this disrupts family life. Explanations of physical changes and their effects, of which he may not have been aware, allow him to improve his self-image. A suggestion that he allot more time to dressing may allow him to reduce the irritation of his family, thus improving family relationships. Psychotherapy can often be brief; and once a secure relationship is established, sporadic interviews, with the knowledge that the therapist is available if needed, may be sufficient.

In summary, it can be said that an excellent beginning has been made in solving the problems of the senescent, but that much more remains to be done. Further research is particularly necessary to separate the facts about senescence from bias and fantasy.

REFERENCES

Berezin, M. A., & Cath, S. H., eds. (1965), *Geriatric Psychiatry: Grief, Loss, and Emotional Disorders in the Aging Process.* New York: International Universities Press.

Birren, J. E. (1963), *Human Aging: A Biological and Behavioral Study*. Chicago: University of Chicago Press.

——— (1965), *Handbook of Aging and the Individual*. Chicago: University of Chicago Press.

——— Butler, R. N., Greenhouse, S., Soholoff, L., & Yarrow, M., eds. (1963), *Human Aging: A Biological and Behavioral Study*. Bethesda, Maryland: U. S. Publich Health Service Publications, No. 986.

Granick, S. & Patterson, R. D. (1971), *Human Aging 2. An Eleven-Year Follow-Up*. Rockville, Maryland: Biomedical and Behavioral Study. Rockville, Maryland: National Institute of Mental Health.

SUGGESTED READING

Levin, S. (1963), Depression in the Aged. *Geriatrics,* 18: 302-307.

World Health Organization (1959), Mental Health Problems of Aging and the Aged. *Technical Report Series,* No. 171.

Zinberg, N., & Kaufman, I., eds. (1963), *Normal Psychology of the Aging Process*. New York: International Universities Press.

Group for the Advancement of Psychiatry (1971), *The Aged and Community Mental Health: A Guide to Program Development,* No. 81. Washington, D.C.: Group for the Advancement of Psychiatry.

CHAPTER TWENTY-EIGHT

Neurologic Aspects of Aging

LOUIS LINN, M.D.

The life process in health and disease, in youth and in old age, consists essentially of an ongoing series of adaptations to stress. Depending upon how effectively one adapts, an individual may be judged healthy—that is, functioning with unimpaired efficiency, he may be dying, or he may display a number of intermediate reaction patterns representing the full spectrum of disease, all of which are, in effect, the continuations of life in the face of handicaps. Viewed thus, a symptom or even a complex disease process is best understood as a reaction pattern having adaptational significance. For human beings, the life process is always *biopsychosocial:* without exception, it is the outcome of complex interacting forces which may be categorized in terms of biology, psychology, or sociology. The weight of each factor varies from case to case and, indeed, from day to day in a single case. A rational treatment plan depends on a full consideration of all three factors in any given instance.

In this chapter we will consider a biological factor: we will explore the way that progressive structural brain changes associated with old age affect the biopsychosocial equilibrium.

The Aging Brain

Sometime during the sixth decade of life the brain begins to lose weight. Millions of nerve cells disappear completely. This change is for the most part secondary to decreased blood flow resulting from generalized arteriosclerosis, heart disease, and stroke. Toxic and metabolic factors associated with disease elsewhere in the body, as well as nutritional impairment secondary to socioeconomic deprivation, contribute elements that act destructively on the aging brain.

Along with these structural alterations occur a variety of other changes. The electrical activity of the brain tends to slow down, particularly in the region of the temporal lobes. Over-all sleep time decreases. The percentage of time spent in Stage I sleep (so-called REM sleep or dream sleep) also decreases. The I.Q. as measured by the Wechsler Adult Intelligence Scale tends to drift downward with age. The ability to learn new facts is significantly impaired.[1] In addition, there is a generalized blunting of perceptual acuity.

A diminished capacity to perceive two stimuli simultaneously provides the basis for the Face-Hand Test for organic brain disase (Bender, 1952). If a normal alert adult with eyes closed is touched on his face and hand simultaneously, he recognizes both touches accurately and promptly. In settings of diffuse organic brain disease, including cerebral arteriosclerosis, the subject reports the face touch correctly, but does not report the hand touch at all or displaces it up towards the face and locates it incorrectly. Persistent errors on double simultaneous stimulation provide presumptive evidence of organic brain disease. This test is normally positive in children up to the age of four or five. It then becomes negative until age 60 after which it tends to become positive again. In the intervening years the test provides a useful presumptive sign. In elderly patients who are depressed and who give a positive reponse, the test tends to become negative as the

[1] According to one theory, the impairment of memory for recent events, which is characteristic of old age, is the result of a neurochemical exhaustion state caused by using up the RNA reserves, a chemical some people believe necessary for the storage of new data in the "memory bank" of the brain.

depression lifts. In all instances of a persisting positive response, further neurologic studies are required to demonstrate absolutely that organic brain disease is in fact present.

The aged brain has a diminished capacity to adapt to the effects of sedative medications; a quantity of sleeping pills easily tolerated by a younger person may produce disorientation and delirium in the aged. This vulnerability to sedative medications provides the basis for the Sodium Amytal Test for organic brain disease (Weinstein & Kahn, 1955). When sufficient amytal is injected to produce nystagmus and slurring of speech, disorientation may appear in a person who was previously oriented. This is a positive response. Up to age 60, a positive response is presumptive evidence of organic brain disease. Thereafter, the percentage of positive responders increases steadily with increasing age, in the absence of additional organic brain disease.

With all of these demonstrable evidences of impaired brain functioning in the senescent, it may come as a surprise to learn that the severity of their actual clinical psychiatric impairment is only slightly related to the severity of the brain damage found at autopsy. In the past, there was a tendency to overestimate the importance of irreversible brain damage in the etiology of the mental disorders of old age. This led to an attitude of pessimism concerning the value of treatment and, at times, to actual neglect. How remarkably labile and how responsive to treatment the old can be is exemplified by the following case history.

A woman, age 80, was referred for psychiatric evaluation because of a personality change consisting of extreme irritability, persecutory trends, periods of forgetfulness, and actual confusion. These changes had started abruptly about three months previously. The referral diagnosis was Psychosis with Cerebral Arteriosclerosis, secondary to recent small strokes.

During the interview, the patient was encouraged to discuss her life history. She wept bitterly and described in detail a lifetime of marital disharmony which she had accepted with considerable ambivalence out of an inordinately conscientious concern for her family and public opinion. After 55 years of marriage her husband retired from work, and they moved to a housing project for elderly people. This setting and the unaccustomed round-the-clock presence of her husband evoked an unendurable sense of entrapment. As she ventilated her feelings of despair, she showed no detectible signs of organicity. Indeed, her account was lucid and coherent, and her emotional tone was entirely appropriate to the content of her ideas.

By providing her with supportive psychotherapy and, in particular, by sanctioning her need to defend herself against her husband's clinging dependency, the patient achieved a sustained improvement.

On physical examination, the patient showed signs of aging. The Face-Hand Test, which was positive at the beginning of the first interview, became negative by the end of the first interview and remained negative on subsequent examinations.

What is one to conclude concerning the role of organic brain disease here? Extensive clinical data tells us that the aging of the brain does indeed impair the capacity to cope. Stresses that might have been mastered a decade earlier become overwhelmingly traumatic if brain alterations resulting from aging have entered the picture. This case cannot be deciphered by referring to the biological or brain-damage issue alone or to the psychological issues raised by the altered marital situation. The issue here is one which at the very least is psychobiological in nature.

In addition to individual life stresses such as those just described are certain life stresses which affect entire populations of the old, particularly if they come from a low socioeconomic stratum of society. If two groups of old people matched in all respects except for socioeconomic factors are compared, it will be found that the psychological and behavioral changes associated with aging occur earlier in the lower socioeconomic stratum. Furthermore these changes are more severe and more likely to result in admission to a state hospital. In fact, the senescents of the lowest socioeconomic stratum make up one out of every four admissions to our state hospitals throughout the country.

The Nature of the Biological Vulnerability

At this point it is fair to ask what is the nature of the biological vulnerability of the aging brain. The outstanding feature of the aging brain is its increasing dependency on external stimuli for continued normal functioning. If an old person is placed in a setting of sensory deprivation, as, for example, in a hospital after certain types of eye surgery, he tends to lapse almost invariably into episodes of disorientation (Linn, 1965). In most instances these episodes are swiftly and easily terminated by simple interventions of a family member the patient knows and trusts. On the other hand, continued separation from loved ones in a setting that is strange, lonely, painful, and terrifying can precipitate a lasting state of delirium. If one attempts to control the patient's terror with ill-advised use of sedative medications, the biological factor becomes still more heavily weighted on the side of mental disorder.

A familiar sensory input not only informs the senescent patient about his whereabouts, it also reassures him and hopefully serves to cheer him. In the absence of these supportive sensory inputs, he is easily catapulted into states of anxiety and depression. He is less able to draw on resources from within to maintain a continued state of sensory orientation and a normal mood state.

It is interesting that REM sleep, which some believe represents the innate mechanism for ongoing self-stimulation, falls off considerably with advancing years. The aged brain is peculiarly dependent on external stimulation for continued normal functioning. Given an intact family setting, access to friends and hobbies, and continued appropriate responsibilities at work and in the community, the subject may be so continuously "turned on" that his age-based vulnerability may go entirely unnoticed by himself and by others. A subject with the same level of brain functioning, who is socially isolated, who is deprived of family and community bonds, as well as of work and appropriate responsibilities, may find that the capacity to function on the basis of intellectual and emotional resources from within is insufficient to maintain a normal clinical picture.

The Varieties of Brain Lesions in Old Age

What can we say about the nature of the brain lesion itself? The impact of a given brain lesion depends on its size, the degree to which it is localized or diffuse, its rate of growth or change, and its location. A lesion of a given size which grows very slowly may be an accidental finding at autopsy and without clinical significance during the lifetime of the patient because the slow rate of lesion growth has permitted the brain to adjust to its presence. On the other hand, an identical lesion which appears suddenly—following a stroke or head injury, for example—may produce dramatic alterations in the patient's psychiatric picture.

In addition, the location of the lesion is important; a lesion of a given size may produce a rather circumscribed language abnormality called aphasia if, for example, it is confined to the speech area (a rather small area in the temporal lobe of the left hemisphere). Such a patient may be unable to pronounce the name of objects and yet be able to use them correctly or even to describe their use in rather sophisticated language. The effect of such a language impairment depends on the patient's premorbid personality. One may become severely depressed over it; another may become subject to tantrum-like outbursts, which result in further deterioration of functioning; still another may proceed cheerfully to develop substitute or accessory linguistic devices to overcome the basic handicap.

A lesion that is identical in every respect to the one responsible for the previously described aphasia may have an entirely different effect if located in the vicinity of certain centers that regulate consciousness and the general level of alertness. Such a lesion can produce widespread alterations in the subject's relationship to the world so that he becomes totally disconnected from reality. He becomes psychotic, in short, and lives in what may be described as a kind of waking dream. He tends to be disoriented for time, place, and person and may be unaware that he is sick or that he is in a hospital.

Just as a small lesion strategically located can produce widespread disorganization of brain functioning, so can an extensive lesion produce widespread functional disorganization simply because it is extensive. Subarachnoid hemmorhage, a rapidly growing brain tumor, a diffuse infection of the brain as in encephalitis, or in toxic states due to liver, kidney, or endocrine disease, toxic drug reactions, may all be cited as examples of extensive lesions that produce widespread functional disorganization.

In summary, one cannot speak simplistically of the neurologic aspect of aging. There are certain behavioral and psychological phenomena that tend to occur more frequently in relation to the aging brain; however, these may be present only in latent form and become clinically manifest only when other psychological and social factors also enter the picture. By the same token, we cannot generalize about other neurologic lesions affecting the brain. Whether a given lesion is a result of hemmorhage, thrombosis, embolism, brain tumor, infection, or toxicity, is of secondary importance in determining the clinical psychiatric picture. The impact on the over-all psychiatric picture will depend on the location and size of the lesion, the rate of its growth, the degree to which its effect on brain functioning is focal or diffuse, and not at all on the specific etiology per se. In addition the premorbid personality, the presence of specific psychological stresses, as well as the handicaps and frustrations attendant on a low socioeconomic stratum all contribute their elements in determining the final clinical psychiatric picture.

Psychological Manifestations of Organic Brain Disease

In relation to the senescent patient with diffuse organic brain disease, one often hears the statement that "the patient is confused." While the patient is, indeed, often bewildered, frightened, and disoriented, it is important to emphasize that there is much that is orderly in the symptom patterns he develops, and that some of the confusion, at least, is in the examiner's mind and in his failure to understand the patient. An orderly examination of an elderly patient depends on the use of an orderly set of questions. It is useless to ask a specific question unless we know the normal range of responses to that question. If we ask a hospitalized patient the date, for instance, it is well to know that errors for the day of the week, of the month, and even for the month itself are very common and not at all pathognomonic of organic brain disease. On the other hand, an error in the year usually is significant. The patient with organic brain disease who responds incorrectly tends to give a specific year. He does not choose some random year, but rather one which he will cling to and which he will repeat no matter how systematically one endeavors to correct him. Indeed, we cannot properly say that the patient's memory is impaired so much as that he deliberately and persistently chooses to remember incorrectly. Typically, the erroneous year is one which just precedes the onset of the patient's illness, as if to say that, for the patient, time stopped when his illness began. If we ask the patient the time of the day, errors are not significant unless they cross a meal time, and indicate that he confuses morning, afternoon and evening.

When questioned about orientation for place, the responses again are not random, but tend to follow a specific pattern. The patient may name the hospital correctly but locate it closer to his home, or he may give the name of a hospital he was in several years previously for some minor illness. The subject often misidentifies people about him, insisting that he knows them from a variety of benign settings in the past, even if they are, in fact, strangers to him.

It will be noted that these errors are consistent with a general attitude of denial of illness on the part of the patient. Indeed, if the patient is asked to describe the nature of his disability, he may state explicitly his belief that he is not ill at all, or that he is in the hospital for some minor illness, or that his concern is for some relative who is seriously ill, but that he himself is in good health. If such a patient is asked to account for his whereabouts on the previous night, he may deny that he was actually in his hospital bed and claim instead that he was in a social situation characterized by good health, physical mobility, and pleasant company.

We noted earlier that lesions affecting consciousness or the general level of alertness are particularly prone to disrupt total mental functioning and result in florid psychotic reactions. Here again the picture is complex. Clinical manifestations depend not only on premorbid personality, on psychological and social stress, but on the degree to which consciousness is impaired. Extreme impairments are most often associated with states of elation or apathy; intermediate impairments with paranoid states; minimal impairments with depressive reactions. In the transitions from one level of impairment to another, intermediate "defenseless" states may emerge in which extremes of terror associated with delirium are the principal features of the clinical picture. Thus, as a patient improves, he may show a spectrum of psychotic reactions in which severe depression paradoxically heralds the onset of recovery.

Organic Brain Disease and Late Life Depression

It is often said that depression is the most common psychiatric disorder of old age. One can go further and say that a tendency to depression is the universal fate of man if he lives long enough. Depression is the clinical syndrome reflecting a patient's response to loss and his attempts to cope with loss. In the old, loss of love objects presents a universal psychological problem. The loss of accustomed work role presents a number of social problems. And the loss of general physical health and brain power represent a major loss on a biological level.

In response to a major loss, people tend to go through a series of stages. Initially there are reactions of protest—an active struggle to deny the loss and a predominance of clinging reactions or of irritability and rage. When it is clear that the loss is irrevocable, grief and despair are the dominant responses. It is during this time that suicide is most likely to occur. If the patient survives this stage, then various forms of long-term adaptation appear; disengagement and social isolation may occur, with hermit-like retreat as one solution. Patients with basic ego strengths, particularly those who are gifted and creative and who have an extensive reservoir of socioeconomic resources to draw upon, are capable of amazing degrees of recovery from the reactions of depression in late life.

What is most important about the depressive reactions of late life is that it takes brain power to become depressed. The extensively damaged brain provides a setting that somehow facilitates wishful thinking and regression. Such a brain-injured patient may become silly, elated, apathetic, or paranoid as part of the previously alluded to delusional system that we call denial of illness. As the patient's brain damage subsides, however, his capacity for denial also subsides. As the grim reality of his illness becomes inescapably apparent, the previously cheerful patient becomes depressed. Thus, the emergence of a severe depression is often a paradoxical sign in the sense that it signals clinical improvement. By the same token, depression, which is the commonest psychiatric symptom in old age, is also the most hopeful sign. Depression is never caused by brain damage. It is a feeling which can be generated only if a substantial part of the brain is still intact. It is a realistic cry for help and an attempt to re-establish a remembered state of previous intact functioning. For this reason, late-life depressions deserve our most serious and even heroic therapeutic efforts, regardless of the patient's age or general physical condition.

REFERENCES

Bender, M. B. (1952), *Disorders of Perception.* Springfield, Ill.: Charles C Thomas.

Linn, L. (1965), Psychiatric Reactions Complicating Cateract Surgery. In: *Complications After Cateract Surgery,* Part Two, ed. F. H. Theodore. Boston: Little, Brown.

Weinstein, E. A. & Kahn, R. L. (1955), *Denial of Illness.* Springfield, Ill.: Charles C Thomas.

SUGGESTED READING

Busse, E. W. (1967), Brain Syndromes Associated with Disturbances in Metabolism, Growth and Nutrition. In: *A Comprehensive Textbook of Psychiatry,* eds. A. Freedman & H. Kaplan. Baltimore: Williams & Wilkins, pp. 726-729.

Ferraro, A. (1959), The Senile Psychoses. In: *American Handbook of Psychiatry,* ed. S. Arieti. New York: Basic Books, pp. 1021-1108.

Goldfarb, A. I., (1959), Geriatric Psychiatry. In: *American Handbook of Psychiatry,* ed. S. Arieti. New York: Basic Books, pp. 1564-1587.

Linn, L. (1955), *A Handbook of Hospital Psychiatry.* New York: International Universities Press, pp. 201-216.

CHAPTER TWENTY-NINE

Psychological Testing

MIRIAM G. SIEGEL, Ph.D.

Through the use of psychological tests, the clinical psychologist contributes to the understanding of personality dynamics and to the formulation of treatment plans. The challenge of each testing experience is the portrayal of human uniqueness. This objective involves logical yet sympathetic regard for the total person, his distress, his disturbance, and his health. The most enlightening psychological report is neither too general nor too specific. It distinguishes between disease and transitory impairment of functioning, accepts limitations on the scope of testing, and exerts restrains on predictive expectations.

Uses of Tests

Clinical experience has demonstrated the value of psychological tests. Standardized scoring systems and quantitative measurements provide safeguards against subjective distortions and bias. The estimate of intelligence, its quality, how it is used or not used, is of unequalled value. Tests provide explicit measures of the discrepancy between intellectual potential and actual performance. They show impaired efficiency related to organic disorder and psychological conflicts. In exposing the underlying personality structure, tests make a signal contribution in confirming or contradicting equivocal clinical observations. At the inception of treatment, tests add to the initial orientation of the therapist, to dynamic understanding of the defensive pattern, to transference phenomena, to prognostic assets and liabilities. In longitudinal studies, test data obtained during the initial phase of therapy serve as a baseline for determining future maturational progress and the effectiveness of therapy. Test findings contribute to the selection of the proper treatment modality, referral for residential treatment, establishment of remedial programs for learning disabilities, for vocational choices.

Test Behavior

To the subject, the psychologist represents one member of the therapeutic family. Behavioral manifestations in the test situation often repeat those encountered in treatment settings. However, the shift in milieu, the transposition from therapist to tester, and the introduction of stress associated with standardized demands, elicit revealing changes of attitudes. The psychologist's observations of the subject's behavior are reinforced by test data.

The examiner remains alert to separation anxiety in its gross and subtle forms. In extreme cases, neither parent nor child can tolerate even a brief absence from one another. In those rare instances when the tests must be administered in a parent's presence, their symbiotic interplay is acted out. Separation anxiety has many disguises: arduous farewells as though the child were embarking on a perilous voyage, histrionic displays of affection, loving reunions, kissing, and body merging. Important clues appear in the mother's willingness or reluctance to remain neutral, or to intervene through bribes and threats. The parent's anxiety and narcissistic expectations are expressed in overconcern with the child's achievements. Adolescents come fortified with a friend, adults with a spouse or fiance. At the end of the examination, separation fears may emerge, unpredictably, with a displaced target—the testing psychologist. Some clinging adolescents find each departure traumatic, even from a figure that initially posed an authoritarian threat. Obsessive adults who mask anxiety with skepticism and intellectualized curiosity are unwilling to terminate the test contact without chewing over the procedures. Requests for textbooks on testing are not uncommon. For some subjects, the tests become a painful ordeal. They show a simmering rage, as if they were trapped. Their grudging compliance explodes in an impulsive flight from the office. Their fears of relationship and of exposure are reinforced by panic in their test reactions. Barriers to the test relationship, avoidance of intimacy, fear of intrustion into privacy represent silent but potent obstacles to testing.

During the tests, motility patterns are carefully noted. Rigid posture and excessive restlessness may be rooted in conflicts about impulse control. Organic brain damage may produce pathological restlessness, purposeless or even bizarre movements. Overexcitement also stems from traumatic sexual stimulation, with intolerable inner tensions that lack acceptable outlets for discharge. Volatile behavior at home or in the classroom may create the impression of organic damage where none exists. Masturbation equivalents appear in rocking, twitching, sensuous manipulations of clothing and body parts. In some adolescents, the fear of being found out contains autoerotic guilt that can be mistaken for paranoid distrust. Fear may impel the subject to avoid eye contact with the examiner. Or hostility is expressed in a menacing glare. A fixed gaze may also represent attempts to latch onto a segment of reality. Clothing, in terms of cleanliness, appropriate choice, seductive exposure, or body concealment, provides the tester with further clues. Acceleration or retardation of speech is a significant behavioral aspect of testing. Impediments, stuttering, moments of heightened stress, modifications in grammatical usage are meaningful. To enhance their infantile facade, some children assume the use of baby talk. In testing, as in other clinical contacts, words may be used for communication or avoidance. The subject's speech provides numerous diagnostic and dynamic clues. He may use language as an aggressive weapon, as a means of denial, or, in psychotic deviation, in bizarre ways.

Hunger, both affective and literal, dominates some testing experiences. Depressed children with an entrenched anticipation of oral disappointment come fortified with their own supplies. Their continuous self-feeding of candy, crackers, or gum reduces ease of communication and clarity of speech. Testing requires a measure of trust, whose presence or absence is diagnostically revealing. Phobic fears, masked in the therapeutic contact, may emerge in the unfamiliar test surroundings. Test anxiety brings characteristic defensive patterns to the fore. An exaggerated passive compliance is often belied by contradictory attitudes in test reactions. Depression is mirrored in an apathetic approach, limited mobilization of energy, elusive goals, pessimistic expectations, or a readiness for retreat. Observations related to dependency needs and frustration tolerance are illuminating. Exaggerated requests for assistance may take the form of infantile whining or subtle seductive maneuvers. The examiner's reassuring, nonpunitive approach helps the subject to tolerate frustration, to allay intolerable anxiety, and avoid flight. Limitations must be set, however, on the insatiable and often inappropriate demands of children who have suffered from severe emotional deprivation.

Types of Tests

To obtain a fully rounded, undistorted picture of the whole person, a complete battery of tests must be used. Each test measures different yet interrelated aspects of personality. The psychological examination is administered on an individual basis, in contrast to paper and pencil tests used in school and group settings. The psychologist's choice of tests is intended to obtain data relating to inner strengths, weaknesses, and degree of disorganization. Broad categories include measures of intelligence, personality, educational achievement, vocational aptitudes, and interests. The present discussion is limited to several tests that are useful in therapeutic practice.

Both intelligence tests and personality tests are indispensable for representative measures of potential and functioning. In the revisions of the Wechsler Tests, acceptable time-tested items are retained. Others that are obsolete, ambiguous, or unfair to cultural minorities are discarded. The choice of intelligence tests depends on the age level. The Wechsler Preschool and Primary Scale of Intelligence (WPPSI) is used for children below the age of six. The Wechsler

Intelligence Scale for Children (WISC) is geared to the young school-age child. The Wechsler Bellevue Intelligence Scale (WB) or the Wechsler Adult Intelligence Scale (WAIS) is given to adults and adolescents. The Rorschach Test is basic to the evaluation of the personality structure. Stories from the Adult Thematic Apperception Test and the Children's Apperception Test enrich the dynamic picture. The Bender Gestalt Drawings provide information about visual motor development and organic dysfunction. Human Figure Drawings reflect body-image representations. This integrated approach to testing is in contrast to earlier psychometic aims, whose primary stress was on numerical scores, intelligence quotients (I.Q.'s), and percentile ranks. Dynamic synthesis and analysis are emphasized, rather than mechanistic, interpretative procedures that result in isolated personality tendencies.

Intelligence Tests

Intelligence tests, unlike the unstructured personality tests, contain specific tasks that measure intellectual efficiency at the time of testing. They reveal intellectual assets based on native endowment and the present functioning level, whether intact or disrupted. Years ago, in their initial stage, I.Q.'s were considered fixed and unyielding to change. This has been modified toward a less static view of the individual. Discrepancies between potential and actual achievement are related to complex psychological and socioeconomic factors. A home barren of sensory and verbal stimulation hinders intellectual growth as well as maturational development. Educational opportunities in the broadest sense, both at home and at school encourage intellectual curiosity; their absence restricts it. Psychological factors and organic impairment reduce the level of mental functioning. A careful scrutiny of achievements and deficiencies on the intelligence test reveals the crystallization of some functions, the disturbance of others, vicissitudes of maturation, and the defensive structure that maintains mental equilibrium.

A description of items from the various Wechsler tests will demonstrate the rationale of intelligence testing. They consist of 12 subtests. The Verbal Scale contains six parts: Information, Comprehension, Arithmetic Reasoning, Similarities, Vocabulary, and, as a supplementary subtest, the Digit Span. The Performance Scale also includes six subtests: Picture Completion, Picture Arrangement, Block Designs, Object Assembly, Coding or Digit Symbol and the Supplementary Mazes. After a specified number of failures, the subtest is discontinued. Some items are timed, others are not. A manual with directions for administration and scoring standards is available to the examiner. Through the use of weighted scores, three I.Q.'s are obtained: the Verbal I.Q., the Performance I.Q., and the Full Scale I.Q. The relationship of each subtest score to others within the total test configuration, and tendencies within each subtest represent the basis of evaluation. The deviation from the average subtest score, either upward or downward, furnishes a quantitative measure of intellectual functioning. The analysis of the subdivisions of the Wechsler, in conjunction with other tests in the battery, clarifies the quantitative aspects of intelligence.

Questions on the Information subtest range from simple to difficult ones. One aspect of intellectual efficiency rests on the assimilation of knowledge. Performance on the Information subtest is negatively affected by growing up in an inadequate socioeconomic environment. A low score may be misinterpreted as evidence of intellectual limitations. Anxiety interferes with the recall of Information, yet this may be a transitory phenomenon. Psychotic disturbances are expressed in unpredictable errors and lacunae of knowledge. Isolated instances of internal contradiction may not be pathological, but they alert the examiner to other signs of deviation. Forgetting and not knowing may be momentary or they may be indications of a serious disturbance. The inaccessibility of a bit of Information is frequently associated with repression, and the inability to recall it is accompanied by visible distress. Relief is evident when the forgotten item is blurted out later, sometimes in an inappropriate context. An exaggerated anxiety about forgetting may relate to an awareness of impaired functioning. Blandness in this context may represent a weakening grip on reality. Some obsessive-compulsive subjects obtain a conspicuously high score on the Information subtest without the corroboration of a corresponding level of conceptual performance in their other test productions. They disguise feelings of inadequacy and cling to reality through pedantic display of erudition. The abundance of information at their disposal is linked to their lack of creative imagination in the Rorschach and other personality tests. Amassing information serves the purpose of absorbing anxiety and achieving security, but this goal is not attained. For some subjects, not knowing is a painful blemish on their narcissistic omnipotence. At the other end of the defensive spectrum, negativism to acquiring knowledge, aversion to knowing and understanding, are translated into inhibitions of normal curiosity. Such pseudostupidity is associated with conflicts about learning. A low Information score also indicates depression and withdrawal of interest from the environment. In schizophrenic thought disorders, specific aspects of reality and knowledge may acquire symbolic meaning, and the response is bizarre.

The Comprehension subtest consists of 14 items. On the WISC, it begins with, "What's the thing to do if you cut your finger?" Similar appropriate items are included in the Wechsler Test for other age groups. The Comprehension subtest tests logical thinking, evaluation of reality, judgment, and appropriateness of affect. It often provides clues to emotional immaturity and lack of impulse controls. When judgment is impaired by excessive doubting, the subject includes too many alternatives, and the ability to act may become paralyzed. "What should you do if while sitting in the movies you were the first person to discover a fire?" produces numerous alternatives in regard to judgment and control. The "nonconformist" bristles at, "Why should we keep away from bad company?" For some, their defensive rebellion is deeply entrenched. Others, who are less threatened and less rigid in their need for defiance, use intellectualized compliance to meet the conventional demands of society. "What's the thing to do if you find an envelope in the street that is sealed, addressed, and has a new stamp?" may evoke concealed or overt psychopathic trends. Each Comprehension item provides diagnostic and dynamic clues. A discrepancy may exist between an intellectual awareness of socially acceptable standards and inappropriate acting-out behavior. In some subjects, verbal glibness and superficial conformity in this subtest are contradicted by the opposite reactions in the personality tests. The deficiency in human contact and the loss of object constancy common to institutionalized and deprived children are evident in their blunted and often primitive responses on the Comprehension subtest. Some social situations presented to them are so thoroughly beyond their life experiences as to produce bewilderment and reinforce feelings of inadequancy. Sensitivity to sociocultural factors that have interfered with intellectual growth is an important requirement in test interpretation.

In the Arithmetic Reasoning subtest, the ability to concentrate on the task, reasoning, and the manipulation of numbers are primary factors. In contrast to other subtests on the Verbal Scale, facility with words is not decisive. The subject must make a conscious effort to examine, choose, and organize established arithmetical patterns. Emotional conflict and anxiety interfere with this effort and depress the score. Obsessive doubting also impairs attention to the immediate stimulus. In some schizoid individuals, the capacity for exclusive concentration is confined to arithmetic and disturbed in related tasks. Weak skills in Numbers at the preschool level may be detected in the WPPSI. Poor arithmetic reasoning is indicative of a maturational lag, of temporary loss of intellectual efficiency, or of critical personality disorganization. In accordance with the general principles of test analysis, accuracy of choice among these possibilities relies on the total test pattern.

The Similarities subtest measures cognitive development. It repeats the characteristic construction of the other subtests and includes items of gradual increasing complexity. Scoring criteria relate to the level of abstraction that is achieved. Cognition involves logical thinking, conceptualization, problem solving, and abstract skills essential for learning. These functions are adversely influenced by developmental lags, emotional maladjustment or an empty cultural environment. This subtest retains a high degree of diagnostic sensitivity. It reveals cognitive weakness in incipient form at the preschool level, and it has predictive value for future academic achievement. The Similarities subtest measures ability to recognize abstract grouping and their relationships. This entails spontaneous determination of the connection between two seemingly disparate objects. A low score may relate to limited intelligence or, in better endowed subjects, to maturational arrest, defective reality testing, schizophrenic or organic disorganization.

One Similarity on the WISC refers to a cat and a mouse. Some children whose thinking is fixed on a concrete level tenaciously refuse to explore a possible likeness. They become anxious, antagonistic, and repeatedly stress the differences. Another child, who relies on concrete rather than abstract thinking, enumerates the body parts—fur, legs, tails, eyes. In this instance, the part assumes the properties of the whole or the general: the choice that is reached after a complex process of organization and selection of memory images is too limited and not sufficiently exclusive. Conflictual fantasy and infantile drives color some responses. "The cat eats the mouse," has oral sadistic overtones. Weakened reality testing is suggested in, "The mouse eats the cat." Aggressive and sexual preoccupations are expressed in, "They both have claws," or "They both have babies." Ostentatious formulations, reiterations, doubting, and intellectualizations are consistent with an obsessive orientation in other test reactions. A subject with a superior score on the Similarities subtest may show inhibition and lack of spontaneity in his use of this skill. Schizophrenic subjects express their conceptual deviation through references to abstruse aspects of the objects.

The Digit Span test consists of two parts. In the first, the subject directly repeats series of numbers given by the examiner. The second part involves repetition of digits in reversed order. Repeating a sequence of numbers, of course, requires less effort than reproducing them backwards. In each instance, release from extraneous thought and emotional distraction is essential for successful achievement. The Digit Span is a test of memory, although not in its full clinical sense. Recent memory may be intact, yet anxiety disrupts immediate attention. A loss on the Memory Scale may be transitory or it may signify a break with reality. Memory, especially in reversed sequence, is impaired in brain-damaged subjects. The total test configuration determines whether learning occurs on a rote or conceptual level. The child who combines superior Information and Memory with a weak Similarities score, substitutes rote repetition for logical organization. His educational problems may not become disabling until he reaches the higher grades with their increased demands for cognitive thinking.

Vocabulary is the final test on the Verbal Scale. Scoring, here, is determined by the calibre of the definition. Although the Vocabulary level is essential to the evaluation of general intelligence, this subtest score cannot be used as a reliable gauge of native endowment in subjects who have grown up with cultural disadvantages or insufficient mastery of English. A full battery of tests provides other reliable avenues for the assessment of "nonverbal subjects." Words represent essential tools for thought, modulation of feelings, and delay of impulses, and a home deficient in oral communication and consistent emotional care retards speech development. The amount and variety of stimulation in the early years are more significant than subsequent educational experiences. The child who enters first grade with an inferior vocabulary is seriously handicapped in his equipment for learning. The residue of such deprivation often persists in the adult's primitive usage of language.

Vocabulary is relatively stable and less susceptible to deterioration than the other functions measured by the Wechsler. Language development relies on an accumulation of knowledge and experience. Words, like Information, may be repressed. A "not knowing," "not understanding," may represent a defense against anxiety aroused by intrapsychic conflicts and forbidden impulses. Because they constitute one aspect of his verbal content, the subject's definitions are examined for deviations and diagnostic clues.

Performance Tests

The Wechsler Performance Scale consists of five nonverbal subtests. Several parts require vocalization to communicate the subject's response to the examiner, but the content is not based on language skills. In the Picture Completion subtest, the subject is confronted with drawings of commonplace objects in which an essential element is missing. Only one response is correct. The task is to find the gap in the pattern, to discover the basic inconsistency. This involves a complicated interrelationship of concentration, reasoning, and anticipation. Failure is determined by multiple factors. A narrow cultural horizon contributes to unfamiliarity with the outside world and decreases the score. Differentiation of details, discrimination between the essential and nonessential, represent aspects of reality testing. Weakened concentration on the Picture Completion may be associated with fantasy withdrawal and loss of interest in the environment. Affective stress disturbs this form of visual perception.

Obsessive doubters worry about the form and identity of the object. A young boy with severe body-image confusions patted his meager chest as he examined the picture of the cow; he missed the uncleft hoof and substituted, "The part where you get the milk." The paranoid subject, who is overalert to impending dangers in his environment, expresses in the Picture Completion his distorted sense of reality.

The Picture Arrangement subtest, like the Picture Completion, requires less motor action than the other subtests on the Performance Scale. A sequence of cardboard pictures, some conventional, some sophisticated, must be rearranged into a meaningful story. As a corollary to the Comprehension on the Verbal Scale, this subtest relates to judgment and the ability to translate an understanding of social situations into concrete behavior. In creating the sensible story sequence, the subject is required to plan and foretell the consequences of his initial actions. Without an integration of attention, reasoning, selection, and motor control, the pictures cannot be organized into a realistic pattern. Deviations in the Picture Arrangement relate to limited awareness of social relationships. The smooth verbalizations of some subjects expose their attempts to create a favorable impression on others. This, however, does not represent a true recognition of social situations, and a defensive purpose is established by an erratic, infantile, even chaotic approach to the Picture Arrangement. The pressures of maintaining a facade are corroborated by the personality tests. Narcissistic characters and schizoid individuals with an "as if" emotionality use this "social" awareness for devious ends, as a manipulative ploy. Bizarre arrangements on this subtest provide added evidence of defective reality testing and schizophrenic distortions in other test data.

The other three Wechsler performance subtests specifically investigate visual motor development. They are sensitive indicators of functional disturbance in various diagnostic categories. The Block Designs subtest uses blocks of varying colors. After sample demonstrations by the examiner, the subject is asked to reproduce geometrical forms on a card placed before him. The time limits are generous, and a bonus is given for extra speed. The visual motor coordination involves initial scrutiny of the total pattern and differentiation of the parts from the whole. Rigidity or flexibility results in considerable individual variation. Some subjects immediately perceive the pattern, and their responses are quick and efficient. Others approach the subtest in a piecemeal, disorganized fashion that results in aimless, unguided, motor action. Other tests in the visual motor coordination group help determine whether this defect is of a temporary or lasting nature.

The Object Assembly subtest, unlike the Block Designs test, does not utilize geometric designs. The task is productive, not reproductive. The scoring again involves liberal time allowances and speed bonuses if difficult problems are solved quickly. This subtest is based on a jigsaw combination of familiar objects, a manikin, a horse, a human profile, and others. The broken-up parts may be identified and arranged quickly into a cohesive whole. Subjects with well-developed perceptual ability may show an impairment based on motor deficit. Identification is delayed, and the object is recognized only after preliminary tentative moving about of the separate parts. In this subtest, two processes are involved: visual recognition and spontaneous progression to motor action. Subjects with weak spatial organization have difficulty with this complicated visual motor task. The response may be imaginative and organized, or concretistic and limited.

A qualitative analysis of the approach to the Object Assembly is illuminating. Doubts about identity may be manifested in excessive concern about the manikin's gender. Worry about size, about doing and undoing in the placement of the legs frequently has connotations of castration anxiety. The "compassion" of some children for the cut-up object may relate to body-image anxiety. If extreme, it suggests defective reality testing. Or a subject directs his resentment against the examiner who disassembles an object after his efforts to assemble it. The restructuring of the object, however transient, relates to the self-image. Individual restlessness may be displaced to the object. With dramatic sound effects, an overexcited little boy tried to move the car around. His distress at the inevitable fragmentation was inappropriate; his fantasies about the crash and his role in dismembering the object he had created were associated with his phobic fears and aggressive tendencies.

In the Digit Symbol subtest, or the WISC Coding, the subject is shown a sample line of symbols and numbers on the top of the sheet. Below this, are rows of empty squares with a random placement of the numbers. He is asked to write in the empty square the symbol associated with that number in the sample. A similar test on the WPPSI for preschoolers, who have not yet developed this symbol-number association, is the Animal House. The child is presented with a board with animal pictures and different colored cylindrical pegs. He has to find the right color house for each animal. Time and accuracy are scored. This reproductive form of visual coordination relates to associative learning ability. Subjects with a neurological deficit suffer from an impaired connection between visual perception and reproduction of the symbol. The inability of the motor apparatus to carry out the visual instructions might be likened to an electrical short circuit.

Psychogenic disturbances are also expressed in this subtest. Psychomotor speed is slowed up in depressed, anxious, fantasy-ridden subjects. The obsessive doubter who is overconcerned with accuracy, precision, checking, and rechecking, accomplishes little within the time limit. Strains and defensive devices noted in other Wechsler subtests are confirmed or contradicted in the Coding. A lackadaisical or negativistic approach to other tasks may contrast with a spurt of energy in copying the symbols. An unstable hasty response may result in illegible symbols. This approach interferes with learning and study habits. Some subjects are more efficient when they are on their own, without the distraction of personal contact. Others are made anxious by enforced isolation and withdrawal of supervision. The child's response to the Coding often approximates his adjustment in the classroom.

Visual motor activity may be habitual and, like certain verbal functions, characterized by automatic patterns. Unfamiliar tasks require increased flexibility. In these Wechsler subtests, conscious judgment is transmitted into motor action. Success or failure is determined by interrelated neurological and psychological factors. The equilibrium between verbal judgment and motor action is impaired in brain-injured subjects. Their visual organization may be intact, but the carrying out of the verbal demand is retarded. Yet a deficiency in these Wechsler subtests does not provide incontrovertible proof of a neurological deficit. In other pathological reactions, the disorganizing panic that sets in creates a pseudo organic impression. The overideational obsessive and schizoid subject exposes, in these subtests, the disabling anxiety that accompanies the loss of his language support. Clues to native intellectual endowment are also provided by the visual motor achievements of verbally inarticulate subjects.

Conclusions on the Wechsler Tests

The concluding analysis of the subject's Wechsler reactions is based on his numerical subtest scores. Some variations in performance are not uncommon. A superior visual motor organization in the Block Designs may be associated with weak verbal conceptualization in the Similarities. Wide "scatter" and fluctuations between verbal I.Q. and performance I.Q. are diagnostically significant. Discrepancies are evaluated in terms of cultural determinants, characterological tendencies, degree of intactness, of acceleration and arrest of various functions. Losses may represent temporary inefficiency or lasting impairment. Diagnostic and dynamic clues, ego patterns, and the defensive structure, as revealed in the conventional intelligence test situation, are correlated with the data in the personality tests. Interrelationships within the total test battery are of major significance. In numerous ways, verbal or unspoken, the subject shares meaningful and unconscious material with an observant examiner. The Wechsler test also provides information about discrepancies between group and individual test results. On the former, the bright but doubt-ridden child, becomes paralyzed and produces little. The emotionally labile impatient youngster who performs poorly in group tests also presents an inaccurate picture of his intellectual potential. A child with insufficient language stimulation often produces an inconsistent pattern. The Wechsler, in conjunction with the personality tests, exposes hidden resources in the culturally deprived child whose retarded educational achievement creates a spurious impression of a limited intellectual endowment.

The Bender Gestalt Test

Suspected brain damage is a frequent indication for psychological testing. The Bender Gestalt test is a useful instrument in this area of investigation. It consists of nine figures of varying degrees of complexity, presented one at a time. The subject is required to copy them on a blank piece of paper. The subject's reproductions are evaluated on psychological, intellectual, and neurological levels. Further corroboration or contradiction of organic dysfunctioning is provided through other tests.

Gestalt psychology emphasizes the presence of an inner dynamic factor that binds single parts into a total configuration. Psychological experimentation with this visual perceptual process has produced significant results for practical use in psychological testing. The Bender Gestalt Test provides information about the maturational growth pattern and functional versus organic impairment. In children whose visual motor coordination is not yet fully matured, a significant relationship exists between intelligence and Bender performance. In studies at early age levels, the Bender has been used as a predictive tool for future school achievement. Disorganization associated with brain damage as expressed in visual motor tests may duplicate a Wechsler perceptual deficiency. Inconsistencies are significant, and gradations of loss vary from subtle to gross forms, from "soft" to definite organic signs.

Beyond its neurological aspects, the Bender Gestalt Drawings reveal psychological conflicts and developmental problems. The obsessive-compulsive subject spends inordinate time and energy in his relentless struggle for perfection. In one psychotic subject, this reached such extreme proportions that the test had to be abandoned. His inappropriate response suggested an ineffectual attempt to fasten onto bits of reality. Regressive features, unreliable concentration, and unstable or reinforced lines have dynamic implications. Fluctuations in size between constriction and expansiveness mirror swings between repressive needs and explosive impulsivity. Figures of grandiose size may be associated with magic omnipotence. Pencil pressure may be so timid as to make the figures barely visible, or so forceful that the paper is torn. The degree of frustration tolerance is compared with related attitudes on the other tests.

Projective Tests

A subject's response to specific structured test demands represents one aspect of his psychological organization. In contrast, his reactions to fluid stimuli that lack the firmly established boundaries of the Wechsler tests are the principal concern of the projective test. A projective test is a method of studying personality through unstructured stimuli such as inkblots, drawings, and stories. The subject is not hampered by conventional patterns, and, in his interpretation of the ambiguous material, he divulges unconscious mental processes and content. Because there are no manifestly correct or incorrect answers, he may not recognize the deeper psychological significance of how he handles the task. Projective tests are unique instruments for penetrating the deeper recesses of the personality. In encapsulated form, the subject reveals his less rational, less disciplined patterns, his ego strengths and weaknesses, his fantasies, moods, self-image, his defenses, and the processes through which he preserves his psychic equilibrium. This indirect method reveals the internal organization of personality, the specific human substance that eludes the questionnaire, with its emphasis on separate isolated traits rather than their dynamic interplay. In the initial stages of a clinical evaluation, hidden, inner aspects of the personality system are not readily uncovered. Although the psychologist may elicit a transference reaction similar to the therapist's, the projective tests are sufficiently stimulating to disclose material that may not emerge until a later period of treatment. Ernst Kris's reference (1952) to "regression in the service of the ego" is pertinent to the creative aspects of projective testing. Not only the subject's regressive potential, but his ability to recover, his confusion of fantasy and reality, critical judgment, relaxation or reinforcement of defensive guards, his spontaneous communication and denial, are all demonstrated through the use of sensitive projective instruments. The analysis of tendencies toward health and pathology reaches a convergence in the final comprehensive report of the test battery that includes projective techniques.

The Rorschach Test

The Rorschach is the most widely used projective test in the clinical battery. Hermann Rorschach was a Swiss psychiatrist who began to experiment with inkblots in 1911. His choice of this medium was not original. Inkblots previously used by experimental psychologists were limited to the study of the imagination, and their findings were fragmentary and uncoordinated. Rorschach recognized the diagnostic value of inkblots and standardized their use for clinical purposes. He experimented with a variety of blots and published his findings in 1921. The significance of his contribution is the transformation of a vague uncertain technique into a clinically meaningful tool that stresses the uniqueness of personality and also directs attention to the deviant. This test is relatively independent of the sociocultural background of the subject. Norms have been established for different age groups.

The administration of the Rorschach is simple, although its interpretation is not. The 10 inkblots, five black and grey with various nuances of shading, two black with red areas, and three multicolored, are handed to the subject one at a time in prescribed order. He is asked, "What could this be? What does this look like?" This initial exposure constitutes the Performance Proper. The examiner records the responses verbatim and also notes significant data, reaction time, pauses, fluctuations in speech, giggles, coughs, manipulation of the cards. After the 10 blots have been presented, the subject is asked to look at them again. In this second contact, the Inquiry, ambiguous responses are clarified for scoring purposes, and latent, previously repressed material is elicited. The associative response to the inkblots reflects a complex perceptual organizing process. Memories, drive derivatives, and fantasies are integrated into a specific image. Rorschach associations are scored on four levels: Location, Determinants, Content, and Popular or Original response. Each adds its special meaning to the Rorschach configuration. Relationships among the scoring symbols are more significant than single measurements. Location describes the mode of approach to the inkblot. Some subjects emphasize the whole blot, while others cling to small details that ordinarily escape notice. Oppositional trends are expressed in emphasis on the white areas, rather than the blot itself.

The Determinants, the second scoring category investigates those qualities in the blots which motivated the response. Form—the use of formal outlines—indicates adherence to reality and rational controls that may be weakened or reinforced to meet defensive needs. Obsessive compulsive rigidity in this regard may be coupled with emotional constriction and fear of impulsivity. In contrast, a labile character pays minimum attention to the formal contours of the Rorschach. A propensity for hysterical acting-out behavior is marked by imbalance and loss of critical reflection and self-correction associated with the Form score. One way of deviating from the use of Form in the blots is through the medium of Color. The connection between Color and affect is recognized in esthetics and folklore, and confirmed through scientific research. Intensity of feeling is expressed in emphasis on color. Blunting or blocking of affect produces inhibition of its use. The examiner notes the trigger points for mature and inappropriate reactions. Color is scrutinized for deviant possibilities. The excessive crudity in the Color response that accompanies organic disorganization is consistent with other test signs of a neurological disorder.

In developmental studies of young children, precocious and artificial controls relate to depression and impairment of normal spontaneity. Those who are guarded and obsessional permit only a small trickle of conventional feeling to emerge in their Color responses. Against a background of schizophrenic withdrawal, a controlled Color response may refer to tentative reaching out for contact. Color analysis exposes the hollow affect in the "as if" subjects. Psychopathic characters may use accepted emotional conventions as a manipulative manuever. Like other Rorschach tendencies, the multiple possibilities of Color must be assessed in relation to other test data.

Another Determinant refers to Movement responses, human, animal, or inanimate. A wide spectrum of personality tendencies, intellectual achievements, stirrings of the imagination, identification, passive and aggressive trends, are indicated through the use of Movement. Ideational and conceptual factors are expressed in human movement. Animals reflect more infantile tendencies. The ratio between Movement as indicative of fantasy life, and Color as a representation of affective energies, is a fundamental measure of the subject's mental balance. Reactions to light and dark shadings of the blots (Chiaroscuro) refer to anxiety. Shading may be as vigorously avoided as the other Rorschach Determinants, yet distress is communicated through shifts in mood, uneasiness, and nonverbal signs of discomfort.

The third scoring category, the Content of the association, mirrors the cultural and socioeconomic milieu of the subject. The Content may be primitive and diffuse, or sophisticated and exact. Within a continuum of Content, responses range from an unsocialized private world to strict conformity with reality. Fantasy-ridden subjects may be flooded with unique personal content, while rigid compulsive characters prefer "safe" banalities. Inhibited and stereotyped Rorschach responses may relate to depression, restrictive anxiety, intellectual limitations, and other factors.

The fourth Rorschach scoring category deals with the Popular or Original response. Ten responses have been established as indices of conventional thinking. A percentage of these responses is essential for common sense and reality balance. An overabundance of Popular responses may express rigidity, impoverished background, or restraints on imaginative thinking. At the other extreme, too few Popular responses may indicate tendencies toward depression and isolation. In some pathological states, severe limitations of the Popular response mean that attempts to respond to the demands of reality are abandoned. The Original response is evaluated against the background of the total personality organization. Original responses indicative of creativity are differentiated from those whose seeming originality is a sign of schizophrenic disorganization. Disparities between outer facade and inner attitudes are sometimes reflected in the Popular-Original pattern. As an example, a rebellious, socially deviant adolescent veneer may represent a thin disguise for underlying passivity and conventionality.

A numerical tabulation of formal scoring categories and percentages is the first step in the interpretation of a Rorschach record.

This preliminary procedure forms the basis for a psychodynamic analysis. The eventual composite personality picture stresses the dynamic interplay of the test variables. In anxiety states, for example, the emotional properties of the blots are construed as threatening. This may lead to near panic, flight, a lowering of intellectual level, and regressive phenomena. The subject responds to a potentially disturbing stimulus by an interference in his spontaneous productivity. Its significance is determined within the total test context. The continuum between normality and psychopathology is demonstrated in Rorschach interpretation. Like the other projective techniques, the response to the inkblots indicates that a liability in one function may contribute to strength in another. The task of the interpreter is to determine whether this trend represents consolidation or disruption of the personality.

Human Figure Drawings

The Human Figure Drawing is a major projective technique. The subject is asked to draw a person, and through this nonverbal communication centered about his body image, he provides an additional opportunity for the study of visual motor organization and possible organic impairment. Like adults, children may be uneasy about body exposure. However, they are generally less self-conscious about their drawings. Artistic ability is discounted, although it may embellish the body image. In the directions, the gender is deliberately left ambiguous. Some doubtful subjects ask "A boy? A girl? Can he be doing something? Full face? Profile?" To obtain a valid spontaneous response, the examiner remains reassuring but evasive. After the first drawing, another of the opposite sex is requested. Children sometimes draw their family group and spontaneous pictures of their choice.

In his conscious and unconscious selection and organization of images, the subject expresses his view of himself and other meaningful figures in his world. His body images may be transient or fixed, forceful or ephemeral, active or passive, isolated or involved, complete or fragmented, endowed with lively excitement or depressive lethargy. He reveals his ideas about the arrangement of body parts and organs. The drawings are evaluated on developmental and content levels.

Appropriate maturational criteria are available for children, and this "test age" is compared with performance on the intelligence test and chronological age norms. These body expressions are often weighted with conflict and fantasy. The impatient subject neglects details; the worrisome one fears to omit any. Schizophrenic subjects who are superficially well defended in other tests express their deviation in bizarre figure drawings. The psychotic body image stresses the flux or rigidity of the inner world, the essential loss of identity, and attempts to re-establish a sense of self. The drawings of neurotic individuals reflect a more reliable grip on reality. Total body configuration is more meaningful than reference to single parts. The sequence of the gender choice, male versus female, relates to the subject's own sense of identity. Through the language of drawings, some women reveal their flight from femininity, and the man with a supermasculine facade exposes his passive feminine core. Like the other projective tests, these body-image representations reveal defensive aspects of the personality. Oral and anal details provide clues to regressive needs.

Comparisons of Bender and Human Figure Drawings are revealing. Contradictory tendencies relate to differences in the demands of the two tests. The structured reality demands of the Bender produce in some subjects a need for absolute precision. In contrast, their human figures may be very fluid. Clothes are used both to exhibit and conceal, to seduce, and to protect. Fashion and cartoon disguises are designed to meet individual needs.

Hands placed within the body may represent a narcissistic or autoerotic gesture. Arm movement toward the external world may be wooden, active, alert, searching, aggressive. Lips may be distorted into a smile that exposes dangerous teeth. The conscious intent is friendly, but the manifest image is sadistic. The eyes are rich in interpretative possibilities. In some drawings, a vacant unseeing stare betrays isolation. Piercing black eyes drawn by paranoid individuals express their hostile intentions. Inhibition of the visual function as expressed in drawings is not uncommon in children who suffer from a learning disability. Facial expressions may be depressed, angry, bewildered. Figure drawings provide a direct channel to the inner world of subjective experience. With a pictorial clarity that defies verbal communication, they present the essential human substance.

Apperception Tests

Storytelling as a projective technique is essential in a well-rounded test battery. Among the many available tests, the Thematic Apperception Test (TAT) devised by Henry A. Murray in 1935 is widely used for older children and adults. The Children's Apperception Test (CAT), later devised for young children, consists of 10 pictures. Of the 30 TAT pictures, approximately 15 are given to each subject. The selection depends on sex, age, and relevancy. Each picture is handed to the subject, one at a time, and he is asked to tell a story about it. He is confronted with a wide variety of emotionally charged stimuli. The TAT as a projective technique elicits thought content, fantasies, moods, specifics of environmental interaction, cultural determinants, and early family experiences. The CAT and TAT may disclose an inner life and imagination that is rich and colorful or impoverished and drab. Consistency within the stories reveals the basic personality organization and permits differentiation of open and spontaneous, or furtive and concealed modes of fantasy expression.

The interpretative process begins with the subject's preliminary reaction to the first picture. He may press for further guidance, just as he might have asked for more exact directions on the Wechsler test. In an exhibition of self-derogation, some subjects construe this as a test of imagination and immediately stress their lack of this skill. Brief descriptive enumerations rather than interpretative stories relate to intellectual impoverishment, antagonism to the task, or withholding. The skilled examiner reads clues in the subject's attitude to determine whether further probing would be fruitful. Anxiety and suspicion may be so intense that attempts at clarification are abandoned. Questions about the stories, though couched in gentle terms, may be looked upon as punitive, prying, cross-examining, or a violation of privacy. In his willingness or reluctance to tell stories, the subject often repeats his approach toward the other tests. Some schizophrenics consider a sharing of their thought content as an emptying-out process related to fear of loss of identity. This fear contributes to disguised or open hostility against the testing procedures and the examiner.

Comparisons between Rorschach and Apperception responses frequently indicate considerable consistency. However, differences in accessibility and productivity are as revealing. Anal conflicts about retention and elimination are expressed in worry about what can be shared and what must be censored. Such ambivalences color the total test battery. The doubtful subject who responds with, "I see two stories," is encouraged to tell both, and each is interpreted in terms of latent and overt trends.

Stories are examined for identification and misrecognition of objects, slips that are unnoticed or spontaneously corrected, loss of coherence, rambling, circumlocutions, extraneous data, shifts in imaginative and intellectual level from story to story, appropriate or inappropriate settings, intellectualizations, esoteric references, and ostentatious verbalizations. At all age levels, reality testing, capacity for logical organization, affective components, signs of normal and pathological ego development are noted. In telling his story, the subject chooses and organizes old memories and experiences. In the process of selection, he exposes his drives, needs, inner stress, strivings, anxieties, and defenses. The fictitious aspect of storytelling may be dissolved, with developing awareness and communication by the subject. Mediocre reactions at variance with superior Wechsler achievements relate to the style of intelligence, paucity of imagination, or defensive rigidities. Excessively fluid fantasy and weakened reality testing have pathological significance. In some subjects, responses differ with the changing stimulus. The response to one Apperception picture may be characterized by rigidity, to another by conventionality, to a third by release of strong affect. Some subjects cannot disengage themselves from their inner preoccupations, and a single obsessional thread may run through all their stories. A reality object in the picture may be distorted to correspond to such preoccupations. A lengthy tedious recital of picture details may indicate an avoidance of threatening fantasies and impulses. Concern with minutiae that are ordinarily disregarded appears in some paranoid subjects, whose excessive sensitivity to details alerts them against imagined dangers in their environment. The unstructured nature of the projective stimuli sharpens the watchfulness of some suspicious individuals. Shifts in mood and level of anxiety related to meaningful figures in the subject's world are significant. Apperception themes reinforce one another and are dynamically interrelated.

Aggressive trends may be expressed in direct or nonobvious forms. Themes of punishment may be emphasized or conspicuously absent. Stereotyped parental figures may be avoided and the distance between generations increased by the substitution of a grandparent for a parent. Apperception stories are examined for the nature of object relationships and for indications of active participation or passive submission. Infantile fear of abandonment is encountered at all age levels. Masochistic characters describe the self-destructive maneuvers they employ to provoke the feared rejection. The psychologist who is not acquainted with the subject's life situation uses caution in the evaluation of reality specifics, on the basis of the TAT stories. These take on added significance in the therapeutic setting and provide guidelines for further exploration. The diagnostic impressions of the Apperception Test rely on a detailed study of multiple factors and interrelationships. Affective components are examined for lability, hysterical overreaction, and intensity and quality of depression Delinquent and psychopathic trends may be indicated by a display of blandness, projection, or lack of self-critical judgment. Antisocial content is often linked to primitive rebellion against parental figures. The stories may present clues to the parental contribution to the child's disturbance. Goals may be realistic, constructive, independently achieved. A negative termination reflects disappointment, frustration, even suicidal propensities.

In the first TAT picture, a boy is contemplating a violin which rests on a table in front of him. The subject's story tells something about his attitudes to learning, aspiration, ambitions, his motivation toward therapy. If his reality testing is disturbed, he may transform the violin into a less relevant object, a broken train, a kite, or a gun. A note of magic omnipotence is injected when, without mobilization of effort and energy, the story dissolves into a daydream in which the subject presents himself as a famous, all-powerful child prodigy. Conversely, the boy may be viewed as discouraged, depressed, fatigued, sleepy. In an indirect fashion, the subject describes conflicts of his own that interfere with learning and achievement. Oedipal, castration, masturbation components, retreat from competition with a threatening father image, are suggested inferences to the violin as a fragile, cherished family heirloom. The alternatives of play and work, negativism toward parental pressures assume numerous forms: open refusal, unenthusiastic compliance, shrewd manipulations. This initial story is evaluated within the context of subsequent productions.

The CAT evokes an exciting world of childhood experiences—eating, sleeping, elimination, sexual differences, pregnancy, birth of siblings. Picture V is a bedroom scene of bears, a crib, and an adult bed. Picture VI presents a darkened cave with two dimly outlined figures of bears in the background and a smaller bear lying in the foreground. Repressed primal scene anxieties in one picture may be withheld until the following one. These stories refer to sleeping arrangements and the oedipal situation. Some children tell about their visit to the parental bed and a cuddle between father and mother bear. The parents' acceptance or rejection of this intrusion is revealing. In their stories, children reveal separation fears, sexual curiosity, preoccupation with marital activities. Phobic fears about the durability of the cave may be aroused. Worry about a hurricane and collapse of the cave suggests uneasiness about the solidity of the home. The Apperception fantasies offer vast dynamic material that animates and specifies data obtained from the other psychological tests.

Organization of Test Data

The subject who has completed the total test battery has been exposed to a wide variety of stimuli. Samples of his behavior and his reactions to intelligence and projective tests are obtained in the form of a mass of raw data. The standardized scoring of these data forms the basis of the dynamic interpretation. Emerging traits and patterns are synthesized into the description of a single individual. The practiced examiner translates a private world of subjective experience into a common clinical vocabulary that is meaningful to the other disciplines. A piecemeal enumeration of personality traits has limited value. A communication from the psychologist characterized by unsubstantiated conjectures and excessive use of psychiatric labels and jargon also distorts the personality picture. The psychological test report achieves its greatest usefulness when it is anchored within the framework of ego psychology, formulated in a nondogmatic way, recognizes its limitations, and avoids overgeneralization.

Preparation for Testing

Some practical aspects of psychological testing should be considered. These problems are connected with the ongoing treatment rather than directly with the testing procedures. Preparation of the subject for the examination involves his relation to the therapist and the transference ambivalences. The unfamiliar test situation may evoke irrational fantasies and magic expectations. The psychologist may be viewed as a punishing or loving parent. Parental anxiety may emerge in the preliminary contact. Some parents reveal their pessimistic expectations. Because all previous efforts at testing the child have failed, the contemplated tests will also result in a fiasco. In such instances, a mother's preparation of the child provides dubious reassurances, her negativistic anticipations are transmitted to him, and the mutual symbiotic bond is acted out during the tests. Efforts should be made to counteract preconceived ideas that psychological tests provide proof of serious inadequancy or severe mental illness. An inexperienced therapist who is concerned about exposure of his lack of treatment skills may also intensify the subject's test anxiety. When tests are given during the intake process or emergency situations, a gradual preparation may not be possible. The examiner who is alerted attempts more active reassurance during the tests. Preparation should be open and should stress the psychologist's friendly interest and nonauthoritarian role. In some instances, elements of suspicion and hostility cannot be eliminated, even with proper preparation. These negative reactions may be overtly manifested during the testing or defended against by assuming the opposite attitudes, that is, by reaction formation.

Criteria and Contraindications for Testing

If it is therapeutically advisable, psychological test results are most useful when they are given early in the clinical contact. They clarify psychodynamics that might remain obscure or withheld, measure personality change, and serve as a baseline for longitudinal development studies. Whether the examination is introduced during an initial or later stage, the timing must be sensitive to the subject's therapeutic needs. The therapist must also be aware of the potential harm that may outweigh the benefits of tests. In some acute situations, the benefits to be accrued from a clarification of psychodynamics may be negated by the rupture of a fragile therapeutic relationship. In quiescent psychotic states, the uncovering of inner conflicts may produce intolerable anxiety. Nevertheless, the aftereffects of testing are more often benign and productive. Conflicts and fantasies that confront the subject during his testing experience are used constructively in subsequent therapy sessions. The subject may use the tests as a medium for communication with the therapist or he may share repressed material with the psychologist as a substitute for the therapist.

If the clinical interview provides a clear, unambiguous picture of dynamics and diagnostic impressions, the psychological test may be superfluous. The hostility and negativism that have been directed against the therapist may reappear in a restricted response to the psychological examination. The change in physical surroundings and the total frame of reference, however, rarely fail to produce enlightening results. Except as part of a larger research design, routine testing is generally not practical. The indiscriminate use of testing interferes with the sharpening of diagnostic skills of the young therapist. Some subjects try to use tests as an alternative to therapy, or to ward off a more lasting relationship. With more positive goals, tests also serve as a springboard to treatment.

Testing is essential in disturbances related to intellectual and educational functioning. A professional worker of middle-class background may confuse verbal facility with a superior intelligence. Easy use of language and mimicking of parental vocabulary help to maintain a facade that is inevitably dissipated with increased conceptual educational demands. Seductive charm substituted for mental acuity offers small consolation during an objective intelligence test. At the other end of the spectrum, clinical workers are familiar with the nonverbal, apathetic child who creates an impression of limited endowment. Depression, passivity, negativism, a blunted cultural environment, all interfere with intellectual growth. Projective tests and nonverbal tasks on the Wechsler elicit hidden abilities that are not based on language development. Test performance is decreased by inhibitions related to cultural loss, emotional interference, or a combination of both factors. Superficial assessment of intellectual potential based on the use of one test rather than a battery may lead to inappropriate educational and therapeutic planning. Discrepancies between projective and intelligence test performance and the subtle interplay between affective and ideational factors, underline the need for an intensive psychological study of children with learning difficulties.

A request for vocational recommendations is sometimes included in a referral for testing. This may represent the subject's interpretation of a clinical study. Vocational testing requires skills, training, and knowledge that are available to the specialist in this field, rather than to the psychologist in general clinical practice. If the vocational choice is impeded by psychological problems and identity conflicts, testing by the clinical psychologist leads to the proper referral, therapy, and eventually, to the correct vocational decision. If changes in the environment are indicated—placement in a residential school or foster home—tests help in gauging the ability to tolerate separation and to control impulses. Such information assists in choosing the appropriate institutional setting. In adults, testing may clarify conflicts associated with impending marriage or divorce, hospitalization, and other critical situations. Tests during the normative adolescent crisis help to separate the "ordinary" turmoil from the more profound deviation. Despite the presence of anxiety during periods of stress, the intrinsic personality pattern remains fairly stable in psychological tests.

Prediction and Retesting

Prediction is a major function of all scientific instruments, including psychological tests. This area must be regarded with caution. Future developmental trends can be anticipated, but not established with certainty. An unfavorable environment may precipitate dormant pathology. More fortunate life experiences may help to restrain a latent illness.

Repeated psychological examinations are used in current research programs that involve longitudinal studies. Test results before, during, and after treatment provide objective criteria for evaluating personality changes in terms of normality versus pathology, adaptive potential, object relations, and related areas. In retesting, a comparison with the initial test results will disclose, in favorable instances, symptomatic improvement, increased flexibility and impulse control, and modification of the defensive organization and of other ego functions. Pathological tendencies that have become submerged in the ordinary life of the individual may be exposed in retesting. An increase of I.Q. in subjects with intellectual inhibitions and pseudostupidity is a clear sign of improvement. In another retest, an increased verbal I.Q. may represent a negative reinforcement of obsessional defenses. Changes in manifest behavior, increased cooperation, and reduced anxiety and restriction confirm positive trends that are also demonstrated in the test results. Strivings for conformity, interrelated with affective components, have a varied significance in retesting. The rigidly conforming subject with passive compliant attitudes in his first test may display favorable changes through a more active, emotionally meaningful participation. Conversely, another who had been dominated by antisocial behavior shows improvement by increased conventionality in thinking and more reliable impulse control. In general, retesting determines whether changes have occurred in fundamental personality organization or whether superficial adjustments have led to an improved everyday functioning and relief of symptoms.

Use of Test Results with the Subject

Within the setting of a clinical team, the interpretation of test results is frequently assigned to the caseworker or psychiatrist. It is essential that sensitivity and caution be exercised in communicating this emotionally charged information to the subject and his family. Decisions about the sharing of content with the subject are made on the basis of the therapist's judgment about pertinent information and the current state of therapy. There is consistent agreement on the destructive and unethical aspects of offering a copy of a psychological test report to a parent, to someone who is emotionally involved with the subject, or who lacks adequate professional training. Unconscious needs and fantasies often emerge during a discussion of the test results. The parent with irrational expectations may deny painful aspects of the child's intellectual and emotional problems. Clinicians are familiar with the parent to whom the child represents a narcissistic extension of himself. The child becomes a medium for the fulfillment or frustration of the adult's aspirations. Test findings may motivate an exploration of tangled threads from previous generations. Disturbances in a mother's and father's primary family interaction with their parents and siblings are often mirrored in the child's test reactions. A mentally defective or psychotic family member may contribute to the parent's fear of a deviant child. The tests arouse complex ambivalences in a parent who anticipates a child with a defect. Favorable evidence to the contrary may be greeted with dismay, the validity of the results is suspected, and the examiner's professional qualifications are doubted. "Shopping around" for another psychological examination may represent efforts to obtain test results in agreement with the parent's unrealistic anticipations. Confirmation of feeblemindedness may be sought in cases of pseudostupidity, or, conversely, genuine mental retardation may be denied. Despite repeated evidence to the contrary, through psychological and neurological tests, some parents remain convinced that their child's predicament has an organic basis. When an organic disorder is considered more acceptable than a psychological disturbance, parental efforts to alleviate their own guilt may be present. The psychological examination cannot be considered as an isolated event separate from the subject's therapeutic experiences and his relationship with the external world.

REFERENCES

Dileo, J. (1970), *Young Children and Their Drawings.* New York: Brunner/Mazel.

Haase, W. (1964), The Role of Socio-Economic Class in Examiner Bias. In: *Mental Health of the Poor,* ed. F. Riessman, et al. New York: Free Press of Glencoe.

Haworth, M. R. (1966), *The Children's Apperception Test: Facts About Fantasy.* New York: Grune & Stratton.

——— (1968), The Children's Apperception Test: Its Use in Developmental Assessments of Normal Children. *Journal of Projective Techniques and Personality Assessment,* 32:405-427.

Hirsch, E. (1970), *The Troubled Adolescent: As He Emerges on Psychological Tests.* New York: International Universities Press.

Koppitz, E. (1964), *The Bender Gestalt Test for Young Children.* New York: Grune & Stratton.

Pitcher, E. G., & Prelinger, E. (1963), *Children Tell Stories.* New York: International Universities Press.

Rabin, A. I. & Haworth, M. R. (1960), *Projective Techniques with Children.* New York: Grune & Stratton.

Rapaport, D., Gill, M. & Schafer, R. (1968), *Diagnostic Psychological Testing,* ed. R. Holt, Revised Edition. New York: International Universities Press.

Schafer, R. (1948), *The Clinical Application of Psychological Tests.* New York: International Universities Press.

——— (1954), *Psychoanalytic Interpretation in Rorschach Testing.* New York: Grune & Stratton.

———(1967), *Projective Testing and Psychoanalysis.* New York: International Universities Press.

Siegel, M. (1946a), A Description of the Rorschach Method. *The Family: Journal of Social Casework,* 27:51-58.

——— (1946b), The Rorschach Test in Diagnosis and Prognosis. *The Family: Journal of Social Casework,* 27:102-109.

——— (1948), The Diagnostic and Prognostic Validity of the Rorschach Test in a Child Guidance Clinic. *American Journal of Orthopsychiatry,* 18:119-133.

Tomkins, S. (1947), *Thematic Apperception Test.* New York: Grune & Stratton.

Wyatt, F. (1958), A Principle for the Interpretation of Fantasy. *Journal of Projective Techniques,* 22:229-245.

SUGGESTED READING

Bender, L. (1956), *Psychopathology of Children with Organic Brain Disorders.* Springfield, Illinois: Charles C Thomas.

Dennis, W. (1966), *Group Values Through Children's Drawings.* New York: John Wiley & Sons.

Elkisch, P. (1945), Children's Drawings in Projective Technique. *Psychological Monographs,* 266, Vol. 58, ed. John F. Dashiell. Evanston, Ill.: American Psychological Association.

Frank, L. (1948), *Projective Methods.* Springfield, Illinois: Charles C Thomas.

Halpern, F. (1953), *A Clinical Approach to Children's Rorschachs.* New York: Grune & Stratton.

Harris, D. (1963), *Children's Drawings As Measures of Intellectual Maturity.* New York: Harcourt, Brace & World.

Kellogg, R. (1969), *Analyzing Children's Art.* Palo Alto: National Press Books.

Kris, E. (1952), *Psychoanalytic Exploration in Art.* New York: International Universities Press.

Levinger, L. (1966), Children's Drawings as Indicators of Sexual Discrimination. Unpublished Thesis, New York University. Ann Arbor: Michigan University Microfilms.

Schactel, E. (1966), *Experiential Foundations of Rorschach's Test.* New York: Basic Books.

CHAPTER THIRTY

Community Psychiatry

LOUIS LINN, M.D.

Psychiatry as a clinical science has moved into the Era of Community Psychiatry. Whether one chooses to describe this transition as evolutionary or revolutionary, the fact remains that fundamental changes have occurred. If we are to understand the nature of this most recent change we must review those changes which preceded it.

To begin with, the humanitarian ideas associated with the names of Pinel, Rush, and others ushered in the Era of Enlightened Psychiatry during which the mentally ill were rescued from the mockers, the jailers, and the witchburners. The next change is usually associated with Freud, whose emphasis on the role of psychogenesis, particularly the role of unconscious factors in mental disorder, is commonly credited with introducing the Era of Scientific Psychiatry. However, he must share this honor with Kraepelin, whose contribution of a precise nosology compelled clinicians to observe carefully, refine their diagnostic armamentarium, and perfect their skills in descriptive psychiatry, all of which made it possible to achieve a systematic classification of the major mental disorders. It became possible, for example, to identify mental disorders with organic brain disease and, in certain instances, to institute specific treatments. Similarly, psychodynamic insights opened the way to an understanding of the so-called functional disorders and to the possibility of effective psychotherapy in selected cases. Furthermore, an appreciation of psychogenesis focused attention on the role of the family and the social environment, on the emotional needs of children, and, in addition, was responsible for introducing to clinical psychiatry the concepts of primary prevention and early treatment.

The third phase, the Era of Effective Symptom Control, is generally unappreciated. Following World War II, the combination of Freudian psychodynamics applied with hospital settings to create a therapeutic milieu and the psychopharmacologic advances during the nineteen fifties, increased our capacity to control psychotic symptoms. With this, locked doors and the forbidding isolation of the traditional insane asylum gave way to an open-door policy which let not only patients out but the community in.

The most important consequence of effective symptom control was that it became possible to treat the major mental disorders in the patient's own community. It was this fact primarily which ushered in the Era of Community Psychiatry—the theory and practice of psychiatry applied to a specific community *or to a population living within a specific geographic district.* Community Psychiatry may also be defined as a point of view that, for the majority of patients with reversible mental illness, the treatment locale of choice is the community in which the patient and his family reside. The reasons for this point of view are not hard to find.

(1) Treatment facilities thus located are more swiftly available to the frightened, depressed, or poorly motivated patient. Many patients will walk to a neighborhood clinic, but will resist traveling to a distantly located treatment facility. This increases the likelihood of early treatment and "crisis intervention."

(2) If the neighborhood treatment facility consists of a Community Mental Health Center—that is, a complex of services providing 24-hour emergency care, a full range of outpatient clinics, a 24-hour inpatient service, elective part-time hospitalization services, plus a full range of consultative and rehabilitative services—the patient will not be lost in a noncoordinated network of community agencies. Whereas

the disastrous impact of staff conflict on hospitalized patients has been well documented, less attention has been given to the same phenomenon when it occurs on a community level. Thus, an additional benefit of this treatment arrangement is continuity of care and avoidance of wasteful and antitherapeutic duplication of effort.

(3) Community psychiatry is family-centered, a factor of great clinical importance. We can hardly conceive of normal emotional growth outside the context of normal family living. Moreover, accurate diagnosis and, particularly, the evaluation of psychodynamic factors presuppose an accurate knowledge of the patient's family. While it is often necessary to remove a patient from his home during the opening phase of treatment, one cannot achieve a realistic closing phase without including the family in the treatment plan. Probably the greatest obstacle to the "working through" of insights gained in psychoanalytic psychotherapy is to be found in continued exposure to a traumatic home environment. In short, psychotherapy as we understand it today is family-centered. Needless to say, the latter is rarely possible unless the patient and his family both live in proximity to the treatment facility.

(4) As hospitals tend increasingly to be occupied by patients for shorter periods of time, the importance of aftercare grows correspondingly. Currently, the emphasis of treatment is on rehabilitating the patient in the community proper. This means that the treatment plan must now include cooperative arrangements with community facilities which the patient will use for education, work, recreation, and the like. Some have taken the growing emphasis on outpatient care as a fallacious belief that "the shorter the hospitalization the better." It would be equally fallacious to believe the opposite. Our ideal is optimal hospitalization. This will vary in time from patient to patient, depending on age, diagnosis, severity and chronicity of illness, family circumstances, etc. In many instances the availability of elective part-time hospitalization will add flexibility and speed to the process of converting the hospitalized patient to ambulatory status.

(5) Perhaps the most important consequence of the Community Psychiatry concept is its emphasis on primary prevention. When we focus our attention on the family, on early case-finding and crisis

intervention, we are but a short step from a concern for the broader social environment of the patient. New psychiatric programs are developed most effectively if we start by defining the mental health needs of a given geographic district and then develop district-specific facilities and programs calculated to saturate the district with services aimed at all levels of prevention and treatment. The needs of a young community with a high percentage of school-age children, for example, will differ considerably from those of a largely geriatric community. Similarly, the needs of an urban-poor community will differ from those of a prosperous suburban one.

The Era of Community Medicine

At this point in the evolving patterns of patient care we have arrived at the *Era of Community Medicine.* Community Medicine encompasses all the foregoing propositions. It goes further, however, and sees social stress as a factor that affects all organ systems as well as all patterns of human behavior. In this sense, psychiatry is only one of many specialities directing their efforts at a specific community for purposes of saturating its population with all levels of prevention, treatment and rehabilitation. The essence of community medicine has been embodied in a statement of Rene Dubos. The Four Horsemen of the Apocalypse, he said, still range freely over the entirety of our globe. But death is now acquiring new allies:

> Horsemen of destruction that were rarely seen in the past are increasingly threatening the life and soul of modern man. Vascular diseases ruin his heart and brain; cancers run riot; mental disease break his contact with the world of reason. [As in the past] two kinds of medical philosophy are guiding the approach to the control of these modern endemics. One is the search for [devices] capable of reaching the site of the disease within the body of the individual patient. The other is the attempt to identify those aspects of modern life thought to be responsible for the disease problems peculiar to our times [1959, p. 165].

It is particularly in this latter search—in the socially oriented field of primary prevention—that the psychiatrist in Community Psychiatry joins his colleagues in all other specialties to further the development of community medicine.

The Era of Community Health, Education, and Welfare

Just as the basic concepts evolved by Community Psychiatry foreshadowed the Era of Community Medicine, so have developments in Community Medicine heralded the appearance of the Era of Community Health, Education and Welfare. It has become clear that mental health is inseparable from general health. By the same token, general health is inseparable from education and welfare.

The basic plan enunciated in this chapter, namely, the need to direct our efforts at a specific community for purposes of saturating it with a full range of programs to meet all of its needs, must now be broadened to include a systematic concern for education and welfare as well as health. Indeed, it is fair to say that social welfare is the fundamental base from which we must proceed. Unless we build solidly at this level, programs in education and health are destined to be ineffective.

Perhaps an actual case history will clarify what we mean by Community Psychiatry.

Marcial, described elsewhere (Linn, 1966), was a well-developed, well-nourished boy, age nine, the fourth in a Puerto Rican family of six siblings. His tragic story is all too familiar, and precisely because it is in some ways so commonplace, it is a story of great importance. The father of sibling number one deserted the mother before baby number one was born. Babies two, three, and four were the products of father number two who, in turn, deserted the mother early in the number-four pregnancy and came to New York City. When Marcial (number four) was one month old, his mother left him with her parents in San Juan and set off for New York City with siblings one, two, and three to search for her missing husband. Marcial did not see his mother again for two-and-a-half years. When he arrived in New York City he was suffering from severe malnutrition. He showed a delay in all developmental indices. He could not talk or walk. He was treated for malnutrition in a hospital in New York City for several months and subsequently transferred to a convalescent home for several more months. He was three-and-a-half years old when he finally regained his family. Father number two was never found, but by that time father number three was on the scene, and babies five and six were born in rapid succession. At this point Marcial was sent off to school.

With this history as a background, it will come as no surprise that by age eight, as a second-grade pupil, Marcial was deeply disturbed. He had become hyperkinetic, inattentive in school, destructive, and assaultive. In addition, he became a compulsive fire-setter. He set fires both in school and at home. He was refractory to all disciplinary efforts. On several occasions he fled from home, was away all night, and had to be retrieved by the police. He was brought to a Mental Health Center by the school authorities as an emergency (walk-in) referral, with the plea for assistance in placing him in a city hospital with locked ward facilities. The Mental Health Center psychiatrist was readily able to confirm his physical overactivity and his inattentiveness. In response to questions, Marcial stated that he could "hear the devil telling him he was a bad boy because he was jealous of his little brothers." After a physical examination and laboratory studies, he was placed on trifluphenazine and was admitted to the Day Hospital for observation and treatment.

In the Day Hospital he created an uproar. He taxed the patience and the energy of the entire staff and enraged all the other patients. In spite of maximal surveillance, he succeeded in setting several fires in the building. At the end of each day, the staff decided they had given the patient the maximum benefit of the treatment program, and yet, always, they decided to try one more day before transferring him to Bellevue. One day he was placed on an amphetamine in addition to the phenathiazine, and almost immediately he became more tractable. Because of the mother's unrealiability, all medications were administered in the Day Hospital. Appropriate laboratory studies were repeated routinely while the patient was on medication.

Older siblings dropped Marcial off at the Day Hospital on their way to school and picked him up on the way home, with or without the mother. Discussions with the mother and siblings helped them to be more tolerant of Marcial's "naughtiness" at home. The youngsters in the family had milk and cookies and played games together in the Day Hospital and in the late afternoon went off to their home as a family unit.

Parenthetically I should say that severely disturbed youngsters cannot tolerate group experience. In the family group, interactions with siblings tend to be destructive. In the classroom they cannot share the teacher with other children. These youngsters must first develop the capacity for group interaction in a one-to-one treatment setting, with the help of appropriate medications directed at target symptoms. Only after some initial improvement has occurred can they enjoy the further benefits of group interaction.

After about two weeks, Marcial improved enough to be included in a weekly children's play group with the recreational therapist. Because of this improvement older patients started relating to him with more tolerance. In their own group psychotherapy, adult patients discussed the hostility Marcial provoked. In time, several of them arrived at wholesome insights concerning their role as parents in relation to their own children. The social worker notified the Board of Education about Marcial; a special teacher was sent to the Day Hospital to do schoolwork with him in that setting. This teacher discovered a severe reading disability. The psychologist tested him and found that his I.Q. was within the lower limits of normal and that there was no evidence of psychosis at this time. His responses to the Sentence Completion Test indicated continued guilt about his feelings of sibling rivalry. Even though he did not appear overtly depressed, he expressed self-depreciatory ideas suggestive of a severe depressive reaction.

By the following month he had improved so much that it was possible to return him to his regular classroom. On the way to school he would stop off at the Day Hospital for his morning medication. He attended school for half a day and received remedial reading lessons. He came to the Day Hospital for lunch and spent the rest of the afternoon at the Mental Health Center. He became involved in therapeutic group activities. His mother and his siblings were also involved in this phase of the treatment program. Arrangements were made for him to spend a few weeks in a therapeutically oriented camp for emotionally disturbed youngsters that summer. It was the expectation that he would be able to resume schooling in the fall and attend the afternoon clinic on a weekly basis.

With this case history as a paradigm, we can now describe the essential qualities of Community Psychiatry.

(1) Treatment facilities must be located in the very neighborhood in which the patient lives. This is called the *Principle of Districting.* The simple geographical fact of locating our clinic within walking distance of the patient's home and his school opened up a vast range of therapeutic possibilities that would have been impossible in a traditional treatment facility located far from home.

The psychiatrically disturbed child comes for treatment when he has exhausted the love, patience, and stamina of his family, his teachers, and the community. As Silberstein[1] has expressed it, such patients have exhausted their *reservoir of social credit.* When we take such a patient into treatment, we immediately increase his social credit, not only by a direct therapeutic contribution to the patient, but also, by our example, inspiring family and teachers to try a little harder and a little longer. This additional influx of tender loving care usually has the effect of producing some symptomatic improvement in the patient. This, in turn, encourages everyone to continue his efforts. In this way an *upward spiral* is initiated. By contrast, if the disturbed (and, I might add, *disturbing*) youngster is admitted to a remotely situated hospital, he is commonly excluded from the family. His parents and siblings tend to close ranks against this "troublesome presence," and with the passing of time it becomes increasingly difficult to achieve re-entry for him. In most instances the educational process grinds to a halt for the hospitalized youngster, and he falls increasingly behind his age group in his schooling. Finally, the richest activities program in an inpatient setting is a poor substitute for the stimulation provided by ordinary existence in the community. As a consequence, there is a progressive loss of the social skills. In short, in the traditional nondistricted inpatient treatment setting, a *downward spiral* is almost unavoidably initiated.

(2) *Community Psychiatry* treatment facilities contain five basic elements: an emergency (walk-in) service, an outpatient clinic, part-time hospitalization facilities (Day Hospital and Night Hospital), a full range of consultative and liaison activities with the ancillary services helping the patient (schools, social agencies, etc.), and a full-time (24-hour) inpatient service. A psychiatric facility which includes all these elements is called a *Comprehensive Community Mental Health Center* (CCMHC). It is not necessary that all of these elements exist under a single roof—only that they are in a functional relationship to one another.

In the Marcial's case, we did not have to make use of overnight facilities. However, we are in direct operational contact with city and state hospitals, which provide us with elective coverage for patients who must sleep away from home.

[1]In a personal communication.

(3) In Community Psychiatry, treatment is *crisis oriented,* i.e., the child is provided with help at the time that his social credit is first exhausted, not after two years on a downward spiral when irreparable damage has been done.

(4) A corollary of crisis-oriented therapy is that it is also *short-term therapy.* The patient is helped over recurrent periods of emotional decompensation and is readmitted for treatment on an elective basis as often as he needs it, and for as many years as he needs it.

(5) Treatment is *family-centered.* Community Psychiatry hypothesizes that individual psychopathology is inextricably bound up with psychopathology within the family group. According to this hypothesis, it is impossible to treat one member of a family without helping the other members.

(6) *Continuity of care* is the ideal. Patients who have been the victims of family and community disorganization are particularly traumatized by a treatment program consisting of separate stages which are fragmented and too often in actual conflict. The previously enumerated elements of the CCMHC are designed specifically to achieve continuity of care.

(7) Community Psychiatry regards mental health as a public health issue. It thus not only concerns itself with problems of prevention, but seeks to provide service for all who need it. It is the ideal of service for all that underlies the Mental Health Center's emphasis on group psychotherapy, on therapeutically useful group interactions of all kinds (such as those provided by work, play, and education), and the use of medications for the relief of specific target symptoms wherever possible.

The Four Spheres

In relation to the target population, one can discern what could be termed four distinct spheres of discourse. Sphere One is the nonpatient, nonclient world, i.e., the world of functioning people; Sphere Two is the patient-client world; Sphere Three is the community mental health center; Sphere Four is the administrative apparatus, including federal, state, local, and private funding agencies whose regulations give structure and set limits to programs.

A systematic discussion of community mental health planning must consider each of these spheres separately and in relation to the following separate items: (a) the goal of the program; (b) the leaders of the program; (c) the basic procedures of the program; (d) a means for evaluating the effectiveness of the program.

Sphere One consists of individuals and families of functioning people, their schools, their community and religious centers, their playgrounds and shopping centers, their tenant councils, their neighborhood political organizations, etc. Those in Sphere One are well motivated; their capacity for self-help is maximal. This is the reservoir from which we recruit the successful indigenous nonprofessionals in self-help community action programs. By and large, they can mobilize resources for themselves and their family members to prevent breakdown.

Primary prevention is the principal goal of Sphere One. A subsidiary goal is early case-finding so that treatment can be initiated before irreversible changes have occurred both in the patient and his family. Sphere One programs involve the mobilization of all devices to strengthen normal family living. It sponsors work training programs aimed primarily at the male members of the community. It emphasizes the importance and dignity of the female role as homemaker, particularly in relation to young children. Sphere One programs are largely educational. They are led by educators in family living and by family-planning experts who not only provide contraceptive advice, but who regard family planning in its broadest sense. Home economists and remedial teachers are included. Mental health professionals have a decisive role in formulating educational programs for teachers, clergy, and police concerning the nature of the normal developmental process, the recognition and management of individuals showing the early signs and symptoms of mental disorder. They also provide consultation concerning problem cases, program development, and legislation.

Sphere Two consists of those whose capacity for self-help has been impaired to the point that they have become or should be patients or clients of one of the community-helping agencies. Here we find multiproblem families whose members, with their individual problems, have become the responsibility of separate and often conflicting agencies. Interdisciplinary consultation is the key instrument in Sphere Two. The coordination of separate community efforts is its goal. Mental health professionals must be trained to offer the same skills in relation to the consultative process that they have in relation to psychotherapy. A knowledge of group process and of psychodynamics sensitizes the skilled consultant to fine details of meaning so that he can distinguish between the shadow of manifest behavior and the often crucial substance of unconscious motivation. It increases the consultant's compassion and his tolerance for anger in others. All the similarities to psychotherapy notwithstanding, the consultant must keep in mind his basic goal, to improve the work effectiveness of his consultee. If he sets himself more ambitious goals, he is sure to come to grief.

By the same token the consultant must recognize limitations when they exist, based on emotional impairment in the consultee. Communities characterized by family disorganization have great difficulty evolving their own leaders and in accepting any leadership, however competent. The inability of young people from disorganized homes to accept the leadership of teachers and other authority figures must be understood in terms of transference, that is, as a generalized distrust based largely on disillusionment with their own absentee parents. The failure to take into account this transference aspect of the problem has led to an overestimation of the capacity of such groups to evolve their own leadership, or to participate in disciplined group actions for their own welfare, and, finally, to an ill-considered rejection of skilled and well-motivated exogenous leadership.

Allusions to the role of transference in the reactions of communities that have become disorganized by poverty and social injustice are regularly misinterpreted as a lack of concern for social injustice itself. Needless to say, a consultant who disregards the latter is as inept as a psychotherapist unconcerned with adverse social realities when these plague his patient.

Sphere Three consists of the community mental health center. It also consists of the psychiatric patients and their families as they present themselves for treatment at the center. The complex of services constituting the center may be housed in a single building or may result from the unification of existing services already operating in the community. In addition to the elements of service previously alluded to, the center is the program-generating agency for the designated population. It defines the basic problems after a demographic study of the community. It is responsible for training and research. It participates in all levels of mental health care. It makes provisions for help to all members of the community, regardless of age, diagnosis, social, cultural, or economic status. It initiates treatment promptly during periods of crisis and remains available in an open-ended way after the crisis has subsided.

It has been said that this type of care is for "poor people," that it is "mass psychiatry" or a diluted version of the "real thing." This is not the case. Many of the leaders in Community Psychiatry are psychoanalytically trained clinicians, who learn about Community Psychiatry by giving quality care to a small group of very ill patients who can afford to pay for it. From these patients they learn about crisis intervention, the flexible use of full and part-time hospitalization, continuity of care, active intervention in relation to school and work, the use of sheltered residences, the need to enlist the cooperation of potentially destructive family members, etc.

Sphere Four relates to all those issues involving administration on a local level as well as in relations with city, state, and federal government. It is the regulatory apparatus that impinges on all aspects of the three preceding spheres. In this sphere are the agencies that provide and control the expenditure of funds. They also initiate and stimulate the development of new programs and monitor the quality of service within the community. Some regard Community Psychiatry as consisting essentially of administrative chores and profess a lack of interest in the field for that reason. To the extent that they are discussing Sphere Four they are right; however, this point of view fails to take into account the other spheres.

REFERENCES

Dubos, R. (1959). *Mirage of Health*. New York: Doubleday.

Kolb, L. C. (1968), Remarks at the Twentieth Mental Health Institute. Washington, D.C.: *Psychiatric News,* 3:1.

Kubie, L. S. (1968), Pitfalls of Community Psychiatry. *Archives of General Psychiatry,* 18:257.

Linn, L. (1966), The Fourth Psychiatric Revolution: Implications for General Medical Practice. *Proceedings of Rudolf Virchow Medical Society,* 25:42.

——— (1968), The Fourth Psychiatric Revolution. *American Journal of Psychiatry,* 124:1043.

SUGGESTED READING

Bernard, V. W. & Crandal, D. L. (1968), Evidence for Various Hypotheses of Social Psychiatry. In: *Social Psychiatry,* ed. J. Zubin & F. Freyhan. New York: Grune & Stratton.

Goldston, S. E. (1965), *Concepts of Community Psychiatry: A Framework for Training.* Washington, D.C.: National Institute for Mental Health. Public Health Service Publication No. 1319.

Redlich, F. C. & Pepper, M. (1968), Are Social Psychiatry and Community Psychiatry Subspecialties of Psychiatry? *American Journal of Psychiatry,* 124:37-44.

Whittington, H. G. (1969), *Psychiatry in the American Community.* New York: International Universities Press.

Name Index

Subject Index